WHAT NIETZSCHE MEANS

WHAT NIETZSCHE MEANS

BY

GEORGE ALLEN MORGAN, Jr.
Associate Professor of Philosophy in Duke University

GREENWOOD PRESS, PUBLISHERS
WESTPORT, CONNECTICUT

Library of Congress Cataloging in Publication Data

Morgan, George Allen, 1905–
    What Nietzsche means.

    Reprint of a 1943 issue of the ed. published in
1941 by Harvard University Press, Cambridge, Mass.
    Bibliography: p.
    Includes index.
    1. Nietzsche, Friedrich Wilhelm, 1844–1900.
I. Title.
B3317.M65 1975   193   74–2555
ISBN 0–8371–7404–X

TO THE MOTHER OF
EVE AND JACK
AND
THIS BOOK

incipit vita nova

PREFACE

THIS book is not intended for a museum. It is about a
thinker who happens to be dead, personally, but whose
thought is terribly alive in the agonies of our time. Countless spiritual currents, potent for good or ill, run through
him. Whether we consider the bedlam of the arts, or psy-
choanalysis with its emphasis on the unconscious deter-
miners of conduct and belief; the gospels of biology and
social science, or the writing of history; the mystic nos-
talgia of physicists, or the reaction against liberal theology;
fascism, socialism and "the revolt of the masses," or the
aimlessness of industrial civilization, the wavering of democracy, the debacle of European Christendom, and the
rebellion against science and reason and truth itself — there
we find Nietzsche. He has the courage to experience the
myriad anxieties that fester the modern soul, and a will
to overcome them with new vision.

I turned to Nietzsche as to an oasis of life in the desert
of the post-war period. Amid the sands of humanitarian
optimism, when western civilization was a foolish ostrich,
he met my thirst for a mind fresh and fearless and deep. The
present volume is a by-product of my sojourn, written that
men of good will may drink more freely at the same spring.

There are a hundred valid and valuable ways of studying
Nietzsche, and neither one nor all are ever likely to capture
the whole of his elusive essence. My initial plan was to develop a constructive interpretation of certain themes in his
thought, but as the work progressed so many novel riches
of content and structure came to light that it seemed an
impertinence not to give them a hearing first, for their own
sake.

The fact is that Nietzsche has suffered, probably more

than any philosopher, from the wildest sort of subjective interpretation and criticism. Since the way he wrote makes it so easy to mistake or twist his meaning, and the way he lived makes it still easier to explain his meaning away, it is necessary to establish what in the light of the evidence he probably *did* mean, quite regardless of why, psychologically or historically, he came to think as he did, what effect his thoughts may have had, or how anyone else may choose to evaluate them. That is what I have tried to do, and it is all I have tried to do. The other inquiries are perhaps more glorious and more important, but they presuppose this one, and deficiency here has vitiated most of them to date — the author all too frequently passing a triumphant verdict on something that probably never existed outside his own head. I might have appended some history and criticism to the present study; my excuse for not doing so is that it would require at least another volume and another decade if it were not to be contemptibly superficial.

There is a kind of criticism, of course, which is involved in the very process of probing a thinker's meaning: one has constantly to put questions to him and then try to find his answers, if he has any. To bring all this intellectual give-and-take into the text, however, would make a work of unreadable — and unpublishable — length. But an alert reader may often perceive, in footnotes or between the lines, where a question of analysis or relationship of meanings, or of adequacy of proof, has been brought to a premature halt for lack of further tangible support in Nietzsche's writings.

One serious objection I must anticipate: it will be urged that Nietzsche's thought is so profoundly connected with his life that the two cannot validly be separated. That is true, but let us distinguish its proper import. His life, in the philosophically relevant sense, is something experienced within and digested into the very marrow of his thought,

not an affair of events and dates, still less of someone else's
theory *about* his life — whether Freudian, antiquarian, or
syphilitic. In fact these externals are more apt to be positive hindrances to a deeper insight, and are commonly
employed as such by the persons who make so much of
them. Like Kierkegaard, Nietzsche is an "existential"
thinker; his philosophy is indeed lived, not merely cere-
brated. In this regard I have carefully endeavored *not*
to separate his thought from his life. But almost by definition these are things that elude analytical expression; one
can only hope to lead the reader to the point where he may
listen to them rather than *see* them.

The somewhat austere purpose of the present study also
explains the occasional inclusion of material which may
have little intrinsic value. It is of course impossible and
undesirable to consider Nietzsche's views on every minor
subject, but arguments for central doctrines, such as eternal
recurrence, naturally have to be stated as carefully as possible even when they are evidently invalid, and sometimes
an idea which will strike a contemporary reader as trite or
trivial has to be developed for the sake of its bearing on other
phases of Nietzsche's philosophy.

One danger has been constantly before me: it would be
very easy to over-systematize Nietzsche, and to give his
thought an order that is mine rather than his. Any exposi-
tion makes this inevitable to some extent, but for the most
part I have followed an order that is really discoverable in
the documents, checking the tendency to round it out as
one so frequently might, in the belief that it is better to
leave loose ends where they occur. In my own judgment
there is a surprising amount of coherence in Nietzsche, but
I will not labor the point: since consistency is finally a
matter of nice interpretation, unsympathetic minds will
always be able to see him as a mass of contradictions. It
does not matter. Chesterton once remarked that the world's

greatest books are scrapbooks. The value of Nietzsche's philosophy does not stand or fall with its architecture; he belongs with Plato, Augustine and Pascal rather than Aristotle, Aquinas and Spinoza. Nevertheless, where logical structure exists it does minister to truth in its own humble way; so I have sought to show Nietzsche's thought in its measure of wholeness — without, I hope, muzzling its bite.

The most useful aid to any careful study of Nietzsche is Richard Oehler's *Nietzsche-Register*. In addition I am indebted to the works of Charles Andler, Georg Simmel, Ernst Bertram, Karl Jaspers, Karl Löwith and Kurt Hildebrandt for many kinds of information and suggestion, and it is also fitting to recall with gratitude the names of some early pioneers in the field: Georg Brandes, Alois Riehl, Raoul Richter, the Horneffer brothers, C. A. Bernoulli, Henri Lichtenberger, A. M. Ludovici, Thomas Common, Oscar Levy and H. L. Mencken.

The present book has been befriended in many ways during its nine years' gestation. Professor Carl Joachim Friedrich first called my attention to the philosophic importance of Nietzsche's later works. A short first draft was written in the tactful quiet of the MacDowell Colony, in Peterborough, N. H. The Harvard Department of Philosophy allowed me the privilege of lecturing on Nietzsche, relieved me of part of my teaching duties for one year, and has recently granted exceedingly generous aid in publication. Similarly generous aid has been given, on three occasions, by the Research Council of Duke University. Dr. W. Cary Maxwell rendered valuable advice with regard to translating the German. Final arrangements for publication are largely due to the kindness of Professor Ralph Barton Perry. And for much counsel throughout, concerning both form and content of this study, I am under great

obligation to Professor and Mrs. Alfred North Whitehead,
Professor Eugen Rosenstock-Huessy, Mr. and Mrs. Henry
Copley Greene, and Mrs. Copley Morgan. To all the fore-
going I wish to express sincere thanks.

G. A. M., JR.

DUKE UNIVERSITY

CONTENTS

PART ONE

ECCE HOMO

I. ON READING NIETZSCHE

§ 1. Why Read Nietzsche?, 3. Opinions of the many and of the few. Nietzsche and the present — his acuteness and cleansing force — some kindred spirits. Beyond the isms. § 2. *Vita heroica*, 6. Personality — beginnings — vocation — Wagner — disillusion — suffering, vision, creation — solitude — madness. § 3. The Main Documents, 12. Two decades of writing — the literary remains — periods — the problem of understanding. § 4. The Masked Fisherman, 14. Reticence and communication — Nietzsche uses masks — the limits of print — modern readers are lazy. Angling for men — the perfect reader — difficulties of a new language. Stages of revelation — the last mask. § 5. Has Nietzsche a System?, 21. The challenge — pedants and the universe — the craving for certainty — aping science. System as inevitable growth — retrospective awareness of unity. Promise and fulfilment in Nietzsche's work — how he changes — dialectic of his periods. Logic vs. insight.

II. HORIZONS

§ 1. Portrait of the Philosopher, 30. He makes the values of history — is a synthesis of all opposites — writes in blood — lives his experiment — turns life into flame. His perils today — being the bad conscience of his time — using scientists. Philosophy in action. § 2. "God is Dead," 36. Nietzsche's instinctive atheism — the self-overcoming of Christendom — and a look beyond. Nietzsche's uncompromising honesty — and hope. § 3. Solitude and Community, 39. Pessimism of the orphaned soul — the communion of true culture — ultimate value. § 4. Untimeliness, 43. Nietzsche vs. Nineteenth Century — a sterile age — "the euthanasia of Christianity" — "modern ideas" and modern idols — culture-philistines call the tune. § 5. Truth vs. Life, 47. Pessimism invades the intellect — metaphysicians now dishonest — there is no truth — the delusions of science — from Kant to despair. Falsehood as reality — levels of illusion — to live or to know? § 6. Nihilism, 52. Man demands meaning — lost in the cosmos — pessimism without reservations. The free spirit survives — and sees the problem of a civilization.

PART TWO

LIFE

III. THE WILL TO POWER

§ 1. The Secret of Life, 59. Nietzsche a philosopher of life — will to power as total tendency: aggressive, growing, formative, destructive, extravagant, self-overcoming — the rhythm of risking, getting, spending. § 2. Types of

Evidence, 66. Scientific studies — life amid nature — plants and animals — human relations — clairvoyant psychology. § 3. Value Perspective and Memory, 68. Life must have preferences. It retains past experience and digests it into hereditary character — which resists new experience. Life learns only what it needs to learn. § 4. The Organism and its Processes, 71. The organism a social hierarchy — association and settling of powers — sources of inner adjustment — the importance of conflict. External behavior — internal division of labor — decadence. § 5. Stability and Evolution, 77. No automatic or general progress — species tend to mediocrity — their formation — storage of power — fixation. Advance due to stability and instability — in evolution, will to power sacrifices many for few — explains apparent design. Résumé.

IV. MAN

§ 1. The New Psychology, 84. Overcoming moral resistances — restoring soul to body. External and internal phenomena are symptoms — self-knowledge and self-deceit — "with the clue of the body" — the self as oligarchy — "the genius of the heart." § 2. The Meaning of Will, 90. The superstition of "mental faculties." Will as process and complexity involving self-command — does not work by magic — its meaning in "will to power." § 3. Dynamics, 94. Urges as forms of will to power — not conscious or simple — seek release, domination — compete incessantly — are the only controls. Results of conflict: dreaming, wishing, projection, introversion, sublimation — attraction of opposites — the value of conflict. § 4. Development, 101. Urges learned. Integration an achievement — its types and degrees — "become what you are." Instinct the basis of perfection — storage and decadence — the individual "a piece of fate." § 5. Self-Consciousness, 106. Tool, not master — phantastic interpretation of the unconscious — sign and cause of maladjustment — utterly useless? Evolved by needs of social intercourse — a superficial mirror — slave, enemy and source of instinct. § 6. Man in Evolution, 111. Man the "unfixed animal" — because of "bad conscience," introversion of predatory instincts — which also gave him fresh possibilities. Priests, "chain sickness" as further factors. "Last man" vs. "superman."

V. THE STANDARD OF REVALUATION

§ 1. All for Life, 115. A revolution in values. Approximating the standard: life, not more nor less — grades of life — enhancement vs. decadence — power. § 2. The Meaning of Power, 119. Nietzsche's appreciations contrasted with the power formula — he believes in a variety of individual values. His "power" chiefly vital or intellectual — external power only a means — often opposed to intrinsic power, but enhances it. Why individuals, not groups, are ultimate ends. Strength of will the first criterion, but many others — "power without grimaces." § 3. Dimensions of Power, 125. Organization — "plastic force" and health — will to power shapes and simplifies — harmony and subordination. Spiritualization — why it means greater power — explains the value of weakness. Extensive dimensions also essential: number, strength, contrast — philosophy of antagonism. Apollinian-Dionysian — wholeness. § 4. The Apollinian Virtues, 133. Nie-

CONTENTS XV

tzsche's appreciations related to power — nobility, individuality, style, form, measure — integrity, necessity, *Wohlgeratenheit*, sincerity, cleanliness, purity. Time another dimension — rhythms of life — perfection and its levels — excess of life, creation — magic moments.

VI. THE GENEALOGY OF MODERN MORALS

§ 1. Morality as a Problem, 141. Platonic-Christian moral values hitherto supreme — even perverting philosophy. Ethics as soporific. A plan for comparative study — its part in criticism and reconstruction. § 2. Historical Perspectives, 145. Pre-moral, Moral, and Extra-moral periods. Morality of Mores conservative and cruel — its effects upon later men. Transition to Moral Period one of several great reversals in moral history. § 3. Healthy and Decadent Types, 148. The two kinds of life. Decadence and *ressentiment* — Buddha as physiologist. Asceticism the type of introverted *ressentiment* — its extroversion in communists and others. Decadent values. § 4. Flock Types, 152. Group and individual moralities. Flock Morality expresses fears of a mediocre, classless group — its double scale of values — its softening. § 5. Master and Slave Types, 155. Ruling classes originate values — "good" and "worthless," respect and contempt. Character of the aristocrat — his morals a discipline for strength — passion of distance and lust for tyranny — distortion in the priestly type. Slave Morality. § 6. Absolute Morality, 160. Today a mixture of all types. Trends in the Moral Period: "slave rebellion" — guilt — de-naturalization. Absolute Morality the outcome. § 7. The Dialectic of Self-Transcendence, 163. Self-overcoming as law of moral evolution — how evil becomes good. The old morality supersedes itself — we should become heirs of all the past. The dialectic not inevitable.

VII. MORALS IN REVOLUTION

§ 1. Grounds for Suspicion, 168. Morals from a primitive past are dubious — ethical intuitions naïve. § 2. Morality as Misunderstanding, 170. There are no "moral phenomena" — no free will or guilt or selflessness — morals a form of immorality — the second innocence. § 3. Morality as Poison, 175. Any absolute morality hostile to life. The "good man" most harmful — life requires enmity as well as benevolence. Pity as a modern vice — dread of suffering is decadent. Ascetic Christianity a crime against life. § 4. Sacred Selfishness, 179. Turning evil into good — cruelty as ingredient of culture — egoism as self-development and self-expression distinguished from perverted forms. § 5. The Value of Evil, 184. Fearfulness a condition of fruitfulness — not another absolute — man must become better *and* more evil — the Great Economy uses all energies, even priests and pity. § 6. Morality for Vitality, 187. Relative morality affirmed — not a return but a rise to nature — not libertinism. Christianity useful for taming, now outgrown. Moralities as voluntarily adopted hypotheses. § 7. Ethical Pluralism, 190. Men are not equal, nor should morals be — neither collectivism nor individualism, but gradation — let each type have its own philosophy. Rights based on power, not universal. Punishment without guilt. § 8. Means to Might, 193. Consciousness signifies little — rationalism unreasonable. Actions as symptoms of unconscious causes.

Resolute experiments, not experimentalism, in morals. The difference between taming and training — morality as discipline. The body comes first. § 9. Morals for Individuals, 200. Distinctive individuals the ultimate ends — they arise in the autumn of a people. Their problems require Individual Moralities. How one becomes what one is: solitude — finding oneself — attaining wholeness — self-love the last of the virtues — from "I will" to "I am." Individuality requires its opposite.

VIII. ART AND ARTIST

§ 1. Ex vita, 206. Art vs. pessimism. The artist not a leader — art for life's sake — aesthetics is applied physiology — should begin with creator, not contemplator. Artist as conqueror — contemplation active, not disinterested. § 2. Frenzy, 209. Rausch the Dionysian element of art — distinguishes artist from Christian — from scientist. Heightened suggestibility and communicativeness. § 3. The Evolution of the Arts, 211. Development from Apollinian and Dionysian type-phenomena — the visual group — the emotional group — architecture — Greek tragedy, a supreme affirmation. § 4. Instinct and Discipline, 215. Instincts of play and deception in art — falsehood essential. Communication and language-instincts. Spiritual dependence of artists — value of traditional schooling — and of conventions — imitation and originality. Self-discipline for freedom. § 5. Appreciation, 220. Rausch in the contemplator. Biological theory of beauty and ugliness — judgments vary with power. "Classical" vs. "Decadence Aesthetics," self-enjoyment vs. self-escape — romanticism — Wagner. § 6. Excellence, 225. Classic ideal combines all dimensions of power. Nobility, of and among artists — monologic, social, demagogic art. Integrity of workmanship — varieties of modern dishonesty — romanticism and naturalism. Form as expression of life — "the great style." Perfection vs. Wagner — beauty above sublimity. § 7. Art, Culture, Life, 232. Art cycles — self-limitation, the classic period, baroque — relations to other phases of culture. The dangers of art — art as gratitude, refreshment, promise.

PART THREE

FIRST AND LAST THINGS

IX. THE REVALUATION OF TRUTH

§ 1. Truth as a Value, 241. "Truth" the last stand of the ascetic ideal — why primarily a moral question. § 2. The Biology of Error, 243. A historical critique of reason — mind evolving — began as simplification — natural selection of fictions. Concepts falsify change — levels of simplification — we have created "the world which concerns us." A priori judgments — pragmatic value not truth. § 3. The Sociology of Science, 248. Influences of social life on the mind — language a crude medium — group-pressure for its conventional use — acquires moral sanction — becomes ideal of Absolute Truth — develops into "scientific conscience." Scientific method Nietzsche's test of truth. § 4. The Death of the Absolute, 252. Against claims to certainty — self-criticism of mind is fallible — "immediate certainty" self-contradictory — there are no "facts" — logic and mathematics — living on hypotheses. "There is no Truth" — absolute Being, absolute knowledge, equally baseless and self-contradictory. § 5. Appearance is Reality, 256. "A kind of truth" is possible — "mere appearance" goes with the Absolute — gradations of appearance — getting beneath fictions — perspectivism. § 6. Truth within Life, 261. Varieties of perspective — power the measure of truth. Truth no longer an absolute duty — let science think our senses through — truth and falsehood must live together. Future of the passion for truth.

X. THE MUSIC OF CHAOS

§ 1. A New Interpretation of all Happening, 266. Nietzsche on metaphysics. His pre-Socratic cosmology — flux, multiplicity, chaos, antagonism, overcoming, making, destroying — the will to power. § 2. Beyond Mechanism, 271. Value of mechanism — its superficiality — the end of matter — motion a puzzle — dynamic quanta. § 3. Physics and the Will to Power, 273. The inner nature of force — by analogy to man — will as cause — we are related to nature. Every force makes a perspective of all — will to power explains duration. Error the differentia of life. § 4. Unity, Endurance, Order, 279. Nothing simple — relative unities as power structures — endurance as similarity of change. Natural laws evolve and decay — determinism a tautology — permits novelty. § 5. A Finite Universe, 284. Eternal recurrence as a new religion — possibility of proof — beware the credulous. Time endless — space and energy finite — therefore finite potentialities — identical recurrence inevitable. The world cycle — an irrational necessity. Eternity within time.

XI. DIONYSOS

§ 1. Reality and Value, 291. Values exist through valuation — are plastic vital perspectives — but not deduced from life. Ultimate aims a matter of "taste" — yet taste is a voice of life. Value and reality both perspectival — but values belong chiefly to surfaces. Man as maker of values. § 2. The Birth of Value, 296. New values born in exaltation of body, to "lawgivers" who move the world — de gustibus disputandum — how Nietzsche recommends his. § 3. For the Strong, 299. Optimism and pessimism only symptoms — "yes" or "no"? The strong can contrive a new perfection — the superman — Dionysos. § 4. Eternal Recurrence, 303. Extreme nihilism or extreme affirmation — putting weight on this life — active fatalism — existence as enigma — innocence. § 5. The Tragic Meaning of Pain, 307. A clue from tragedy — suffering related to future, and to joy — "pessimism of strength" — pain secondary — Dionysos vs. the Crucified. § 6. Amor fati, 311. The alchemy of value. Formula for supermen — conquering heaviness — laughter — redeeming the past. Affirmation includes negation — the mystic ring.

PART FOUR

HISTORY AND PROPHECY

XII. THE RISE AND FALL OF CULTURES

§ 1. A Philosophy of History, 319. Nietzsche's attitude to the past — philosophic interpretation required — intuitive method — biological functions of history. History not rational — cyclic and dialectical patterns —

the evolutionary setting. § 2. Modernity Indicted, 324. Typical vices in society, politics, business, science, education, art, religion, philosophy, morals — haste, discontinuity, uncertainty, weak will, self-consciousness, fragmentariness. § 3. Decadence and Nihilism, 327. Modern culture decadent — individual and social, normal and pathological decadence. Nihilism a conjunction of decadence and Christian morals — which were originally made by decadents. § 4. The Secrets of Greece, 331. Greece the pinnacle of history so far — how to guess its riddles. A typical culture-cycle — from mixture to purity — from barbarism to control of force — a series of victories over chaos. Importance of Greek religion — functions of war, state and competition. § 5. Greek Acme and Decline, 337. The age of early tragedy and philosophy. Decline premature, though soon inevitable — its symptoms parallel ours. General causes of cultural decadence. § 6. Christianity, 341. The revaluation of values in Platonism and Judaism — Jesus initiates a peace-movement — his disciples misinterpret him — St. Paul re-establishes Judaism — the march on Rome — Christianity infects the barbarians. § 7. Europe, 346. Mingling of cyclic and dialectical patterns. The cycle: Middle Ages — Renaissance — Revolution and decline. Rome vs. Judea: Renaissance — Reformation — Revolution — Napoleon. Flock movements: Jesuits — democracy. Europe kept alive by tension — our debt to Christianity — our curse.

XIII. A PHILOSOPHY OF THE FUTURE

§ 1. Signs of Strength, 351. No blue-print for Utopia. An ambiguous age — sound elements — the "new barbarians." § 2. The Coming Crisis, 354. Parallels with China and India — liberalism undermines itself — makes ideal slaves. Active nihilism produces healthy reaction — eternal recurrence as "hammer." "Who shall be master of the earth?" § 3. The Birth of Humanity, 358. Beyond nationalism — the world system run for a new aristocracy — victory of ideas. "Good Europeans" carry culture through barbarism to "The Great Noon," when humanity will become a reality by having a single aim. § 4. World Culture, 362. Cycles in the future — thousand-year experiments. The change of scale — conscious direction — heirs of universal history — new myths for old. § 5. Justice and the Law-giver, 366. The ethics of Caesar — life naturally unjust — justice as will of the strongest — reconciled with kindness. § 6. The Caste System, 369. Why aristocracy? Natural order of castes — class hygiene and the treatment of decadents — sound mediocrity as base of the culture pyramid — culture vs. the state. § 7. The Lords of the Earth, 373. The highest caste trains for super-humanity — the end for which others exist. Its perfection, beauty, austerity, spirituality, terrible kindness — educating the whole man — "die at the right time."

EPILOGUE 377

NOTE ON REFERENCES AND ABBREVIATIONS 379

SELECT BIBLIOGRAPHY 385

INDEX 393

PART ONE

ECCE HOMO

CHAPTER I

On Reading Nietzsche

*Another century of readers — and the mind itself
will stink.* (VI 56)

1. WHY READ NIETZSCHE?

LIKE St. Paul, whom he so hated and admired, Nietzsche
has been "all things to all men." Probably no
thinker has excited a wider ambit of conflicting
interests, sordid and spiritual, shallow and profound. To
the timidly conventional a Satanic mind, clothed in the
abominations of Antichrist and deserving his bad end; to
the blasé a *sauce piquante* of irresponsible wit; to the fanatical a stick to beat things with — sometimes himself; a
tasty morsel for gossips and psychological morticians; a
monster of ruthlessness for some readers, a floodgate for
sentimental yearning in others; prophet, mountebank,
iconoclast, clown — all these and many more has Nietzsche
been to the masses.

Can anything be good which attracts so many flies? Certainly his motley following has aroused prejudice against him
in cleanly and discriminating minds. Yet perhaps a sound
instinct has guided the vulgar, and even the torrents of
abuse are an involuntary tribute to greatness. And that
Nietzsche is often used for propaganda by each side of a
struggle, as in the World War, suggests that he may be
*mis*used by both.

Fortunately there have been a select but increasing few
who have looked beneath the gaudy colors of the popular
Nietzsche Myth. They have seen the heroic sufferer be-

hind the jester and the man of mildness beside the man of force, and from them a more tolerant attitude to Nietzsche has been spreading out among the general public. So it has come to pass that today his writings command a degree of open-minded, if puzzled, attention. To readers of this sort the present volume is addressed.

Although his work ended fifty years ago, Nietzsche's philosophy is so profoundly relevant to the modern world that he is in many respects more our contemporary than that of his fellow-Victorians. Apart from a few details, he does not require translation into the present; he speaks directly within it, so much are his problems our problems and his predicament our own. Concern with his philosophy is not a matter of intellectual curiosity. It is a necessity of life.

Nietzsche's predicament, the given setting in which his thought strikes root, is a world of weakened and fast disintegrating traditions: religious faith, social structure, moral standards, the ideals which give sense to life — all broken or about to break. His endeavor is to understand and evaluate this plight, to detect its causes and foresee its possible outcome, and, thus grounded, to build toward a future civilization with a more adequate philosophy. Therefore his thought, though it begins in the contemporary scene, is not confined there. He is too deep for that. The hot pursuit leads him back to the first questions of metaphysics, and his philosophy, like Plato's, runs the full gamut from loftiest theory to concrete action. It is philosophy in the grand style once more.

Nietzsche's attack is distinguished by its many-sidedness, its penetration beneath the surface of things, its radical fearlessness. He leaves scarcely an aspect of modern life untouched. Breath-taking as they often are in isolation, his dissections gain force when seen as parts of a whole. The canvas he paints is nothing smaller than a comprehensive indictment of western civilization. This amplitude of gaze ranks him apart from those minor prophets who daub one or two patches forever.

Nietzsche not only considers many aspects of the world; he approaches them from many points of view. His thought on any topic is not a simple-minded opinion but a significant strife of ideas through which he works toward some complex synthesis. Whether successful or not, that effort electrifies the mind to wrestle in turn with issues of ineluctable importance. To this is due in no small measure the vitality, the fertility, the inexhaustible suggestiveness of Nietzsche's philosophy. He almost compels originality.

His habit of cutting under the obvious, peering around and behind things and standing them on their heads, will always try the patience of sensible people, but it would be a grave mistake to consider this effect its chief merit. Nietzsche gives one a new concept of depth. The objects he describes take on half a dozen dimensions instead of the conventional two or three. One may return with a new love of surfaces, but the old Euclidian innocence of mind is lost forever.

Nietzsche is generally known to be radical in his thinking, and that is probably why so many fear him. But only the weak-minded need fear. To the strong he is either a friend or a "beautiful enemy." That he is radical means simply that he digs remorselessly for the roots of things, and does not hesitate to draw the conclusions implied by his premises. No one since Socrates has so tenaciously stung the mind with his questioning. Where most of us stammer and slink into compromise, Nietzsche strikes out at whatever seems dead and false in modern life. He is an incomparably cleansing, tonic force.

All camps, therefore, will find him a man to be reckoned with, as friend or foe. He foresaw in a measure the rise of fascism and, though not a fascist, welcomed it for ulterior purposes of his own. Correspondingly, he has been the most thoroughgoing critic of liberalism and Christianity. When he wrote, the one was smug, the other triumphantly expanding. Today both are threatened by major world forces; the prestige of each is seriously impaired. Frightened liberals and Christians will be tempted to deny all faults, like a driver shutting his eyes before a crash. The determined and responsible, however, will welcome criticism, in the belief that cutting out gangrene is the first condition of survival.

The centrality of Nietzsche for our time most readily appears in the galaxy of brilliant men related to him — many profoundly affected by his thought, the rest in some way spiritually akin. To mention a few: Nicolas Berdyaev, William Ernest Hocking, Eugen Rosenstock-Huessy, Max Scheler, Oswald Spengler, Nicolai Hartmann, Henri Bergson, Alfred North Whitehead, Hans Vaihinger and the pragmatists, José Ortega y Gasset, Albert Schweitzer, the psychoanalysts, the school of *Existenz-Philosophie* and the Kierkegaardians; among men of letters: Luigi Pirandello, Gabriele d'Annunzio, H. L. Mencken, Theodore Dreiser, André Gide, Stefan George, Thomas Mann, and a host of others.

So much for the exciting foreground. Nietzsche himself is above the schools and camps, and to identify him with any one is to trivialize him. He *lived* our chaos, this cauldron of the nations, and saw perhaps — who knows? — the door beyond.

2. VITA HEROICA

In the deepest sense, the whole of Nietzsche's philosophy *was* his life, but let us pursue at first the human circumstances of his career. Beginning in October, 1844, it lasted forty-four years, until something like a paralytic stroke shattered his creative powers at the turn of the year 1888–89. He lingered, broken, until death in 1900.

Physically well-formed, and robust until illness took him, reserved and rather formal in manner, with an innate dignity of bearing already evident in his earliest school years: such was Nietzsche as we might have met him. When he was not distracted by the agonies of existence, friends found him charming, sensitive, humorous, fond of gay talk, gifted with vivid imagination, and touchingly considerate. Simple Italian townsfolk, with whom he lived for a time, used to refer to him as "the little saint."

His ancestry, of which he was proud, included many clergymen on both sides of the family. He was deeply attached to his father, a Lutheran pastor, whose early death profoundly affected the life of the child Friedrich. In after days he always spoke with veneration of his father and of the sincere Christian piety he had known as a boy.[1]

Six years, from 1858 to 1864, were spent at Pforta, one of the oldest and most distinguished of German boarding schools. There he obtained a thorough grounding in classical and Germanic studies, developing at the same time marked interests in history, poetry, music, and philosophy. The variety of his talents perhaps accounts for the fact that he was slow to decide upon a career. From 1864 to 1869, with the exception of a year of military service and illness, he studied at the universities of Bonn and Leipzig. First enrolling in theology, largely because of family pressure, he soon went over to classical philology under the brilliant Friedrich Ritschl. Ritschl recognized his genius, and gave him a flaming recommendation to the University of Basle which brought him there as professor of classics at the unheard-of age of twenty-four.

This precocious success was not an unmixed blessing. It

[1] Cf. XIV 358; XV 14 f.; L.G. 21/7/81; L.O. 23/6/81. (For explanation of symbols, see note preceding the bibliography.)

fastened him too soon to an exacting professional routine against which he rebelled inwardly because it kept him from the true vocation already stirring within. For Nietzsche was never simply a scholar. His work always had a philosophical perspective, was always tied by a secret thread to the living issues of the day. In fact he planned for a time to take his doctorate in philosophy instead of philology, and just before the call to Basle he was at least playing with the idea of a change to chemistry.[2]

The inspiration of his classical studies was the hope of a rebirth of true Hellenic culture in Germany. In his student days he had discovered the two chief pillars of his hope — Schopenhauer and Richard Wagner. The latter had the special merit of being alive: here was genius incarnate, here was a *real* Aeschylus or Pindar,[3] not just a book: here was the actual hero who could create Greece anew.

Despite its inconveniences Nietzsche retained his post at Basle for a decade. The first years saw the acme of his intimacy with Richard and Cosima Wagner. The days spent with them at near-by Tribschen were the happiest of his life. He plunged enthusiastically into the growing Wagner movement and devoted his own productive energies more and more explicitly to philosophical and cultural questions. But when Wagner moved to Bayreuth, deserting Hellenic idealism for the sake of popular artistic success, the eventual parting of the ways became inevitable. Wagner compromised with modernity. Nietzsche sickened under this mortal blow to his hopes[4] until in 1879 he found it necessary to retire from his professorship.

The last decade of his career was spent in lonely wandering, poverty, intense physical and mental suffering, and creative work of the first magnitude. After the loss of

[2] L.R. 16/1/69.
[3] L.R. 3/9/69. Cf. L.W. 22/5/69, 21/5/70, 2/1/72.
[4] Cf. Kurt Hildebrandt, *Gesundheit und Krankheit in Nietzsches Leben und Werk* (1926), pp. 44–68.

Wagner in 1876 Nietzsche went through a period of intellectual asceticism, but in August, 1881, a surge of inspiration gave him a renewed vision of the future, to which the rest of his life was dedicated. Thereafter, life was a struggle for victory against heavy odds. Living in drab attic rooms, often without fire in winter; near-sighted almost to blindness, sitting alone night after night unable to read or sleep, bruised and humiliated by his difficulties in dealing with people and practical affairs; alternating between hideous pain, an almost irresistible impulse to suicide, blackest despair and self-doubt, and periods when he grasped confidently the vocation which, coming ever more plainly to view, alone held him to life — such was Nietzsche's existence during the years when his greatest masterpieces were written. Not his too-human traits but the conquest over them, the living on despite them, is the impressive fact about Nietzsche's humanity.

His loneliness was rooted in a radical difference of perspective which almost no one could be found to share. "In an absurdly early period, at the age of seven," he wrote, "I knew already that never a human word would reach me...."[5] Wagner was the one friend who for a time penetrated this loneliness, he testified, and nothing ever compensated for the loss of his friendship. Of it he wrote later:

Now that is gone — and what is the use of being *right* in many respects where he was wrong! As if this lost sympathy could be erased from memory thereby! — And I have lived through similar things before.... They are the hardest sacrifices which my course of life and thought has demanded of me, — even now my whole philosophy wavers after an hour of sympathetic conversation with utter strangers: it seems to me so foolish to wish to be right at the cost of love, and not to be *able to communicate* one's most precious things lest one dissolve the sympathy.[6]

[5] XV 47. Cf. XIV 396; II 3 f.; V 238 f.; L.Mu. 18/10/87; L.O. 12/10/86, 17/6/87.
[6] L.G. 20/8/80. Cf. VIII 201; XV 37; L.O. summer/86 (after returning from Germany), 12/11/87.

Later unsuccessful attempts at deeper intimacy were based
on the same privation and brought violent disappointment.
Of his acquaintance with Lou Salomé he wrote to a close
friend:

> The peculiar distress of the last year and the year before
> consisted quite literally in this, that I thought to have found
> a human being who had wholly the same task as I. Without this
> hasty belief I should not have suffered ... to this degree from
> the feeling of *isolation* ... for I am and was prepared to carry
> through my voyage of discovery *alone*. But as *soon* as I had
> dreamed but once the dream of *not* being alone, the danger was
> terrible. Even now there are hours when I do not know how to
> endure myself.[7]

One by one Nietzsche's earlier friends were estranged
by the development which his thought took. Franz Overbeck remained personally devoted but could not share the
vision closest to Nietzsche's heart. Finally the last family tie
was virtually broken when his sister married an anti-
Semite. Nietzsche met his destiny alone.

This personal solitude was aggravated by the fact that
after 1873 his books were practically unsold and unread.
Most of his best work had to be published at his own expense. The stolid indifference of the public, especially in
Germany, baffled his chief purpose — to attract sympathetic
minds through his writings — and partly explains the fierce-
ness of his later style. It is as if he had to scream in order to
be heard at all. The total absence of any human response
to *Thus Spake Zarathustra* almost broke him.[8] Fame, if not
understanding, came ironically when he was beyond call.

Ill health dogged him.[9] From 1873 onward his constitu-
tionally poor sight was further weakened by frequent and
protracted spells of migraine. Thus for much of the time

---

[7] L.O. c. 8/12/83. Cf. 9/82, 10/82, early 12/82; I 406 f.

[8] L.O. 17/6/87. Cf. XIV 93; Salis-Marschlins, *Philosoph und Edelmensch*
(1897), p. 31.

[9] The best accounts of his health are: Hildebrandt, *op. cit.*; Karl Jaspers,
Nietzsche, Einführung in das Verständnis seines Philosophierens (1936), pp. 76 ff.;
Erich F. Podach, *The Madness of Nietzsche* (1931).

he was unable to work at all, and at his best could use his eyes very little for reading or writing. The sick spells took a turn for the better after 1880, but they remained wretched enough.

No definitely psychotic symptoms appeared until the delusions of grandeur a few days before the final catastrophe, although a certain over-excitement of mood during the preceding four months may be considered a warning signal. It is important to insist upon this fact because Nietzsche's subsequent insanity has been used by quacks to discredit his philosophy. All of his works were written before the delusions appeared. Criticism of his philosophy must be based upon judgments of value for which the critic, not medical science, is personally responsible. To write otherwise is cowardly and dishonest.

However, Nietzsche's thought was lived rather than merely written, and for this reason it will always be of interest to ask whether his madness was an integral part of his life or a brute accident senselessly coming from without. It is inevitable that the superstitious should regard it as a judgment of God. The preponderance of medical opinion inclines to a diagnosis of progressive paralysis. But the diagnosis can never be proved for lack of modern clinical data, and it was certainly an atypical case. For one who follows as best he can the titanic struggles of Nietzsche's spiritual life it is difficult to resist the belief that they at least contributed to the Icarus-like tragedy. Nietzsche entertained the possibility that the vehemence of his emotions might produce such an end, and although he did not expect the blow just when it came he seems at times to have anticipated that the fulfilment of his mission would bring death, as in the lines about the pine tree:

Too near me is the clouds' abode, —
I wait the soonest thunderbolt.[10]

[10] VIII 354. Cf. VI 15, 18; L.G. 14/8/81, 13/7/83; L.O. c. 28/8/83, c. 26/12/83; L.S. 6/7/83. Such is the projected death of Zarathustra in XII 392, 394, 401 ff., 418 (cf. VI 9 f.).

3. THE MAIN DOCUMENTS

Apart from juvenilia and philological papers, Nietzsche's works occupy the full two decades following his move to Basle. The most important are as follows. His first book, *The Birth of Tragedy*, written 1870/1, appeared early in 1872. Then came the four *Untimely Views* (1873–76): *David Friedrich Strauss, The Use and Harm of History for Life, Schopenhauer as Educator,* and *Richard Wagner in Bayreuth. Things Human, Too Human,* begun in 1876, was published in 1878. It was soon followed by two supplements, then by *Dawn* (1880/1) and the first four books of *The Gay Science* (1881/2). *Thus Spake Zarathustra* was written in four parts at intervals from 1883 to 1885, followed by *Beyond Good and Evil* (1885/6), the fifth book of *The Gay Science* (1886), and *Toward the Genealogy of Morals* (1887). In 1886 Nietzsche wrote a set of prefaces for some of his earlier books which contain valuable self-comment. The last year, 1888, brought a brilliant series of short pieces: *The Case of Wagner, The Twilight of the Idols, The Antichristian, Ecce Homo,* and *Nietzsche contra Wagner,* of which the last three were not published until years later. There is also a collection of verse composed from time to time during most of his life but for the most part not published then.

In addition Nietzsche left a mass of notes and unfinished material which is of special importance because he did not live to round out his philosophy. Selections from it fill eight volumes of the long-standard octavo edition and much more is promised in the critical edition now appearing. Some of the most valuable of the fragments from the later years were pieced together by editors according to a plan sketched by Nietzsche himself, and published under the title, *The Will to Power,* which he had once intended for his great systematic work. Such a philosophic magnum opus had been planned ever since the writing of *Thus Spake Zarathustra*, which he called the "vestibule" of his building,[11] but in 1888 he changed his purpose to a shorter, less exhaustive treatise in four parts, to be entitled *Revaluation of All Values*. Of these only the first part, *The Antichristian*, was finished. Hence *The Will to Power* remains the most complete single presentation of Nietzsche's mature philosophy.

It is customary to divide Nietzsche's writings into periods, but the number and dating of these vary considerably. There is no reason to quarrel about them; no doubt many are legitimate, for different purposes. In so far as any division can claim pre-eminence it must be that which Nietzsche himself recognizes as marking the crises in his own development. To this the present study will refer whenever a rough differentiation into periods seems necessary. It comprises an early period of romantic metaphysics and enthusiasm for a Hellenic-German renaissance under the aegis of Schopenhauer and Wagner, containing *The Birth of Tragedy* and *Untimely Views*; a middle period of disillusion with romanticism, essaying a maximum of intellectual self-discipline, dating from *Things Human* to *The Gay Science*, approximately; and a later period, from *Zarathustra* onward, in which Nietzsche moves from detachment to affirmation and attack.

Such, in brief outline, is the form in which Nietzsche's philosophy confronts us: spread over twenty years in the life of a profoundly developing man with intense spiritual passions and a supremely supple intellect; subject to the ebb and flow of experience; a full half consisting of fragments and private jottings, much of the remainder written in aphorisms devoid of evident sequence; at the same time vast in extent and never reaching a final authoritative expression. Only the most patient and self-critical effort, therefore, can hope to discover what Nietzsche meant.

[11] L.O. 7/4/84.

4. THE MASKED FISHERMAN

We shall not understand this brilliant chaos unless we keep in mind how and for whom Nietzsche was writing. He wrote above all with extreme reticence. Born perhaps of his instinctive feeling of difference, this trait characterized him from early childhood.[12] He appears to have believed that utterly complete communication is impossible, that even between people who are most akin there is an ultimate, impassable gulf.[13] And with regard to what *was* communicable he maintained an attitude of great reserve. "Taciturn" (*schweigsam*), "hermit," "abyss," "labyrinth," "cavern," are favorite epithets for his disposition.[14]

Since full communication is impossible we necessarily always wear a mask, and Nietzsche soon learned that a deliberate choice of masks or "foregrounds" was advisable. He writes:

Thus I learned betimes to be silent, as well as that one must learn to talk in order to keep silence properly: that a man with backgrounds needs foregrounds, be it for others, be it for himself: for foregrounds are necessary in order that we may get a rest from ourselves and in order to make it possible for others to live with us.[15]

Nor is it a matter of one mask before one reality. Nietzsche speaks of a whole series or labyrinth of masks behind masks, in which one can never be sure of having reached bottom:

The hermit ... will doubt whether a philosopher *can* have "final and proper" opinions at all, whether within him yet a deeper cave does not lie behind every cave ... an abyss behind every reason, beneath every "foundation." Every philosophy is a foreground-philosophy — this is a hermit's judgment: "There is something arbitrary about the fact that he stopped *here* ...

---

[12] L.S. 20/5/85, 8/7/86; L.F.N. I 30; H.K.A. I 279.
[13] VI 316 f. Cf. XIV 419; XVI 330.
[14] Cf. XIV 355; XV 35 f.; L.O. early 4/83; L.S. early 7/83.
[15] XIV 348. Cf. 61; III 288; VI 81, 255, 272 f.; VII 60 f.; XIII 285 f.; L.S. mid-7/81.

that he no longer dug deeper *here* . . . — there is also something suspicious about it." Every philosophy also *conceals* a philosophy; every opinion is also a hiding place, every word also a mask.[16]

This statement alone is enough to laugh out of court all unimaginatively literal-minded interpretations of Nietzsche. To stop with what merely happens to seem obvious on a first or second reading is to disgrace oneself.

Nietzsche used masks as protection against impertinent intrusions and as a kind of delicacy toward others.[17] In matters of philosophy he had a reasoned basis for this reserve in the conviction that true communication, so far as it is possible at all, is so only between men of a kind (*"inter pares"*). Others fatally mangle our every effort — he writes:

One finds out at last that people *mean*, feel, scent, wish different things in the *same words*. . . .
This is said in order to explain why it is difficult to understand such writings as mine: with me inner experiences, valuations and needs are otherwise. For years I have had intercourse with men and pressed self-denial and courtesy so far as never to speak of things close to my heart. Indeed I have lived almost only so with men.[18]

Hence the use of masks and foregrounds; Nietzsche could not bear to have his deepest concerns caricatured by the shallow. "I am proud enough for an *absolute* incognito, even in miserable circumstances," he declared: "but *half* esteemed, *half* tolerated, *half* mistaken for another, I feel as in Hell . . . ." [19] Accordingly he wrote in a manner deliberately intended to make fools of unworthy readers:

---

[16] VII 268. Cf. 66. Perhaps Nietzsche's ultimate reason for the inevitability of "masks" is his denial of the absolute unity of personality, which implies that nobody is ultimately any *one* thing (cf. XIV 396). Compare his epistemological "perspectivism" and his rejection of the categories of "substance," *Ding an sich*, etc. (see Chaps. IX and X below).
[17] VII 60 f., 258 f.; VIII 204 f.; L.G. 23/7/85.
[18] XIV 411 f. Cf. VII 61; XVI 330; L.S. 20/5/85, 8/7/86.
[19] L.O. early 4/83. Cf. c. 11/2/83; I 407; also drafts of letters to Frl. Meysenbug and Paul Rée, *Ges. Briefe* V 504 ff.

My writings are very well protected: whoever, having no right to such books, takes them and thereby mistakes them immediately makes himself ridiculous — a little attack of rage drives him to pour out what is inmost and most ridiculous in him . . . .[20]

Nietzsche was in fact far less willing to express himself fully in print than in speech. It was his rooted conviction, for reasons already given, that "The best and essential is communicable only *from man to man*; it can and shall not be 'public.' "[21] He approved the practice of ancient Hindus, Greeks, and others who carefully distinguished an exoteric philosophy to be taught in public from an esoteric one to be reserved for the initiate:

Our supreme insights must — and are meant to! — sound like follies, under certain circumstances like crimes, if they come, unlawfully, to the ears of those who are not qualified and pre-destined for them.[22]

And he was all the more anxious to maintain a general re-serve in print because he detested the lazy and hasty habits of modern readers. One reason for his use of the aphoristic style was that it kept his real meaning from those unfit to grasp it.[23] But even orally, Nietzsche testifies, he never ex-pressed his philosophy with complete freedom, for lack of anyone capable of adequate understanding.[24] Therefore we cannot dogmatically infer gaps in his actual thinking from apparent gaps in his written or reported thought. Such conclusions can only be tentative.

Masks, on the other hand, may reveal as well as conceal. One must never lose sight of the fact that Nietzsche believed in and passionately desired some kind of genuine communi-cation with his fellows.[25] He did not write for the sake of

[20] XIV 359. Cf. 360, 416; XV 54 f.; VII 46.
[21] L.O. c. early 11/84. Cf. c. 2/7/85; Salis-Marschlins, *op. cit.*, p. 32.
[22] VII 49. Cf. XIV 418 f.; V 340.
[23] VI 56; XI 115; XII 177; XIV 360 f.; V 341; IV 10. Cf. X 43 f.
[24] XIV 355 f., 396, 412; L.S. 20/5/85.   [25] L.S. 20/5/85, 8/7/86.

mystification, but rather to attract kindred minds with whom he might work in the intimacy of direct conversation. He was "fishing for men," as he called it, and often referred to his books as "fish hooks" or "landing nets."[26] His efforts were tireless:

> I made my longest attempt ... on Richard Wagner. Later I thought of "seducing" the German youth.... Still later I prepared a language for the heads and hearts of dauntless men who might be waiting for my strange business somewhere in a corner of the earth. Finally ... I contrived "Thus Spake Zarathustra."[27]

Even after *Zarathustra* the fishing continued, this time for allies in the work of revaluing the old values.[28] We must not infer, however, that Nietzsche considered his books mere occasional pieces of no permanent worth: he also wrote for a select few scattered across centuries.[29]

For men to whom he would really appeal, Nietzsche indicates quite plainly how he wishes to be read. Proper reading is an art and a difficult one, little known today outside the circle of skilled philologists:

> For philology is that venerable art which requires of its worshipper one thing above all, to step aside, give oneself time, become tranquil, become slow —, as a goldsmith's art and connoisseurship of the *word*, which has to turn out nothing but fine, cautious work and achieves nothing if it does not achieve it *lento*.... It teaches how to read *well*, that is, to read slowly, deeply, delicately and circumspectly, with mental reservations, with doors left open, with delicate fingers and eyes ... My patient friends, this book wants perfect readers and philologists only: *learn* to read me well! —[30]

The perfect reader is "a monster of courage and curiosity," "yet in addition something pliant, cunning, vigilant, a born adventurer and discoverer."[31]

[26] VI 27 f., 345 ff.; XIV 355 f., 380 f., 393; IX 428 ff.; L.O. early 11/84, 31/3/85; L.R. 15/12/70; L.G. 3/8/83. Cf. XI 380.
[27] XIV 356.　　[28] XV 102.　　[29] XII 216; VIII 213 f.
[30] IV 10. Cf. V 344; XI 116; VIII 307; IX 428; XIV 362; XV 57.　[31] XV 55.

Nietzsche is of course aware that the aphorist style presents peculiar difficulties. An aphorism is a link in a chain of thought: the reader must learn to reconstruct the chain from the links. As a model of the sort of imaginative elucidation required, Nietzsche offers, in the third treatise of *Toward the Genealogy of Morals,* an opening aphorism which the rest of the treatise interprets.[32] He predicts in fact that university professorships will one day be founded for the interpretation of *Zarathustra,* and hopes that his works may receive the rigorous, serious study now lavished on classics like Aristotle.[33] This implies that he wrote with sufficient care to repay exact interpretation, and the inference is justified: niceties of mood or syntax often make a great difference. For example, a casual reader might think that Zarathustra's remark, "I should believe only in a god who knew how to dance," actually commits him to such a belief. But Nietzsche warns elsewhere: "Zarathustra himself is, to be sure, merely an old atheist . . . . Zarathustra says he *should* — but Zarathustra *will* not . . . Let us understand him correctly." [34]

The earlier quotation about the relation of words to individual experience deserves double emphasis. We shall not compass Nietzsche with a dictionary. Only the most sensitive awareness of his idiom, coupled with a congenial gift for echoing novel life in our own souls, will bring us near him. This is his deepest demand upon the reader, unfortunately seldom fulfilled:

After all no one can hear more from things, books included, than he already knows. For that to which one has no access from experience one has no ear. Let us imagine an extreme case: that a book . . . is the *first* language for a new series of experiences. In this case simply nothing is heard, with the acousti-

[32] VII 297; XI 115; XIV 354; VI 56.
[33] XV 49; XII 215 f.
[34] VI 58; XVI 381.

cal illusion that where nothing is heard *also nothing is there* . . . This in the end is my average experience . . . .[35]

He asks above all that we suffer the same problems and share with him the same passions, the same intellectual integrity, the same fearlessness.[36]

For the elect, Nietzsche intended his use of "masks" to have a progressively educative effect:

Suppose one conceives a philosopher as a great educator, mighty enough from his lonely height to draw long chains of generations up to himself: then one must also grant him the unearthly prerogatives of the great educator. An educator never says what he himself thinks, but only what he thinks of a subject in relation to the profit of him whom he is educating.[37]

As an esoteric philosopher, Nietzsche believed in many stages of insight, and the need of preparation for apprehending deeper truth.[38] So he wrote to Overbeck in 1886, "I must first supply a multitude of educative premises until I have finally trained my own readers, I mean readers who may be *allowed* to see my problems without breaking on them." [39]

Hence we find that Nietzsche's writings were a gradual revelation of his ulterior meaning and purposes. First he spoke through the masks of Greeks, Wagner, Schopenhauer;

[35] XV 51. Cf. L.O. 5/8/86. Nietzsche is one of the philosophers who use ordinary speech instead of inventing a new technical vocabulary. He realizes that the clash between his meaning and the philosophy embedded in language often makes him seem to contradict himself (XIII 52). His writings are full of such linguistic traps for the unwary. Only a critical study of the context and of parallel usages can decide what his words probably mean in each case. Two of the most common sources of confusion are his use of the same word, e.g. *die Moral*, for a meaning which he rejects and for one which he affirms, and secondly his habit of writing forcefully from one point of view at a time — thus in some respects he greatly values modern science, in others he scorns it, and naïve scholars have concluded that he must have been "for" science at one time and "against" it at another.

[36] VII 296; VIII 213 f.; XI 384; XIV 356 f.; XV 108.

[37] XVI 352. Cf. XIV 419.

[38] Cf. XIII 53; XIV 349; XV 248.

[39] L.O. 12/10/86. Cf. XIV 382.

then through the "free spirit." [40] With Zarathustra he broke
his silence much more boldly, though not to completion.[41]
Moreover, Nietzsche testifies that most of his writings are to
be "dated back" because they deal with experiences which
occupied him several years earlier.[42] This can be verified
from his literary remains; for instance, some fundamentals
of "immoralism" were already stated in 1873, and drastic
criticisms of Wagner were jotted down in January, 1874.[43]
It is much easier to perceive the continuity in Nietzsche's
development if we realize that his writings were a gradual
overcoming of reticence about what had long possessed his
soul, and it is impossible to accuse him of caprice, as the
superficial do, if we see the germs of a later style developing
at the very time when the earlier one is at its height.

In December, 1888, Nietzsche wrote to his friend Gast,
". . . I now no longer write a sentence in which I do not
come forth *wholly* . . . ." [44] Masked fisherman no longer,
the "Lawgiver of the Future" was fulfilling a pledge written
some five years earlier in a Zarathustra fragment:

> The *slightest* concealment *cripples* his entire strength: he
> feels that he has *evaded* an idea till now . . . .

> The least withholding, the subtlest silence hinders *all great
> success*: as soon as man is *humanity completely* [*vollkommen
> die Menschheit*] *he moves all nature.*[45]

Just before the catastrophe, therefore, Nietzsche was beginning a new phase in his career,[46] wherein he planned to come
out as openly for his ideas as was possible in public. But
this was cut short: what he left is the series of masks.

---

[40] XV 66 f., 72 f.; XIV 393, 395 f., 400.
[41] L.G. 22/3/84; L.S. 20/5/85; L.O. 14/9/84. Cf. XIV 351.
[42] III 3 ff. Cf. XI 378 f.
[43] X 189 ff., 427 ff.
[44] L.G. 16/12/88.
[45] XIV 293.
[46] Cf L.F. 14/12/87; L.G. 16/12/88.

5. HAS NIETZSCHE A SYSTEM?

The present study endeavors to discover the implicit wholeness of Nietzsche's thought as we may detect it through the shifting masks. But *is* there any whole? Almost everyone insists that Nietzsche perpetually contradicts himself.[47] Is he not only unsystematic but deliberately anti-systematic? Only the sequel can answer these questions convincingly. But let us listen now to Nietzsche's own professions in the matter.

True indeed, he does oppose some kinds of system building. In one sense he is unsystematic because the universe is:

There are schematic minds, those which hold a thought complex to be *truer* when it can be inscribed in previously designed schemes or tables of categories. There are countless self-deceptions in this field: almost all great "systems" belong here. But the *fundamental prejudice* is: that order, perspicuity, system must belong to the *true being* of things, conversely that disorder, the chaotic, uncalculable appear only in a false or incompletely known world — is an error in short —: which is a moral prejudice derived from the fact that the truthful, trustworthy man is wont to be a man of order, of maxims, and in general something calculable and pedantic. But it is quite indemonstrable that the nature [*an sich*] of things behaves according to this recipe for a model official.[48]

Nietzsche also disdains dogmatic finality or completeness in philosophy — the claim to have the last word, answer all questions. The will *to* system — attempting to round out one's views in order to make the weak points seem as good as the rest — he considers intellectually dishonest. Moreover, the craving for certainty is a sign of weakness, for strength loves uncertainty and adventure: in this respect he champions the methods of science against the traditional methods of philosophy. He equally dislikes the general

[47] E.g. Jaspers, *op. cit.*, pp. 8 f., 13 f., and *passim*.
[48] XIII 57 f.

pretentiousness, "the big, virtuous, unqualified words," of the older philosophies.[49] And most fundamental of all, perhaps, is his vivid sense of the variousness of existence, its infinite possibilities of interpretation: beyond any given scheme one may imagine alternatives. Hence he says, "I am not narrow enough for a system — and not even for *my* system . . ."[50]

Nietzsche dislikes the affectation of "being scientific" (*Wissenschaftlichkeit*) — for example, the premature elaboration of technique; the pretense of pure "objectivity," where valuations and therefore personal experience are involved; arranging ideas in a neat logical order which falsifies their origin:

> Let us not hide and spoil the *actual way* in which our thoughts have occurred to us. The profoundest and least exhausted books will most likely always have something of the aphoristic and sudden character of Pascal's *Pensées*. The driving forces and valuations are far beneath the surface; what emerges is an effect.[51]

On the other hand, Nietzsche does admire some kinds of unity: organic growth, though not finality; coherence, without rigidity. He likens the proper development of a philosophy to that of a tree:

> We have no right to be *fragmentary* in any respect: we may neither err piecemeal, nor piecemeal strike the truth. On the contrary our thoughts, our values, our yea's and nay's and if's and whether's grow out of us with the inevitability with which a tree bears its fruit — all together related and corresponding with one another and evidences of one will, one health, one soil, one sun.[52]

Because it lives, such a system remains for a long time, perhaps always, incomplete, and Nietzsche esteems the power required for it:

---

[49] XIII 54 f., 72 f., 116 f.; XIV 353 f., 413; III 28, 201 f.; IV 255, 356; VIII 64; XVI 268; VII 3 f.

[50] XIV 354. Cf. V 332. It is a chief merit of Prof. Jasper's book, *op. cit.*, that it emphasizes the restless infinity of Nietzsche's thought.

[51] XV 450 f.   [52] VII 289. Cf. V 328.

Such dogmatic men as Dante and Plato are *farthest* from
me and perhaps thereby most fascinating: men who dwell in a
trimly built and firmly believed house of knowledge. . . .
It requires an entirely different strength and flexibility to
keep hold of oneself in an incompleted system with free, unbounded vistas, than in a dogmatic world. Leonardo da Vinci
stands above Michelangelo, Michelangelo above Raffael.[53]

If a growing system ever attains a kind of completeness, it
does so only at the end, like the ripened fruit of a tree, and
it has great worth just *because* it is an inevitable growth
rather than something *voulu*:

As sceptical ages, *suffering* from uncertainty, go over to
a rigid faith, men with a repugnance to premature dogmas and
restrictions *allow* a total belief, on the other hand, to be
wrested from them only slowly and late (because they do not
suffer from uncertainty, but get pleasure). These latter kinds
of extorted total belief and generalization have decisive *value*:
they have grown *despite* the opposing tendency.[54]

This ideal of a philosophic unity developed in the teeth
of resistance naturally finds expression in Nietzsche's comment on his own work. He is unafraid of change, and allows
his thoughts to take him where they will, his passions to
speak with immediate sincerity. But he believes that something enduring is secretly at work there, and he discerns in
periodic retrospect that they have been all of a piece. The
following selections from his letters are representative —
they range from 1868 to 1888:

Moreover without my intention, but precisely on that account
to my delight, all my writings are taking a quite definite direction; they all point like telegraph poles toward a goal of my
studies which I shall soon have firmly in view too.[55]

The unconscious, unpurposed congruence and intimate connectedness of thought going through the motley arranged mass
of my recent books has aroused my astonishment: one can not

[53] XIII 55.
[54] XIII 72. Cf. 58 f.; XVI 349; L.O. 30/8/87, 18/10/88; L.S. 26/12/87.
[55] L.R. 1–3/2/68.

get rid of oneself, therefore let us dare to let ourselves go *extensively.* —

I confess what I now should very much desire — that sometime another man should make a kind of résumé of the conclusions of my thought and, in so doing, compare me with previous thinkers.[56]

... I have now resolved to devote the next five years to the elaboration of my "philosophy," for which I have built a vestibule with my *Zarathustra.*[57]

Thinking through the problems *of principle* ... brings me again and again, despite the boldest attacks on the part of my inner "sceptic," to the same decisions: they already stand, as veiled and obscured as possible, in my "Birth of Tragedy," and everything that I have learned in addition meanwhile has grown into and become part of them.[58]

That the long logic of a quite determinate philosophical *sensibility* is involved here, and not a confusion of a hundred indiscriminate paradoxes and heterodoxies: of that, I believe, nothing has dawned even on my most benevolent readers.[59]

Very curious! I have understood my own writings for four weeks .... It is like the mother with her child: she loves it perhaps, but in perfect stupidity about what the child *is.* — I now have the absolute conviction that everything is well done from the beginning — everything is one and means one.[60]

Nietzsche sees this unity of thought chiefly in retrospect because he believes it dangerous to look for in advance, lest premature self-analysis destroy the unconscious integrity of life.[61] But his lasting concern for it is equally shown by the earnestness and regularity of his retrospection — on New Year's Eve, and in the series of autobiographies which, ending with *Ecce Homo,* began at the age of thirteen.[62]

[56] L.G. 16/8/83.
[57] L.O. 7/4/84. Cf. 24/3/87; L.S. mid-6/84.
[58] L.O. 7/85. Cf. XIV 413; L.G. late 8/83.
[59] L.B. 8/1/88. Cf. L.G. 12/4/87; VII 288 f.; V 328.
[60] L.G. 22/12/88. Cf. L.B. 4/5/88.
[61] Cf. I 389 ff.; XV 43 f.; VII 287 f.; XI 385; X 191; H.K.A. III 291.
[62] Cf. L.Mu. end of 12/64; *Aus Meinem Leben,* H.K.A. I 1 ff.

In his last self-comments Nietzsche not only affirms but specifies the essential identity in his thinking.[63] A few examples: the problem of good and evil occupied him continually from his fourteenth year;[64] *The Birth of Tragedy* already contained the heart of his philosophy — the problem of science in its relation to art and life, the contrast of aesthetic and moral interpretations of existence, the distinction between "strong" and romantic pessimism, the Dionysian Weltanschauung and its revaluation of values;[65] *Untimely Views* were promises of which the rest of his life was the fulfilment:

> The essay, "Wagner in Bayreuth," is a vision of my future: on the other hand my inmost history, my *becoming*, is recorded in "Schopenhauer as Educator." Above all, my *vow!* . . . *What* I am today . . . oh how far I still was from it then! — But I *saw* the land — not an instant did I deceive myself about course, sea, danger — *and* success![66]

Nietzsche of course does not claim an absolute identity in all his writings; rather, his ideal of philosophy as a fruit of life implies change, including the discard of things outgrown. His first period, he recognizes, contained extraneous elements which had to be sloughed off: idolization of Schopenhauer and Wagner, and the associated hope of a German cultural renaissance; romantic idealism, with its "lofty moral attitudes," inflated rhetoric, conscious clinging to illusions, and underlying pessimism.[67] Much distortion in

---

[63] The most important sources are the 1886 preface material and *Ecce Homo*. That Nietzsche is not simply reading into his earlier work the point of view of his last period is proved by the presence of very similar self-comment from early in the middle period (1875–79: XI 116 ff.).

[64] VII 289. XIV 347 indicates that the problem occupied him a year earlier. In a draft of a letter to Wagner, July, 1876, Nietzsche says that he has carried about with him the things discussed in *Richard Wagner in Bayreuth* since his fourteenth year (*Ges. Briefe* V 341).

[65] I 1 ff.; III 12; XI 117; XII 213 f.; XIV 363 ff.; XV 61 ff.; LO. 7/85.

[66] XV 72. Cf. XIV 381 f.; L.O. summer/84; L.R. winter/82–83.

[67] I 1 ff.; XIV 364, 372 f., 375 f.; V 324 f.; XII 212; XVI 362; L.R. winter/82–83. Cf. L.R. c. 20/12/71.

the works of this period, he acknowledges, is due simply to the use of borrowed formulae:

> How much I now regret that then I did not yet have the courage (or the presumption?) to permit myself a *language of my own* in every respect for intuitions and ventures so distinctive — that I laboriously sought to express in Schopenhauerian and Kantian formulae alien and new valuations which radically went against the spirit of Kant and Schopenhauer . . . . ! [68]

In other respects Nietzsche drops some of his early philosophy simply because he has grown older. Each stage of life has its own perspective, he believes, and his youthful work will remain valid for men of that age:

> What I wrote in those days [*Untimely Views*] . . . would not become *truer* through my depicting it again more delicately, limpidly and rigorously now, when my hand and my eye have perhaps learned something more. Every period of life understands the "truth" after its own fashion; and he who steps before those paintings with young, effervescent senses and great aspirations will find as much truth in them as he is able to see.[69]

But Nietzsche attributes more than negative significance to his intellectual development: it follows a dialectical pattern with cumulative effect. He likes to think of philosophies "as methods of educating the mind: with their one-sided demand to see things exactly so and not otherwise, they have always developed a particular power of mind best." [70] Accordingly he speaks of having several philosophies, and recommends that one live through a series of viewpoints, finally uniting all in one comprehensive vision.[71]

[68] I 10 f. Cf. XV 62. He doubtless has particularly in mind the "artists' metaphysics" in *The Birth of Tragedy* (cf. I 8; XIV 364 f.). He also says of the early studies of the origins of morality, made in his second period, that they are "noch unfrei, noch ohne eine eigne Sprache für diese eignen Dinge." (VII 291.)

[69] XIV 380. Cf. 373; III 139.

[70] XIII 82. Cf. 41.

[71] XII 13 f.; V 5, 8; II 11 ff.; XIV 337, 352; XV 9 ff.

A late sketch gives the pattern of his own periods:

The road to wisdom....
The first step. Revere (and obey and *learn*) better than anybody. Collect in oneself all things worthy of veneration and let them struggle together. Carry everything heavy.... Period of community.

The second step. Break the revering heart when one is *most tightly bound.* The free spirit. Independence. Period of wilderness. Criticism of all that is revered (idealization of the unrevered), attempt at inverse valuations.

The third step. Great decision whether fit for the positive position, for affirmation. No god, no man longer *above* me! The instinct of the creator.... Give oneself the right to act.[72]

Therefore his dramatic turning-points were not a wild reversal of extremes, for no reason. He testifies that in his second period, the "great detachment," he deliberately took sides against *himself* and for the things to which he had formerly been unjust. The quest for "knowledge at any price" was at once a "cure" for romantic pessimism and self-disgust — over the disillusion with Wagner — and a means to more just and realistic views of men and things. Above all, it was an adventure of the "free spirit," "wandering" in foreign lands, over "wilderness" and "open sea," "seeking" his lost self, a time of gradual "convalescence" — these are his metaphors and symbols for the experience.[73]

At the same time, Nietzsche sees the second period as the outcome of what was deepest in the first: it contained the wider action of the same undaunted will to destroy shams

---

[72] XIII 39 f. Cf. XII 121 f.; XIV 310 ff.; VI 33 ff.

[73] III 5 ff.; II 6 ff.; V 3 f., 245; VI 396 ff.; XI 121 ff., 383; XII 213 f.; XIV 348 ff., 386 f., 389 f., 393; XV 73 f., 77; L.Bü. 12/82; L.R. winter/82-83. In his second period Nietzsche devoted himself with special zest to the study of natural science (XV 77), and evident good will toward science characterized his general attitude. But to identify the philosophy of the second period with "positivism" is very shallow indeed. His *"Erkenntnis"* is something quite different from ordinary science, though glad to make use of it (cf. V 245), and admiration for the scientific spirit is evident well before *The Birth of Tragedy* was written: see the sketch of Democritus and footnote on Comte, XIX 371 ff., 374 n.

and face the worst sides of existence, and deepened pessimism to include knowledge, art, and morals. He writes:

> The Schopenhauerian man drove me to scepticism toward all that was revered, esteemed, hitherto defended (also toward Greeks, Schopenhauer, Wagner), genius, saint, pessimism of knowledge. By this *roundabout way* I came to the *summit* . . . .[74]

The criticism of morality was itself a moral activity, a "refinement of morality." [75]

Again the transition from the second to the third period was not so much rupture as fulfilment. The second having been a process of seeking "himself" through self-estrangement, the third began when he "found himself" — gained a renewed vision of his task and faith in his right to it.[76] The third does not discard the essence of the second; it takes it up, modified and limited, into a more inclusive whole. A letter of 1883 says:

> Of all good things that I have found, I am least willing to have thrown away or lost the "gaiety of knowing" . . . . Only now, with my son Zarathustra I must *rise* to a *much loftier* gaiety than I could ever depict in words before.[77]

"Gaiety of knowing" is to be limited by a renewed will to art, to appearance, because the creative will is revived.[78] "Not in vain," he writes, "have I made for years the loneliest of all sea voyages: I *have* discovered my 'new country' . . . now indeed I have still to *conquer* it . . . ." [79] In his

---

[74] XI 120. Cf. I 427 ff.; III 4; XV 443, 487; L.O. 31/12/82.
[75] XIV 312, 399.
[76] II 9 f.; III 7 f., 10; VI 223; XIV 390, 404 f.; XV 84 f.; L.O. c. 8/12/83. Cf. IV 112 ff., 319.
[77] L.O. c. 8/12/83. Cf. L.G. 2/4/83. As late as Oct., 1885, Nietzsche writes of having the right "den Sinn seines Lebens in die Erkenntnis zu setzen" (L.O. 17/10/85). For further evidence of the retention of the "free spirit" in the third period cf. VII 39 ff., 287; VIII 302. In this period Nietzsche envisages a higher type of man than the "free spirit," but he regards the works of the second period as the necessary means to the understanding of that higher type (XIV 349).
[78] V 10 f.; VIII 208 f.
[79] L.O. c. 8/12/83. Cf. 9/82.

third period, therefore, he moves more and more from the attitude of universal questioning toward one of peremptory command: from problems to decisions.[80]

Whether or not Nietzsche "has a system," we may conclude, depends upon the point of view, but there can be no doubt that he deserves to be read seriously as a philosopher. It is hoped that the ensuing chapters will explode the myth of his capricious inconsistency, but there is no need to claim him faultless in this respect — what thinker has been? Insight is more important than logic, and it sometimes comes separately.

[80] XV 106. Cf. VIII 217 f.

CHAPTER II

Horizons

Our very strength *suffers us no longer in the old rotten ground* .... *and even perishing is better than becoming half-and-half and poisonous. Our very strength forces us to sea, yonder where till now all suns have set* .... (XV 435)

1. PORTRAIT OF THE PHILOSOPHER

ONE does not understand a thinker simply by reciting his conclusions. By themselves, they are so many dead specimens in a museum. First we must know the setting within which they grew — the driving purpose, the problems which, as Nietzsche describes it, tortured him day and night.[1]

A philosopher often reveals his purpose most plainly when he tells us what philosophy is. Nietzsche would have us discriminate, in this respect, between "philosophical laborers" and philosophers proper. The laborers — among whom he includes even Kant and Hegel — work on inherited traditions of value: they "conquer" the past, sum it up in new formulae. But the real philosophers conquer the future: they create new values and scales of value, and are thereby the prime movers of history, men of the longest foresight, with responsibility for the destiny of man. They are not so much lovers of pre-existing truth as creators of what shall be held true. These sovereign minds are "commanders and law-givers":

They say, "It shall be thus!"; they first determine the Whither and For What of man, and thereby dispose of the preliminary

[1] L.O. Frühjahr/86, summer/86 (after returning from Germany), 14/4/87.

work of all philosophical laborers, all conquerors of the past —
they take hold of the future with a creative hand.... Their
"knowing" is *making*, their making is a legislation, their will
to truth is — *will to power*.[2]

Nietzsche finds that in former ages the great philosophers
and religious founders — Plato and Mohammed, for example
— have eased the terrific responsibility for their deeds by
shifting it to a supernatural authority, but this self-mis-
understanding often led them astray. He implies that the
coming philosophers will do without this illusion: they will
know that they are really creating, not receiving, values.[3]
    What sort of man has the right to such an enterprise? [4]
Clearly he must be a truly universal being, a man of the
greatest personal "size." Thus Nietzsche describes his own
development:

> For the task of a *revaluation of values* perhaps more capacities
> were needed than have ever dwelt together in an individual;
> also, above everything, contrasts [*Gegensätze*] of capacities,
> without allowing them to disturb, destroy one another.
> Hierarchy [*Rangordnung*] of capacities; distance; the art of
> separating without antagonizing; mix nothing, "reconcile"
> nothing; an enormous multiplicity which is nevertheless the
> opposite of chaos — this was the prerequisite, the long, secret
> labor and artistry of my instinct.[5]

That is why the philosopher seldom "comes off"; he has
to be an epitome of human nature, from loftiest to basest
desires, and therefore risks incurable conflict and self-
disgust. His omnivorous curiosity can easily dissipate all
personal identity; he must be deep in love and hate, yet
just; sensitive and plastic, yet firm as granite.[6]
    The philosopher's powers, as Nietzsche conceives them,

---

[2] VII 161 f. Cf. 160 f., 339, 406, 114; XVI 97, 347 f., 350; XV 94, 438, 446 f.;
XIV 332; X 24; I 414 f.
[3] XVI 348 ff.; XV 447.
[4] Cf. VII 165 f.
[5] XV 44.
[6] XVI 350 f. Cf. VII 419 f.; XIII 20 f., 23 f.; XIV 336.

are not the product of mere mental gymnastics; they must
feed on vivid experience. Values will not yield themselves
to the detached observer. "One must be capable of passionate admirations, and creep with love into the heart
of many things. Cold grey eyes do not know what things
are worth . . . ." [7] Only when the philosopher has thus lived
through the whole scale of human existence can he face
adequately the problem of the hierarchy of values:

> Not until now, in the noontide of our life, do we under-
> stand . . . how we had first to experience the most manifold
> and contradictory states of distress and happiness in body and
> soul, as adventurers and circumnavigators of that inner world
> called "man," as surveyors of every "higher" and "one-above-
> another" likewise called "man" — penetrating everywhere,
> almost without fear, disdaining nothing, losing nothing, tasting
> everything . . . — before we might finally say, we free spirits,
> "Here — a *new* problem! Here a long ladder on whose rungs
> we ourselves have sat and climbed — which at some time or
> other we ourselves have *been*! . . . ." [8]

Nietzsche does not mean experience in the trivial sense
either. The philosopher must use the very marrow of his
being, not "present mere brain events"; he has to vivisect
himself and write in his own blood.[9] Therefore truth is
essentially a matter of courage: " 'How much truth does a
mind *endure*, how much truth does it *dare*?' — for me this
became the proper standard of worth. Error is a *cowardice.*" [10] In these terms we can understand his scorn for
the ideal of philosophy as a life of safe retirement and
"objective" contemplation, aloof from the dangers and

[7] XIV 347 f.

[8] II 12 f. Cf. V 7 f.; VII 161; XV 11; X 24.

[9] XIV 361; VII 420; VI 56; III 5; IV 325; XI 383; XV 72. Cf. IV 354;
V 276; XI 382; L.G. end of 8/83; L.O. c. 19/4/83. Nietzsche's letters and autobiographical documents teem with hints at the experiential sources of his thought.
For example, cf. XV 9 ff., 18 f., 63, 67, 77, 90 f., 108; XIV 363 f.; L.G. 26/8/83,
23/7/85, 27/10/87, 20/12/87, 1/2/88; L.O. 5/9/81, c. 25/12/82, c. 28/8/83.

[10] XVI 383. Cf. XV 3, 36, 55, 64, 118 f., 158; VIII 169; L.O. 12/2/87; L.B.
2/12/87.

HORIZONS

disappointments of existence: the true philosopher lives
very "unphilosophically," and "feels the burden and duty
to a hundred attempts and temptations of life: — he risks
himself incessantly, he plays *the* bad game."[11]
There is a place for cool detachment of course. Philosophy is not dumb emotion. Nietzsche objects to intellectual-
ism, not to the intellect. High mentality using full-bodied
passion is but another example of the opposites which the
ideal philosopher will embody:

... he just *cannot* but transpose his state each time into the
most spiritual form and distance — this art of transfiguration *is*
philosophy precisely.... We are no thinking frogs.... We
must continually bring forth our thoughts out of our pain and,
motherlike, give them all we have in us of blood, heart, fire,
zest, passion, torment, conscience, destiny, fate. Living — for
us that means continually transmuting all that we are into light
and flame....[12]

In our own time, Nietzsche perceives, the philosopher
meets greater dangers than ever:

The scope and tower building of the sciences have grown
monstrously, and therewith the probability as well that the
philosopher becomes tired while still a learner, or lets himself
be caught and "specialized" somewhere: so that he never comes
to his summit at all, namely to the survey, general view, *downward view*. Or he gets up there too late, when his best time
and energy are already past; or damaged, coarsened, degenerated
so that his vision, his total value judgment means little any
more. Precisely the acuteness of his intellectual conscience may
make him hesitate and be delayed along the way; he fears the
temptation to be a dilettante ... he knows too well that one who
has lost his self-respect no longer commands, no longer *leads*,
even as a knower .... In addition to this, to redouble the philosopher's difficulty, he demands of himself a judgment, a Yes
or No, not about the sciences but rather about life and the value
of life — he learns with reluctance to believe that he has a right

---

[11] VII 147 f. Cf. 62, 149 ff., 158 f.; XV 451, 473; XVI 85.
[12] V 8. Cf. 30; III 3, 11; IV 328 f., 362 f.; XIV 348, 398 f.

or even a duty to this judgment, and has to seek his way to that right and that belief only on the basis of the broadest . . . experiences, and often hesitatingly, doubtingly, mutely.[13]

Again, our age misleads the philosopher by showing him partial and decadent ideals — philosophy as criticism or as science. Nietzsche takes care to mark these off from his own conception. To identify philosophy with criticism is to disgrace it, he holds, for criticism is only one of the tools of the philosopher. He will use it severely, of course. He has to be the "bad conscience of his time," if he is to shape *new* values. Therefore he must obtain distance, detachment; and since he too is a child of the time, this requires that he conquer himself — including his first, romantic revolt *against* the time: in this sense he should become "timeless." It will be well to remember that Nietzsche, in criticizing his age, by his own confession criticizes part of himself, of life as he has known it.[14]

Science also Nietzsche considers invaluable as a tool, and he deeply regrets the inevitable limits of his own scientific knowledge. But he holds that the scholar and scientist differ essentially from the philosopher: their declaration of independence in recent days — a phase of the democratic movement — has obscured the fact that they really belong to an inferior rank. They are specialists, means, not ends: slaves working under orders — directly those of the guild, ultimately those of some philosopher. "The scholar is the herd animal in the realm of knowledge," essentially imitative, in need of a leader. The philosopher is the natural leader; his business is not to specialize but to rule; and if philosophy is

[13] VII 146 f. Cf. XVI 348 f.; XV 447.
[14] VII 158 ff., 162; V 340; VIII 1 f.; XI 135; XV 9, 11, 447. Cf. X 45, 102; I 474 f. Likewise the great philosopher will be a sceptic and freethinker, strong enough not to need a supporting faith — but also a free-*actor*, one whose will is not weakened by scepticism, nor bound by the timidities of democratic freethinkers (V 282; VII 63 ff., 152–58; XIV 396 f.; XVI 342).

generally disdained by scientists today, it is largely because the so-called philosophers — "epistemologists," "positivists," and the like — are themselves only humdrum specialists, and poor ones at that.[15]

Against all the weakly modern ideals, Nietzsche would have the philosopher unite theory and practice, thought and action. Philosophy in the past, he maintains, has too often been a mere compensatory *Umdichten* of reality, a projection of wishful fantasy into the nature of things; it has therefore been chiefly a quietive, an excuse for inaction, peddled as a specific for "consolation," "resignation," and "spiritual peace." He himself takes the opposite view:

> The most important question in all philosophy . . . seems to me to be how far things have an unalterable character and shape: so as, when this question is answered, to go, with the most reckless courage, for the *improvement of the side of the world known to be alterable*.[16]

Beyond the conceptual re-interpretation of existence he sees a higher task: "to *set* a *goal* and mould actuality toward it" — "interpretation by deed." [17]

Nietzsche faced his own future in this spirit. In his mature period he scorned the suggestion that his main concern was with books.[18] Rather, he taught that the philosopher, as the man of greatest vision, must guide humanity toward his new ideal.[19] He recognized that such a purpose involved

[15] VII 143 ff., 148 f., 150 ff., 158 ff.; XV 446 f.; III 283 ff.; V 330, 341 f.; VI 183 ff.; XIII 13; XIV 75; X 20 f., 24, 114; I 410, 477–92; L.D. mid-8/68, c. 20/10/68. Cf. XVII 340; H.K.A. III 328 f. Nietzsche's criticism of the scientist as philosopher does not mitigate his esteem for scientific method, nor his use of that method in philosophy. See below, pp. 251 f. Nor does it conflict with admiration for the scientific spirit in contrast to certain *kinds* of philosophy (as in IV 295 f., 352 ff.).

[16] I 514. Cf. 492 f., 513 f.; XIII 23 f.; XIV 401, 75; XVI 72, 74, 84 f.

[17] XVI 97.

[18] L.S. 19/6/81, 11/83; L.O. c. 11/11/83.

[19] VII 85, 137 f.; XIV 397; XVI 351 f., 359. In Nietzsche's earlier writings the philosopher figures in a less decisively creative but none the less active rôle, as the "physician of culture" (X 180 ff.), art and religion being considered the radically originative forces (X 114, 183, 188): later their functions are absorbed by the philosophic ideal.

"more than was ever called philosophy," and therefore described it as a synthesis of several hitherto separate types — "To become artist (creator), saint (lover) and philosopher (knower) in one person: — my practical aim!" [20]

From the time when Nietzsche grasped the full scope of his life-work — his Aufgabe, as he called it — he devoted his energies to its completion with absolute singleness of heart. The rest of his books were to prepare for a dramatic crisis in history, which he was planning to precipitate finally by the publication of Revaluation of all Values. The final writings had a deliberately violent tone because they were incitements to world revolution. Thenceforth his philosophy was indeed to be written in blood.[21]

2. "GOD IS DEAD"

Beyond question the major premise of Nietzsche's philosophy is atheism. He never seriously doubts it; rather he describes himself as an atheist "by instinct." [22] Despite — or because of — an ecclesiastical family background and an earnestly pious childhood, his religious belief, in the orthodox sense, drops away forever during his student days.[23]

[20] L.O. c. 20/8/84; XII 213. Cf. 214 f.

[21] It is a mistake to imagine that Nietzsche's revolutionary violence is a sudden whim of his last months. Most of the daring claims of Ecce Homo are already made in the 1886 preface material and in letters dated 1883 and 1884. The sense of destiny and the devotion to a supreme Aufgabe are expressed in letters beginning as early as the summer of 1881. Cf. L.S. 19/6/81, mid-7/81, 29/11/81, early 8/83, early 3/85; L.R. 15/7/82, 22/2/84; L.O. summer/83, c. 11/11/83; c. 10/3/84, c. 2/5/84, 21/5/84, before 10/7/84, 14/5/87; L.M. 2/84, 5/84; L.G. 20/12/87; XIV 357, 361, 364, 409 — also the draft of a letter to M. v. Meysenbug, Ges. Briefe V 493. Compare XV 49, 115 ff., 125.

[22] XV 26. Cf. 70. V 168, VI 379 f., and XIII 314 make it a matter of "taste" [Geschmack] rather than arguments or virtue. Atheism is a term with several meanings. Nietzsche was primarily a Christian atheist. The metaphysics of The Birth of Tragedy included a non-moral artist deity (I 45). The later metaphysics excluded all supernatural entities, but Nietzsche wrote that "properly, only the moral God is refuted" (XIII 75), and that many other gods are still possible (XVI 380 f.). XII 169 declares that the sole true proposition of all Religionsphilosophie is the Epicurean one, "If there are gods, they do not care for us" (cf. III 194). A late fragment suggests the deification of the culminating epoch in the cosmic cycle of eternal recurrence (XVI 115, 170).

[23] The early piety is evident in the juvenilia, some of which have been pre-

Since atheism seems obviously true to him, he seldom offers arguments for it, and one has to search his writings to find reasons for his attitude. When found, they come to this: that there is no evidence for the existence of the Christian God, and that all experience is evidence against it, "because all happening is neither kind, nor intelligent, nor true." [24] Belief in a being so unlike life as we know it seems utterly irrational to Nietzsche, and he therefore deems psychological and historical explanation of it the most effective refutation: it is the projected wish-fulfilment of human needs baffled by the real world.[25] And as such it enshrines values to which Nietzsche is irreconcilably opposed because they are a "crime against life." If the Christian God *existed* he would not be divine: "We deny God as God . . ." [26]

However little pain the loss of religious belief may give Nietzsche, to live out its consequences is a task of the first magnitude.[27] His mature period opens with the pronouncement, not of simple atheism, but of a catastrophic historical experience: "God is dead!" [28] That is to say, something on which men have lived for centuries has vanished; the heart of Christendom has stopped, and the rest of its body faces death, for the spirit has departed from its members. This is more than a personal experience; it is the knell of a civilization. Nietzsche likens our predicament to the legend that long after the death of Buddha his shadow was

served from his eleventh year onward (cf. H.K.A. I 31). No *struggle* over religious doubts is expressed in his youthful letters, and very little in the juvenilia: H.K.A. II 55 or L.F.N. I 314 is practically the only significant passage. A later, probably autobiographical, note estimates that the peak of a modern person's religiosity comes in his tenth year (XI 63).

[24] XVI 270 f., 380; XIV 72; II 52 ff., 116 f.; V 216, 279; X 402; VII 77 f.; XII 167; H.K.A. III 322 or L.F.N. I 332.

[25] VI 42 ff.; IV 89; II 117-22, 135 f., 138, 140; XV 242 f., 384 f., 425; XIII 298 f.; VIII 49 f., 97 ff., 231 ff.; L.F.N. I 330 or H.K.A. III 319.

[26] VIII 281. Cf. 232 ff.; VI 379 f.

[27] A boarding school essay (1862) already recognizes the difficulty of constructing something to take the place of Christianity (L.F.N. I 313 f. or H.K.A. II 54 f.).

[28] V 147, 271; VI 12; XIII 316. Cf. I 127; III 247; VI 378 f.; IX 128.

WHAT NIETZSCHE MEANS

. to be seen in a cave: it will be long before all the
.dows of God have disappeared. Our first reaction may
even be one of relief and encouragement, but later our culture will undergo a period of "rupture, destruction, downfall, revolution," a "stupendous logic of terror," an eclipse
of the sun unlike any yet known on earth.[29]

To lead mankind through this crisis becomes the central
problem of Nietzsche's philosophy: to free every phase of
life from the moribund remnants and to rebuild on a new
basis that should justify the loss of the old by the creation
of a yet higher form of existence: [30] "Perhaps just that renunciation," he writes, "will also lend us the strength with
which renunciation itself can be borne; perhaps man will
rise ever higher from the time when he no longer *flows
away* into a god." [31]

As an atheist, Nietzsche is moved by a passion for integrity which permits no compromise. He scorns half-
hearted devices for buttressing a faith that has inwardly
collapsed: "bridges of lies to the old ideal," finite gods,
the will to believe in what comforts us.[32] He hates the inward falsity of modern Christians who profess the old faith
and live a worldly life.[33] He demands purity (*Reinheit*),
intellectual honesty, freedom from self-deception above all:
given the way we now think and live, what we now *know*,
"it is indecent to be a Christian today." [34] Indeed he claims
that this very sincerity which now demands radical atheism
is the outgrowth of the scrupulous Christian piety it is destroying:

...we have outgrown Christianity because we have dwelt,
not too far from it, but too near it; nay more, because we have

[29] V 147, 164, 271 f.; XIII 316 f. Cf. XV 137 f.; H.K.A. II 55 or L.F.N. I 314.
[30] V 147 ff., 163 f.; XIII 317.
[31] V 217. Cf. IV 313, 330; XII 167, 170 f.; XV 241; H.K.B. I 181.
[32] VIII 286 f.; XII 167; XV 267 f.; IV 8 f. Cf. I 224 ff. Hence Nietzsche's
disdain for romanticists like Wagner who, after a riot of freedom, collapse
finally at the foot of the cross (II 117; VII 230).   [33] VIII 265; XV 282.
[34] VIII 263, 296; II 117; VI 265; XV 22 f., 112 f., 116 f., 123; XIII 317.

grown *out from* it — it is our stricter and more fastidious piety itself which *forbids* us to remain Christians today. —[35]

Christendom was a whole, he maintains. If an essential part is broken we should not dally with patching up fragments; we should work out a new whole.[36] Nietzsche's integrity is constructive as well as destructive.

Nor, finally, does he let the loss of the old faith turn him sour or force him to resignation. He does not pose in despair, nor mount a pedestal to denounce the universe and display his own superior nobility. Nietzsche begins and ends as a man of affirmative good will. Very early he writes to Rohde: "Ah, my true fellow, one has no alternative: one must be in hope or despair. Once for all I have decided for hope." [37]

3. SOLITUDE AND COMMUNITY

The death of God brings a profounder loneliness than man has yet known, and this was added to the human loneliness of Nietzsche's life. To Overbeck he declared, ". . . for all those who somehow had a 'god' for company, what *I* know as 'solitude' did not yet exist." [38]

The essay on Schopenhauer begins with the predicament of the self alone with its struggles and its destiny: What am I? What shall I do with my life? We have to be responsible to ourselves for our own existence. Each of us knows that he is a unique person, but few have the energy, courage or insight to throw off the husks of convention and achieve a sincere realization of their potentialities, and no one can do that for us. But unless we do "become ourselves," life is meaningless. "There is no drearier and more repulsive

---

[35] XIII .318. Cf. VI 377, 380; VII 480 f.; V 272 ff., 302; XII 137; XV 331.
[36] VIII 120; XV 82.
[37] L.R. 31/12/73. Cf. XIV 381; XV 65 f., 106, 117; I 11; V 245, 324 f.; VI 62, 115.
[38] L.O. 2/7/85. Cf. IV 313; XIV 336; XV 205.

creature in nature than the man who has shunned his genius...." [39]

So in another essay Nietzsche urges:

... ask yourself why you, an individual, exist, and if no one else can tell you, then do but try to justify the meaning of your existence *a posteriori*, as it were, by setting yourself a purpose, a goal, a "whereunto"... Perish of it, by all means — I know no better life purpose....[40]

This self-given goal turns out to be identical with the true or "higher" self, the unique potentiality which the individual should realize: "... your true nature [*Wesen*] lies, not concealed deep in you, but immeasurably high above you, or at least above what you ordinarily take for your self." [41] Realizing your "higher self," therefore, means fulfilling your loftiest vision, noblest ideal.[42] Thus Nietzsche's initial craving to "become himself" is something very different from ordinary "self-expressionism" or self-indulgence: it is one of the deep ethical roots of his philosophy.

This passionate idealism, this will to conceive life grandly and throw oneself into it without reserve, reveals Nietzsche's profoundly religious nature as well as did his uncompromising sincerity.[43] He says that he has never been ambitious for fame, but that he finds it unbearable "not to be occupied and grown together" with what seems to him "most momentous in the world." [44]

On his way to the goal of self-fulfilment Nietzsche en-

---

[39] I 388. Cf. 387 ff., 430 f. Compare the signs of early resentment toward the warping influences of his own childhood: L.F.N. I 313 f., 316 f. or H.K.A. II 54 f., 58.

[40] I 366. Compare the praise of quixotism in L.B. 8/1/88.

[41] I 391. Cf. 413, 444, 514; VI 94.

[42] II 400. Cf. III 8, 10; XV 43 f., 72, 78.

[43] In *Ecce Homo* Nietzsche expresses scorn for idealism, but it is clear from the context that he means the *old* idealism which he is combating (cf. XV 48, 73 f., 153). Examples of idealism and of the use of the term *"Ideal"* in a favorable sense during Nietzsche's last period will be found in XIV 274, 351; XII 369; XVI 381. Nietzsche also testifies that he has had specifically religious experiences (XVI 380; XIV 348, 367, 391 f. Cf. XV 90; VII 272).

[44] XI 381. On ambition cf. XVI 194; L.O. c. 2/5/86.

counters perilous difficulties. The individual has to liberate himself from environmental influences which are false to his essential being, for the "unfree man" is "a disgrace to nature."[45] But emancipation is not enough; nature, freed from "unnature," desires "transformation through love."[46] For the free man still has to face a sharp conflict between the higher self and the lower, between the ideal aspired to and the contemptibly imperfect present.[47] From this arise the twin dangers of either being torn to pieces, or hardening his heart and giving up the ideal; in the latter event, "the uniqueness of his being has become an indivisible, incommunicable atom, a stone grown cold."[48] Only the love, only the fidelity of lower self to higher, and of higher to lower, can save the whole — and at bottom "we yearn immeasurably to become whole."[49]

Thus in the solitude of his own soul does Nietzsche touch one of his deepest problems: how to love and use the basest qualities in nature, which are essential to complete fruition, without compromising the noblest; how to love the highest values without being driven thereby to disgust with existence as a whole; how to combine negation and affirmation: in short the problem of evil, of pessimism. Nietzsche testifies that the root of his pessimism lies in our common incapacity for assisting the realization of the ideal we behold,[50] and that in fact pessimism is his temperamental disposition, disgust with life his greatest danger: serenity and gaiety his victories.[51]

[45] I 585, 383, 387 f., 414 f. This is ostensibly about Schopenhauer, but there is no doubt that Nietzsche is giving his own experience here.
[46] I 586.
[47] I 411 f. Cf. VI 60. The connection of love and contempt [*Verachtung*] occurs with significant frequency: cf. VI 14 ff., 261 f., 94, 388, 418; VII 95, 170; XVI 343; VIII 363; XI 67 f.
[48] I 414. Cf. VI 62.
[49] I 444, 506 f., 514, 548.
[50] I 441.
[51] V 3 f.; XI 382; XIV 376, 406; XV 23, 123, 158, 205 f.; VI 141 f.; L.R. 14/5/74. 23/2/86; L.O. *Frühjahr*/86.

The individual, he suggests, can escape obsession with his own limitations by generalizing his ideal, and by seeking fellowship with others in common devotion to it. Let him "work at the consummation of nature" by living for the production of the man of genius, whether in himself or in others. The perception of one's own limitations, and discontent with these, are the root of true culture: a community of men dedicated to the generation of great individuals who shall achieve perfection.[52] In such devotion one attains the best fulfilment compatible with one's own defects:

... how does your life, the life of the individual, obtain the greatest value, the deepest meaning? How is it least wasted? Surely only through your living for the advantage of the rarest and most valuable specimens . . . .[53]

At this point we meet Nietzsche's ultimate intuition of value, that positive inspiration which underlies all his philosophy. The man who professes the goals of culture thereby declares:

"I see something above me, greater and more human than I myself am; help me, everybody, to attain it, as I will help everyone who knows and suffers from the same thing: in order that at last the man should again arise who feels himself abundant and unlimited in knowing and loving, in vision and ability to achieve, and hangs upon and in nature with all his entireness as judge and standard of the value of things." [54]

This quality of individualized and perfected human existence, therefore, is what makes life finally worth living for Nietzsche.

The achievement of human solidarity in the realization of this vision is his path from solitude to community:

The individual shall be dedicated to something super-personal — that is what tragedy demands; he shall forget the fright-

[52] I 439–445.
[53] I 443. Cf. 411; 464 f., 367 f.
[54] I 443. Cf. XVI 359.

ful anguish which death and time cause the individual: for even in the smallest moment, in the shortest atom of his career something sacred can befall him which infinitely outweighs all struggle and all tribulation — that is what it means *to be tragically disposed* [*gesinnt*]. Even though the whole of humanity must die one day — who could doubt it! — the goal is given it, as the supreme task of all coming ages, so to grow together into oneness and community that it shall go to meet its impending extinction *as a whole* with a *tragic disposition*. In this highest task is comprised all ennoblement of men; from its final rejection would result the saddest picture a friend of humankind could put before his soul. That is how I feel it! There is only one hope and one guarantee for the future of what is human: it lies in this, *that the tragic disposition shall not perish.*[55]

4. UNTIMELINESS

Some thinkers are born in their own time, others not. Nietzsche was not. He and his contemporary society were radically out of phase, and he never found the solidarity he sought — not even with a single friend. Nevertheless he recognized that in part he shared the nature of his age. So the inner contrast of higher and lower selves found an extension in the conflict between Nietzsche and the modern world, or between Nietzsche the man of the future and Nietzsche the modern man, the decadent. In the end he was proud to claim that he had experienced *in himself* all the pathological features of the era, because he believed that he had won his battle to transcend them.[56] He was indeed peculiarly fitted to be "the bad conscience of his time."

As a young man still absorbed in the ordeal of finding himself, Nietzsche craved above all some person to whom he could look up and some community of effort into which

[55] I 523. Cf. 74; VI 115. Nietzsche refers approvingly to this passage in *Ecce Homo* (XV 37). The same sense of solidarity appears later in occasional uses of the term *Menschheit* (e.g. VI 87; XVI 82).
[56] Cf. VIII 1 f.; XV 9 ff.; I 416 f.

he could throw himself unreservedly — but in vain. During his last period he could still write:

Why do I not find among the living the men who look beyond me and must see me beneath themselves? Have I only *searched* poorly then? — And I long so particularly for *such*!!

I have become acquainted with no man whom I should have felt as *authority* in his *most general* judgments, whereas I had a deep need for such a man.[57]

The noblest to be found, he tells us, were the *genuine* Christian and the romantic artist. When these ceased to exemplify the highest ideal for him, nothing was left in the contemporary world to serve him as inspiration. For Nietzsche, the nineteenth century was a barren age.[58]

Unfortunately he could not simply ignore its sterility; it was too insistently repugnant. He felt a loathing for the typical manifestations of the time which was almost physical; expressions of disgust and contempt for men came often from his pen. His aristocratic tastes were offended at every turn by modern commonness:

In all times there will be great peril for one who has the desires of a lofty and fastidious soul, but today it is extraordinary. Flung into a noisy, plebeian age, with which he does not care to eat out of the same dish, he can easily perish from hunger and thirst or, in case he nevertheless "falls to" at last, from disgust.[59]

Therefore Nietzsche soon began to make a comprehensive critique of present culture: the series of *Untimely Views*, of which as many as thirteen were planned, was to help him "expectorate" the hostile feelings with which his "untimeliness" filled him.[60]

If Nietzsche was dissatisfied with the few genuine Christians, he was positively revolted by the typical Christianity

---

[57] XII 219; XIII 220. Cf. XIII 213; L.K. 6/7/74; L.S. 3/2/82; H.K.B. II 7 f.
[58] XIV 358 f.; III 7; XII 367 f.
[59] XIV 384. Cf. VIII 263; VII 44; VI 140 ff., 392 f., 419; I 362.
[60] L.R. 19/3/74. Cf. X 473 ff.

of the time. He saw it weak, half-hearted, gradually beating a dogmatic retreat and compromising itself with alien values. Having lost the fear of God, it was degenerating into a religion of comfortable enjoyment and respectability. The best that was left of it was a "gentle moralism," the modest disposition to believe that divine love would make everything for the best: in a word, "the euthanasia of Christianity." Moreover, by lingering on in this enfeebled condition it threatened to become a permanent hindrance to the achievement of any more strenuous ideal.[61]

Nor did Nietzsche think much better of the secular philosophies which offered themselves as substitutes — democracy, liberalism, humanitarianism, scientific and industrial progress — "Modern ideas," he sarcastically called them. They repeated the same essential values on a less heroic scale, and none seemed to offer an adequate goal for living. Their ideals if realized would be contemptible. The mere alleviation of misery, the mere quantitative spread of "happiness" over the greatest number of people, were too negative to satisfy him. To a deeper mind such philosophies seemed but temporary veils over an ultimate conviction of the worthlessness of existence.[62]

For this reason Nietzsche had more sympathy with the pessimistic thinkers of the century. At least they were more profound than Herbert Spencer. Their pessimism, if not valid as a protest against the universe, none the less had merit as a protest against the general spirit of the age. They had courage and sincerity. These qualities, Nietzsche states, were what drew him to Schopenhauer.[63]

[61] IV 58, 88; II 128; XV 203 f., 318; X 289, 298; IX 211; I 397. Cf. I 127. Nietzsche had far greater respect for the Christianity of former times. His view of it might be summed up in the statement that Christianity gave the wrong answers to the right questions (cf. L.S. 22/2/87). His respect for genuine Christianity is also expressed in his pride at having so great an enemy (L.S. 17/9/88; XV 22).

[62] I 2 f., 7, 86, 94 f., 100, 104 ff., 124 ff., 160 f., 358 f., 367 f.; VII 135 ff., 180 f.; IX 142, 161 f.; X 205 f.; XV 204 f., 224, 387 f.

[63] XIV 375, 385; XI 378; I 128 f. Cf. XV 68.

Business and politics, he perceived, were the dominant forces of the time, and, as dominant, barbarous. Instead of subserving higher goals they perverted art, education, and philosophy to their own sordid purposes, making all modern life restless and spiritually empty. He was particularly distressed by the turn of affairs in Germany after the war of 1870, and from that time onward he became increasingly hostile to the spirit of the new empire. "A great victory is a great danger," he warned his fatherland.[64]

Uncivilized in its strength, the age was also weak and false in its so-called culture. The preponderant type of man was the philistine, the "flock animal," who permitted himself occasional excursions into art or philosophy, but was careful to distinguish these amusements from the "serious business" of life, such as making money. Not so much his mediocrity as his shameless self-satisfaction *in* mediocrity, as if he were rightly the measure of all things, aroused Nietzsche's ire. The culture of the "culture philistine" (*Bildungsphilister*) was not a sincere expression of a unified life, but an ornament used to conceal an ugly interior. And because it concealed, it was the chief obstacle to a genuine cleansing and renovation.[65]

Multiplicity, barbarism, smugness, falsity, ugliness, weakness: these sum up Nietzsche's impression of his age:

Taken as an appearance for the eye and compared with the previous appearances of life, the existence of modern men . . . shows an unspeakable poverty and exhaustion, despite the unspeakable variety . . . . Is not the whole like the glimmer and flash of countless pebbles and particles borrowed from earlier cultures? Is it not all inappropriate pomp, apish movement, presumptuous superficiality? . . . . And in between, veiled and concealed only by the rapidity of motion and gyration — grey

[64] I 179 f., 322 f., 420 ff., 446 ff., 486 f., 533 f.; V 77 f.; L.Ge. 7/11/70. Cf. I 109.
[65] I 139, 181, 191 f., 314 ff., 322, 361, 374, 397 f., 517 f., 534 f.; IX 413. Nietzsche soon came to include moral hypocrisy among the greatest vices of his age (XIV 356). His favorite names for modern falsity in general were *Schauspielerei*, *Falschmünzerei*, *Tartüfferie* (XV 199; XVI 248; L.S. 11/83).

impotence, gnawing strife, most industrious tedium, dishonest misery! [66]

To find the whole world sorry was an additional incentive to pessimism. How to adjust to this fact became a chief concern of Nietzsche's philosophy: how to discover what was fundamentally wrong with the age, to explain how things came to go wrong, to find means to set them right again, and — behind all this — to construct a general Weltanschauung in which the very existence of such ugly times as the present should be justified.[67]

5. TRUTH VS. LIFE

We have seen Nietzsche attribute "the death of God" to an uncompromising will to truth, which had been bred by the religion it now undermines. In the end, he believes, this will has destroyed its only adequate object. Instead of leading to a supreme, all-satisfying reality, as once it seemed to do, the quest for absolute truth is becoming a restless unmasking of illusions: everything is false, it concludes, and the result is to intensify the pessimism derived from the self and contemporary civilization, by adding the "pessimism of the intellect." [68]

For a brief period, during his infatuation with Wagner and Schopenhauer, Nietzsche escapes complete scepticism by the half-voluntary illusion that certain types of artistic, philosophic or religious inspiration yield an intuitive apprehension of ultimate reality.[69] But he soon drops this as but a last figment of religious belief, and consequently his

[66] I 527. Cf. 143, 160 f.
[67] Cf. XV 442 f.
[68] Cf. III 19; X 210; XV 443.
[69] The last ghost of this belief seems to be departing in the essay, "On Truth and Falsehood in the Non-Moral Sense" (1873; cf. X 200). It has its apogee of course in *The Birth of Tragedy* (cf. I 8, 34 f., 102). In that book Nietzsche follows Schopenhauer to the extent of holding that Music (more generally, the Dionysian element in art) is a revelation of the ultimate nature of things (cf. I 40 f.). The fragments from this period contrast the Apollinian as *Schein des Scheins* with the Dionysian as *Schein des Seins* (IX 183).

middle period begins (in *Things Human*) with an explicit rejection of all metaphysics, in the sense of the claim to know something absolute, behind nature, in terms of which the riddle of existence can be finally "explained." History and natural science — or, more generally, scientific thinking — thenceforth count as comparatively true; metaphysics and religion as deeper stages of illusion.[70]

Characteristically, Nietzsche spends little time on the arguments of the metaphysicians. They do not impress him as worth the trouble. It is sufficient to look at the history of hopeless contradiction between them, and especially to perceive their ulterior purpose — namely to reinstate some form of quasi-religious belief in "God, freedom and immortality." In short they are patent rationalizations in the service of the old ideal, and after one has accepted the downright atheism of Schopenhauer all previous systems become untenable. It only remains to perceive that even in Schopenhauer the old ideal "sneaked through." [71]

It is natural that Nietzsche, a German, should pay most attention to Kant and Hegel in his rejection of metaphysics. He sees them as, at bottom, merely "procrastinators" of the inevitable rise of atheism. The Kantian dodge was the limitation of rational knowledge, leaving room beyond for the arbitrary postulation of what one wished to believe. The Hegelian dodge consisted of reading a divine process of self-realization into history. Nietzsche considers both men dupes of the dying ideal.[72]

His own position, early metaphysics apart, begins with the sceptical elements of Kant and pushes them further. Metaphysical knowledge is not only impossible but mean-

---

[70] II 33 f., 38 f., 44 f., 47, 116 ff.

[71] III 18 f.; IV 5 ff.; V 301 f.; XV 154. Cf. VII 10 f.

[72] XV 211 f., 216 f., 328, 331 f., 440; V 301; IV 6. Nietzsche admires Hegel for his affirmative Weltanschauung, his development of the idea of process or evolution (*Werden*), his glorification of the historical sense, and certain aspects of the dialectical movement of contradictories (XV 211 f., 442; V 300 f.; IV 8).

ingless. It is incorrect to say that we can never know "ultimate reality," for the very notion of an ultimate or absolute is illegitimate. Hence, in the traditional sense of the term, there is no Truth because there is no "True Being": "everything is false." [73] Even science is anthropomorphic. No one has established its universal validity, or the "*a priori* synthetic judgments" on which it rests — the Kantian proof reduces finally to the tautology that they are "possible" "by virtue of a capacity" (*vermöge eines Vermögens*). Science therefore appears no longer as the dictation of Natural Laws by Reason, but as the clever way in which a particular animal species simplifies its environment.[74]

Thus, though metaphysics is an illusion from the point of view of science, science in turn becomes but another stage of illusion as far as absolute truth is concerned. In *The Birth of Tragedy* Nietzsche already attacks the scientific optimism of his time under the guise of "Socraticism." The "theoretic man" pursues truth in the delusion that reality can be fathomed, and even purged of evil, by rational thought and its applications. But faith in the omnipotence of reason shatters, for the courageously persistent thinker, not only on the fact that science can never complete its work but chiefly on the positive apprehension that reality is irrational.[75] As Nietzsche writes later, "We are illogical and therefore unjust beings from the first, *and can know this*: that is one of the greatest and most insoluble disharmonies of existence." [76]

The sincere search for truth culminates in despair, and Nietzsche mentions this as a third danger which the solitary

[73] XVI 96, 100, 58 ff.; XV 153; II 33.
[74] VII 20 f., 41; X 145, 190 f., 194 ff.; II 36 f.; XVI 19 f., 26, 56 f., 80. This scientific scepticism proves that Nietzsche, even in his middle period, was no, "positivist."
[75] I 104 ff., 108, 124–28; IX 179; XIV 369 f.
[76] II 49. Cf. 48.

self encounters in its development. He predicts that such will be the ultimate effect of the Kantian philosophy. The masses will experience it merely "in the form of a corroding and crumbling scepticism and relativism," but nobler minds will be driven to desperation, as was Kleist. With evident sympathy Nietzsche quotes from him:

> We cannot determine whether what we call truth is really truth, or whether it only seems so to us. If the latter, then after death the truth we accumulate here is nothing any more, and all endeavor ... vain .... My sole, my highest goal has sunk and I have none left.[77]

Nietzsche uses "truth," like many of his terms, in two senses: an old one which he denies, and a new one which he affirms. The despair just described is of course despair of attaining the traditional *kind* of truth. There is another kind which seizes him with horrible conviction:

> To be sure, what I *now* call truth is something quite fearful and repulsive ....
>
> *Do* you understand Hamlet? Not doubt, *certainty* is what drives people crazy ... We are all *afraid* of the truth ....
>
> ... there is only one world, and that is false, cruel, contradictory, demoralizing, without sense ... A world so made is the true world.... That falsehood is necessary in order to live: this too forms part of that dreadful and dubious character of existence.[78]

That is the "truth" which demands courage of the thinker.[79] It is the truth about illusion, and the various stages of illusion previously considered — science, art, metaphysics, reli-

[77] I 408 f. Cf. 413 f.; X 141; XIII 53. "Das Lied der Schwermuth" (VI 433 ff.) is Nietzsche's most personal and acute utterance of this despair. One must read the many expressions of his primary passion for truth in order to appreciate the gravity of the problem as he experienced it: cf. I 428; II 48; IV 297, 345; V 37 f.; XII 8, 127, 397; XIV 231; L.S. 11/6/65; also the draft of a letter to Georg Rée, *Ges. Briefe* V 526.

[78] XIV 382; XV 36; XVI 270 f. Cf. I 55 f., 65, 67 f.; XV 121 f. "The truth is ugly" (XVI 248, 94).

[79] See above, note 10.

gion — are so many means of flight from reality, if literally believed in.[80] Thus Nietzsche envisages several levels of "illusion," each false in comparison to the one beneath it (e.g. the artist's world in comparison to the scientist's); but the last level is not "true being": it is simply the irrational totality which includes the others, and which by traditional (Platonic-Christian) standards *is* a world of illusion, i.e. of relativity and flux, in which nothing ever "really is." [81]

So, for Nietzsche, reality is literally bottomless. There is no ultimate truth in the sense of something eternal and rational which would be the perfect fulfilment of our craving to know. In practice, therefore, the inherited will to truth means not the attainment of truth but the penetration of veil after veil of illusion.[82] At this point the question arises, "whether one *can* abide consciously in untruth? Or, if one *must* do that, whether death be not preferable?" [83]

But the baffling of reason is not all: life itself depends on illusion. Nietzsche believes that we can neither think, feel nor act without falsity. "The sincere person ends by realizing that he always lies." [84] From this point of view the will to truth as a will to destroy illusion appears as a will to death: its unrestricted exercise is hostile to life.[85] Thus the problem of truth is double-edged: it involves a conflict between the demand for absolute truth and its frustration by the nature of things, and a conflict between the desire to know and the desire to survive: it seems impossible to live with truth or to live without it. This is one of the chief issues in

[80] XVI 271; I 3, 125. Cf. VII 54.

[81] For further instances of contrast between various levels of illusion (*Schein, Wahn, Täuschung, Irrthum, Lüge*) see I 7 ff., 33 ff., 58, 104, 128 f., 160 f., 290, 293, 339, 342, 379; II 48; IX 4; X 111 ff., 118 f., 127, 206 f.; XIII 28 f., 50; XII 21–49.

[82] Cf. I 104; II 405, 409, 412; V 237, 273 f.; VII 187, 189; VIII 295; X 162; XII 260; XVI 96.

[83] II 51.

[84] XII 293, 224; II 5, 48 ff.; X 119, 208; VII 55; XIV 16, 87; I 339, 342.

[85] V 275; X 208; XIII 27, 124; XIV 7 f.

The Birth of Tragedy, where it is symbolized by the antagonism of Socrates and Greek tragedy, of science and art.
Nietzsche writes later, ". . . I face this discord with holy terror to this day. . . . *The Birth of Tragedy* believes in art
against the background of another belief: that it *is impossible to live with the truth . . . .*" [86]
Hence a new question — "a problem with horns," Nietzsche calls it: what is the *value* of truth, or of its pursuit?
Why not be deceived? May not illusion be worth more? Is
not truth in any case a relative, not an absolute value? [87]

6. NIHILISM

Man's religious history, Nietzsche observes, has bred in
him a new need: a need to have a meaning for his life as a
whole.[88] "The fundamental fact of the human will" is "its
horror of a vacuum: *it needs a goal* — and it will sooner will
Nothing [*das Nichts*], than *not* will." [89] The atheist discovers that in fact it has willed "Nothing," namely values
which are not only unreal but hostile to reality.[90] Therefore the "death of God" means that the very heart has
dropped out of existence. For apart from the religious
("ascetic") ideal, the human lot as a whole has had no meaning. " 'Why man at all?' — was a question without an answer; the *will* for man and earth was lacking; after every
great human destiny there sounded, as refrain, a still greater
'In vain!' " [91]

We have followed Nietzsche through several phases of
experience, in each of which his atheism precipitated a
tragic contrast between the ideal and the actual: no redemption for an imperfect self, no providence for a sick society,
no truth for a passionate mind. To these should now be
added the plight of man amid the cruelties of evolution and

[86] XIV 368. Cf. I 55 f., 92 ff., 104, 160 f.
[87] I 2; V 274 f.; VII 9, 55, 469 ff.; XIII 340 f.; XIV 12. Cf. XVI 272 f.
[88] V 36 f.   [90] VII 480 ff.
[89] VII 399.   [91] VII 482. Cf. VI 40.

the vast indifference of the physical cosmos, as modern
science describes them:

> The *most general characteristic of the modern age*: man has
> lost *dignity* incredibly in his own eyes. Long as center and
> tragic hero of existence in general; then at least struggling to
> prove himself related to the decisive and intrinsically valuable
> side of existence . . . .
>
> . . . he has become an *animal*, animal without metaphor,
> abatement and reservation, he who in his previous faith was
> almost God ("child of God," "God-man") . . . Since Coper-
> nicus man seems to have got upon an inclined plane — he is now
> rolling faster and faster away from the center — whither? into
> nothingness? into the *"overwhelming* feeling of his nothing-
> ness"? [92]

At this point experience culminates for Nietzsche in an
all-embracing event — nihilism: the conviction of a total
contrast between value and fact.[93] It differs from common
pessimism by being more thorough, retaining no consola-
tions whatever, and by stressing the meaninglessness of evil
rather than its mere existence. Nietzsche believes that he
has fathomed blacker depths of despair than any European
pessimist, and therefore likes to make merry over the
would-be pessimism of Schopenhauer — who, though a pessimist, played the flute after meals — and of other contemporaries who beguiled their gloom in sundry moral or aesthetic ivory towers.[94] The nihilist is beyond all that; he has
literally *nothing* left. Nietzsche defines him thus:

> A nihilist is a man who judges, of the world as it is, that
> it ought *not* to be, and of the world as it ought to be, that it
> does not exist. Accordingly, existing (acting, suffering, will-
> ing, feeling) has no sense: the passion of "in vain" is the nihil-
> ist's passion . . . .[95]

[92] XV 154 f.; VII 474. Cf. V 147 f.; VII 190; X 189; XV 142, 194.
[93] XV 141, 145, 148 ff., 165 f.; XIV 220 f.; XVI 417; V 280.
[94] VII 80, 115, 411; VIII 133; XIV 376; XV 154, 205 f., 443, 487. Cf. H.K.A.
II 68.
[95] XVI 84. Cf. XV 146, 182; VI 197 ff.

And the most vivid description of nihilism as an experience runs:

Nihilist's diary. — The shudder over the discovered "falsity." Empty; not a thought left; strong passions revolving about objects without value: — spectator of these absurd agitations for and against: — superior, derisive, cold to oneself. The strongest impulses seem like tempters and liars: as if we were expected to believe in their objects, as if they wished to seduce us. The strongest force no longer knows what for. Everything is there, but no purposes. — Atheism as ideal-lessness.

Phase of passionate denial and active negation: in it the stored-up desire for affirmation, for adoration, is discharged . . .

Phase of contempt even for denial . . . even for doubt . . . even for irony . . . even for contempt . . .

Catastrophe: is falsehood something divine? Does the value of all things rest on the fact that they are false? . . . Should one believe in God, not because he is true, *but rather because he is false* — ? [96]

"The strongest force no longer knows *what for*" — exactly here the essential heroism in Nietzsche took its most decisive stand. Instead of breaking in the crisis, he resolved to move onward, though not a star lit his way. Something invincible in him compelled tenacity to life. The "Great Liberator," as he called it, saved him in his moment of most desperate anguish: the idea came to him that "life might be an experiment of the knower — and not a duty, not an irresistible fate, not a fraud! — And knowledge itself . . . a world of dangers and victories . . . ." [97]

The old ideals are wrecked — must they be the only ones possible? he came to ask. The world is not worth what we thought — is it therefore worthless? Is it not hasty to conclude that, because the old meaning is false, no new one can

[96] XVI 405.
[97] V 245. Cf. II 52 f.; L.Mu. 18/10/75. Nihilism did not of course encounter Nietzsche only in 1876. It was a recurrent experience of which traces may be found in his letters until near the end (cf. L.R. 23/5/87; L.G. 15/1/88; L.O. 3/2/88).

be discovered? Is it not absurd for man to condemn all existence because it does not conform to his arbitrary specifica-
tions? Perhaps nihilism indicates something wrong with us
rather than with nature. Perhaps it is the modern world,
not *the* world, that is worthless.[98]

With something like these questions in mind Nietzsche
embarks, in his middle period, on a voyage of discovery.
"The free spirit" is his symbol for this movement of his
thought: it scours a trackless sea of possibility in quest of
new "land":

We homeless ones from the beginning — we have no choice
at all, we have to be conquerors and discoverers: perchance we
shall bequeath to our descendants what we ourselves lack —
perchance we shall bequeath them a *home*.[99]

Zarathustra sings of the free spirit's voyage:

If that seeking joy is in me which drives the sails toward
the undiscovered, if a seafarer's joy is my joy:
If ever my exultation cried: "The shore vanished — now the
last chain fell from me —
— the infinite roars about me, far out gleam space and time,
now then, come on, old heart!" [100]

Evidently a life devoted to "knowledge" in this sense is very
different from one of mere curiosity or peaceful scientific
research: the utter detachment from old beliefs means risking every kind of shipwreck, and in a solitude no helping
sympathy will penetrate.[101]

After Nietzsche has discovered his "new country" [102] he
feels, on looking back, that his experience is somehow repre-

[98] XV 163 f., 182; XVI 95, 406 f.; V 7, 279; VIII 143.
[99] XIV 414. Cf. IV 372; XV 435. The motto (taken from the *Rig Veda*) which
Nietzsche chose for *Dawn* indicates his sense of unexplored possibility: "Es giebt
so viele Morgenröthen, die noch nicht geleuchtet haben." The symbolism of
Meer and *Land* appears as early as 1862 (L.F.N. I 314 or H.K.A. II 55).
[100] VI 337. Cf. III 9 f.; V 162.
[101] V 245; XII 8; VII 36 f., 48 f.; XIV 394 ff.; XI 385; II 7 ff. Cf. VII 179, and
the draft of a letter to Georg Rée, *Ges. Briefe* V 526.
[102] Cf. L.G. 2/4/83; L.O. c. 8/12/83.

sentative of what lies in store for the modern world as a whole:

> I have borne a torture until now: all the laws according to which life evolves seemed to me to stand in opposition to the values for the sake of which such as we *endure* to live. That does not seem to be a condition from which many suffer *consciously*: all the same I intend to put together the signs by which I assume that it is the *fundamental character*, the really *tragic problem* of our modern world, and, as secret trouble, the cause or interpretation of all its troubles. *This problem has become conscious in me.*[103]

Thus his philosophy becomes an attempt to deal with the issues set by the coming of nihilism in modern civilization. The crisis arises from the contradiction between Christian ideals and the nature of things which confronts us. The way to victory is the "revaluation of all values."

The rest of this volume will be devoted to an exploration of the "new country" which Nietzsche discovered, beyond nihilism.

[103] XIV 346. Cf. V 163 f.; XV 137 f.; XVI 378; III 11; II 267; XI 384.

PART TWO
LIFE

CHAPTER III

The Will to Power

Whatever I create and however I love it — soon I must
oppose it and my love.... (VI 168)

1. THE SECRET OF LIFE

NIETZSCHE is a philosopher of *life*. The universe interests him chiefly as context. Since nihilism results from a clash between the laws of life and the ideals which have made it seem worth living, and since the revaluation of values seeks to overcome this conflict, he is doubly concerned to find a true statement of those laws:

... the *presuppositions* for all previous goals are destroyed.
Science shows the flux but not the goal: however, it gives the *presuppositions* with which the new goal *must* agree.[1]

What are those assumptions about fact, best supported by science, in view of which we must revise our ideals?

Nietzsche's sister describes the experience which, apparently, first suggested to him both a new conception and a new valuation of life. He was serving in the hospital corps during the war of 1870. After a day of fatigue and horror on the battlefield, he suddenly heard a noise like thunder approaching and fresh Prussian regiments dashed past, eager for combat. It then occurred to him that life at its best was not a wretched struggle for existence but a fight for power.[2]

When Nietzsche, in his last period, proclaims that life is

[1] XII 357.   [2] L.F.N. II 682 f. Cf. I 23 f.

essentially "will to power," he means something much more circumspect and subtle than is commonly supposed or the Prussian experience suggests. He tells us that he borrows the expression "from the strongest of all urges, which has directed all organic evolution so far." [3] By implication, therefore, he uses it in a somewhat extended or analogical sense, proposing "to consider what *all life* shows as a reduced formula for the total tendency." [4] He does occasionally use "will to power," or apparent equivalents, in the ordinary sense of one motive which exists beside others — pleasure, knowledge, social approval, etc.[5] But he makes it quite plain that in his general theory of life he does not mistake one particular *outcome* of evolution for the *source* of evolution. It is rather that he finds "will to power" the most suggestive name for the primal life-force out of which all special organic and psychological functions have evolved and whose generic traits they retain — "The cravings are specialized more and more: their unity is the *will to power* ...." [6]

What are those traits? A survey of them, and of Nietzsche's criticism of rival theories, will take us to the heart of his position.

Life is by nature something active and aggressive, he maintains. Writers like Darwin and Spencer have too much stressed passive adaptation to fixed environment:

In Darwin the influence of "external circumstances" is absurdly *overestimated*: the essence of the life process is precisely the prodigious organizing power [*Gewalt*] creating forms from

[3] XIII 66. Cf. 219.
[4] XVI 101.
[5] Cf. IV 30 f., 178, 228 f., 235; VIII 149, 169; VII 65, 450; XVI 338. This usage is evidently connected with ambiguities in the meaning of "power" to be discussed in Chapter V: when Nietzsche speaks of will to power as one among other impulses he usually means "external power" or domination. Nietzsche also speaks of life both as a striving for power and as a striving for the *feeling* of power (XVI 155. Cf. IV 30 f.). This introduces a possible ambiguity which he does not appear to consider.
[6] XIII 66. Cf. VII 57 f.; XIV 327; XVI 152.

within, which *takes advantage of, exploits* the "external circumstances" . . .[7]

Life takes the initiative and modifies the environment.
"Adaptation" is secondary.[8]

The aggressive aspect of the will to power is often emphasized by Nietzsche and has generally been mistaken for
the whole:

> . . . life itself is *essentially* appropriation, injury, conquest of
> the foreign and weaker, oppression, harshness, imposition of
> its own forms, assimilation and at least, at mildest, exploita
> tion . . . . People everywhere are now raving . . . about coming
> conditions of society in which "the exploitative character" shall
> be lacking: — to my ears that sounds as if one promised to invent
> a life which should refrain from all organic functions. "Ex
> ploitation" is not peculiar to a corrupt or imperfect and primi
> tive society: it belongs to the *essence* of the living . . . it is a
> consequence of the inherent will to power.[9]

Note that exploitation is not identified with will to power.
It is not all of life, then, but Nietzsche does emphatically
mean that these features are necessary, and, as the passage
suggests, this point is decisive for his social philosophy.

The phenomena of growth show the imperialistic character of life most convincingly — Nietzsche uses "will to
power" and "will to grow" almost synonymously: "It belongs to the concept of the living that it must grow — that
it must expand its power and therefore ingest outside
forces." [10] To illustrate this vital necessity, one does not
have to refer to the bloody pages of history; the babe in the
womb and the sprouting plant show the same innocent
vandalism.

As the passage about Darwin indicated, the acquisitive
aspect of the will to power involves more than the mere

[7] XVI 120. Cf. 144 f.; VII 372.
[8] VII 23 f., 372.
[9] VII 237 f. Cf. 368; VI 295. VII 163 suggests that Nietzsche is deliberately
overemphasizing this aspect of life to correct certain contemporary weaknesses.
[10] XVI 179. Cf. XIV 410; XV 232 f.

effort to engulf greater and greater quantities. It is selective
and formative; it organizes and administers what it acquires.
Life, like the artist, is essentially creative.[11]

It is also destructive, even when creative. A sheep is no
longer sheep, it is not even mutton when a child has digested it. Nietzsche holds that creation necessarily involves
destruction, and that the never ending conflict of wills to
power is the condition of advance.[12] By this time it is clear
that he thinks of *many* wills-to-power: every society, every
organism, every cell has its own.[13] He takes pains to under-
line the ruthlessness of animal existence far more than Darwin does: "Life always lives at the expense of other life,"
and "aggressive and defensive egoism are not a matter of
choice ... but rather the *fatality* of life itself." [14]

"Will to power" as a will to *grow* means an upward drive
in life. Nietzsche combats the prevalent theories of "self-
preservation," "will to live" or "struggle for survival," which
imply a horizontal rather than an upward tendency. Will
to power includes them as limiting cases, but they are exceptional; "the rule is rather the struggle for *power*, for
'more' and 'better' and 'faster' and 'oftener.' " [15]

Wanting to preserve self is the expression of a distressed
condition, a restriction of the proper fundamental instinct of
life, which aims at *expansion of power* and in this desire threatens and sacrifices self-preservation often enough.... Not distress but rather abundance and extravagance, even to absurdity,
predominate in nature.[16]

That life often risks itself in the venture for power, reminds us that it is generous as well as acquisitive; that it

[11] XII 106; VII 382 f., 372.
[12] VI 168 f.
[13] Cf. XVI 16 ff., 126, 154, 171, 173 f.; VII 238.
[14] XV 407; XVI 179.
[15] XIII 231. Cf. VII 23 f.; VIII 127; XVI 57, 153; XIV 410. Nietzsche may still
use the term *Erhaltung* on occasion (e.g. XIV 31 f., 337), but never in such a
way as to contradict the position taken here.
[16] V 285.

gives as well as takes. It *must* take — that has been established — but it may also overflow beyond itself. Nietzsche's name for this phase of will to power is "self-overcoming" (*Selbstüberwindung*): [17]

All great things perish through themselves, by an act of self-abolition: so the law of life wills it, the law of the *necessary* "self-overcoming" in the essence of life — to the lawgiver himself, at last, the summons is always issued: "*patere legem, quam ipse tulisti*." [18]

This clearly is not the denial but the fulfilment of will to power; the accumulated strength, which was bred under the old law, undermines it and creates the new.[19] The same form, the same organism does not continue growing forever; if it goes far enough it finally *out*grows itself. The impetus of will to power culminates in a thrust which is at once a venture upward and a leap to death. The simplest illustration is animal reproduction: when the animal has grown to full strength it gives its best energies for its young and so brings about its own decline.[20] In general, Nietzsche declares, the deepest desire of life is "to create beyond and above itself," thereby perishing; where that is lacking, there is decadence [21]— "A full force wants to create, suffer, go under...." [22]

"Will to power," then, turns out to mean not endless greed, but getting and spending, in a kind of rhythm. The primary fact is the out-going, venturesome impulse of life which is at once an exertion and a loss of power: "The prodigality of force" is "the most essential character even

---

[17] There is no good English equivalent. Nietzsche means "creating something beyond self through overcoming self." He does not mean denial of self or flight from self; the self is supremely active, not frustrated.
[18] VII 481. Cf. 53, 364; IV 9; XV 119; VI 167 f.
[19] XII 365.
[20] See note 69 below. Cf. "...des *Wachsthums* der Gattung, d. h. der *Überwindung der Gattung* auf dem Wege zu einer stärkeren Art" (XVI 57).
[21] VI 47 f., 94, 110 f., 168. Cf. VIII 172 f.
[22] XV 305. Cf. VI 9 f., 16 f.

of the most appropriate actions." [23] So even a will to get power presupposes a will to spend it. But particularly in the period of growth, the will to power exerts itself toward acquisition: "The will to *accumulate force* is specific for the phenomenon of life, for nutrition, generation, heredity — for society, state, custom, authority." [24] Then when power has been stored up to superabundance, the will to power manifests itself as an overflow:

> The great man is an end [*Ende*]; the great age, for example the Renaissance, is an end. The genius — in work, in deed — is necessarily a prodigal: *that he spends himself* is his greatness . . . The instinct of self-preservation is unhinged as it were . . . . They call it "sacrifice"; they extol . . . his indifference to personal welfare, his devotion to an idea . . . : all misconceptions . . . He gushes forth, he gushes over, he uses himself up, he does not spare himself — with fatality, disastrously, involuntarily as a river's overflowing its banks is involuntary.[25]

But this phase in the rhythm of will to power is still, like the others, an exertion of power, and not an abrogation of the fundamental aggressive and destructive traits.[26] If anything, Nietzsche seems to stress the last phase as the more important, as if getting were ultimately for the sake of giving:

> The "ego" subjugates and kills: it works like an organic cell: it robs and does violence. It wants to regenerate itself: — pregnancy. It wants to give birth to its god, and to see all mankind at his feet.[27]

"Will to power," in short, means "will to risk power in order to get more power and spend it."

Nietzsche's complex conception of life is beautifully summed up in Zarathustra's discourse "Of Self-Overcoming." It is worth quoting at length, not only for its own

[23] XIII 268. Cf. XVI 104, 121; XV 407; VII 23 f., 412.
[24] XVI 154.
[25] VIII 157. Cf. XV 93.
[26] XIII 177 f.; XVI 208.   [27] XIV 61. Cf. VI 110; VII 412; H.K.A. II 69.

sake, but because it proves that he thought of these things together, as one whole:

All that lives is something that obeys.

And this is the second point: he who cannot obey himself is commanded . . . .

But this is the third: . . . that commanding is harder than obeying. . . .

A venture and risk appeared to me in all commanding; and always, when it commands, the living thing stakes itself thereon.

Nay further, when it commands itself: even there it must pay for its commanding. It must become judge and avenger and victim of its own law.

"But how does this happen?" I asked myself. "What persuades the living to obey and command and, commanding, still to practise submission?"

Where I found life I found will to power; and even in the will of the servant I found the will to be master.

And as the lesser surrenders itself to the greater, that it may have pleasure and power in that which is least: so even the greatest surrenders itself too, and for the sake of power risks — its life.

And life itself told me this secret: "Lo," it said, "I am that *which must always overcome itself.*

"To be sure, you call it will to procreation or urge to the goal, to the higher, farther, more various: but all that is one, and one secret.

"I had rather go down than renounce this one thing; and truly, where there is decline and the falling of leaves, lo, there life is sacrificing itself — for power!

"That I must be struggle and becoming and purpose and contradiction of purposes: alas, he who guesses my will may also guess by what *crooked* ways it must move.

"Whatever I create and however I love it — soon I must oppose it and my love: so my will demands.

"Many things are more highly valued by the living than life itself; yet out of this very valuing speaks — the will to power!" —[28]

[28] VI 166 ff.

2. TYPES OF EVIDENCE

Nietzsche looked upon the will-to-power theory as one of the great unifying ideas in his philosophy. We shall not grasp its full force until we have traced its applications in morals, art, and cosmology, but it will not be amiss to glance now at the major sources of evidence on which he bases the theory.

He was quite serious in wishing to form a conception which should be in harmony with science. After the crisis of 1876, he turned passionately to the study of natural science and became acquainted, at least through German expositors, with much of the best work of his day — that of Claude Bernard, Lord Kelvin, Faraday, and many others.[29]

But though much of his later writing employs biological language and abounds in acute comment on the scientists he read, it would be a serious error to suppose that the will-to-power theory grew only out of such studies, or to file it away in some allegedly separate "positivistic" compartment of his thought. Nietzsche learned from science but was not its slave. He tried to view life from every angle, and history, literature, the arts, religion, society, psychology, and inner experience all had a share in his synthesis.

If we look for his evidence that life is will to power, we encounter first the general spectacle of life amid nature. The way life as a whole and man in particular have exploited the physical environment shows something of what they are after.[30] Modern technology is simply the last, most spectacular phase of the conquest of nature.

Secondly, there are the relations between living beings, so eloquently described in some of their more cruel aspects by Schopenhauer. Nietzsche remarks that a generalization intended to cover all life must apply to plants as well as

[29] XV 77. Cf. Andler, *Nietzsche, sa vie et sa pensée*, II 313 ff., IV 401 ff.; L.F.N. II 521 f.
[30] XVI 155, 277.

animals. "For what do the trees of a primeval forest struggle with each other? For 'happiness'? — For *power!*" [31] Every plant grows, therefore competes with its neighbors for soil, sunshine, and water. Animal species prey upon plants and upon each other, and do not stop with bare subsistence but seek increase. Men in turn make conveniences of plants and animals.

Human relations exhibit the action of will to power more intimately. History is the record of its struggles — men, families, cities, empires all wrestling for primacy — notably Nietzsche's beloved Greeks.[32] Likewise the activities of mind are bent upon mastery: the artist over his materials, the thinker over his subject, and the priest over the souls of men.[33] Nietzsche observes will to power naked, or scantily clothed with cant phrases, in the relations between societies:

Groups are devised in order to do things for which the individual has not the courage. Just for that reason all communities, societies, are a hundred times more *candid* and *instructive* about the nature of man than the individual, who is too weak to have the courage for his desires . . .[34]

Nietzsche finds a fourth type of evidence in himself and, through himself, in the minds of others. He describes his own nature as "the juxtaposition of the most luminous and most fateful forces, the will to power as never a man has possessed it," and again says, "My self-overcoming is fundamentally my strongest power . . . ." [35] Wagner is similarly portrayed: "At bottom an impetuous will burrows in headlong torrent, which by all courses, caverns and gorges, as it were, seeks the light and craves power" — "Each of his urges strove insatiably . . . ." [36]

[31] XVI 164. Cf. 163.
[32] VIII 169 f. Cf. VII 238; below, p. 336.
[33] XIII 177; XVI 225 f.; XIV 46; XV 246 f.
[34] XVI 173. Cf. X 368.
[35] XV 67; L.O. 31/12/82. Cf. c. 27/12/82.
[36] I 504, 507.

Nietzsche's works are full of clairvoyant psychology; its perennial theme is to lay bare the indirection and finesse of the will to power in human nature. Some of his dissections are:

The *masked* varieties of will to power:

1) Desire for *freedom*, independence, also for equilibrium, peace, *coordination*. Also the hermit, "freedom of spirit...."

2) Orderly arrangement, in order, within the larger whole, to satisfy its will to power: *subordination*, making oneself indispensable, useful, to him who has the power; *love*, as a secret path to the heart of the more powerful — in order to dominate him.

3) The feeling of duty, conscience, the imaginary solace of belonging to a *higher* rank than the ones who actually have the power; the recognition of an order of rank which permits one to *sit in judgment*, even over the mighty; self-condemnation; the invention of *new tables of value* (Jews: classic example).[37]

3. VALUE PERSPECTIVE AND MEMORY

Nietzsche's view of the nature of life is not exhausted by the bare notion of will to power. Willing includes "the idea of a valued object," [38] which in turn involves some kind of perception:

The will to power *interprets* .... Mere differences of power could not yet feel themselves as such: there must be something there that wants to grow, which interprets every other something-wanting-to-grow with respect to its value.... In truth, interpretation itself is a means of becoming master of something.[39]

Hence Nietzsche's favorite idea that life is necessarily "perspectival": it is inconceivable without preferences, without

[37] XVI 206 f.
[38] XI 190. Cf. XIII 172; below, pp. 91 f.
[39] XVI 117 f. Cf. XIII 82, 227 f., 230; VI 168. Nietzsche also attributes "a kind of mind," i.e. thinking and feeling as well as willing, to all parts of the organism, regarding the brain as only a centralizing apparatus (XIII 232, 267; XIV 44; XVI 18). Needless to say, he does not attribute highly developed and

an evaluation of its surroundings from its own point of view.[40] And, as this and an earlier quotation stated, all values express will to power.

The character which most separates life from the rest of nature, in his view, is *memory*: "Everything organic is distinguished from the inorganic by the fact that it *gathers experiences*, and is never identical with itself in its processes." [41] In some sense the entire past of life lives on in every organism and cell.[42] Nietzsche's position here rests upon the analogy between biological heredity, the transmission of social traditions, and human memory and habit formation: [43] all retain or re-enact the past in the present, somehow.

He does not think of memory as a passive accumulation, however; life could not carry the burden.[44] He sees in it rather a kind of active "assimilation" (*Einverleibung*):

One must learn anew about memory: it is the mass of all experiences [*Erlebnisse*] of all organic life, alive, arranging themselves, shaping each other, wrestling with one another, simplifying, compressing and changing into many unities. There must be an inner *process* which is like the formation of concepts from many particular cases: the stressing and ever fresh underscoring of the basic scheme, and omission of secondary features. — As long as something can be recalled as a separate fact, it is not yet melted down: the latest experiences still swim on the surface.[45]

The result of a continued process of assimilation, Nietzsche holds, is the production of stable "basic forms" (*Grundformen*) which are transmitted with special em-

---

conscious mental functions to primitive organisms: they are only slowly evolved out of the vaster unity of inorganic existence (cf. VII 57 f.; XI 187 f.; XIII 227 ff.).

[40] VII 4, 7; II 11; XIII 74, 172.

[41] XIII 231. Cf. 232; below, pp. 278 f.

[42] XIII 231 f., 237, 58. Cf. X 149; V 87 f.

[43] Cf. XVI 119, 180 f., 358; XIII 58 f., 233, 236; XV 192 ff.; IV 39 ff.; VII 250 f. Nietzsche does not pretend to explain the *how* of organic memory: cf. XIII 59, 233; XVI 118.

[44] VII 343 f.   [45] XIII 237. Cf. 236, 58; VII 343.

phasis, forming individual, social, or racial character. Their production is not wholly the work of inner forces; it also depends upon the recurrence of similar experiences, which enables the gradual shaping of definite structures. A change in mode of living interrupts the process, tending to unsettle the previously acquired forms.[46]

He thus maintains the essentially Lamarckian view that heredity, being a transmission of past "experience," is the inheritance of characters acquired in some past, however remote. He believes that feelings, valuations, and habits pass from father to son, and that reproduction is possible because every cell, especially every germ cell, contains all the past in condensed form.[47] Correspondingly, he thinks of the development of a new organism as a recapitulation of the past, a kind of "remembering" and re-embodiment of it. However, not the latest but the oldest "memories," those which have been most repeated and therefore condensed into the most persistent "basic forms," are first re-enacted and most stubbornly retained.[48]

This introduces another principle which Nietzsche evidently recognizes but does not name. It might be called "hereditary inertia." The basic forms derived from the past have a resistance to change or a tendency to repetition proportional to the "weight" of the past they embody, that is, to the number and intensity of past experiences which they have "assimilated." Some basic forms are so deeply ingrained that they are virtually impervious to fresh environmental influences. This protects Nietzsche from the more foolish overstatements and refutations of Lamarckianism. He is well aware that many animal structures and functions are not permanently modified now by environmental influences, such as those of domestication.[49]

[46] Cf. XIII 139; XV 192 ff.
[47] XII 160; XIII 58, 207, 209 f., 220; X 174. Cf. III 293.
[48] XIII 236, 58. II 253 f. and XIII 234 suggest cultural and psychological recapitulation theories.   [49] XVI 146. See the discussion of "fixation" in Sec. 5.

His theory of heredity leads to another Lamarckian principle: the development of characteristics, in the race as in the individual, is governed by *need* — "one has only what one has need of." [50] He uses this principle chiefly in its application to human affairs, but he probably holds it valid for all life. He does not explicitly relate it to the will to power. Some passages even seem to contradict the latter by suggesting that men will not become as strong as they might unless they are compelled to do so, as if lethargy rather than will to power were their normal state. [51] What he finally appears to mean is that will to power varies widely in aggressiveness; it is not insatiable in every respect, but becomes canalized and often settles into a routine which limits the urge for growth: its greatest achievements require the stimulus of severe conditions. [52] The slackening of endeavor need not be a total abrogation of those dynamic traits which Nietzsche has declared to be essential for all life, but it is nevertheless an important qualification of the will-to-power theory, and the principle of need is a significant admission of the importance of environmental factors.

4. THE ORGANISM AND ITS PROCESSES

Since Nietzsche claims that all organic functions are specialized forms of will to power, his interpretation of them, if successful, will be an important verification of his theory.

The unity of the living organism and the nice mutual adjustment of its functions have been a source of much controversy. "Mechanists" have tried to explain them wholly in terms of physical science; "vitalists" have argued that some kind of soul or life-principle is required.

The problem is specially acute for Nietzsche because he conceives the organism, not as one simple will to power, but

[50] XVI 382. Cf. VIII 128; XII 191; X 225; V 326.
[51] VIII 150, 170. Cf. XVI 288, 338; VII 65.
[52] VIII 128, 150; XII 191; VII 245 f.; XIV 411; XVI 338; L.G. 20/12/87.

as a multiplicity of wills to power in mutual strife: "Life might be defined as a lasting form of *processes of settling power* [*Kraftfeststellungen*] where the respective combatants grow unequally." [53] The will to power is obviously a principle of separation. How can it also be a principle of union?

In any case the two orthodox theories do not satisfy him:

> So far *neither* explanation of organic life has been successful: neither that from mechanics *nor that from mind*. . . . The management of the organism occurs in a manner for the explanation of which the mechanical world *as well* as the mental can be adduced only *symbolically*.[54]

By "symbolically" perhaps he means something like the process by which he formed the theories of will to power and organic memory from analogies to familiar facts of experience.

In any event the leading idea in his own picture of the living organism is the analogy to human societies. The latter are manifestly full of conflict, yet they possess a certain unity of thought and feeling which enables organized cooperation, division of labor, government. So he thinks of an organism as an oligarchical society of wills to power which struggle with each other to some extent but also make common cause against the outer world — *both* "a war and a peace." [55] Association is a consequence of the will to power because it is a *means* to power: the weaker obey the stronger for the sake of safety and of power over the yet weaker, and the stronger organize the weaker in order to use them as "functions." But command requires self-limitation:

> Each has something to perform, and in order to attain this *regularly* the stronger *foregoes* further encroachments and *accommodates itself* to an *order*: this is part of self-regulation.

[53] XVI 117. Cf. 161, 163; XIII 227.
[54] XIII 242 f. Cf. XII 147.
[55] VI 46; XIII 165, 169; XVI 17 f., 126 f.; VII 344; XII 155.

With respect to the *duties* of the *functions* the mighty One and the function agree; there is nothing "unegoistic" about it.[56]

In general the predatory aspects of will to power are mitigated and mutual sympathy is developed *within* any living association for the sake of joint action against outsiders.[57]

Life was defined as a process of settling or determining power. We are now in position to explain this more fully. When two or more wills to power meet they measure their strength against one another and the result shows which is the stronger — which can command and which must obey. In some cases one succeeds in converting others into subordinate functionaries and thereby forms an enduring association (organism, society), in which relative powers are "fixed" in an order of rank (*Rangordnung*). But since life is not static the powers do not stay settled once for all; they grow unequally, and consequently the internal struggle continues: society is a prolonged experiment in command and obedience. So living association displays a measure of persistent order which is continually being disturbed by fresh disorder. The center of gravity shifts; masters and servants exchange rôles.[58]

How explain the development of order out of fundamental strife? It would seem to require a high degree of intelligence on the part of the will to power. Nietzsche's implicit answer seems to be the application of three principles: the formative property of the will to power, organic memory, and natural selection. The initial organization of a living association is the work of a dominant will which galvanizes comparative chaos into order by translating or projecting its own internal order upon the unshaped group, much as the chick embryo "organizes" the rest of the egg or as an

[56] XII 105. Cf. 106; III 207; VI 167; XIII 169.
[57] VII 368, 237 f.; XIV 323.
[58] XIII 62, 169, 173; XVI 57, 108 f., 215; VI 309; XII 105.

artist projects himself into his materials. So of the "blond beasts" who organized states Nietzsche writes,

> Their handiwork is an instinctive making of forms, imprinting of forms; they are the most involuntary, unconscious artists that exist: — where they appear something new soon stands forth, a structure of power [*Herrschafts-Gebilde*] which *lives*, in which parts and functions are limited and correlated, in which nothing at all is admitted in which a "meaning" with respect to the whole has not first been placed. They do not know what guilt . . . is, these born organizers; in them that fearful artist's egoism rules, which stares like bronze and knows itself justified in the "handiwork" in advance for all eternity, as the mother in the child.[59]

Secondly, Nietzsche maintains that even the subordinate wills to power derive some satisfaction from the association, and those "social" functions which begin under compulsion come by cumulative repetition to be second nature; obedience to "law" becomes instinctive, even pleasant, thereby increasing the internal harmony of the organism.[60] Thirdly, those organisms or societies which do not achieve a measure of internal order do not survive.[61]

Nietzsche stresses the fact that the parts or functions of an organism exhibit strife as well as concord. He finds it supported by some contemporary biology and holds it to be important for understanding the organism:

> If all wished to take a "reasonable" attitude at their posts, and did not wish continually to manifest as much force and hostility as they need in order to *live* — then the driving force would be *lacking* in the whole: the functions of similar rank contend: one must take *heed* constantly, every negligence is exploited, the opponent is *watching*.[62]

---

[59] VII 382. Cf. XVI 127, 343; VIII 92. The masses, or chaos generally, cannot spontaneously evolve order out of themselves (I 368).

[60] XII 103; XI 260. On the first point, see text, pp. 72 f.

[61] Cf. XIII 187, 233; XII 114. Nietzsche would probably add, though I do not remember a passage to this effect, that the principle of "need" would lead the rulers to learn better how to command and the subjects better how to obey.

[62] XII 104. Cf. 147; Andler, *op. cit.*, IV 411 ff.

Even the vertical relations of command and obedience retain an element of hostility, he believes; there is resistance
in obedience, and a command is an acknowledgment that
the other "will" has not been completely subjugated.[63] If
a society becomes too friendly it goes stale.[64]

In the external behavior of the organism, will to power
may manifest itself in apparently opposite ways according to
circumstances. It normally seeks obstacles which it can
master and resists or avoids those which threaten to master it.

> The will to power can only manifest itself against *resistances*;
> so it seeks for that which opposes it — this [is] the original dis-
> position of the protoplasm when it puts forth pseudopodia and
> gropes about itself. Appropriation and assimilation are above
> all a desire to overpower, a shaping, acquiring, and transform-
> ing until finally the vanquished has passed over entirely into
> the sphere of influence of the aggressor, and increased it.

> The strength of the aggressor has a kind of *measure* in the
> opposition which it needs; every growth reveals itself in the
> search for a more powerful adversary . . . .[65]

When one organism is unable to engulf the other it may
"enslave" it and form a new organism, as we have seen. In
some cases the weaker may seek to become parasites of the
stronger and the stronger in turn may resist accordingly.[66]

Nietzsche interprets the specializations of will to power
within the organism by analogy to the division of labor in
human society. The alimentary functions are one such
specialization. The original impulse is "wanting to enclose
everything in oneself"; later, as a result of division of labor,
a limited appetite is developed, and the organism endeavors
to engulf little more than enough to replace losses. But
this limited function is subordinate to a higher will to power
which displays the primitive expansiveness in other fields —
for example in intellectual conquests.[67]

[63] XVI 117; XIII 62, 258 f.
[64] XIII 187; II 355 f.
[65] XVI 123; XV 21. Cf. XIII 274.
[66] XVI 122.
[67] XVI 121 ff.

Nutrition is a result of the acquisitive phase of the will to power; reproduction its overflow when an excess has been acquired.[68] Reproduction in its most primitive form, fission, is due to the acquisition of more than the original "will" can administer.[69] Even in its highest forms, however, it is not the sacrifice of the individual for the species, but rather "the individual's accomplishment proper, and therefore its supreme interest, *its greatest manifestation of power* . . . ." [70]

The functions which serve to orient the organism in its environment — perceiving, feeling, thinking — are developed primarily as means to food-getting. "The entire apparatus of knowledge is an apparatus of abstraction and simplification — directed not toward knowledge but rather toward *taking possession* of things . . . ." [71]

Reproduction reminds us that organisms do not grow indefinitely but follow a characteristic life-cycle of rise and decline. A general reason for such rhythms has already been given in the discussion of "self-overcoming." But Nietzsche discovers a second reason in the division of labor within the organism: it produces "a stunting and weakening of the parts, finally death for the whole." [72]

The life-cycle introduces a distinction of the greatest importance for his practical philosophy: that between rising and decadent life. This implies another limitation of the will to power. The downward phase of the cycle is a kind of normal decadence, and decadence is lapse of will to power:

The thirst for power is indicative of the ascending course of *development*, the thirst for surrender [*Hingebung*], of the descending. The joys of old age all have most deeply this surrender to things, thoughts, persons: one who is striving upward dominates. The invalid has the inclination of old age in advance.

[68] XII 103. Cf. V 53.
[69] XVI 121 ff.; XIII 113, 259.
[70] XVI 144. Cf. XIII 177.
[71] XVI 22. Cf. 117.
[72] XVI 143.

Life itself bears for me the character of instinct for growth ... where will to power is wanting there is decline.[73]

Nietzsche interprets decadence in terms of the social nature of the organism and the fact that the will to power of the whole depends upon a complex interplay of forces. In every case there is:

... anarchy of atoms, disintegration of will ... the vibration and exuberance of life forced back into the smallest structures, the rest *poor* in life. Everywhere paralysis, fatigue, torpor *or* enmity and chaos: both more and more evident the more one ascends to higher forms of organization. The whole no longer lives at all ....[74]

The will to power, therefore, is not present in living organisms at all times in the same degree, but it remains essential for the perpetuation and development of life.

5. STABILITY AND EVOLUTION

Although Nietzsche is usually classified as an evolutionary philosopher, he radically denied that evolution is an inevitable progress. Both his atheism and his hostility to the current liberal ideas prompted this denial:

"Humanity" does not advance, it does not even exist. The total aspect is that of an immense experimental laboratory where a few things succeed, scattered through all ages, and unspeakably many fail, where all order, logic, connection and obligation are absent.

The entire animal and plant world does not develop from lower to higher . . . But rather all together, and one over another, and promiscuously, and one against another.[75]

[73] XI 253; VIII 221. Cf. XVI 281; VIII 48 f., 88 f., 233. Decadence does not imply a *total* lapse of will to power. Nietzsche refers our reigning values to the will to power of decadents (XV 486).

[74] VIII 23 f. Cf. VII 236; L.F. winter/84–85, 26/8/88. This and many other passages make it evident that the category of *wholeness* is highly relevant to Nietzsche's conception of life: cf. I 129 f.; VI 264; VII 382 f.; VIII 154, 163; XIII 271. But he does not develop the point.

[75] XV 204; XVI 147.

He grants that the principle of natural selection — at least in this sense, that only organisms capable of living have survived — is very important,[76] but he does not believe that it makes for continued evolution. On the contrary, though it weeds out some of the very weak it also eliminates the exceptionally gifted, and it ultimately favors mediocrity:

Species do *not* grow in perfection: the weak always master the strong again — that is because they are the large number, also they are *more clever* . . . Darwin forgot the mind (— that is English!); *the weak have more ingenuity* [*Geist*] . . . One must need ingenuity to get ingenuity.... By ingenuity I understand.... wariness, patience, cunning, disguise....[77]

There are other reasons why species as a whole do not progress. Exceptional individuals are by nature unstable, liable to perish:

.... they are extreme, and by that very fact almost decadents to begin with . . . The short duration of beauty, of genius, of the Caesar is *sui generis*.... The higher type presents an incomparably greater complexity — a greater sum of coordinated elements: thereby disintegration also becomes incomparably more probable. The "genius" is the sublimest machine there is — therefore the most fragile.[78]

Moreover, unusual specimens show no general tendency to mate with their likes; their qualities are constantly tending, therefore, to be mixed in and neutralized by the average type in the course of generations.[79] Also, similar beings with similar needs survive better than dissimilar ones, whether sub- or super-normal: because, for example, they can understand and aid each other more effectively.[80]

Nietzsche opposes the common idea of a species as a mysterious higher entity, for whose good the individual is (or

[76] XIII 233. Cf. VII 88 f.; VIII 221; H.K.A. III 386.
[77] VIII 128. Cf. XV 432; XVI 146 ff., 429; L.F.N. I 322 or H.K.A. II 167.
[78] XVI 148. Cf. VIII 202 ff.; VII 88.
[79] XVI 146 f.
[80] XII 73; VII 254 f.

should be) sacrificed. A species, if taken for an entity, is a fiction. Properly, it means simply a group of similar organisms in which change, from generation to generation, is so slow as to be comparatively negligible.[81]

To ask how species are formed is to ask how a set of organisms acquire an abiding uniformity of character. Nietzsche's hypothesis is:

A *species* arises, a type becomes firm and strong in the long struggle with essentially identical *unfavorable* conditions.... Here that indulgence, that excess, that protection under which variation is encouraged, are absent: the species needs itself as species, as something that can obtain a footing and make itself stable at all, precisely by means of its severity, uniformity, simplicity of form.... A type with few but very strong traits... becomes fixed in this manner beyond the change of generations....[82]

In other words, unfavorable conditions tend to isolate the group from external influences which might tend to merge the new type in an older one or upset its formation. The persistent sameness of conditions induces a sameness of attack upon them, therefore in the course of time a sameness of character. And the hostility of conditions compels hostility to internal variations, and puts the will to power on its mettle. Here we see at work the principles of need and of organic memory. If things go well a species builds up tremendous power by this process; circumstances compel it to become strong.[83] This general view of the way in which power is accumulated — I shall name it the principle of "storage" — has great importance in Nietzsche's ethics.

Storage cannot continue indefinitely:

The danger of these strong communities founded on like individuals of firm character is the stupefaction [*Verdum-*

[81] XVI 33, 144 f.; XII 73.
[82] VII 245 ff. Cf. XVI 120.
[83] VII 247.

mung], gradually increased by heredity, which ... follows all stability like its shadow.[84]

If the unfavorable conditions under which the species was shaped relax suddenly, the amassed forces explode in a riot of variation, but the extreme types soon perish by reason of their own disorder, and the mediocre survive.[85] So a species advances only to the point of attaining a clearly marked form; "every type has its *limit*: beyond this there is no evolution." [86]

If stabilization continues long enough, the uniformity of type becomes so dominant in the stream of heredity that finally no further change is possible. Nietzsche calls this condition "fixation" (*Feststellung*), and he thinks that most animal species have already reached it.[87] Since he conceives of life as a process of *Kraftfeststellung*, of "settling" relative powers, fixation might be defined as a state in which the powers within the organism have been "settled" for good and follow an hereditary routine, like static human societies governed wholly by tradition. In terms of the theory of organic memory, fixation would mean the accumulation of overwhelming "hereditary inertia" in the "basic forms." And the possibility of fixation is further evidence that organic memory may curtail the will to power.

Ultimately, therefore, the factors at work in the preservation of species are agents of stability, not of change or evolution. Progress is possible, Nietzsche believes, only in so far as some instability is present: "one must still have chaos in oneself to be able to give birth to a dancing star." [88] But just as too much stability means fixation, too much chaos brings death. The condition for progress is a happy inter-

[84] II 211.
[85] VII 247 f. Cf. XIII 187.
[86] XVI 147.
[87] XII 120; XIV 66 f.; XIII 276. This would explain the difficulty of verifying experimentally the hypothesis that acquired characters may be inherited.
[88] VI 19.

weaving of order and disorder, the one giving endurance, the other a stimulus to change. Without stability, advances cannot be consolidated. According to Nietzsche, the optimum situation is a firm basis of stability which is then repeatedly "inoculated" with not too great doses of "degeneracy" or "weakness" or "sickness" or "novelty." [89] Since he so often denounces the *dominance* of stolid mediocrity, it is important to emphasize how much he values stability in its proper place.[90]

The mainspring of evolution when it does occur is of course the will to power. True advance, he says,

> ... always appears in the guise of a will and way to *greater power* and is always accomplished at the expense of numerous lesser powers. The extent of a "progress" is even *measured* by the mass of all that had to be sacrificed for it; humanity as mass sacrificed to the growth of a single *stronger* species of man — that *would* be an advance . . .[91]

So the counterpart to his contention that a species as a whole does not progress is the proposition that progress consists in the conquest (*Überwindung*) of a species by a select group: it subjects the masses to "slavery" (instrumental functions), and shapes itself, by isolation from the masses and by resisting the dangers of its position, into a new, higher species, much as a human aristocracy is formed. In short, the condition of all development is "making possible a *selection* at the expense of a multitude." [92] This is essentially the process already described as the way in which living associations of wills to power arise.

Since Nietzsche denies the presence of divine purpose in

[89] II 211 ff.; XVI 119 f. Cf. V 159; XVIII 160; XIX 15, 54. In other words, the right interplay of Apollinian and Dionysian factors (cf. I 71 f.).

[90] Cf. V 297; XVI 338 f.; II 213.

[91] VII 371.

[92] XV 238. Cf. XVI 127, 144; VII 246; VI 13. At the same time Nietzsche appears to have another conception of evolution which he uses principally in his psychology and aesthetics, namely the unfolding or differentiation of some *Urphänomen*. See above, p. 60, and below, pp. 211 ff.

nature, he tries to explain the apparent teleology of living organisms and their evolution in terms of the will to power. So he writes:

... that *becoming stronger* brings with it arrangements which resemble a teleological design —: that the apparent *ends* are not intended but, as soon as the supremacy over a smaller power is established and the latter works as function of the greater, an order of *rank*, of organization must awaken the semblance of an order of means and end.

The *new* forms shaped from within are *not* formed for a purpose; but in the struggle of the parts a new form will not stand long *without* relation to a partial utility, and then take shape more and more perfectly according to *use*.[93]

The same organ may pass through a succession of different uses, as it is subjugated by several powers in turn. But this need not be evolution in one direction, he adds, for the succession of "conquests" is due to chance encounters.[94]

Nietzsche makes very tentatively many of the detailed applications of his theory to biological phenomena, but certain general ideas stand out as the ones to which he attaches importance and on which he builds much of his philosophy. They include: the indispensable rôle of the will to power, with its creativeness and destructiveness, its getting and spending, its "storage" of power under the stress of steady difficulty and its rhythmic "self-overcoming" in the evolution of higher forms; the necessary functions of perception, perspectival valuation, organic memory; the "assimilation" of organic memories, yielding stable "basic forms" under the guidance of "need," which dominate heredity and may finally produce permanent fixation; the

[93] XVI 58, 120. Utility cannot explain the development of new organs, he argues, because they are not useful in their early stages; also "utility" is ambiguous, varying widely with ends and conditions (XVI 119 f.). The problem of teleology in organic life occupied Nietzsche early: cf. XIX 385 ff.; H.K.A. III 371 ff. or L.F.N. I 352 ff.

[94] VII 370 f.; XIII 179.

organism as a social hierarchy, in perpetual tension; decadence as disintegration and lapse of will to power; the tendency of groups to approximate an average type; the conflicting agencies of stability and "chaos" and their interweaving to produce advance; the sacrifice of the many for the few as the condition of progress. The next problem is to apply these ideas to human nature.

CHAPTER IV

Man

In man are united creature and creator: in man there is material, fragment, excess, clay, muck, nonsense, chaos; but in man there is also creator, moulder, hammer hardness, spectator divinity and seventh day .... (VII 181)

1. THE NEW PSYCHOLOGY

NIETZSCHE takes pride in being an unequalled psychologist.[1] In fact he suggests: ". . . that psychology again be recognized as mistress of the sciences, for whose services and preparation the remaining sciences exist. For henceforth psychology is the path to the fundamental problems once more." [2]

He believes that psychology now leads to the major issues for the same reason that until now it has been shallow and perverted. The religious and moral tradition — therefore the whole structure which is collapsing in nihilism — has been built on a set of psychological falsehoods which have blocked scientific insight:

The whole of psychology hitherto has been caught on moral prejudices and apprehensions; it has not ventured into the depths. . . . The power of moral prejudices has penetrated deeply into the most intellectual . . . realm — and of course harmfully, obstructively, blindingly, distortingly. A proper physio-psychology has to struggle with unconscious resistances in the heart of the investigator, it has "the heart" against it . . . .[3]

---

[1] XV 57, 123; XIV 386 f.
[2] VII 37.
[3] VII 35 f. Cf. 73; II 60 f.; XIII 162; XV 360 f., 420, 425; XVI 163.

Because Nietzsche considers himself the first to conquer these resistances he even says, "Before me there was no psychology at all." [4]

The first step toward realism, therefore, is to eliminate hallowed superstition. So he demands that man be "translated back into nature." Beneath the glosses of idealism and human vanity we must learn to read "the frightful original text *homo natura*" with the same self-discipline we have brought to the study of physical science.[5] That means denying the traditional separation of soul and body. Nietzsche believes that the soul idea was really invented in order to disparage the body, and although he may still use the customary language on occasion [6] he actually intends to reverse the relation: "I am body entirely and nothing besides; and soul is only a word for something in the body [*am Leibe*]." [7]

With man regarded simply as one of the animals Nietzsche's psychology, both in method and in results, is largely an application of his theories about life in general. He conceives it as "morphology and theory of evolution of the will to power." [8]

But he is not a behaviorist, because his conception of the body is not materialistic. The passage which most explicitly attacks the old-fashioned "soul" also criticizes old-fashioned "matter," and goes on to explain that modifications of the soul hypothesis may still be legitimate in science. What he really rejects is the metaphysical entity supposed to be an eternal and indivisible monad.[9] And this fits very well with the will-to-power theory, since it too attributes to all forms

[4] XV 123. Cf. 63 f., 112 f.; VII 36.
[5] VII 190. Cf. V 149; VIII 229; I 57 f., 63.
[6] E.g. V 159; XIV 393.
[7] VI 46. Cf. 43 ff., 111, 278; XV 124; VIII 187. *Geist* is also distinguished from *Selbst* (VI 46 f.) and from *Seele* (III 58; VI 284). The self or soul is the ruling hierarchy of "centers of will" in the body. See below.
[8] VII 35. Cf. XVI 152.
[9] VII 22 f.

of life quasi-mental traits indicated by such terms as "striving," "valuation," "memory," and the like.

Just as Nietzsche rejected a dogmatic explanation of the organism in terms of either mind or mechanics, but suggested using both as "symbols" of the real process, so in psychology his method combines introspection and sense perception (including the sciences founded upon it) without assigning the last word to either. He calls these methods respectively "internal and external phenomenology." [10] In the mass of notes which were not prepared for publication, he seems to balance the two — now combining them, now pushing each at the expense of the other. Sometimes he speaks of conscious phenomena as mere symptoms of bodily processes; at other times he suggests that physical movements are visible expressions of one or more conscious minds,[11] or again, he observes analogies between them and says that we can speak metaphorically of each in the language of the other.[12] If we infer the true meaning of his method from his use of it, we must conclude that it treats both internal and external phenomena as "symptoms" of the real; the sequel will show that he describes the self with data obtained from both types of observation.

Following his defense of "body" against "soul," he emphasizes the merits of physiology and the demerits of introspection. He rejects the view, so prominent in modern philosophy, that mind can know itself with immediate certainty: on the contrary the inner world is rather more "phenomenal" than the external, and there are no "facts" of consciousness.[13] Consciousness, he believes, is a simplifying — therefore falsifying — medium, and causes neither its own states nor bodily movements.[14]

Paradoxically, it is because we are so close to ourselves

[10] XIV 45.
[11] XIII 164 f., 239 f., 252 ff.
[12] XIII 58 f.; XII 147.
[13] VII 25 f., 54; XVI 5 ff.   [14] XIII 64 f., 235; V 294; XVI 6 ff.; XIV 45.

that we are so remote. Of the view that knowledge should start with the "facts of consciousness" because we are more closely acquainted with the "internal world," Nietzsche writes:

Error of errors! The familiar is the usual; and the usual is hardest to "know," that is, to see as a problem, that is, to see as alien, as distant, as "outside us". . . . The great certainty of the natural sciences in comparison to psychology . . . rests precisely on this, that they take the *alien* [*das Fremde*] as object: whereas it is almost something contradictory and absurd to *intend* to take the not-alien as an object at all . . .[15]

Another and perhaps deeper reason for Nietzsche's distrust of introspection is his belief that illusion is a necessary condition of life and that we therefore instinctively thwart attempts to penetrate it in ourselves: we are unwilling to know the truth there.[16] He profoundly distrusts all direct attempts at self-knowledge; in fact he says that he has always thought but badly and unwillingly about himself, and regards a penchant for self-observation as a sign of degeneracy in a psychologist: [17]

We just necessarily remain strangers to ourselves, we do not understand ourselves, we *must* mistake ourselves, for us, to all eternity, the saying goes, "Each is farthest from himself" . . . .[18]

He sees the comparative advantage of "external phenomenology" not only in its greater reliability but also in its superior fruitfulness. The sense world can

. . . . be observed a hundred times more variously, acutely and accurately. External phenomenology gives us by far the richest material and permits the greater rigor of observation . . . .

Nothing good has yet grown from the self-observation [*Selbstbespiegelung*] of the mind. Not until now, when people

[15] V 295 f. Cf. 20.
[16] Cf. VII 54 f.; XVI 18; XII 318; XIV 45; XV 411 ff.
[17] VII 263; XVI 452 f.; XIII 291. Cf. XII 246; L.F.N. I 369 or H.K.A. IV 126. X 494 seems to imply a different view of self-knowledge.
[18] VII 288. Cf. V 254.

are seeking to inform themselves even about all mental processes; e.g. about memory, with the clue of the body, do they
make progress.[19]

Accordingly, of the two methods Nietzsche assigns priority
to the "phenomenon of the body," "without deciding anything about its final meaning." [20] "With the clue of the
body" becomes his motto.[21]

But he characteristically subjects "external phenomenology" also to careful examination and qualification. The
physical data described by science are a translation of an
"internal process" into the sign language of visual and
tactile sensations.[22] What we ordinarily call "the body"
is only the best metaphor for the real interplay of forces
which composes our nature.[23] When Nietzsche speaks of
"the body" it is well to remember that he may mean it in
this metaphorical sense.

The most definite statement of his view of the human self
shows his method in use:

Starting point from the *body* and physiology: why? — We
gain the correct idea of the character of our subject-unity,
namely as rulers at the head of a community (not as "souls" or
"life forces"); likewise of the dependence of these rulers upon
the ruled, and the conditions of gradation and division of labor
which make possible at once the individual and the whole. Likewise how the living unities perpetually arise and perish and how
everlastingness does not appertain to the "subject"; likewise
that the struggle expresses itself in commanding and obeying
and a running determination of limits of power is part of life.
The partial *ignorance* in which the ruler is kept concerning
the particular doings and even disturbances of the community,
is also one of the conditions under which government is possible.
In short we gain an appreciation even for *nescience*, for seeing
in the large and the rough, simplifying and falsifying, for the

[19] XIV 45; XIII 251. Cf. XIV 353.
[20] XVI 16.
[21] XVI 125, 17, 31; XIII 250 f.; XIV 353.
[22] XVI 18, 103 ff., 112 f., 153; XIII 64, 66, 69.   [23] XIII 249.

perspectival. However, the most important thing is: that we understand the sovereign and his subjects as *of the same kind*, all feeling, willing, thinking — and that we learn to infer an accompanying [*zugehöriges*] subjective, invisible life wherever we see or guess motion in the body.[24]

Thus Nietzsche uses the clue of the body to suggest a complex relational structure, something manifold and in perpetual flux, in short the hierarchical society already familiar to us from his theory of the living organism: the self or "subject" is simply the ruling oligarchy in this society. But the members of the society borrow from "inner phenomenology"; they all in some sense "think," "feel," "will." This is evidently the modification of the old "soul hypothesis" which Nietzsche desires.[25] Soul and body are no longer defined in antithetical terms, and the crucial problem is no longer how they interact but how both are related to the phenomena of sensation and inner consciousness.

While Nietzsche leans heavily upon "external phenomenology" in forming his theoretical framework, most of his concrete psychological insights evidently come from introspection. His distrust of it merely leads him to adopt cautious and indirect procedures. One method is a surprise attack. An open approach is disastrous:

> Never observe *in order* to observe! It gives a false perspective, a squint, something forced and exaggerated. Experiencing [*Erleben*] as *intending* to experience — that does not succeed. In the experience one *must* not look at himself; every look becomes the "evil eye" then.[26]

So Nietzsche likens his study of a particular topic to the way in which a traveller goes to sleep with the intention of waking at a certain hour: the psychologist gives himself up wholly to the experience, but at the decisive moment "something springs forth and catches the mind *in the act*." [27]

[24] XVI 17 f. Cf. 16 f.; XI 235; XIII 247 f.
[25] VII 23. Cf. 30.
[26] VIII 121. Cf. 66; III 356.   [27] V 5 f. Cf. 341; III 361; XV 11.

A second indirection is to study history, a field which seems to Nietzsche to offer endless opportunities for psychological research. We reveal ourselves most deeply in what we do and say, and most of what we are is a prolongation of the past. The historical psychologist sees his own experiences more profoundly when they are thus reflected, and thereby knows both himself and general human nature better.[28]

No set of rules, of course, can adequately describe Nietzsche's peculiar gifts as a psychologist. In many respects he is a confessed and admiring follower of the great French moralists, from La Rochefoucauld to Stendhal, and he bitterly regrets the lack, in his contemporaries, of their subtlety and psychological perceptiveness.[29] At bottom his psychological skill was perhaps a kind of clairvoyance, like theirs. So he speaks of the "genius of the heart," of his own "Dionysian dowry," and claims to know a soul's inward parts by "smell." [30] The ultimate secrets of soul guessing, naturally, can *only* be guessed.

2. THE MEANING OF WILL

Along with the soul, Nietzsche rejects another notion which dominated the older psychology: mind as a "thinking substance" possessing "faculties" through which it produces particular thoughts, feelings, and so forth. He regards as pure fiction any such separation of an "agent" from the process, any belief in something permanent beneath the process, something simple behind the complexities of experience. He admits that something of the sort may be embedded permanently in the language we have to use, but as far as possible he endeavors to substitute process for substance and complexity for simplicity.[31] Let us re-

---

[28] III 121 f. Cf. VII 69 f.; V 44 f.; II 12 f., 364 f.; IV 61; XI 47, 114; above, p. 24.   [29] II 57 f.; XV 35, 112 ff.; XIV 356 f.
[30] VII 271; XV 57, 22. Cf. VII 255.
[31] XVI 13, 26, 31, 43, 50 f., 55 f., 61, 63, 109; XIII 261; XII 148.

member this when, as so often, he continues to use language
fraught with the old connotations.

He also denies the separation of "mental faculties," so
characteristic of the old psychology. There is no such thing
as pure thought, mere feeling, naked will; each involves
the others. For instance:

"Thinking," as the epistemologists apply it, does not occur
at all: it is a quite arbitrary fiction obtained by picking out one
element from the process and subtracting all the rest, an artificial arrangement for purposes of intelligibility.[32]

Thought or reason is "a relatedness [*Verhältniszustand*]
of diverse passions and cravings"; "every passion contains
its quantum of reason"; feelings are implicit judgments;
will includes feeling and thought.[33]

These remarks afford clues to the meaning of "will" in
Nietzsche. Without some such help it seems a hopeless
paradox that he should make will to power the essence of
life and yet declare that "there is no will at all." [34]

Other passages make it clear that Nietzsche is really denying *previous* conceptions of will, notably Schopenhauer's,
which illegitimately abstract all specific content from the
process. Properly, "there is no 'willing' but only a 'willing-
something' "; directedness is an essential\character of volition; mere "will in general" is nonsense.[35] Also, such
theories project "the will" behind the process as an agent
which "does" the willing.[36] So when Nietzsche denies the
faculty he does not necessarily deny the fact: "That belief
in will is necessary in order to 'will' — is nonsense." [37]

Further, Nietzsche objects to the conception of will as
something unanalyzable and mysterious. In this, he thinks,

[32] XVI 7.
[33] XV 419; IV 40 f.; XIII 269; XIV 38 f.
[34] XIII 263; XV 172; XVI 135.
[35] XVI 133, 137 f., 155 f. Cf. L.F.N. I 343 or H.K.A. III 353.
[36] XVI 15.
[37] XIII 263.

Schopenhauer and the rest have been misled by popular prejudice, which assumes that everybody knows what "will" is, and that one word must stand for one thing. Nietzsche replies:

Above all, volition seems to me something *complicated*, something that is a simple entity only as a word .... In every volition there is, firstly, a plurality of feelings, namely the feeling of the state *from* which, the feeling of the state *toward* which, the feeling of this "from" and "toward" itself, then too an accompanying muscular feeling which ... begins its play as soon as we "will" .... Secondly, thought as well: in every act of will there is a commanding thought; — and let no one suppose himself able to separate this thought from the "willing," as if will should still remain then! Thirdly, will is not only a complex of feeling and thinking, but before all a *passion* [*Affekt*]: specifically, the passion of command. What is called "freedom of will" is essentially the passion of superiority with respect to the one who must obey ... — this consciousness is in every will, and likewise that strain of attention, that direct gaze which fixes on one thing exclusively, that absolute valuation "this and nothing else is needful now," that inner certainty that obedience will occur, and all else that pertains to the state of the commander. A man who *wills* — commands a something in himself which obeys, or of which he believes that it obeys.[38]

He holds that Schopenhauer in particular debased the notion of will by making it the same as desire, neglecting the element of self-command.[39] Lastly, he discards the idea that volition causes bodily action by a kind of magic. This belief is due, he says, to a confusion of the "command" and "obedi-

[38] VII 28 f. Cf. XIV 38 f.; XI 188; XIII 263 ff., 281; V 165 f.

[39] XV 202; XVI 132. Certain passages identify the "command" with a sudden explosion of force (XIII 263, 264. Cf. 159, 267). Another denies that the tension of a force striving for release is a "willing" (XVI 133). The fact that the latter passage is part of the same fragment which distinguishes will from striving or desire suggests that desire may be the tension of pent-up forces, will their explosive release.

Some passages (XI 188; XIII 64, 252) still speak of "will" as if it were synonymous with "impulse," "passion" or "desire." This may indicate an inconsistency, but it is more probably a careless use of language. Will does not exclude desire; it is desire plus "command."

ence" concealed beneath the synthetic notion of self or ego:
the commanding gets identified with all the work of the
subordinates which execute it, and we come to think that
"will" does it all by simple decree. In fact, however, there
is a long series of commands and obedience as the order
passes down the hierarchy of "souls" or "wills" which make
up the living body, and is finally translated into physical
movements. The "will" of which we are conscious knows
practically nothing of the intricate mechanical detail of
the ensuing action, still less is it able to produce it all alone.
To will is really to make an experiment to see what we can
do, and if the experiment is often successful it is because
we usually command only when it is probable that we shall
be obeyed.[40]

The foregoing account of will is ostensibly an analysis
of conscious volition. How far may it be taken as a statement of the meaning of "will" in "will to power"?[41] We
are thrown back on conjecture, but on the whole the most
probable account seems to be as follows. Nietzsche attributes will in some sense to all living beings, but his thought
moves through several dialectical stages. In his polemic
against the superstitious popular conception he takes the
point of view of mechanistic biology or "external phenomenology," and shows how little such "will" has to do with
the real bodily action.[42] Then he finds a mechanistic the-

[40] VII 29 f.; XIV 38; XIII 249 f., 265 ff.; V 165; XI 287 ff. Nietzsche sometimes
denies efficacy of any kind to *conscious* will. See the discussion of consciousness
in Sec. 5.

[41] The evidence is conflicting and indecisive. Some passages from the period
of *The Gay Science* restrict "will" to beings having intellect, and intellect to higher
organisms with well developed nervous systems (V 166; XII 143. Cf. XIII 234).
But another passage of even earlier date, though it also makes will imply intellect, uses both to interpret the nature of physical force (XI 188). In the last
period several passages extend the notion of will to all parts of the organism
and regard the nervous system only as an "apparatus of centralization" (XIII
239 f., 243, 267). This I take to be the final drift of Nietzsche's views; the dis-
crepant passages may tacitly refer only to conscious volition, or may represent
a temporary emphasis on "external phenomenology."

[42] Cf. XVI 131 f.

ory inadequate in turn and supplements it with the conception of a society of primarily unconscious wills to power. The analysis of "will" given in this section may be taken as giving clues to the general meaning of "will to power," but consciousness must be subtracted, and perhaps other complexities in the analysis. *Just* how far Nietzsche uses "will" in a generalized or metaphorical sense in "will to power," it is impossible to say. It is fairly clear that he means to retain the notion of "commanding" and the notion of directedness or intentionality.[43]

3. DYNAMICS

As a psychologist, Nietzsche is not satisfied with painting mental scenery; his main concern is with the dynamics of human nature, the complex interplay of forces moulding thought, character, and conduct. The combination of internal and external phenomenology has led him to conceive the self as a society of dynamic factors. He describes them, of course, as specialized forms of will to power:

> Our intellect, our will, likewise our sensations, are dependent upon our *values* [*Wertschätzungen*]: these correspond to our urges and their conditions of existence. Our urges are reducible to *the will to power.*
> The will to power is the most fundamental fact which we can get at.[44]

His names for these differentiated modes of will to power in man are "impulse" or "urge" (*Trieb*), "instinct," "passion," "affect," and "desire," and as a rule he appears to use them synonymously.[45] They represent a change from biological to psychological language. Whether or not it is more than a change of language, he does not say. Presumably the

---

[43] XVI 17, 107 f., 155 f.; XIII 263 f.; VI 166 f.

[44] XIV 327. Cf. VII 35; XII 304; XIII 64, 69; XVI 152.

[45] *Trieb* is synonymous with *Instinkt* in XIII 256, with *Leidenschaft* in XII 100, with *Begehrung* and *Wille zur Macht* in XIII 66. Will to power is called an *Affekt* in XVI 152.

new terms stand for members of the ruling oligarchy in the bodily society of wills to power.[46] In any case, wherever Nietzsche writes as a psychologist, "urges" are his dynamic elements. In this respect also he breaks with the older psychology: "passion" is always and necessarily the mover in human nature; reason is not an independent controlling power but the instrument of passion.[47]

True to his critique of "faculties," Nietzsche warns against the specious simplicity of *conscious* urges:

The separate so-called "passions" (e.g. man is cruel) are only *fictitious unities*, inasmuch as that which enters consciousness as homogeneous, from different basic urges, is synthesized by imagination into a "being" [*Wesen*] or "faculty," into a passion.[48]

Nietzsche again emphasizes complexity and process:

Urges are *higher organs*, as I understand it: actions, sensations and states of feeling grown into one another, organizing, nourishing each other —[49]

Despite Nietzsche's polemic against psychological description in terms of *conscious* purpose, it is evident that his adoption of "urge" or "instinct" as dynamic category, as well as the whole will-to-power theory, makes his psychology teleological or purposive in some sense. But he attacks the view, held by some pessimistic writers, that an urge seeks satisfaction in the sense of seeking the appeasement of desire, as if desire were essentially painful. On the contrary, satisfaction is found in unimpeded activity, not in some result of the activity, and *"happiness* would be the *equilibrium of the releasing activities of all urges."* [50] So urges

[46] Cf. XIII 70, 245.
[47] XV 419; XIII 245.
[48] XIII 70. Cf. 261; XII 148. XVI 134 f. goes the whole way with "external phenomenology" and makes all "affects" fictitious interpretations of physiological states (cf. XIII 252 f., 267).
[49] XIII 256. Cf. 255.
[50] XIII 257. Cf. 254 f.; XII 305.

exhibit the primary, power-spending aspect of the will to power. "Every urge, while it is active, sacrifices force and other urges: it is finally checked; otherwise it would ruin everything by extravagance." [51]

Impulses also manifest the acquisitive aspect of will to power: "every urge is desirous of ruling." [52] There is consequently a perpetual rivalry among them. Each arouses its opposite and others as well. An impulse acts "by *seizing* the stimuli and *transforming* them. In order to seize them it must struggle: i.e. *restrain*, repress another urge." [53] Nietzsche thinks the urges obtain their "nourishment" from experiences or incoming stimuli; each one lies in wait for "booty" and "as it were fingers every state into which a man gets," which it seeks to interpret to its own satisfaction. Hence "each moment of our life lets some tentacles of our being grow and some others wither, according to the nourishment which the moment does or does not bear in itself." [54] Thus, though urges may vary enormously in degree of alertness or in the amount of expression obtained, they are never, strictly speaking, inactive, for an urge *is* essentially a kind of activity (*ein bestimmtes Tätig-sein*).[55]

Nietzsche therefore pursues the psychology of dynamic conflict into its endless ramifications. In fact the chief significance of his view that the self is a group of wills to power is the consequent ubiquity of strife within it. Let us consider his theory of conflict and of its typical consequences.

Since urges are the sole motive forces, they are also the sole agencies of inhibition. "The will to overcome a passion [*Affekt*] is finally only the will of another or several other passions." [56] Here again Nietzsche is combating traditional psychology, which usually made conscience or reason independently controlling powers in human nature.

---

[51] XV 407.
[52] VII 15. Cf. VI 51.
[53] XIII 255. Cf. XI 283.
[54] IV 120 ff. Cf. XIII 70.
[55] XIII 255.
[56] VII 101. Cf. IV 105 f.

Nietzsche recognizes a number of ways in which urges, when frustrated in their normal outlets, find indirect expression. Dreaming and wishing are examples. He intimates that dreams may have the function of compensating to a certain extent for the absence of "nourishment" for certain impulses during the day. This, he thinks, would explain something of the extraordinary variety in the character of dreams despite the fact that physical conditions are much the same from night to night: different propensities have been starved and therefore take the lead in fabricating the dream interpretations of stimuli.[57] As for wishing, it is a sort of dreaming, an expression of impotence or fatigue, escape from reality: what men call their "ideals" are often compensatory in this way, the magnitude of the ideal being a measure of the degree of frustration. "Man, when he *wishes*, rests himself from what is everlastingly valuable in him, from his actions: in the unreal, absurd, worthless, childish."[58]

Other indirect responses to frustration affect our attitudes to other people. Nietzsche notes that we may believe in another as we should like to believe in ourselves, and, conversely, dissatisfaction with something in ourselves may be projected as a kind of revenge, in artistic work or in our treatment of men; for example the fanatic's cruelty to heretics may be an indirect revenge upon the secret scepticism in his own breast.[59] Nietzsche's famous psychology of *ressentiment* illustrates this principle: the inwardly un-

[57] IV 121 f. Cf. XIII 282 f. He also remarks that dreams reveal truths about ourselves of which we are only obscurely aware, if at all, while awake, and that most men's dreams must be abominable (III 45; IV 127. Cf. III 171, 301; XIII 240, 281). In *The Birth of Tragedy* he gives a conception of dreams as both revealing and tending to heal or release depths of our being not accessible to waking consciousness — an idea which later psychologists have found very fruitful (cf. I 20 ff., 25, 34 ff.).

[58] XV 384 f. Cf. IV 275.

[59] VI 80; XI 294; VII 257. For other examples cf. II 291, 378; III 228; IV 89. The "dramatic *Urphänomen*" as described in *The Birth of Tragedy* is also a kind of projection (I 60 f.).

happy take revenge by making a caricature of the fortunate and their values.[60] Even crimes of violence may be indirect — therefore misunderstood — expressions of inner tortures of maladjusted instinct.[61]

The converse substitution, which might be called "introversion" — Nietzsche's term is *Verinnerlichung* — also occurs. Impulses normally expressed in relations with the outer world may, if blocked, turn inward and act upon other elements in the self.[62] This, he believes, is often a source of inner poisoning: when "the beast" is checked in action it becomes "bestiality of idea." Therefore in some cases one should give vent to an immoral impulse for the sake of health rather than choke it down; for example instead of swallowing anger one might express it verbally or in imaginary revenge.[63] Hence Nietzsche has a good word for the priestly confessional:

...to whom would the people have reason to prove themselves more grateful than to these men ... before whom they can pour out their hearts with impunity, upon whom they can *get rid of* their secrets, cares, and worse (— for the man who "communicates himself" gets rid of himself; and he who has "confessed," forgets). Here a great necessity rules: namely for psychic refuse too there is need of drains and of cleanly, cleansing waters therein....[64]

On the other hand, Nietzsche does not consider all checking of impulses harmful. Temporary asceticism, for instance, can serve to intensify, purify, and spiritualize the passions.[65]

Of a piece with Nietzsche's effort to overcome moral resistance to psychology is his belief that the unconscious

---

[60] See below, pp. 149 ff. Also revenge generally may vent itself upon substitute objects (VI 207. Cf. I 407 f.).

[61] VI 53 f.

[62] See Sec. 6. VIII 160 f. uses *verinnerlichen* in quite a different sense.

[63] XI 202 f.; VII 391; II 80; III 35. Cf. VI 79; XV 18.

[64] V 287. Cf. VI 169.

[65] VII 87, 119; XIV 94; XVI 313.

urges at the base of human nature are terrible and revolting to moral standards. This is symbolized, in *The Birth of Tragedy*, by the satyr as the natural Dionysian man.[66] A later essay runs:

> What does man really know of himself? .... Woe to the fatal curiosity which should once be able to look through a crack out and down from the chamber of consciousness, and which should then divine that man rests, with the unconcern of his ignorance, on the pitiless, the ravenous, the insatiable, the murderous, and as if suspended in dreams on the back of a tiger.[67]

Nietzsche thinks that such an unmasking of impulses is unnatural and a sign of broken instinct. Normally our urges maintain a deft naïveté in the employment of flattering disguises.[68]

But the counterpart of this savage picture is his theory of sublimation or spiritualization (*Sublimirung, Vergeistigung*), the most significant of the ways in which urges attain indirect expression. He writes:

> All passions have a time when they are merely fatal, when they drag down their victim with the heaviness of stupidity — and a later, very much later one when they are married to the spirit, are "spiritualized." [69]

By sublimation Nietzsche evidently means refinement, increased sensitiveness and considerateness of action, and expression in thought and imagination rather than in mere muscular response alone. He holds that the highest things in human culture — religion, philosophy, art — are sublimations of such passions as cruelty and lust. The fact is obscured, however, because: "When an urge becomes more *intellectual* it gets a new name, a new charm and new valuation. It is often *contrasted* to the urge on the older level,

---

[66] I 57 f., 63.
[67] X 191. Cf. VI 54.

[68] XV 411 f.
[69] VIII 84. Cf. 86.

as its contradiction . . . ." [70] Nietzsche is particularly aware of the importance of the erotic instincts in this regard: "The degree and quality of a man's sexuality reach up to the utmost pinnacle of his mind." [71]

He also recognizes other features of mental conflict. An impulse not only arouses its opponent, but gives zest to it: "the more strongly one develops an urge, the more *attractive* it becomes to *plunge* once into its *opposite*." [72] Nietzsche does not analyze this process — perhaps it is due to fatigue — but he gives many examples: pessimism and melancholy incline one toward optimism and gaiety; conversely, deep happiness may express itself in pessimism; passionate natures may be charmed by wisdom and justice or by scepticism; an occasional stupidity makes wisdom taste better; dependent souls may be most zealous for independence, and "precisely for those men who strive most hotly for power it is indescribably agreeable to feel themselves *overwhelmed!*" [73] Also we tend generally to idealize our opposites.[74]

Finally, Nietzsche does not consider mental conflict an evil *per se*. It is a case of that inner "chaos" which is necessary for growth. "One is *fertile* only at the cost of being rich in contrasts [*Gegensätze*]; one stays *young* only on the supposition that the soul does not recline, does not hanker for peace . . ." [75]

[70] XII 149. Cf. 87 ff.; VII 186 f., 355, 357 f.; XVI 141, 228 f., 246; IV 36 f., 75 ff., 110 ff.
[71] VII 95. Cf. 119, 418; XVI 226, 228 f., 232 f., 243; XV 334; VI 78 f.; XII 149; XI 253; VIII 133 ff. Sex and cruelty are already intimately associated in the Dionysian urge as conceived in The Birth of Tragedy, where the theory of sublimation is also plainly suggested (I 26 ff. Cf. XVII 299).
[72] XV 206.
[73] IV 239. Cf. 217; I 2 f.; VI 153 ff.; XI 381, 386 f., 391; XIII 290; XIV 163. Similar relations hold between Apollinian and Dionysian, and between Dionysian and Socratic urges (I 19, 38; IX 180). IV 60 speaks of the feeling of power and the feeling of *Ergebung* as "the two kinds of happiness."
[74] IV 275.
[75] VIII 86. Cf. XII 119.

4. DEVELOPMENT

Nietzsche emphasizes the plasticity of human nature, excepting in principle only the general characteristics of will to power. All specific urges or needs have been "learned" and none are eternal, though some are now so deeply "fixed" as to be practically permanent. He admits no absolute distinction between "second nature" and "first nature." [76]

This view continues his Lamarckian biology. Since valuation and organic memory belong to all life, it is possible to explain the genesis of instinct as the cumulative inheritance of valuations and actions:

All human urges, like all *animal* ones, have been developed and placed in the foreground as *conditions of existence* under certain circumstances. *Urges* are the *after-effects of long-fostered valuations* [*Wertschätzungen*] which now function instinctively, as a *system* of judgments of pleasure and pain. First compulsion, then habituation, then want, then natural propensity (urge).[77]

As the last sentence suggests, there are intermediate stages in the development of an urge, notably that of "half-instinct" which only reacts to stimuli and does not move spontaneously.[78] The process of building recurrent experiences into the constitution of man exemplifies the "assimilation" at work in all organic memory.[79]

The rest of Nietzsche's theory of heredity also applies to the genesis of urges. They are acquired because of "need": that is, conditions compel the animal to adopt certain habits or perish — hence the statement that urges begin as "com-

[76] XIII 257; I 309. Cf. II 45; below, p. 111.

[77] XIII 256. Cf. 237, 139, 209 f., 220, 273; XII 148, 150, 317; IV 264; V 76; VII 250 f. The best illustration of this process is Nietzsche's account of the origin of the truth-impulse (X 162, 189 ff.).

[78] XII 150.

[79] Cf. XII 64, 145, 148, 150; XIII 168, 173, 219 f., 233; XVI 408 f.; V 150, 152; VIII 308; above, pp. 69 f.

pulsion." And the environmental setting must be comparatively stable, else activities are not repeated long enough for cumulative effect. But, owing to "hereditary inertia," an impulse may be inherited long after it has ceased to be a condition of existence.[80]

This account resolves apparent contradictions in Nietzsche. He may favor or oppose an attempt to change human nature according to the time scale in mind. Where important changes are to be obtained, he usually thinks in terms of several generations. He says that neither the absence of passions which one has, nor the possession of those one has not, can be more than shammed in one generation; but in two or three, what *was* pretense has *become* reality. Thus he can mock the actor (*Schauspieler*) and at the same time hold that "all character is a *rôle* to begin with." [81]

Given the self as a group of urges, the attainment of a measure of unity amid their natural conflict becomes a problem analogous to that of the unity of the biological organism, and Nietzsche's solution is essentially the same. He considers integration an achievement, not a datum; an exception, not the rule:

Do not suppose at all that many people are "persons" ... many are indeed *several* persons; most are *none*. Wherever the average qualities, on which continuance of a type depends, prevail, being a person would be a waste.[82]

Evidently an indefinite number of degrees and patterns of integration are possible. He describes three typical ones:

1) the *dominating passion*, which brings with it the highest form of health there is: here the coordination of the internal systems and their working in one service are best attained — but that is almost the definition of health!

2) the *opposition* of passions, the two-ness, three-ness, many-

[80] Cf. XIII 173, 139, 255 ff.
[81] XIII 280. Cf. 282 ff.; V 82 f.; IV 272; VIII 22 ff.
[82] XVI 298.

ness of "souls in one breast": very unhealthy, inward ruin, disintegrating ... unless one passion finally becomes master. ...

3) the *juxtaposition*, *without* being an opposition and co-operation [*Füreinander*]: often periodic, and then, as soon as it has found an order, also healthy . . . The most interesting men belong here, the chameleons ... they are happy and sure, but they have no development .... [83]

These differences of integration make it possible for him to interpret such expressions as "strong will" or "weak will" without supposing the existence of "will" as a separate entity. The first pattern is his idea of strong-willed character, with its "precision and clarity of direction" derived from the dominance of one urge; the others are types of weakness. [84]

In *Ecce Homo* he describes his own development as an ideal instance:

Our distant, future destiny rules over us, even when we as yet have no eye open for it; for a long time we experience only riddles. The choice of men and things, the selection of events, the shoving aside of what is most agreeable, often what is most revered — it terrifies us ... but it is the higher reason of our future task.

Meantime the organizing "idea" which is called to rule grows and grows in the depths — it begins to command, it leads slowly *back* from bypaths and wrong paths, it prepares *single* qualities and abilities which one day will prove themselves indispensable as means to the whole ... before it lets anything be known of the dominating task .... [85]

Such is evidently the norm expressed in Nietzsche's motto, "Become what you are," and also in his problem of realizing the "higher self." [86] What one *is* (if one is anything, in this sense) lies hidden in the dominant instinct, the

---

[83] XVI 210. Cf. 142; I 393.

[84] XV 172.

[85] XIII 33; XV 44. Cf. XIV 387; III 8; XII 164. II 12 generalizes the personal experience.

[86] See above, pp. 39 f., below, pp. 202 ff. — especially note 154.

"tyrant in us," the hidden destiny; *becoming* what one is means growing the other impulses in the self around this central one: the fruition of inborn talent.

Integration accordingly depends upon fortunate heredity. Nietzsche speaks of the "enlightened despotism" which every great passion exercises.[87] But how do passions become enlightened? He says that impulses are originally crude and destructive of the whole: not just any kind of domination by any violent urge will produce a harmonious entirety.[88] As in the case of the unity of the organism, his answer is in terms of organic learning plus natural selection. Of the impulses which have gone into the making of scientific thought he writes, "Many hecatombs of men have been sacrificed before these urges learned to understand their togetherness and to feel with one another as functions of one organizing power in one man!" [89] In like manner the ruling power must become enlightened and learn self-limitation in the exercise of its authority.[90]

"Instinct" means somewhat more than "urge," in Nietzsche's usage. By it he means an urge which, through generations of practice, has embodied a high degree of "intelligence" or skill. In this sense he speaks of instinct as "assimilated virtue" and "regulated habits." [91] Talents are ancestral accomplishments.[92] Sure instinct is the "result of a long form of similar activity on the part of a species of man"; its unconscious automatism is "the presupposition of every kind of mastery, of every kind of perfection in the art of life." [93] These are the reasons for the importance of instinct in his ethics. At the same time his admiration is not

[87] XVI 342.
[88] VIII 84; XV 407; XII 114; I 394.
[89] V 155.
[90] XII 105. Cf. III 213.
[91] XVI 409; XIV 413.
[92] IV 346.
[93] XV 193 f.; VIII 301. Cf. XV 458, 470; VIII 92 f. The high esteem for instinct appears very early in Nietzsche; cf. L.F.N. I 338, 369 or H.K.A. IV 126.

uncritical: instincts are open to suspicion just because they carry a hidden past.[94]

His theory of the gradual building up of instinctive powers illustrates the process of "storage":

> How do men come by a great force and a great task? All virtue and skill in body and soul has been acquired painfully and in detail, by much industry, self-conquest, limitation to little, by much tenacious, faithful repetition of the same tasks, the same renunciations: but there are men who are the heirs and masters of this slowly acquired, manifold wealth of virtues and skills — because, by reason of fortunate and judicious marriages, and also happy accidents, the acquired and accumulated forces of many generations are not squandered and frittered away but bound together by a firm ring and will. At the end namely there appears a man, a prodigy of force, who demands a prodigious task.[95]

Conversely, Nietzsche says, decadence consists in the disintegration of instinctive order: "To *have* to combat the instincts — that is the formula for decadence: as long as life *ascends*, happiness equals instinct." [96]

The hereditary basis of "what one *is*" leads him to take a strict view of our potentialities as individuals. To be sure, we can change our masks:

> We contain the *sketch* for *many* persons in ourselves.... Circumstances bring out one shape in us: if the circumstances change very much, one also sees two, three shapes in himself. — From every moment of our life there are still many possibilities.[97]

But the core of our being remains "a piece of fate" which renders moral exhortation absurd:

> We do not believe that a man becomes different unless he is already: i.e. unless, as occurs often enough, he is a plurality of persons, at least of tendencies to persons. In this case what

[94] XIII 251.
[95] XVI 358. Cf. XV 429.
[96] VIII 74. Cf. 92 f., 154; VII 236; XIV 124; XV 462 f.
[97] XIII 280. Cf. 179 ff., 256, 281; XIV 37.

one gets is that another rôle steps into the foreground .... The look is altered, *not* the essence . . . He who is a criminal by fate and aptitude unlearns nothing . . . .[98]

5. SELF-CONSCIOUSNESS

Nowhere does Nietzsche break more radically with psychological tradition than in his treatment of mind or consciousness — the two had come to be largely synonymous. Since Descartes at least, modern thought usually identified man's self with his conscious mentality or stream of thought, and even man's passions and inspirations were reduced to modes of awareness. But we have seen how Nietzsche makes the self a hierarchy of urges which determine character and conduct for the most part unconsciously. It remains to ask what place is left for mind.

The polemical aspect of his discussion may be summarized as an attack upon three customary assumptions.

(1) Consciousness is not an autonomous, sovereign power, nor is it the true self. It is an instrument of the ruling oligarchy of urges — "an organ, like the stomach." [99] It neither initiates nor executes action, and does not even control the succession of its own states: the series of conscious states is not causally connected but "perfectly atomistic," a mere symptom of the struggle of impulses going on beneath.[100]

(2) Consciousness is not a mode of access to infallible, absolute truth — witness the criticism of "internal phenomenology." Observing the marvelous "interpretation" of nervous stimuli in dreams, and believing that waking experience is not radically different in nature, Nietzsche

[98] XV 424. Cf. VIII 89; XV 382 f.; VII 191; XIII 38.
[99] XIII 257. Cf. 71, 164, 267; XVI 36 f. Nietzsche appears to identify consciousness and *self*-consciousness, and to use "Geist" sometimes as synonymous with "Bewusstsein."
[100] XVI 6 ff., 129; XIII 65, 241, 246, 267; XIV 36; XI 283 f., 288 ff.; XII 150 ff.; VIII 94, 266; V 153; IV 128 f. This is a continuation of his critique of conscious volition. Some such view of consciousness in general is already hinted in *The Birth of Tragedy* (I 29, 45).

suggests "that all our so-called consciousness is a more or less phantastic commentary on a text which is unknown, perhaps unknowable, but felt." [101]

(3) The value of consciousness has been absurdly over-rated. Philosophers have assumed that progress lay in becoming more and more conscious, whereas unconscious instinct is the type of perfection, consciousness being rather the sign of some maladjustment:

> In every apperception [or "act of becoming conscious" — *Bewusstwerden*] a discontent of the organism is being expressed: something new is to be tried, nothing is adequately in order for it, there is trouble, tension, excessive irritation — all that is precisely what apperception is . . .[102]

It appears also to be an occasion of maladjustment. "Mind is the life which itself cuts into life" and "comprehension is a *finish* [*Ende*]." [103]

At times Nietzsche pushes the polemic against consciousness to an extreme, as when he writes, "All that becomes conscious is an end-phenomenon, a close — and causes nothing . . . ." [104] This would seem to contradict his theory that consciousness is an instrument or organ — an instrument must be effective somehow —, his belief that consciousness disintegrates instinct — also a kind of efficacy —, and his apparent intention, as a philosopher, to influence events by making men conscious of certain things.[105]

His ulterior purpose is to attack the moral assumption that a voluntary action is caused by its conscious motive. Fortunately, his more moderate statements accomplish this end without implying the paradox that consciousness does literally nothing. They suggest that a conscious aim is not

[101] IV 123. Cf. XVI 9, 39.
[102] XV 470. Cf. 449, 469; XVI 38 f.; V 49; VII 379; I 91–5.
[103] VI 151, 364; XV 194. Cf. I 94 ff.; V 48 f., 294; IX 34 f.; XVII 317 f.
[104] XVI 8. Cf. 131, 140, 445; XIII 65, 159, 246; XIV 36; VIII 94, 266.
[105] Cf. XIV 74, 103; II 42; XVI 363; XII 64 f. So XII 118 says that in great ages egoism tends to become self-conscious.

the *prime* mover in action, and that the stream of consciousness is not the full causal series involved in producing the actual response: it is rather a "symptom" of the main process, useful at best for orientation and direction, often a mere disguise of what is really happening.[106]

In any case Nietzsche is aware of a problem set by his general position: if consciousness is well-nigh superfluous, how account for its existence?

> The problem of consciousness (more accurately: of the becoming conscious of self) stands before us only when we begin to comprehend to what extent we could do without it .... Namely we could think, feel, will, remember, we could likewise "act" in every sense of the word: and nevertheless all that would not need to "enter our consciousness".... The whole of life would be possible without beholding itself in a mirror, as it were: as in fact by far the preponderant part of this life — and indeed even of our thinking, feeling, willing life — still takes place for us without this reflection.... *Why* consciousness at all, if it is *superfluous* in the main? [107]

Nietzsche answers that consciousness was evolved as an aid to intercourse with the external world.[108] He observes that refinement and intensity of consciousness generally accompany special capacity for communication and that capacity usually develops in response to need; that consciousness signifies a need for readjustment; and that conscious thought operates in terms of language, a social product developed in the first instance for communication. From these facts he concludes:

> ... *consciousness in general has developed only under the stress of the need for communication* .... That our very actions, thoughts, feelings, movements come into our consciousness — at least a part of them — is the effect of a fearful, long "must" ruling over man: as the most endangered animal he *needed*

---

[106] V 310 f.; VII 52 f.; XIII 119, 132 ff., 157–64, 215, 246; XVI 129 ff. See above, pp. 92 f.

[107] V 290 f.   [108] XVI 22, 36 f.

help, protection, he *needed* people like him, he had to know how to express his distress, to make himself intelligible — and for all that he first had need of "consciousness," that is to "know" what he lacks, to "know" how he feels . . . . Man first learned as a social animal to be conscious of himself — he does so still, he does so more and more.[109]

The social origin, the passage continues, explains why consciousness is superficial, general, and falsifying: it brings to light only our "herd nature," what we have in common with others, and ignores our individual selves.

Nietzsche also explains its shallowness by means of its rôle in our dealings with the environment. As a field marshal must have simplified data if he is to achieve a ready grasp of the course of battle, so consciousness supplies the ruling urges with selected and simplified versions of fact. Consciousness is "the hand with which the organism stretches farthest, to get hold of things all around," essentially a means to power.[110] As an instrument for administrative orientation, it is "accessible only to generalizations" and therefore fundamentally superficial. Nietzsche speaks of it as the "surface" or "skin" of an action "which, like every skin, betrays something but *conceals* still more." [111]

The social theory of the origin of consciousness helps to explain Nietzsche's apparent identification of consciousness and self-consciousness, and also his favorite mirror metaphor:

Conscious sensation is sensation of sensation; likewise conscious judging contains the judgment that judging is taking place. The intellect without this redoubling is unknown to us, naturally. But we can show its activity to be much the richer.

Consciousness always contains a double reflection [*Spiegelung*] — there is nothing immediate.

---

[109] V 291 ff. Cf. XII 155; XIII 247.

[110] XIV 46. Cf. XIII 234 f., 241, 249; VII 187 f. In this case it is not clear whether consciousness still means "self-consciousness" for Nietzsche.

[111] XIV 328; VII 53. Cf. XIII 65; XI 289; VII 343 f.; XV 44; XVI 131.

... thoughts *appear* to us; apperception, the reflection of the process in the process, is only a comparative exception (perhaps a refraction by contrast [*Brechen am Contraste*]).[112]

If conscious states are like mirror images we can understand why their succession is not a causal nexus, and also why they show only the surface of things.

Nietzsche relates conscious mentality to instinct in at least three ways: mind is primarily the slave of instinct, but it can also undermine instinct, and in time its dominant traits may *become* instinct. The first relation has been sufficiently discussed; he observes one form of it — now called rationalization — in the invention of specious reasons for what we do on impulse or habit.[113] The second he attributes partly to the evolutionary status of consciousness. It is the most recently developed organ, therefore most imperfectly adapted to the needs of the whole, and continually a source of danger.[114] But he sees a deeper antagonism between consciousness and instinct which no further development is likely to abolish: consciousness questions, doubts, suggests alternatives, whereas the "first imperative of instinct" is "*one does not ask* about certain things." Hence the first requisite for creating an instinctive tradition is to get rid of consciousness.[115] Just this disinclination to self-doubt or to consider alternatives explains why the strong tend to be less prudent than the weak: since the latter find direct modes of satisfaction more difficult, they are compelled to adopt foresight and cunning, in short to become intelligent.[116]

The third relation — that mind may become instinct — undoubtedly illustrates the theory of "assimilation" which accounted for the genesis of urges in general. Though Nie-

---

[112] XI 48; XIII 245; XI 278. Cf. IV 124; V 291; XI 177, 187; XVI 140; XV 469.
[113] Cf. IV 40, 270; V 310 f.; VI 53 f.
[114] V 48; XIII 164 f. Cf. XVI 137.
[115] VIII 153, 300 f.; XIV 122. Cf. VIII 38 f.; II 215; XV 411 ff. See also note 103 above. Compare the corresponding definitions of *Dummheit* (VII 118; IV 28).
[116] Cf. VIII 128; VII 319 f.; XI 50, 52 f.; XVI 231; IV 227.

tzsche ridicules the idea that conscious beliefs and states
of feeling have important immediate effects on action, he
holds that opinions held for generations gradually become
assimilated and thus transform human nature decisively.[117]
The same impulses can be ennobled or degraded by connecting them with a good or a bad conscience, respectively
— witness the history of erotic impulses under the influence
of Greek or of Christian beliefs — and indeed man has been
differentiated from the other animals through the influence
of religious and moral convictions.[118]

Finally, mind itself has become an independent instinct:

Reason is a slowly evolving auxiliary organ which for vast
ages, fortunately, has *little* power to determine man; it works
in the *service* of the organic urges and slowly emancipates itself
to *equality of status* with them — so that reason (opinion and
knowledge) struggles with the urges as a distinctive new urge
— and late, quite late, to *preponderance*.[119]

Mind as an urge for knowledge, with embodied instinctive
skills, functions mostly, of course, *beneath* consciousness.[120]

6. MAN IN EVOLUTION

The theory of evolutionary "fixation" stated that species
may get into such a rut that hereditary inertia prevents
further change. Nietzsche believes that most species have
actually reached this stage. It is the distinction of man to
be "the still unfixed animal"; for him alone among animals
there are as yet "no eternal horizons." [121]

That is because man is sick, and the resulting inner

---

[117] VIII 265 f.; XII 64.

[118] IV 42 f., 74, 116; II 194; III 371 f.; V 155 f.; XII 263; XIII 144, 174 f., 224.
Other instances of the transmutation of consciousness into instinct will be found
in VII 347; X 399.

[119] XII 157. Cf. XVI 99.

[120] Cf. XV 470. "Intellect" is distinguished from "consciousness" in XI 48;
XIII 240, 246.

[121] XIV 67; V 175; VII 88; XII 120, 206 f. XIV 39 states that man is *festgestellt*
in many instincts.

"chaos" has prevented stagnation. Nietzsche's name for man's sickness, or at least for one of its most virulent forms, is "bad conscience," and his theory of its origin, formulated in *Toward the Genealogy of Morals*, explains why man has remained plastic.

The theory assumes that men, at first living wild, were suddenly compelled to settle down under ruthless political domination exercised by some conquering band of "blonde beasts." This change was the most radical in man's history, comparable to the experience of those sea animals that were compelled to become land animals or perish. Its suddenness allowed no time for the old nomadic instincts to adjust themselves to outside conditions. Consequently:

> ... they had to search for new and, as it were, subterranean satisfactions. All instincts which do not discharge themselves outwards *turn inwards* — this is what I call the *making inward* [*Verinnerlichung*] of man: thereby what is later called his "soul" springs up in man for the first time. The entire inner world, originally thin as if stretched into a frame between two skins, has unfolded and branched out, has got depth, breadth, height, in proportion as the outward discharge of man has been *checked*. . . .Hostility, cruelty, pleasure in the chase, in sudden assault, in change, in ravage — all this turning against the possessor of such instincts: *that* is the origin of "bad conscience." . . . . But with it was induced the greatest and weirdest disease, from which humanity has not recovered to this day, the suffering of man *from man*, from *himself* . . . .[122]

So the disease did more than merely prevent the fixation of the human species. It opened up hitherto undreamed-of possibilities. Nietzsche continues:

> ... with the fact of an animal soul turned against itself on this earth ... there was something so new, profound, unprecedented, enigmatic, contradictory *and full of future*, that the aspect of the earth was fundamentally changed thereby. . . .

[122] VII 379 f. Cf. 381 ff.; XV 411. The picture of the subjugated peoples appears to be somewhat different in VII 236.

Since then, man *also* counts among the most unexpected and exciting lucky throws that the "great child" of Heracleitus, be it called Zeus or Chance, makes; — he awakes an interest in himself, a suspense, a hope, almost a certainty, as if by him something were announcing, something preparing itself; as if man were not a goal but only a path, an episode, a bridge, a great promise . . .[123]

Nietzsche traces some of the subsequent vicissitudes of man's sickness and plasticity. Always there is the double aspect of danger and promise. Thus he writes of the priests who learned to exploit man's "bad conscience" for their own ends:

From the beginning there is something *unhealthy* in such priestly aristocracies ... but as to what has been invented by these very men as remedy for this their morbidity ... humanity itself is still ill with the after-effects of these naïve priestly cures! .... With priests exactly *everything* becomes more dangerous, not only remedies and arts of healing, but also pride, revenge, sagacity, debauchery, love, thirst for power, virtue, disease; — to be sure it may also be added, with some justice, that man in general first became *an interesting animal* on the soil of this *essentially dangerous* existence form of man, the priestly one; that here the human soul first got *depth* and became *evil* in a higher sense; and those are the two fundamental forms of superiority of man over other animals so far! . . .[124]

So Nietzsche speaks of the "chain sickness" produced in man by the fetters of moral and religious error, yet holds that just those errors have educated man above the level of animality.[125] The successive dominance of several scales of value, each making unlimited claims, has both ennobled the urges valued in each case, and produced conflict among them which makes man sick in comparison to other animals — whose instincts are harmonious because they perform limited tasks.[126]

[123] VII 381.
[124] VII 310 f. Cf. 424 ff.
[125] III 371 f.; V 155 f..
[126] V 155 f.; XV 335.

The same is true of man's present predicament: there is danger of relapse into fixation at a tame level, and there is promise of advance to unequalled heights. These lines of change lead to the "last man" and the "superman," respectively.[127] Nietzsche describes the former thus:

Alas! There comes the time when man will give birth to a star no more. Alas! There comes the time of the most despicable man, who can no longer despise himself.

A little poison now and then: it makes pleasant dreams. And much poison finally, for a pleasant death.
One still works, for work is a pastime. But one takes care lest the pastime fatigue.

No shepherd and one flock! Each wants the same, each is the same: he who feels differently enters the insane asylum of his own accord.
"Formerly everybody was crazy" — say the smartest, and wink.[128]

Nietzsche concentrates all his passionate energies to prevent this petering out of humanity, and, instead, to send it on, in an adventure of "self-overcoming," toward the realization of its highest potentialities. He is willing to admit a generous share of the unforeseen: "Nothing can be predicted, but with a certain elevation of the type Man a *new* force can reveal itself, of which we previously knew nothing (— namely a synthesis of opposites [*Gegensätzen*]!)"[129] Yet he has now laid down general principles of vital advance, supplied means of understanding the raw material of human nature, caught sight of its latent possibilities, and suggested the laws by which it can be re-fashioned.

[127] VI 16, 19 f.; XII 360, 416; XIV 66 f.; XVI 335.
[128] VI 19 f.
[129] XIV 44 f. Cf. VI 113.

CHAPTER V

The Standard of Revaluation

> *Humanity has always repeated the same mistake:...*
> *it has made a standard of life out of a means to life ...*
> *instead of finding the measure in the greatest enhance-*
> *ment of life itself, in the problem of growth and ex-*
> *haustion.... (XV 401)*

1. ALL FOR LIFE

NIETZSCHE directs all the forces of his mature philosophy toward a "revaluation of all values," lest we lose heart in nihilism and yield the earth to the "last man." His German, *Umwertung*, is but poorly rendered by "revaluation." He intends more than a routine inventory: he means revolution, a thorough overturn of the old scale of values.[1] Nor does he wish to be the sterile sort of revolutionary who merely juggles existing terms into another pattern: he claims to create *new* values, as the alchemist makes gold of base metals — "he alone enriches; the others merely exchange."[2] What is the standard by which Nietzsche condemns the old hierarchy and erects the new?

We can best reconstruct that standard by a series of approximations. The first of these, and the most certainly his, is life. He writes: "What are our values and tables of moral goods themselves worth? *What comes of their rule?* For whom? In what respect? — Answer: for life."[3] This

---

[1] Cf. VII 137; V 205; VI 113, 169; XIV 382; XV 116 f.; XVI 164, 339, 363. Nietzsche does not regard himself as the first value revolutionary in history: Judaized Christianity was an *Umwertung* of pagan values (VII 71, 315). XV 338 states that there have been several revolutions of like nature.

[2] L.B. 23/5/88; VI 73, 169, 193 f.; XVI 351.

[3] XV 333. Cf. 169, 249, 339; VIII 193, 226; VII 290.

might be called Nietzsche's *a priori*; its importance in his thinking could hardly be exaggerated.[4] Loyalty to life — "remaining true to the earth"[5] — is the essential basis of his demand for a revaluation of values. About the Christian or "good" man, the supporter of the old ideals, he concludes:

...so he ends...by understanding nature as evil, man as depraved, being good as grace.... In sum: *he negates life*.... With that he should consider his ideology of good and evil refuted.[6]

In adopting life as his standard, Nietzsche intends to exclude both supernatural and fragmentary values: nothing beyond life and nothing less than it shall be accepted. "The death of God" explains the rejection of other-worldly ideals: they have become nihilistic. The fragmentary ones arose because some instrument of life was mistaken for its end, some part for the whole.[7] Such is the case, he thinks, with consciousness and its most prized forms, pleasure and happiness:

The *"conscious* world" can *not* be considered as *starting point for value*: necessity for an *"objective"* assignment of value [*Wertsetzung*].

Of the immensity and complexity of cooperation and opposition exhibited by the total life of every organism, its *conscious* world of feelings, intentions, valuations, is a small section. We have no right to postulate this bit of consciousness as purpose, as "why," for that total phenomenon of life: consciousness is plainly but one more means in life's unfolding and expansion of power. For that reason it is naïve to postulate pleasure, or spirituality, or morality, or any particular from the sphere of consciousness, as supreme value....

That is my *fundamental objection* to all moral-philosophic

[4] XVI 164 does say that life is only a means to growth in power. Nietzsche is alluding to his extension of the will-to-power hypothesis to include all nature; life then becomes a special case of the universal urge. On the human level, however, life remains unchallenged as the arbiter of values.

[5] VI 13.
[6] XV 398.
[7] XV 401; XVI 166.

cosmodicies and theodicies, to all *"wherefore's"* and *highest values* in previous philosophy and philosophy of religion. A kind of *means* has been *misunderstood as an end*: conversely *life and its enhancement of power were degraded to a means.*[8]

But life exists in many forms, and the life of the few and of the many, the stability of life and its advance to higher levels, are quite different points of view.[9] So Nietzsche recognizes that a further approximation to a definite standard of value is necessary: he must grade the *kinds* of life.[10]

[8] XVI 165. Cf. 166, 137, 139 ff., 170; VI 46 f. In view of the frequent attention given to hedonism by Nietzsche it may be well to summarize all his thought on the subject of pleasure, both psychological and ethical:

a) Man seeks power, not pleasure or "happiness," for he willingly endures pain in order to grow in power (XVI 161, 163 f.).

b) Pleasure and displeasure are not ultimate valuations. They are "late and derivative intellect phenomena" which reflect organic judgments about the increase or decrease of our power by some given event. They vary according to our degree of power. It is our unconscious, instinctive judgment of value which first *makes* anything pleasant or unpleasant. (XVI 7, 133 f., 159, 161; XV 336; XII 143 ff.; XIII 172, 238 f., 269, 271 ff.; VI 47 f.)

c) Pleasure and displeasure, being conscious feelings, are merely accompanying — not motivating — phenomena; and they are instruments in the service of the whole organism, not ends to which the organism is a means. (XVI 8, 133, 137, 139 ff., 152, 160, 165 f., 445; XIII 157 f., 134; VI 47; XV 165.)

d) As symptoms, however, they are not utterly unrelated to value. Pleasure is essentially a feeling of increase in power; happiness consists "in the dominant [*herrschend gewordnen*] consciousness of power and victory." (XVI 375, 152, 157 f.; XV 455; VIII 218. Cf. VIII 226 f.)

e) But pleasure and displeasure are not complete opposites and cannot be used infallibly even to identify true values. Many pleasures are intensified by a subtle mixture of displeasure, and indeed growth in power involves the displeasure produced by resistance which is then overcome. (XVI 17, 124, 158 ff., 162 ff.; XIII 274. Cf. I 28; VII 180 f.)

f) The consequence of hedonism is nihilism, since there seems to be more displeasure than pleasure in the world. (XV 164; XVI 161, 166, 223.)

g) Hedonism is a symptom of weakness, decadence; it indicates morbid sensibility and the absence of a strong will which could set up a justifying goal in life. (XVI 75, 166, 212, 223; V 84 f.; XIII 152.)

h) A strong man despises hedonism and its "pessimism of sensibility": he is bent upon his goal, in the pursuit of which he regards how he or others happen to feel as matters of secondary importance. A rich and self-confident nature "fragt den Teufel danach, ob sie selig wird, — sie hat kein solches Interesse am Glück irgendwelcher Gestalt, sie ist That, Kraft, Begierde, — sie drückt sich den Dingen auf...." (XVI 212, 75, 437, 446; XV 158, 164; VII 180; XIII 177; IV 149 f.)

[9] VII 339. Bare *life* cannot be made into an ethical imperative, for no one can live otherwise than "according to life" (VII 17).

[10] XVI 92.

This central doctrine of "gradation" (*Rangordnung*) has been hinted several times already, in his aristocratic intuition of value, and in the implicit value judgments of his theory of evolution and of human nature. It appears more openly in his oft-repeated expressions of the supreme goal as the abundance, thriving, growth, enhancement, intensification, heightening (*Steigerung*) of life.[11] And it is finally stated in sharpest accents when Nietzsche makes the contrast between healthy and decadent, rising and declining, strong and weak, abundant and starved, vigorous and exhausted life: when he champions "pagan" against "anemic" ideals.[12]

But what distinguishes healthy from decadent, and what is the specific nature of the life we propose to enhance? Will to power.[13] Accordingly Nietzsche takes the fulfilment of the basic urge of all life for his criterion of value: "There is nothing in life that has value beside the degree of power — assuming that life itself is will to power."[14] That very will dictates all value-perspectives:

All "purposes," "goals," "meanings" [*Sinne*] are only modes of expression and transformations of the one will inherent in all happening: the will to power.... *Willing* in general is nothing else but willing to become *stronger*, willing to grow — and also willing the *means thereto.*

All valuations are only consequences and narrower perspectives *in the service* of this one will: valuing *itself* is only this *will to power.*[15]

Power, then, is the standard of value which Nietzsche affirms with all the eloquence at his command, in the martial words of *The Antichristian* and *The Will to Power*:

[11] XV 321, 363, 401; VII 290; XVI 115, 136, 439.
[12] V 324; VIII 48 f., 193, 89, 92 f., 140; XVI 92, 278, 439; XV 174 f., 389.
[13] XV 333.
[14] XV 184. Cf. XIV 87.
[15] XVI 137 f. Cf. 100, 415; VI 168; XV 232 f.

I have the good fortune, after whole thousands of years of straying and confusion, to have rediscovered the way that leads to a yes and a no.

I teach no to all that weakens — that exhausts.

I teach yes to all that strengthens, that stores up power [*Kraft*], that justifies the feeling of power.[16]

We have yet to inquire what power means.

2. THE MEANING OF POWER

As stated so far, Nietzsche's position seems to have extreme logical simplicity: there is just one species of ultimate good, namely power, and the worth of any particular life is measured by its amount of power.[17] But over against the stark monism of the power formula stand the multitude of vivid appreciations which give such color to Nietzsche's writing. How could a man who felt the variety of things so keenly propose to reduce all values to one? Strength of passion and of will apart, here are the qualities for which his words dance and glow:

1) Uniqueness, individuality — "Is it not desecration to a degree if the lover thinks, 'I do not really long for this beloved, but for love' — is not every generalization of the goal a desecration?" [18]

2) Integrity, purity, sincerity, and the corresponding hatred of the charlatan, the "actor," of falsity and inner duplicity.[19]

3) Subtlety, delicacy, *nuances*, intellectuality (*Geistigkeit*), culture, nobility (*Vornehmheit*), and the correspond-

---

[16] XV 180. Cf. VIII 217 f. These passages also either state or imply the power standard: XVI 120, 127, 136 f., 169 ff., 277 f., 375, 383; XV 152, 416; VII 371; VIII 132.

[17] In one passage Nietzsche even suggests a purely quantitative treatment (XVI 169). XVI 65, 411 do not contradict the quantitative standard. Jaspers' interpretation of these passages (*op. cit.* p. 267) is based, I think, on a misreading of the texts, which really refer to Nietzsche's attack on the current mechanistic cosmology. X 136 gives an early version of the quantitative approach to value.

[18] XII 136. Cf. 75, 125, 204 f.; I 388; XIV 111; XI 240.

[19] VIII 51, 46 f.; I 314, 383 f., 585; VII 147, 160, 182, 189 f., 259 f.; XI 260 ff., 379 f.; XV 22 f., 112 f., 118.

ing dislike of massive, brutal effects in modern art, of modern idolatry of the state, and of the common, the plebeian, of mass egoism and resentment (*ressentiment*).[20]

4) Greatness, which he places in the nature of a man, not in the size of his effect upon history, and the corresponding attack upon the worship of success, of what merely happens to be in power — for example, the misuse of Hegel to justify the Prussian state or German Empire.[21]

5) Measure, limitation, form, style: the Apollinian element in life and art.[22]

6) Ripeness, serenity, perfection, "the golden nature."[23]

Nor is Nietzsche unconscious of this variety of goods: he emphasizes it. There is not *one* model of perfect man, as moralists have assumed, but many, and he makes no claim that his personal ideal is for everybody. He rejoices, rather, in a diversity of perfected types, as he finds them in the best days of Greece or Italy:[24]

Let us finally consider what a naïveté it is in general to say, "Man *ought* to be thus and so!" Reality shows us a ravishing wealth of types, the luxury of an extravagant play and change of forms....

This is the task: to create an abundance of *aesthetic, equally justified* valuations: each the ultimate fact and the measure of things for an individual.[25]

Accordingly we are compelled to ask whether there may not be a corresponding complexity in the conception of power which he makes his standard of value. The mean-

[20] VII 47, 50, 116 f., 224, 233 ff., 419; XVI 282 f., 250 f., 373 f.; VIII 7, 18, 108 f., 111 f., 113 ff., 142; X 276; XV 114, 409; VI 69 ff.; XIII 194, 352; II 342; XI 363 f.
[21] X 121 f., 273; XII 191 f., 346; XVI 293 f., 213; I 354, 368; XV 48, 442; VII 256.
[22] VII 179; XV 56, 389; XVI 289 f., 387 f.; X 188, 227, 244; III 129; I 183.
[23] VI 468 f.; XIV 147, 171; XV 194, 389; XVI 229, 328, 365, 450; VII 179; VIII 427; XII 124, 366 f.; I 342, 464.
[24] XI 240, 242, 244; XII 124 f., 196, 204 f., 365; XIII 322 f.; XIV 88, 111; II 224; XV 395.
[25] VIII 89; XII 75.

ings of the German *Macht* and *Kraft,* usually synonymous
for Nietzsche, fall roughly into these groups:

1) physical force, compulsion, violence;

2) vital energy, vitality, vigor, robustness, strength;

3) mental or spiritual energy, stamina, grit, moral
strength, strength of mind, ability;

4) social or political ascendancy, mastery, sway, authority, influence, legal or ecclesiastical powers, empire, dominion;

5) supernatural agencies.

The last, of course, must be omitted, but all the rest are
relevant to his usage. The English, "power," has a similar
spread of meaning, but somehow a thinner quality, and it
seems to emphasize the ideas of brute force or social domination, whereas *Macht,* for Nietzsche, gives pre-eminence
to vital or intellectual energies and abilities. This difference is doubtless partly to blame for the popular misunderstanding of him as an apostle of violence for its own sake.
But even in describing the notorious "blonde beasts" he
writes, "At the beginning the noble caste was always the
barbarian caste: their superiority lay, not in physical force,
primarily, but in force of soul — they were the more *complete* men . . . ." [26]

A comparison of the passages in which Nietzsche speaks
of power reveals an emphatic contrast, in his thought, between the two groups of meanings just mentioned, which
for convenience will be called "intrinsic" and "external"
power. Some passages imply a distinction between external
power and value. His scorn for measuring greatness by
success or historical influence has already appeared, and he
makes it plain that men's worth is not the same as their
political power:

There is no harder misfortune in all human destiny than
when the mighty of the earth are not also the first men.

[26] VII 236. Cf. 382.

The *degeneration of rulers and ruling classes* caused the greatest mischief in history! Without the Roman Caesars and Roman society the madness of Christianity would not have come to power.

When Nero and Caracalla sat on high there arose the paradox, "The lowest man is *worth more* than the one up there!" [27]

More explicitly, he says the same of all external power: "Outer goods, wealth, power do not come into consideration; they have no value of their own, but are only useful for something better." [28]

Conversely, he finds the power he does value for its own sake sometimes quite dissociated from external power:

He who is spiritually rich and independent is also the most powerful man in any case . . . .

. . . I have found power [*Kraft*] where people do not look for it, in simple, gentle and obliging men without the least inclination to domineer — and conversely the inclination to domineer has often appeared to me an inner sign of weakness: they fear their slavish soul and cast a king's mantle about it . . . .[29]

The contrast between external and intrinsic power reaches its climax in passages which pit them directly against each other. We have seen his objection to Darwin, that the "weak," by banding together and using low cunning, usually conquer the "strong": "the strongest and happiest are weak," he adds, "if they have organized herd instincts, if they have the timidity of the weak, the majority against them." [30] Yet there is no doubt where value lies. Similarly he says that human "weakness" has always been "powerful" in human affairs.[31]

[27] VI 358; XVI 292 f. Cf. 289 f., 376 f.; XIV 65 f.; X 310, 324; XIII 352; VI 141.
[28] XIV 100 — part of an admiring note on Aristotle's "great-souled man." For the instrumental status of external power see further: VII 235 f.; XIII 176 f., 352; I 411; XII 367.
[29] XI 388, 251. Cf. IV 224; VII 48 f.; XI 367; XIV 100.
[30] XVI 149. See above, p. 78. On the worthlessness of mere numbers cf. I 81 f., 367 f., 442 f.   [31] I 308.

To be sure, he prizes outer controls very highly as means to the development of intrinsic power. Man's mastery of physical forces will be the basis of future progress: *"When power is won over nature, then one can use this power in order freely to develop oneself further: will to power as self-enhancement and strengthening."* [32] Indeed he suggests that external power somehow intimately heightens intrinsic power:

... proprietors are as one man of one belief, "One must own something in order to *be* something." But this is the oldest and soundest of all instincts: I should add, "One must want to have more than one has in order to *become* more."

Wherever the superior is *not* the more powerful *there is something missing in the superior himself*: he is only a fragment and shadow at most.[33]

Also intrinsic power seeks outward influence, if often in subtle and indirect fashion.[34] This shows that the distinction between external and intrinsic, though valid in some sense, should not be pressed uncritically.

The primacy of intrinsic power, so far as value is concerned, is further verified by Nietzsche's conviction, expressed in all periods of his thought, that the ultimately self-justifying ends can only be individual lives, not classes or societies or humanity as such:

Fundamental mistake: to place the goals in the flock and *not* in particular individuals! The flock is means, no *more!* But now people are trying to conceive *the flock as an individual* and ascribe a higher rank to it than to the individual — deepest misunderstanding!!! [35]

The superman idea is merely the logical consequence of this conviction.

[32] XV 434. Cf. XVI 164.
[33] XV 232; XIV 65. Cf. VI 306.
[34] XII 364; XIII 177.
[35] XVI 203. Cf. 127; XV 341 f., 429; XI 142; X 309 f., 323; I 364, 367 f., 442 f.

The conception, hitherto loosely labelled "intrinsic power," becomes more definite if we examine some of Nietzsche's more specific statements about estimating human worth:

> I value man by the *amount of power and fullness of his will* .... I value the *power* of a *will* by how much resistance, pain, torture it endures and can turn to its advantage ....[36]

He develops the point in a letter to his sister:

> I distinguish *strong* and *weak* men first of all — such as are called to rule, and such as are called to service and obedience, to "devotion." What *disgusts* me with *this* age is the unspeakable feebleness, unmanliness, impersonality, unsteadiness, good-naturedness, in short the *weakness* of *"self"*-seeking, which would even like to dress itself up as "virtue." What has done me good hitherto was the sight of men with a *long will* — who can keep silence for decades and not even adorn themselves with pompous moral words on that account — perhaps as "heroes" or "noble minded" people — but who are honest enough to believe in nothing better than in their *self* and their will to stamp it upon men for all, all time.
>
> .... What attracted me to Richard Wagner was *this*; Schopenhauer likewise lived only in such a sentiment.
>
> I know better than anyone, perhaps, how to make gradations [*Rangordnungen*] among the *strong men* too, *according to virtue*; as indeed there are yet a *hundred* varieties among the weak, and very sweet and amiable ones — according to the virtues that belong to the weak. There are strong "selves," whose self-seeking one might almost call divine (e.g. Zarathustra's) — but *every* strength by itself alone is something refreshing and enrapturing for the eye. Read Shakespeare: he is full of such strong men, rough, hard, powerful men of granite. In these our age is so poor — — — and, to crown all, in strong men who had mind *enough* for *my* thoughts! [37]

[36] XV 416.
[37] L.S. 11/83. Cf. VI 163 f., 408. VI 166, VII 346, and I 573, together with the analysis of will as involving a "command" (above, p. 92), supplement this distinction between the strong and the weak. The strong command or govern themselves; the weak need guidance, and therefore the strong tend to dominate

So strength of will is only the most important part, not the whole, of value, and the combination of that with intelligence is what Nietzsche misses most.

That power means more than brute effectiveness, and that kinds of power differ significantly in value, are further approximations to his standard. Other fragments put the matter thus:

The Germans imagine that *power* [*Kraft*] must reveal itself in harshness and cruelty; then they submit gladly and with admiration .... That there is *power* in gentleness and quietness, they do not easily believe. They miss power in Goethe and imagine Beethoven has more: and in that they are mistaken!!

...indeed power is first...but there are kinds of power without grimaces.[38]

3. DIMENSIONS OF POWER

Can we get a more systematic account of the complexities in Nietzsche's idea of power? One statement of the power formula gives a clue: "By what is *value* measured objectively? Only by the amount of *enhanced* [*gesteigert*] and *organized power* . . ."[39] This suggests that power has at least two dimensions, extent and organization, and that both are relevant to an estimate of value.

Many previous discussions confirm the point. Strength of will, for example, consists in the *integration* of urges. Organization plays an equally prominent part in Nietzsche's ideal of "plastic force" [*Kraft*], which he thus describes:

...I mean that force to grow individually from out oneself, to transmute and assimilate the past and the alien, to heal

the weak even without deliberate intention (cf. XIV 66; VII 346; VIII 302). This is another aspect of the interdependence of external and intrinsic power. It also indicates that for Nietzsche the most important kind of the latter, if not its very essence, is *self-mastery*.

[38] XI 363 f. Cf. 33; III 57 f.
[39] XVI 137.

wounds thoroughly, to replace what is lost, to reproduce broken forms out of oneself.

It is only a matter of force: to have all pathological traits of the century, but to counterbalance [*ausgleichen*] them in an exuberant, plastic, restoring force.[40]

Such strength he considers the essence of health, and health is clearly a type of organization.[41]

Again, we have seen that will to power — to growth — gives form to what it conquers:

The greater complexity, the clear separation, the togetherness of highly developed organs and functions, with disappearance of intermediate members — if that is *perfection*, then the result is a will to power in the organic process, in virtue of which *masterful, formative, commanding* forces always increase the field of their power and simplify inside it again and again: the imperative *growing*.[42]

Thus organization implies limitation, definiteness — an important feature in Nietzsche's conception of value.[43]

Another passage distinguishes more clearly the factors of raw energy and organization:

This "will to power" expresses itself in the *interpretation*, in the *manner of spending force*: — transformation of energy into life and "life to the highest power" accordingly appears as goal. The same quantum of energy means different things at different stages of evolution.

What constitutes growth in life is the ever more thrifty and farther-calculating economy which achieves more and more with less and less force . . .[44]

In this instance "energy" and "force" are clearly not equivalent to that "power" which is the measure of value; they refer rather to the extensive dimension of power, the physi-

[40] I 286; XVI 366. Cf. XIV 112; H.K.A. II 355.
[41] Cf. XV 173.
[42] XVI 118. Cf. 127.
[43] Cf. I 160; II 201 ff.; IV 240, 335; VII 177 f.
[44] XVI 115 f.

cal or vital energies which are to be shaped in various ways.[45]

Nietzsche sees that organization itself involves two further dimensions: harmony and subordination. For intrinsic value, he thinks a happy balance of the two ideal: harmony without subordination would lack strength; and the excessive dominance of one faculty, as in modern over-specialization, means the destruction or atrophy of the rest. So he says that the problem of education is to combine the harmonious development of all powers with the discovery and unfolding of the major talent, according to this model:

> ... where at all do we find harmonious wholeness and polyphonic concord in one nature, where do we admire harmony more, than precisely in such men as was Cellini, in whom everything — knowing, desiring, loving, hating — gravitates toward a center, a root force, and where precisely through the compelling and dominating ascendancy of this living center there is formed a harmonious system of motions to and fro, up and down?[46]

Subordination is therefore necessary for the highest harmony, but a dominant power not balanced by others is disastrous: "Every force (religion, myth, desire for knowledge) has, in excess, barbarizing, immoral and stultifying effects, as rigid tyranny (Socrates)."[47]

There is yet another aspect of value which is akin to the idea of organization. Nietzsche indicates it by such words as "noble," "spiritual," and "higher":

> ... a church is above all a power structure [*Herrschafts-Gebilde*] which ensures the highest rank to the *more spiritual* men, and *believes* in the power of spirituality so far as to forbid itself all coarser means of power [*Gewalt*] — by that alone the church is a *nobler* institution than the state under all circumstances.

[45] Cf. IV 357 f.; XVI 243; XV 93 f.; and such expressions as *überströmende Kraft, überströmende Animalität* (XVI 328; VIII 47).

[46] I 393. Cf. 394; X 308 f.; XII 367; XVI 148, 210, 227, 264; VI 203 ff.; XIV 148; XVII 330 f., 336.

[47] X 188. Cf. 12, 227, 310; XVII 334.

There is no doubt: when a species of man has lived for whole generations as teachers, physicians, those who care for souls, and as models ... in the end there arises a higher, finer and more spiritual type.

The sublime man has the highest value, even when he is quite delicate and fragile, because an abundance of quite difficult and rare things have been bred and preserved together through many generations.[48]

But Nietzsche says not only that the most spiritual or intellectual man — other things being equal — is most valuable, but also that he is strongest.[49] Therefore he makes "spiritualization" or "sublimation" part of the power standard.

What are his reasons for including "spiritualization" in the meaning of power? One of them is that if power is measured by resistance overcome, the most spiritual man is strongest because he surmounts the greatest difficulties. The passage last quoted illustrates this, as does his portrait of the philosopher: particular skills have to be acquired singly by generations of practice, and focused finally in the nature of one individual.[50] It is also confirmed by Nietzsche's belief that the most intellectual are able to lead the hardest life — one of spiritual independence and adventure — and to do the most difficult thing: create new values.[51]

Further reasons come from his psychology of sublimation.[52] We saw that it means an increased refinement in the use of instinctive energies, and that he regards it as the source of the highest cultural values. Now he observes

[48] V 308; XIV 98; XVI 358 f. Cf. 148; III 302; VII 172 f.
[49] VIII 302; XIV 28. Cf. XVI 357; XI 388; XIV 97.
[50] VII 146 f., 165 f., 172 f. Cf. XVI 350 f., 358.
[51] VII 48 f., 161; V 230 f.; VIII 302.
[52] See above, pp. 99 f. Nietzsche's valuation of *Vergeistigung* must be carefully distinguished from that of *Geist*. He can speak scornfully of the latter in some of its forms (VI 141; VIII 128), and says that it requires blood (*Geblüt*) to ennoble it (XVI 329). *Vergeistigung* is not the development of *Geist* alone; it is the marriage of *Geist* and passion (VIII 84).

that the more considerate uses of power require strength, while brutality is a sign of weakness:

> Where the means of power are not great enough, *intimidation* appears, *terrorism*: to that extent all punishment for the sake of deterrence is a sign that the positive, *outflowing virtue* of the mighty is not great enough: a sign of scepticism about their own power.[53]

Within the self, likewise, sublimation of dangerous impulses is more considerate treatment than harsh repression, and requires more self-control:

> *Take* all that is fearful *into service*, piecemeal, step by step, tentatively: so the task of culture demands; but until it is strong enough for that it must combat, moderate, veil, even curse it.[54]

Nietzsche also says that power varies in depth of control, and that the finer forms of power constitute fuller possession:

> Every living thing reaches about itself with its force to grasp as far as it can, and subjugates the weaker to itself.... The *increasing "humanization"* in this tendency consists in this, that one feels more and more *delicately* how difficult it is really to *assimilate* the other: how crude injury indeed shows our power over him, but at the same time *estranges* his will from us still more — so makes him less conquerable.[55]

The same would presumably be said of a man's relations to his own passions.

We can now interpret the rough distinction between external and intrinsic power as one of degree. The former is power of a relatively low grade of organization or sublimation. Hence the exceptional individual is richer in high grade power than the mob which usually beats him in the struggle for survival; and if he is more spiritualized than

[53] XIII 198. For the non-violent influence of the strong see references in note 37.
[54] XVI 375.
[55] XVI 203 f. Cf. VIII 86.

groups can ever be, there is reason for making him, rather
than them, the ultimate end.

We can also explain some of the most paradoxical passages in Nietzsche — those which disparage power and value
weakness:

One pays dearly for coming to power: power *stupefies*. . . .
"*Deutschland, Deutschland über Alles*," I fear that was the end
of German philosophy . . .

Power is tedious — just have a look at the "Reich"! . . .
Would existence on earth be at all bearable, if woman had not
become a genius of amusement and charm, if she had not become
woman? But one must be weak for that . . .[56]

The explanation is that a stably consolidated system tends
to express its energies in accustomed channels, and the stimulus of weakness or instability is required if subtler and
more indirect modes of activity are to be developed.[57] This
has appeared in the relation of spiritualization to mental
conflict, and in the general principle that a combination
of stability and "chaos" is necessary for evolutionary advance.[58] Nietzsche uses the same idea in his conception of
"great health" (*die grosse Gesundheit*) as an abundance
of "plastic force" which ever risks itself anew in experiments with danger, using "disease" as a stimulus to
"health." [59]

The extensive dimensions of power have yet to be considered. For sublimation, you must have something to
sublimate:

Spiritualization set as *goal* . . . . But unless sensualization is
present the spirit becomes very thin.

The force and power of the senses — that is the most essential
in a successful [*wohlgeratenen*] and complete man: the splen-

---

[56] VIII 108 f.; XIV 244. Cf. VII 312; II 342; VIII 128. Here he is disparaging
relatively external power, of course. He may also have had Sparta in mind: cf.
XVIII 151.   [58] See above, pp. 79 ff.
[57] II 211 ff.   [59] V 342 ff., 159; II 8; VII 395; XVI 240 f., 366.

did animal must be given first — else what does all "humanization" matter? [60]

In more general terms, "the highest intensity of life does indeed stand in necessary relation to its broadest expansion," as Nietzsche remarks in a comment on Guyau, interpreting "expansion" of course in terms of will to power.[61]

Other things being equal, the sublimation of many passions would constitute greater power than that of a few, and similarly for the case of stronger or more antagonistic ones. Therefore, we might say that the extent of power is measured in terms of at least three variables: the number, the strength, and the variety or contrast of the things controlled.

Nietzsche actually emphasizes all three, in various descriptions of eminent forms of power or value: the dimension of *number* — "the higher type presents an incomparably greater complexity — a greater sum of coordinated elements"; [62] *number* and *strength* — "the highest man would have the greatest multiplicity of urges, and have them also in the relatively greatest strength which can still be borne." [63] Variety adds the notion of difference or *contrast* between the elements which are organized, and Nietzsche implies its importance by his admiration for the "whole man" or "synthetic man" as distinguished from the human fragment (*Bruchstück*), the former being the one who compasses the full gamut of human nature.[64] Contrast is most extreme between opposites (*Gegensätze*). So he holds that the highest power is power over opposites, and that the greatest men are those who unite the most antagonistic traits:

[60] XIV 97; XVI 385. The highest intellectual development also tends to exhaust the vitality of the next generation (III 302).
[61] XIII 113.
[62] XVI 148. Cf. 127, 351; I 442; XIV 148.
[63] XVI 344. Cf. 323; XIII 123 f.
[64] XVI 287, 297, 359, 385; VIII 111; VII 236; XIV 91.

Man, in contrast to the animal, has trained up an abundance of *opposite* [*gegensätzlicher*] urges and impulses in himself: by reason of this synthesis he is lord of the earth.

I believe that from the presence of opposites, and from the feeling of them, precisely the great man, *the bow with the great tension*, arises.

... the *highest* man ... would be *that* man who represented most intensely *the antithetical* [*Gegensatz-*] *character of existence*, as its glory and sole justification . . .[65]

And in general, advance to higher levels is made by a synthesis of hitherto incompatible powers.[66]

The tension between opposites has a peculiarly important place in Nietzsche's thought on the nature of power. He believes it an essential source of energy in life:

In truth a strong *antagonism* belongs in everything, in marriage, friendship, state, confederation, corporation, learned societies, religion, that something proper may grow. Resistance is the form of *force* — in peace as in war . . . .[67]

Consequently tension is the condition of human advance [68] — here again we touch his view that "chaos" is needed to offset the tendency to stagnation — and society, when tired and overcivilized, must for a time revert to barbarism to obtain fresh energies. This is one ground for his justification of strife, war, and violence.[69]

We have discovered that his power standard of value includes at least two "vertical" dimensions — organization (with the components of harmony and subordination) and spiritualization — and three "horizontal" ones — number, strength, and contrast of elements.[70] In terms of his Greek symbolism, the first group might appropriately be called

[65] XVI 344, 345, 296. Cf. 230, 264; L.G. 21/1/87.
[66] XIV 44 f.; XIII 176. Cf. II 256 f.
[67] XII 119. Cf. XV 404; XI 313; IV 182.
[68] VII 180, 5.
[69] II 355 f., 221 f.; III 295.
[70] A further and obvious one, duration, will be mentioned later.

the "Apollinian," the second the "Dionysian" dimensions.[71]
But let us note that the ideal of completeness or wholeness
(*Ganzheit*) was connected with both groups, and seems indeed to imply more than either, namely something like
self-containedness or self-sufficiency.[72] That too may be
considered a form of power, perhaps a third Apollinian
dimension, and Nietzsche's high rating of it will appear
more fully in the sequel.

One cannot be sure that this account covers all the dimensions he had in mind, and his writings suggest many more
complexities of relationship between them. But the main
conclusion is clear, that his standard of value has a richness
of content which may do greater justice to his concrete
appreciations than at first appeared.

4. THE APOLLINIAN VIRTUES

Intellectuality and intrinsic greatness have been incor-
porated in the power standard. We are now in position
to do the same for the rest of Nietzsche's leading values.
They also turn out to be modes of the vertical dimensions
of power and may therefore be called the Apollinian virtues.
Together with strength of will, they go far to complete his
moral ideal.

He gives greatest care, perhaps, to *nobility* (*Vornehmheit*) — the English as usual is inadequate. He clothes this
value with flesh and blood to an extent quite unusual in
ethical literature. The heart of it appears to be this: it
distinguishes, separates, gives "distance"; it is self-sufficiency,
pride — the opposite of vanity —, independence, responsibility to self, self-reverence.[73] The emphasis here is clearly

[71] Cf. I 22 f., 36; XVI 386 f.
[72] On wholeness in general see above, note 64; p. 41, note 49; p. 77, note 74,
and passages quoted on pp. 74, 77, 121, 127, 203.
[73] VII 164, 233 ff.; VI 312; XVI 330 ff.; XI 367, 390; XIII 344, 347; XIV 100;
XV 113 f.; IV 193 f. Cf. also the contrasting nature of the ignoble or common
(VIII 115; XI 390). I am unable to account for Nietzsche's extraordinary valua-

upon the "vertical" dimensions of power. *Noblesse oblige:*
a gentleman does not do certain things because they are
beneath him, and Nietzsche acknowledges that the ideals
of medieval chivalry marked a higher nobility than that of
his beloved Greeks.[74] Likewise the statement, quoted earlier,
that the church is a nobler institution because it relies
wholly on spiritual power, implies that spiritualized power
is a form of nobility.[75]

Nietzsche values *individuality* primarily as a variant of
nobility: he emphasizes its self-sufficiency and distinctive-
ness. For the rest, he thinks of it as style and integrity: an
individual is one whose life has sincere unity of style.[76]

Style and *form* are also related to nobility: the great
aristocracies have been lovers of form in life as well as in
art and landscape. At the same time there is evident connection with the dimension of organization in the power
standard. The will to power shapes and simplifies what it
conquers. So Nietzsche attributes aristocracies' love of style
to their sense of power: "The strong, mighty ones want *to
form and to have about them nothing more that is alien!*" [77]
Style is unity of form imposed by a central organizing power,
as in the fragment, "Connection of the aesthetic and the
moral: the great style demands one strong fundamental will
and abhors incoherence most." [78] And Nietzsche defines
culture as "unity of artistic style in all vital functions." [79]

tion of *cynicism* (XV 54) except as a variant of nobility, to wit as a form of
extreme independence.

[74] IV 191 f. On the first point cf. XV 20. Nevertheless the Greeks were a
major source of Nietzsche's ideal of *Vornehmheit* (XIX 6).

[75] The aspect of nobility most difficult to express in terms of the power standard
is recognition of, and reverence for, high grades of value in others. Nietzsche
explains that this too is a way in which a noble soul honors *itself*. He might
add that the feeling *of* distance develops a feeling *for* distance (VII 243, 249,
252. Cf. 166, 235; VIII 272 f.; XII 322; XV 93).

[76] IV 339 f.; XI 238, 242, 367; XII 118, 125; XIV 309. See below, pp. 200 ff.,
especially for evidence on the latter points.

[77] XVI 329. Cf. 118, 331; IV 193 f.

[78] XIV 148. Cf. 145; XVI 227; V 219 f.

[79] I 183, 186, 314. I 187 distinguishes this from the sterile *uniformity* of
contemporary barbarism.

Measure, also akin to nobility, is one of the most neglected of his ideals.[80] Many readers miss this because he seldom mentions it — and for a reason:

Of two quite lofty things, measure and the mean, one had best never speak. Some few know their powers [*Kräfte*] and signs, from the paths of the mysteries of inner experiences and revulsions: they revere in them something divine and shrink from the audible word. All others hardly listen when they are spoken of, and imagine it is a question of tedium and mediocrity . . . .[81]

The difference between measure and mediocrity is that between slackness and tension: the weak are moderate from want of force; the strong love measure as delight in controlling force:

The belief in the *joy* of *moderation* was lacking hitherto — this joy of the rider on fiery steed! — the moderateness [*Mässigkeit*] of weak natures confused with the moderation [*Mässigung*] of the strong ones!

The precept, "Nothing too much," is addressed to men of overflowing force — not to the mediocre. Self-control and training are only one *stage* of elevation: higher stands the "golden nature." [82]

In the language of *The Birth of Tragedy*, Apollo is the god of measure, but he cannot live without Dionysus.[83]

The Apollinian dimensions of power culminate in a quality, perhaps best called *integrity*, which includes and sums up the preceding virtues, much as Justice does Plato's. Nietzsche expresses it in many terms. It is the ideal of a consummate unification of power, where style is not externally grafted on but has grown organically from within, and in which no foreign or undigested elements remain:

[80] XIII 194; XIV 113; II 127 f.; III 57 f.
[81] III 129. Cf. VI 249.
[82] XVI 290, 328. Cf. XI 33; VII 179; II 202 f.
[83] I 36 f.

the integrating force has as it were completely permeated the whole.

So he sometimes speaks of "necessity" (*Notwendigkeit*), not in a logical or metaphysical but in a vital or aesthetic sense — for example, when he compares the development of a philosopher's thought to the growth of fruit on a tree, or when he says that true form is a "necessary organization" (*Gestaltung*) rather than a mere agreeable appearance.[84] He pleads for such an inner inevitability of style in his great essay *On the Use and Harm of History for Life*, holding up as the genuine conception of culture the Greek model of "a new and improved nature [*Physis*], without inside and outside, without disguise and convention . . . a unanimity between living, thinking, seeming and willing." [85] So he protests against the concealment of genuine individuality behind convention, and admires the pre-Socratic philosophers — "strict necessity prevails between their thinking and their character." [86]

On the biological plane, integrity of power depends upon a fortunate synthesis of hereditary factors, which he calls "successful" or "well-bred" (*wohlgeraten*). It means "being all of a piece," "carved out of whole wood," bound and belonging together, not patchwork. Psychologically, it consists in perfect harmony and adjustment of instinct, leading a man to choose what is good and avoid what is harmful for him.[87]

Nietzsche illumines now one side, now another, of the ideal of integrity by such terms as "honesty," "purity," "cleanliness," "sincerity," "genuineness," "candor," "probity" (*Ehrlichkeit, Reinheit, Reinlichkeit, Wahrhaftigkeit, Echtheit, Redlichkeit, Rechtschaffenheit*), and he implies it

---

[84] VII 289; I 528. Cf. VIII 120.   [85] I 384. Cf. 91, 372 ff., 526 f.
[86] IV 339 f.; X 13. See above, pp. 39 f.

[87] XV 12, 51; XVI 361; VIII 92. Cf. the descriptions of the opposite, *missraten* (VIII 229, 239; VII 88). Similarly, the ideal of *Ganzheit* as an outcome of cultural or individual development is a variant of the ideal of integrity. See note 72.

by his diatribes upon modern affectation and falsity. Of the latter he contrasts two kinds: toward others, and toward self. Both express the underlying falseness of contemporary life, its "physiological contradiction." [88] The first species is *Schauspielerei*, pretending to do more than one can.[89] The second is dishonesty with oneself, "uncleanliness," a much graver fault in his eyes.[90]

He describes the purification of a race as a process in which initially coarse and conflicting forces are limited and harmonized, and so connects purity with the power standard.[91] And he pays a handsome tribute to purity of culture in his picture of the Italian Renaissance as:

> ...a glow of sincerity and aversion to pretence and mere effect (which glow blazed forth in a whole profusion of artistic characters, who with supreme moral purity demanded of themselves perfection in their works and nothing but perfection)....[92]

So far in the analysis of power we have neglected time. It would be a mistake to imagine that Nietzsche considers it irrelevant to value. On the contrary, he says that "dura-

[88] VIII 46 f., 51. Cf. I 314 f.

[89] Cf. XV 193 f., 463 f.; VII 147; VI 248, 372 f.; V 296 ff.; VIII 27 f. How Nietzsche reconciles his love of honesty with his theory of "masks" (see above, pp. 14 ff.) is something of a problem. The solution may be that *Schauspielerei*, being the use of "masks" in order to make an impression on others, is a form of vanity and therefore ignoble — the "noble" use of masks being a form of modesty and self-protection, or the like (cf. XVI 330 f.). *The Birth of Tragedy* approves the use of masks to express symbolic truth, condemns "masked," i.e. imitation, art (I 73, 75, 77, 120 f.). Sincerity (*Wahrhaftigkeit*) is a special virtue of the critic and "free spirit" in a time of general insincerity and mixed values. It purifies, cleans. Its merciless revelation of the ugliness and falsity of men is the first step toward eliminating hybrid elements. Nietzsche calls this "the suffering of sincerity" and "heroism of the sincere" (VII 189 f.; XI 262 f.; X 324; I 427 f.). It is a destructive phase, to be followed by a constructive one (I 322). But when pushed to the extreme sincerity discovers the tragic problem of truth and illusion, stated above, pp. 47 ff. (cf. XII 293) — an unresolved difficulty which as yet threatens to undercut the whole of Nietzsche's ethics.

[90] XI 261 f., 379 f.; XV 22 f.; VII 160, 259 f.

[91] IV 240 (quoted below, pp. 332 f.). Cf. I 416 f. Nietzsche describes a similar process in the individual: IV 357 f.

[92] II 224.

tion is a value of the first order." [93] Accordingly time might be counted a seventh dimension of the power standard. The omission of time was a necessary over-simplification, but it has made his conception of value too static. One should never lose sight of the fact that back of his explicit theory of power lies the vaguer notion of life in its fulness — life with its perpetual flow, its rhythms and seasons.

"Perfection" (*Vollkommenheit*), in one of its senses, has more time in it than do the rest of his value terms. It means an ideal culmination or "ripeness" of some vital process, whether it be an act, an artistic creation, an epoch of life, an entire life, a series of lives, or a human culture. He describes it as "the perfection and final ripeness in every culture and art, the really noble in works and men, their moment of smooth sea and halcyon self-sufficiency, the gold and coldness which all things show that have completed themselves." [94]

The upward movement of life — the phase of "becoming" what one "is" — involves struggle, which Nietzsche symbolizes in the figure of the tragic hero; its culminating perfection — "being" what one "is" — he symbolizes by the god: "Higher than 'thou shalt' stands, 'I will' (the heroes); higher than 'I will' stands, 'I am' (the gods of the Greeks)." [95] Consummate perfection, when by good fortune it comes to pass, embodies all the riches of accumulated growth, lets fall every unassimilable fragment, and crystallizes into limpid splendor. Nietzsche says that Michelangelo saw:

... the problem of the victoriously completed one, who first had need to overcome even "the hero in himself"; the man most lifted up on high, who rose above his compassion even, and

[93] V 297. Cf. II 313; IV 205.

[94] VII 179. Cf. XV 193 f., 389, 469 f.; II 6; VIII 7, 34; VI 468; XII 124, 366 f.; XIV 265; I 342, 440. *Vollkommenheit* is used apparently in a different sense in XVI 118, 127; XV 35.

[95] XVI 328. Cf. 357; VI 33 f.; VIII 93. On the hero and his contrast with the god see further VI 172 f.; XII 294 f.; XIV 253.

mercilessly smashes and destroys what is unsuitable for him [*das ihm Unzugehörige*] — radiant and in undimmed divinity.[96]

That is undoubtedly a vision of the superman. But there are many lesser perfections. Nietzsche's scale of values has room for higher and lower types, each capable of greater or less perfection on its own level. Thus man, though *strongest* of the animals, is least *perfect*; the philosopher is a higher type than the artist, but on the whole less successfully developed; and in general, the higher the type the greater the odds against the achievement of perfection.[97]

Our account of the power standard has also ignored the out-going, self-transcending movement of will to power. Nietzsche places its typical occurrence at the peak of life, giving away what has been acquired: "Perfection: that is the extraordinary enlargement of one's feeling of power, opulence, the necessary frothing over all brims . . ."[98] The highest forms of love and creativeness are expressions of an "excess of life"; forces stored to the bursting point "overflow," and the great man is a prodigal who lavishes his riches upon the world.[99] Nietzsche evidently prizes creativeness — "the virtue that gives" — for its own sake. "The highest individuals," he says, "are the creative men . . . ."[100] Is the grade of creativity another measure of power and therefore a new dimension in the standard of value? In any case this aspect should not be forgotten in the full meaning of the power standard.

Since life is in perpetual flux, perfect "being" can only come to pass. Though duration is an important dimension of value, the highest values are among the most fleeting:

[96] XIV 147. Cf. VI 172.
[97] VIII 229; XIV 336; XII 113; XVI 148. The complexity of Nietzsche's standard is well illustrated by XVI 364.
[98] XVI 229. Cf. VI 110 f.; above, pp. 63 f.
[99] Cf. VIII 157; V 53; XV 66, 94, 175, 420; XVI 441.
[100] X 309. On his valuation of creativeness see further: VII 180 f.; XV 33, 93 f., 101, 197; XVI 292, 343; VI 19, 48, 73, 91 ff., 123 ff., 130, 153 ff., 169, 206, 236, 296 f.; I 8, 45, 413; IV 361 f.; V 334; VIII 9, 86 f., 123 f., 134.

"The destiny of men is arranged for happy moments — every life has such — but not for happy ages." [101] But the magic moment can be that "something sacred" "which infinitely outweighs all struggle and all tribulation," and with this we again salute an ultimate intuition of value.[102]

[101] II 343. Cf. I 146; VII 179; XIV 260.
[102] See above, pp. 42 f.

CHAPTER VI

The Genealogy of Modern Morals

*The great epochs of our life lie where we win the
courage to re-christen our Evil as our Best.* (VII 101)

1. MORALITY AS A PROBLEM

WE ARE now ready to approach the destructive
phase of Nietzsche's revaluation: *"Moral* values
were the supreme values hitherto: does anyone
wish to call that in question? . . . If we remove these
values from that position, we change *all* values: the
principle of their previous *order of rank* is overthrown
thereby . . ."[1] So he aims his attack with the question:
which values shall have first place, and what shall be the
hierarchy of values?

The reigning values being *moral* ones, to revolutionize
the hierarchy is necessarily to undertake a critique of the
European moral tradition, which Nietzsche takes to be
Platonic or Christian — "Christianity is Platonism for the
'people.' "[2] "Immoralism" and "beyond good and evil"
are his slogans for this destructive phase of his thought.[3]

He believes that the old values have ruled so completely
that philosophy has unconsciously worked in their service.
Morality has been "the real Circe of the philosophers" since
the time of Plato; the clue to the remotest doctrines of their
metaphysics lies in the secret purpose from which each
system grew. Even their logic, their trust in reason and its
validity, is a moral phenomenon, and their systems have
collapsed primarily because they were based on morality.

[1] XVI 363. Cf. XV 141 f., 343, 345.
[2] VII 5.   [3] XV 122; V 339.

Hence "the moral problem is more radical than the epistemological." [4]

Small wonder then, says Nietzsche, that moral philosophy in particular has been a mere soporific. Morality has had unconditional authority, which means that real criticism was forbidden. Philosophers did not even come within sight of the interesting problems. Their "foundations of morality" were in fact:

... only a learned form of good *belief* in the prevalent morality, a new means of its *expression*, therefore itself a set of facts within a determinate morality, nay, in the last analysis, a kind of denial that this morality *may* be taken as a problem: — and in any case the opposite of an examination ... of just this belief! [5]

In seeking to "found" morality they took it for granted: they supposed men already knew good and evil.[6]

To see morality as a *problem* requires emancipation from its authority, in short — by *its* standards — immorality, and Nietzsche believes that he is the first to do so. We do not automatically know what is good. We must inquire. Above all, what is the value of the old values themselves? This attitude of critical questioning is one meaning of "beyond good and evil." [7]

As a preliminary to the critique of morals Nietzsche plans a descriptive study on a scale both comprehensive and intricate. The real issues, he believes, emerge from a comparison of many moralities, and previous thinkers have failed to grasp them largely because of an arbitrary selection of data — because they thought only in terms of local beliefs.[8] He makes acknowledgments to his erstwhile

[4] XIV 410; IV 4 ff., 8; VII 14 f.; XV 122, 393, 431, 438 ff.; XIII 120. Cf. XVI 91.
[5] VII 114. Cf. 183; IV 4 f.; XIII 114.
[6] VI 287 f.; XIII 96 ff., 105.
[7] VII 290, 293 f.; XV 333; XIII 96 f., 114 f., 155 f.; II 432 f.; III 205, 227; IV 5, 13; VI 288; V 276 f., 339 f.
[8] VII 114, 294. Nietzsche's perspective of historical relativism began early: cf. L.F.N. I 315 or H.K.A. II 56.

friend, Dr. Paul Rée, and to English psychologists, for having at least attempted a natural history of morals, but he objects to their atomistic psychology and above all to their lack of historical sense. Instead of spinning hypotheses in the air, explaining the past by mixing Darwinism with delicate contemporary morals, one should get at the past in terms of the actual sources.[9]

Nietzsche considers this a task, not for one man, but for generations, and he looks for learned companions to help him begin it.[10] He regards his own results as fragmentary and tentative parts of a larger whole. *Toward the Genealogy of Morals* does not even give a full picture of his own views.[11] The element of caution and tentativeness in his thought is too often overlooked.

"Moral science" seems to him too pretentious a name for the present stage of the investigation. He would have the preliminary work consist in:

... collection of material, conceptual formulation and classification of a vast realm of delicate feelings and distinctions of value, which live, grow, procreate and perish — and, perhaps, attempts to make clear the recurrent and more frequent formations of this living crystallization — as preparation for a *theory of types* of morals.[12]

Further, he would distinguish the history of moral feelings from that of the moral concepts in terms of which feelings, and the actions they prompt, are rationalized.[13] Then there are associated beliefs about matters of fact which the moral historian should consider — opinions men have held about

[9] VII 295, 301 ff. Nietzsche is not objecting to the use of hypotheses as such — he uses them deliberately (XI 192) — but to hypotheses unrelated to available inductive evidence. Thus he proceeds to offer linguistic evidence for his own view (VII 306).

[10] V 44 f.; VII 295.

[11] XIV 345 f.; L.O. 4/1/88.

[12] VII 113.

[13] IV 40. Cf. XIII 129. Nietzsche intended to include the history of moral philosophies in his account of the genealogy of morals (XIV 345 f.).

the origin or effects of their particular morality, about free
will, divine sanctions and the like.[14]

Drawing nearer to his critical purpose, he plans an ex-
planatory interpretation of moralities in relation to the
conditions and urges from which they arise, and which they
both express and modify: "morals as effect, as symptom, as
mask, as hypocrisy, as disease, as misunderstanding; but also
morals as cause, as remedy, as stimulant, as hindrance, as
poison." [15]

He recognizes that description and explanation are one
thing, the standard of criticism another, and asserts with
special emphasis that a genetic account of a morality is not
the same as an evaluation of it: its present worth is quite
distinct from that of its beginnings [16] — and also independent of the truth of its owner's beliefs about it.[17]

On the other hand the facts *are* relevant to criticism in
several ways. Some have a preparatory or forensic value.
The discovery of unsavory origins, he suggests, may help
to put the mind in a critical attitude. If natural origins
are discovered, alleged supernatural ones — and therefore
supernatural authority — lose hold on our minds, and in
general a study of the past makes us suspect the specious
absolutism of the present moral consciousness.[18]

But of course the facts become directly relevant to criticism, in terms of Nietzsche's standard of value, when they
reveal the grade of life which a morality expresses or tends
to breed. With this in view he calls for a very complicated
inquiry:

My endeavor [is] to understand the moral judgments as
symptoms and sign-languages, in which processes of physiologi-

[14] V 278. Cf. VIII 97 ff.
[15] VII 294. Cf. 115 f., 338 n.; XIII 118. Nietzsche includes the influence of
physical factors such as nourishment and climate (V 44; XIV 318).
[16] XIII 129 ff., 138; XV 333; V 277; IV 49 f. Cf. III 205 f.; VIII 369 f. Conversely, the present purpose of something should not be projected into the past as
an account of its origin (VII 369; XIII 132, 179).
[17] V 278; XIV 401 f.; XIII 131.   [18] XV 104 f., 333; IV 39 ff.

cal success and failure, also the awareness of conditions of conservation and growth, are indicated . . . .[19]

The question, "What is this or that table of goods and morality *worth?*" has to be placed in the most varied perspectives; especially, one cannot analyze acutely enough the "worth *for what.*" For example something that obviously had value with respect to the greatest possible durability of a race (or to enhancement of its powers of adaptation to a definite climate, or to preservation of the greatest number), would by no means have the same value if it were a question of developing a stronger type.[20]

We should remember this many-sidedness, lest we mistake parts of his thought for the whole.

Psychological and historical facts are relevant to the critique of morals because it is first necessary to understand *what* is being valued. So Nietzsche reproaches mankind primarily for its self-deceit, namely its failure to see what Christian morality really is.[21] But he undertakes a natural history of morals for more than a destructive purpose: he would use all past experience to build the future.

2. HISTORICAL PERSPECTIVES

Nietzsche divides the moral history of man into three major periods: the *Pre-moral*, occupying vast pre-historic ages; the *Moral*, entered by various portions of the race during the last ten thousand years; and the *Extra-moral* (*aussermoralisch*), now about to begin. He distinguishes them briefly as follows: in the first, men derive the value of an action from its consequences without regard to psychological motive. In the second, they judge it by its origin, which is supposed to be a conscious intention (*Absicht*). In the third, the conscious antecedents of an act will be

[19] XV 334 f. Cf. 82 f., 122 ff., 333 ff.; VII 464.
[20] VII 338 n. f. Cf. XIII 118 f., 214 f.
[21] XV 123.

regarded as an ambiguous symptom; its value will depend rather upon its *unconscious* source.[22]

Some features of morality, Nietzsche suggests, extend down into the animal world, but man first distinguished himself from the animals when he learned to relate his actions to enduring welfare.[23] He was not a rational utilitarian to begin with, however, but lived in groups dominated by custom and superstition. This type of life, which occupied the pre-historic period — therefore by far the greater part of man's past — Nietzsche calls "the Morality of Mores" (*Sittlichkeit der Sitte*). The customs themselves may have originated in supposed experiences of use or harm, but this morality proper consisted in nothing more than blind obedience to custom, based on a superstitious fear of some vague power.[24]

Morality of Mores, therefore, was rigidly conservative, collectivistic, harsh, and superstitious. Individuals usually acted without thinking of themselves as *individuals* at all; collective conscience made the whole group feel guilty when anyone violated a custom, whether intentionally or not, and supernatural punishment was expected to follow. On the other hand, to be free, individual, novel, was to be immoral, and such freedom from custom as we now possess had to be purchased by incalculable suffering. In those days, self-torture and insanity were the only ways in which

[22] VII 51 ff. II 63, 95 give a somewhat different division of the main stages up to the present.

[23] IV 32 ff.; II 95.

[24] IV 16, 28; II 97 f. This account may seem at variance with the previous description of the Pre-moral Period. I think the most probable interpretation is, as here stated in the text, that regard for consequences is the origin of the customary valuation of acts but not the way in which this valuation, once established, persists. VII 51 f. merely says that the retroactive force of the success or failure of an act led (*anleitete*) men to think well or ill of it (cf. XV 359; IV 28, 31, 44 f.; II 97 — but XIII 190 suggests a possibly different view). At any rate Nietzsche's main thesis remains: that the Pre-moral Period disregarded the psychological antecedents of actions. IV 16 implies the contrary, but I can only interpret this as a slip of the pen or as evidence that Nietzsche's view had changed when he wrote *Beyond Good and Evil*.

a moral originator could transcend custom and inspire belief, even self-belief.[25]

The harshness of Mores corresponded to the harshness of life in the small primitive communities which were perpetually at war. Such conditions bred a love of cruelty quite opposite to the altruistic attitude which some authors consider the origin of morals generally. And since the same cruelty was attributed to the gods, voluntary suffering became a means of obtaining their favor. Nietzsche sums up the characteristic moral values of pre-historic man as follows:

... suffering was accepted as virtue, cruelty as virtue, dissimulation as virtue, revenge as virtue, disavowal of reason as virtue; on the other hand well-being as danger, inquisitiveness as danger, peace as danger, pity as danger, being pitied as disgrace, work as disgrace, insanity as divinity, change as immorality and portent of perdition! [26]

He indicates that the period of customary morality had several lasting effects. It made man dependable and uniform to a certain extent — a foundation on which subsequent moral developments could build.[27] Again, the phantastic beliefs about natural phenomena and their relation to avenging spirits kept men from observing the real causes and effects of their actions. Thus began the "moralization of existence": men mistook the sequences of guilt and punishment for those of cause and effect.[28] Finally, our present moral feelings are shot through with valuations and factual judgments from the Morality of Mores.[29]

There are also marked contrasts between past and present. Nietzsche holds that moral development, like evolution generally, does not advance in a straight line according to a

[25] IV 16 ff., 21 ff., 26; II 97 f.; V 156 f.; VII 421 ff.; XV 338. Cf. XIII 188.
[26] IV 27 f. Cf. 25 f., 17; VII 292, 422; II 97.
[27] VII 345; IV 24, 27. Cf. II 65.
[28] IV 17, 19 ff., 38 f. Consequently the moral realm has progressively shrunk as men have learned to think causally (XV 378).
[29] IV 27 f., 39 ff.

single purpose, such as the expansion of altruism.[30] So he writes:

> People lack knowledge ... of what reversals the moral judg-
> ment has already undergone, and how in the most fundamental
> sense "evil" has actually been re-christened "good" several
> times already. I have referred to one of these displacements
> with the contrast, "Morality of Mores." [31]

The transition to the Moral Period, with its shift of attention from consequences to origins of action, was a major
reversal. Nietzsche suggests that it represented an early
attempt at self-knowledge, based on a concern for "origins"
which reflected the dominance of aristocratic values.[32] Since
he appears to place the rise of aristocracies and the "making-
inward of man" near the beginning of historic times, we
may conjecture that he dates the Moral Period from the
same epoch.[33]

He attributes to this period far more than the change of
emphasis in moral judgment. He traces within it a be-
wildering complexity of moral types and interweaving developments, and it is difficult to decide whether he does not
assign the beginnings of some of these to the Pre-moral
Period. At any rate before we can consider the upshot of
the Moral Period as a whole we must examine singly some
of the elements which have gone into its making.

3. HEALTHY AND DECADENT TYPES

Nietzsche first divides the kinds of morality according
to his basic distinction between kinds of life — healthy and
decadent:

> Every time has, in its measure of power [*Kraft*], a measure
> showing which virtues are permissible, which forbidden. Either
> it has the virtues of *ascending* life: then it fundamentally opposes

[30] Cf. VII 369 ff., 419 f., 423, 292.
[31] XV 338.
[32] VII 52.   [33] Cf. VII 378 ff. See above, pp. 112 ff.

the virtues of declining life. Or it is itself a declining life —
then it also needs the virtues of decline; then it hates everything which is justified only out of abundance, out of exuberance
of forces.[34]

Once more, in the realm of morals, he discovers radical
antitheses.

He says that a healthy morality both expresses and fosters
health. It is directed by sound instincts, and its values affirm
life — will to power. Presumably all the special moral types
have both healthy and decadent variations, but he describes
"Master Morality" as the perfect example of a healthy
morality, in sharpest contrast to decadent forms.[35]

Degenerating life naturally prefers opposite values, especially on the negative side: it hates the expressions characteristic of abundance. But, according to the passage quoted,
whereas the healthy *have* the virtues of rising life — that is
the meaning of health — the decadent merely *need* the virtues of decline. That is, they do not necessarily possess
habits appropriate to their condition. Nietzsche believes
that in fact they usually choose what is bad for them, since
decadence *is* disintegration and maladjustment. We must
therefore distinguish Decadence Moralities proper, which
are characteristic *expressions* of decadence and therefore
increase it, from those modes of life *appropriate* to decadence, which he prefers to call "hygiene." If a decadent
chooses the latter he must have some remnant of healthy
instinct.[36]

Nietzsche says that the psychological center of degeneracy
is a feeling of impotent resentment (*ressentiment, Rach-
und Nachgefühl*). A decadent is not only unlucky in action,
but hypersensitive. He is too feeble to resist stimuli, unable to ignore or forget; everything wounds him. So he
cannot control his emotional response, and the most natural

[34] VIII 48. Cf. IV 272 f.
[35] VIII 48 ff., 88.
[36] VIII 142 f., 220; XV 11 f., 19 f., 340.

one, in such a condition, is resentment, longing for revenge on something — anything. The sufferer instinctively seeks a cause of his suffering — an agent who is to blame, against whom violent emotions may be released. At bottom, Nietzsche thinks, resentment is caused by a desire to stun pain. It differs from healthy revenge particularly in that, being impotent to express itself by immediate action, it poisons and consumes within. Therefore the decadent is most harmed by it as well as most prone to it.[37]

The hygienes which Nietzsche considers more or less appropriate to decadence have this in common, that they tend to eliminate *ressentiment* rather than express it, and do so by diminishing pain. Such modes of life, he believes, were taught by Jesus, perhaps by Epicurus and Pyrrho, and most realistically by Buddha, "that profound physiologist." Nietzsche himself practiced something of the sort as a temporary cure. In the narrow sense, these hygienes are not moralities at all; they work in terms of suffering rather than of sin, virtue and salvation. The logic is this. Since feeling and reaction bring suffering, it is best for decadents to cultivate peaceful ways of living which reduce feeling and reaction to a minimum — a sort of "Russian fatalism" which accepts events without rebellion. "Resist not evil" is the rule: all forms of enmity and strife must be avoided; universal love should take their place. More extreme forms can reach a condition of self-induced hypnotism analogous to animal hibernation. Nietzsche believes that such practices sometimes help a decadent to get well, and at least do not make him worse. But he adds that they treat only the symptom — suffering — not decadence itself, and implies that the best treatment would be not moral but medical.[38]

---

[37] VII 339 f., 320, 43; XV 18 f., 170 f., 409 f. Earlier hints of the psychology of *ressentiment* occur in IV 274 and VI 207. How much Nietzsche based this theory on personal experience is shown in XV 9 ff., 18 ff.; L.O. c. 28/8/83; L.G. 26/8/83, 20/12/87.

[38] VII 443 ff.; VIII 236 f., 251 ff., 270; XV 11 f., 18 ff., 171, 259 ff., 293, 467 f. He regards Stoicism as a variant of this type (XV 340 f.).

Decadence Moralities proper are themselves symptoms of degeneration, the sort of morals decadents characteristically adopt. But since resentment may be directed toward oneself or toward others, there are two corresponding types of morals.

An example of the first is ascetic morality centered upon the idea of sin. To a sufferer seeking an object for his resentment the priest replies that all suffering is due to sin. Thereby self-hatred is produced: [39]

The need of *redemption*, the essence of all Christian needs ... is the most sincere form of expression of decadence; it is the most convinced, most painful assent to it in sublime symbols and practices. The Christian wants *to get rid* of himself. *Le moi est toujours haïssable.*[40]

Unlike Buddha, the ascetic priest inflames the craving behind *ressentiment*: he stuns pain by debauching emotion. For this purpose he uses the whole pack of wild passions — "anger, fear, lust, revenge, hope, triumph, despair, cruelty" —, releasing now one, now another in alternate orgies of penitence and salvation. Such excesses give temporary distraction but make the sick worse. They do have the social utility of segregation, of preoccupying them with themselves, and inducing self-destruction in some cases. On the other hand the ascetic ideal is contagious. Its emotional dissipations have impaired the general level of health and taste, especially in Europe.[41]

Nietzsche illustrates the second type, which directs *ressentiment* outward, by anarchists, socialists and communists, who make "society" to blame for their misery, and by Christianity in many of its historical developments. All these make life bearable for the unfortunate, by taking revenge upon the fortunate. They do this most insidiously

[39] VII 439 f.
[40] VIII 50.
[41] VII 72 f., 437 f., 441, 452, 455 ff., 459 ff., 464; XV 310 ff. Cf. II 145 ff.; IV 54 f.

by a revaluation of values: they slander the manly passions and virtues, health, happiness and enjoyment, self-reliance and power, making them a reproach to the fortunate, while they glorify the opposite qualities, possessed by the weak and decadent. So they achieve a compensatory imagination of moral superiority. But their revenge is not imaginary: they have succeeded in giving the healthy a bad conscience, and in arousing their pity to the point of general disgust with life.[42]

Several or all types of Decadence Morality, as Nietzsche describes them, have the same essential values: selflessness, pity, and hedonism — dread of pain and longing for "bliss." And he criticizes these values largely because they spring from decadence — "What is *worthless?* . . . . all that comes from weakness, from envy, from *vengeance.*"[43]

4. FLOCK TYPES

Nietzsche employs another primary division which cuts across the previous one: group morals and individual morals. But he appears to hold that all morality has hitherto been of some group type.[44]

He opposes the theory that evolutionary selection has shaped moral judgments for the preservation of the species as a whole. Each particular morality has been developed with reference to the interests of some limited group which lived in competition with others. The contrast between their respective codes was often heightened to antagonism, because every group tends to think ill of what is foreign, and to resist the influence of rivals — another instance of the antitheses within morality.[45]

[42] VII 432 ff.; XV 124 ff., 409 f.; VIII 141 f., 243 f., 267 ff., 304; XVI 198 f. Cf. IV 89, 215, 258.
[43] VIII 304. Cf. 253 f.; XV 170 f., 180, 305, 406, 408 ff.; VII 175, 269 f.; XVI 75, 212, 223.
[44] V 156; XII 112 f.; XI 244. On individual morals see below, pp. 200 ff.
[45] XIII 141 f.; V 156; XV 336; XVI 89.

The oldest type of group morality is "Flock Morality" (*Heerden-Moral*). By a "flock" or "herd" Nietzsche seems to mean primarily a community in which class divisions are unimportant. He says that the basis of flock formation is weakness and fear — the strong are by nature independent. A herd therefore emphasizes solidarity and equality. It tolerates variation neither above nor below the average, for it hates difference or independence. So Flock Morality both appeals to, and tends to produce, mediocrities — the common run of people. And men generally have inherited strong gregarious instincts, because they have lived mostly in flocks since they were apes. By extension of meaning, then, Nietzsche applies the term "Flock Morality" to the sort of values supported by these instincts and therefore attractive to average people, whether they happen to be living in a herd or not. In short, Flock Morality includes the typical middle-class morality of today.[46]

Nietzsche does not conceive of Flock Morality as a simple, unchanging type. It has a complex character and history, based on a peculiar duality of values. Externally, a herd manifests unvarnished egoism; for the sake of self-protection, it esteems warlike virtues when exercised against outer danger — the "shepherd" or leader especially should have them. Conversely for internal relations, a herd prizes harmlessness and helpfulness, and therefore disapproves the very qualities which it admires for external purposes. The ambivalent attitude of a herd to its leader seems to reflect this double scheme of values. On the one hand the flock animal needs a leader, for it cannot direct itself; and gregarious life has bred powerful instincts of obedience which are deeply satisfied when they find someone, like Napoleon, who can command them. On the other hand a flock perse-

[46] VII 129, 132 ff., 135 f., 451; V 156 f.; XV 345 ff.; XIV 66 f., 248; XVI 283 f., 336; XIII 111, 212; XII 116, 278. This description of the flock implies that "Morality of Mores" is a form of Flock Morality, and V 156 f. verifies the implication.

cutes natural leaders — the exceptionally strong — and would like to get on without any at all. "One flock and no shepherd," is the motto of Flock Morality today.[47]

Nietzsche points out that Flock Morality has changed its emphasis during the course of history. Fear, its chief motive, has been drawing its consequences, one after another. Earlier times were dangerous. Therefore the herd fostered warlike impulses, and valued actions only with reference to group welfare. So in the early days of Rome, an act of compassion for another *individual* was simply non-moral, neither good nor evil; only the *res publica* counted. But when external danger diminished, fear turned toward other members of the herd, and produced a second scale of values. The very impulses which had been admired seemed doubly alarming when they were no longer drained off in war. Consequently they were branded immoral, and the safe, peaceful, mediocre qualities — those which do *not* arouse fear in one's neighbor — became the supreme virtues. This is the state of Flock Morality today. Its cardinal teachings are "equal rights" and "sympathy with all suffering," and its ideal is a conditon of comfort and safety for all, in which pain has been abolished — in short the complete absence of anything to fear. That would be the final consequence of the "imperative of flock timidity." As we move toward it, Flock Morality itself grows slack (witness contemporary sympathy with criminals), for lack of dangers which would force it to be severe; and it would ultimately abolish itself as no longer needed.[48]

Let us note in conclusion that Flock Morality has come, though from other motives and with different shades of meaning, to share the values of decadent morals: altruism, pity, freedom from pain.

[47] XV 353, 351, 290; VII 129 f., 132 ff., 136; XVI 338; XIV 68.
[48] VII 132 ff., 137, 64; XVI 337 f.; XIV 66 ff. Cf. VI 245–52; XIII 187 f.

5. MASTER AND SLAVE TYPES

Whereas Flock Morality arose in classless societies and tends to produce them, Master and Slave Moralities are associated with societies divided into upper and lower strata. Nietzsche holds that we have inherited from them a duality of moral valuations which he expresses by contrasting "good and worthless [*gut und schlecht*]" and "good and evil [*gut und böse*]." [49]

He finds a clue to his hypothesis, and a preliminary confirmation of it, in comparative linguistics. Different languages, he maintains, show a parallel development in the meaning of the words used for "good" and "worthless." The terms first indicate membership in the upper or lower class, respectively, perhaps singling out some trait typical of the class. Later they drop social status as such, but retain the reference to qualities of character. He cites examples from French, English, Italian, German, Latin, and Greek. [50] "Gentleman" and "villain" illustrate his thesis.

Accordingly he concludes that the values of Master Morality come from the masters themselves. He points this thesis against a current theory that moral judgments began with the approval of unselfish actions by those to whom they were useful. Not the recipients of goodness, Nietzsche says, but the good themselves originated aristocratic values, without much regard to unselfish actions as such. And it was not cool calculation of any sort, but a "hot gushing-forth" of value judgments from the mighty, inspired by "the passion of distance." Master Morality was a kind of self-affirmation, self-glorification: through it the nobility affirmed itself as good, set off against the baseness of the lower class. Not actions but men were the first objects of moral approval;

[49] Awareness of this duality is found as early as II 68 f.
[50] VII 306–10; XI 256.

the worth of actions was secondary, depending upon the kind of man they typified.[51]

So the emphasis in Master Morality is active and positive. It calls those traits "good" which make a man respected, even feared — power, pride, frankness, the ability to be a good friend and a good enemy. "Worthless" — base, vile, common, mean, poor, sorry — is a derivative concept, applied to qualities which arouse contempt, such as weakness, cowardice, anxiousness, servility, deceitfulness.[52]

Nietzsche makes this moral type more concrete by describing, in detail, the aristocratic temper. A healthy aristocracy considers itself, not an instrument of king or society, but the end for which the rest exist. It is deeply egoistic, and takes the sacrifices of the many as a matter of course. Its members believe that duties exist only between equals — the lower orders may be treated as one pleases. They are hard, ready for great responsibilities and risks, not afraid of suffering; they do not seek happiness, pleasure, contentment, passive enjoyment; they wish to give, and are unwilling to receive without giving, but their gifts are the overflow of souls rich in power, rather than expressions of pity. They have a profound instinct for honor and gradations of value, revere age and tradition, are given to enthusiastic loves and loyalties. Their deepest quality is self-reverence; with it go self-mastery, delight in form and measure, mistrust of all kinds of unrestraint — including freedom of speech and press. They tend to be imprudent and forthright, for utilitarianism and hypocrisy are signs of weakness. They are whole-hearted both in friendship and enmity, and call enemies as well as friends "good"; their contempt is reserved for the base.[53]

Nietzsche regards a Master Morality as a discipline which

[51] VI 278; VII 303 f., 239 f.; VIII 49 f.; XIII 150, 152, 190; XIV 62 f.

[52] VII 239 ff., 318 f.; II 68 f. Cf. VI 279.

[53] VII 236 f., 239 ff., 243, 249, 251 f., 318 ff.; XIII 152, 177 f., 193 f.; XIV 95; XV 113 f., 304 f.; XVI 326, 330 ff.; II 68 f.; IV 193 f. Cf. VI 68, 305. Nietzsche is

a ruling class has to impose on itself in order to maintain its position in face of danger from without or from below. It is severe, intolerant of variation, and trains a type, namely the type of virile virtue to which the class owes its ascendancy. Noble races retain something of the original "barbarian," or "blonde beast." The type their morals train is one of increasing strength, not mediocrity.[54]

He further explains the dynamic character of Master Morality by two kinds of psychological tension present in healthy aristocracies. The first is the "passion of distance," or feeling of superiority, produced by the contrast with a subject class. It is not shallow snobbery, for Master Morality demands a more exacting life than that of the lower classes:

They talk so stupidly about *pride* — and Christianity has even made it be felt as *sinful!* The fact is: he who *demands and attains great things from himself* must feel himself very remote from those who do not do that — this *distance* is interpreted by these others as "opinion about self"; but the former knows it only as perpetual work, war, victory, by day and night: of all that, the others know nothing![55]

The passion of distance generates reverence for higher gradations of value and an urge to achieve ever more sublime distances:

Every elevation of the type "Man" hitherto has been the work of an aristocratic society — and so it will always be again — a society which believes in a long ladder of gradation [*Rangordnung*] and difference of value between man and man . . . . Without the *passion* [*Pathos*] of distance, as it springs up from the incarnated difference of the classes [*Stände*] . . . that other, more mysterious passion could not grow at all, that craving for ever new extension of distance within the soul itself, the

describing a healthy aristocracy. He recognizes of course that aristocracies become decadent (VII 236; XVI 328).

[54] VII 246 f., 236, 321 ff.; XIV 76 f. XIV 69 f. and XVI 328 describe a converse process of weakening through over-civilization.

[55] XIV 101. Cf. V 56 f.; VII 395; XVI 303.

development of ever loftier, rarer, remoter, more widely stretched, more comprehensive states, in short precisely the elevation of the type "Man," the continued "self-overcoming of man"....[56]

The second kind of tension arises between the aristocrats themselves. They are unbroken, mere complete animals from the beginning:

... the strong strive *away* from one another with as natural a necessity as the weak *toward* one another; if the former unite, it happens only in the prospect of an aggressive joint-action .... The instinct of the born "masters" (that means, of the solitary, predatory species of man) is at bottom irritated and disquieted by organization. Beneath every oligarchy there always lies hidden — all history teaches it — the lust for *tyranny*; every oligarchy constantly trembles from the tension which every individual in it needs, to remain master of this lust.[57]

This produces freedom, self-dependence in the members of an aristocracy:

One must have no alternative: either at the top — or below, like a worm, mocked at, destroyed, crushed under foot. To become a tyrant, i.e. *free*, one must have tyrants against one. It is no small advantage to have a hundred swords of Damocles above one: thereby one learns to dance, thereby one comes to "freedom of movement." [58]

Thus Master Morality endorses the principle of equality between aristocrats; [59] and in this respect, as well as in its intolerance of variations, it presents analogies to Flock Morality, though Nietzsche does not discuss the point. But there is a fundamental difference — the difference between slackness and tension, stagnation and self-conquest. Herd

---

[56] VII 235. Cf. IV 194; VIII 148, 272 f.; XVI 326 f.; XVIII 191; L.G. 3/8/83. So seriously does Nietzsche take this idea that he makes it a general rule: the only way to ennoble an urge in the self or a class in society is to give it top rank (V 155 f.; XIII 212 f.).
[57] VII 451. Cf. 321 f., 236.
[58] XVI 204. Cf. 326 f.; VIII 149 f.; XII 118 f.
[59] VII 238, 252; XVI 330.

animals are "levellers"; their values relax life to an average performance. Aristocratic values train a race upwards, make for advance.[60]

Nietzsche gives special attention to one variant of Master Morality: that which develops when the dominant class is a priesthood. Here "clean and unclean" are the characteristic class distinctions which later develop into moral ones. The inactive, brooding mode of life, and the far more unhealthy "cures" with which the priest endeavors to treat his self-induced neurasthenia, make him an essentially dangerous type; and when he is a rival of the warrior caste he easily comes to adopt a scale of values opposite to those usual in Master Morality. Since he is unable to fight openly, impotence poisons his hatred. Then, for the sake of spiritual revenge upon the rival caste, he identifies the poor, the humble, the lowly, the unfortunate, the sick as the good; and promises eternal damnation to the powerful and noble. In this way a priesthood, as in the case of the Jews, may lead a general "slave rebellion in morals." [61]

As in the case of decadence, Nietzsche might distinguish between the mode of life appropriate to a subject class and the one such a class tends to adopt; he clearly implies such a distinction; [62] but with the epithet "Slave Morality" he appears to refer only to the second. Slave Morality, like the decadent types, is a creation of *ressentiment*, and contrasts with Master Morality at almost every point. The one is active, spontaneous, the other reactive; the one affirmative, the other negative. "Evil" (*böse*) is the primary concept in Slave Morality; "good" is derivative. The slave begins by resenting oppression and envying the good fortune of his masters. These emotions, redoubled and poisoned by im-

[60] VII 64, 235; XV 353. Cf. the contrast between Hesiod's good and evil Eris (III 215).

[61] VII 310 ff., 126 f. Stringent criticisms of priesthoods and their methods appear as early as 1865: cf. L.F.N. I 328 f. or H.K.A. III 129 f.

[62] VIII 294 f., 303 f.; VII 367.

potence, vent themselves in a distorted conception of the
masters, whose qualities, thus conceived, are then called
"evil." "Good" is likewise compensatory: it glorifies what
slaves have and masters have not — humility, obedience,
patience, forgiveness. What arouses fear is thus called good
by the masters, evil by the slaves; and as the masters feel
contempt for what is "worthless," so there is a tinge of
contempt in the slaves' idea of a "good" man — harmless,
good-natured, a little stupid. Further characteristics which
contrast with Master Morality are: hedonism, prudence,
utilitarianism; the doctrine of "the dignity of labor" and
the sinfulness of being idle; a passive conception of happiness as rest or peace; vituperation of enemies. Also the slave
is dishonest, with himself and others; "his soul squints."
What he parades as a demand for "justice" is really his own
will to power; and when a slave class has attained power, it
changes to the principles of Master Morality.[63]

6. ABSOLUTE MORALITY

Nietzsche does not mean that his moral types must exist
in pure form. He often perceives them, compromised or
confused perhaps, in the same man or epoch, and he diagnoses modern morals as a hybrid of *all* the types, including
traces of Master Morality. We are "physiologically false"
because our instincts embody opposite valuations.[64]

When we piece his type studies together, certain major
trends in the "Moral Period" emerge. He sees an obvious
kinship between the values characteristic of Decadence,
Flock, and Slave Morality, and a fundamental antagonism

[63] VII 71 f., 242 f., 317–21, 326, 328 ff.; XIII 152; XIV 69 f.; XVI 196, 216.
Cf. I 127; XVI 176. These are typical but not universal slave traits. Nietzsche
speaks with admiration of Epictetus as an exception (IV 354 f.). Also XVI
300 states that strong individuals prosper better in the lowest than in the middle
classes of society. A hint of the underlying psychology of "re-active" morality
is already to be found in an early description of the attitude of weakly natures
toward great men (L.F.N. I 321 or H.K.A. II 129).

[64] VII 239; XV 337; VIII 51; XIII 118; XII 81; L.O. 4/1/88. That we have
inherited elements of Master Morality is further confirmed by II 69; VII 387.

between these and Master Morality. Also, he places aristocratic modes of thinking at the beginning of the Moral Period.[65] One trend, then, was from the dominance of Master Morality to the preponderance of an amalgam of the other three types: such is his account of the Jewish-Christian "slave rebellion in morals" of the past two thousand years. The flock, needing leaders, was seduced by decadents, its morality perverted in the direction of decadence ideals.[66] But in the course of time herd instincts proved more powerful: the decay of ascetic Christianity and the rise of democratic humanitarianism was a return of Flock Morality to its natural form.[67] Nietzsche believes that *Flock Morality is the most important element in present morals,* and that this fact threatens ultimate stagnation for humanity.[68]

A second trend — really occupying Pre-moral as well as Moral periods — was the development of a sense of guilt, the theme of the second treatise in *Toward the Genealogy of Morals.* "Bad conscience," Nietzsche holds, began from self-torture produced by introverted predatory instincts; it was perfected by ascetic priests who read into it the relationship of debtor to creditor. This also had had an independent previous history. From the beginning, the creditor's claim to "satisfaction" was supported by unspeakably cruel penal laws. In time, men believed their tribe to be indebted to its ancestors for its existence and under legal obligation to repay them, sometimes with human sacrifice. The ancestors of the most powerful tribes later became gods; so humanity inherited the consciousness of owing obligations to the gods, even after the passing of the kinship group.

[65] VII 52. See above, p. 148.
[66] XV 300, 345, 351; VII 334 ff. The existence of such a trend is further supported by Nietzsche's description of Slave Morality as a *reaction.* Also VII 304 states that certain flock values come to the fore *after* the decline of aristocratic values.
[67] XV 300 f.
[68] VII 64, 90, 130, 134 ff., 139; XVI 335, 337 f.; L.O. 4/1/88. Cf. IV 133 ff.; above, p. 114.

This belief the priests coupled with introverted cruelty:
man was led to interpret his suffering as punishment for sin
against God, and his will to make himself suffer brought
the agonized conscience to its maximum, in the conception
of unredeemable guilt meriting eternal punishment.[69]

A third major trend, connected with the first two, Nietzsche calls "the de-naturalization of morals." Moralities,
we have seen, were at first oriented toward the welfare of
some group, however imperfectly; this is what he means by
"natural morality" — one that serves some vital need. But
through various stages morals were detached from life and
gradually made hostile to it, as in the case of the typical
decadent and slave values. Greek philosophers, notably
Socrates and Plato, contributed to the process by treating
morals in terms of abstract ideas and inventing another
world for them to inhabit, thereby detaching morals from
their roots in Greek history. Priests taught the existence
of a supernatural moral order, and read imaginary sequences
of sin and punishment into nature. Morals were also de-
naturalized by the separation of act from agent — the belief
that actions are good or bad in themselves regardless of
who does them. In sum, denaturalization took morality
from the service of life, and made moral values absolute,
therefore capable of condemning life itself. Lately, morals
have become independent even of religion. Hence the
culmination of the whole process is nihilism.[70]

Our inquiry thus far has disclosed a diversity of ingredients and origins; it is now pertinent to look for their unity.
Essentially *what* morality does Nietzsche propose to criticize? As just stated, it is one claiming absolute status: its

---

[69] VII 347–54, 378–91, 456 ff. Cf. VI 207 f. This sequence of thought is more
obvious in German: *Schuld* means both "debt" and "guilt."

[70] XV 155, 249 f., 339, 345, 358, 362 ff., 458 f.; VIII 89, 244 ff. Cf. I 10. The
re-naturalization of Flock Morality (XV 300 f.) is a recent reversal of the trend.
One might almost say that Nietzsche conjures up the nihilist movement in
order to prevent the trivialization of man threatened by Flock Morality.

imperatives are categorical, its values supreme; all else must be approved or condemned with reference to them. Secondly, it claims absolute universality of form: it does not offer different ideals for different types of life but insists that a single pattern, a single rule, obtains for all.[71] Thirdly, its content consists in absolute antitheses: certain qualities are utterly good, others utterly evil.[72] Fourthly, these qualities belong to conscious motives for which we are morally responsible; if our motives are guilty we suffer remorse and deserve retributive punishment.[73] Finally, the good qualities are self-denial and pity, the evil ones selfishness and will to power. In short, this morality is nihilistic; its logical conclusion is the condemnation of all existence.

The upshot of the whole Moral Period, and the focus of Nietzsche's critical onslaught, then, might best be styled "Absolute Morality." [74] It is that complex of values which has swayed the world for the past two thousand years; he usually calls it "Christian morality," sometimes simply "Morality" (die Moral).[75]

7. THE DIALECTIC OF SELF-TRANSCENDENCE

The attentive reader will have noticed several applications of Nietzsche's biological and psychological theories to his natural history of morals. The most striking of all is his use of his principle of evolutionary "self-overcoming" as a general law of moral evolution. He has demonstrated the presence of many contrasts in the moral realm. He now conceives the development of moral values as a strife and succession of antithetical ideals.

Any reigning morality condemns all fundamental innovation:

[71] VII 128; IV 185; XV 372 f.; XI 206. Cf. VII 174 f.
[72] XV 83, 397 f.; VII 10, 73; IV 96 f.
[73] VII 52; XIII 119; VIII 97 ff.; II 65; XVI 201.
[74] Cf. I 10; XV 83, 119; XIII 98; XIV 87; XI 214 f.; XII 75, 82, 124 f.
[75] E.g. I 10; XV 118 f.

So far, the strongest and most evil minds have advanced humanity most . . . . The new is . . . under all circumstances the *evil*, as that which desires to conquer, to overthrow the old landmarks and the old pieties; and only the old is the good! The good men of every time are those who dig old thoughts to the bottom and bear fruit with them, the husbandmen of the mind. But every land is finally worn out, and the ploughshare of evil must come again and again.[76]

But when the "evil" in turn becomes established it is transformed into "good"; so

Everything good is the transformation of an evil: every god has a devil for a father.

Forming an ideal, that means *remoulding* one's devil into one's god. And for that one must first have made one's devil.[77]

Nietzsche mentions several examples of goods which were once evils, among them marriage, pity, and settling grievances at law instead of by private feud.[78]

He says further that strife continues after the establishment of the new ideal. ". . . every created god in turn creates a devil for himself. And that is *not* the one from which he arose. (It is the *neighboring* ideal, with which he must *struggle*.)" [79] And in the transition from one ideal to the next, the older is not simply destroyed by an outside force: it brings about its own destruction by an act of self-transcendence which is the inevitable consequence of its previous victory:

[76] V 41. Cf. XII 262; VI 27, 62.
[77] XII 262. Cf. VI 94; VII 101, 182 f.; IV 29, 327 f.; XIV 53, 316; XV 338; XVI 376; XII 90. The last quotation may be an allusion to Nietzsche's adoption of the will-to-power theory. In 1870 he heard lectures by Jakob Burckhardt, in one of which Burckhardt declared power to be *an sich böse* (*Weltgeschichtliche Betrachtungen*, Leipzig: Kröner's Taschenausgabe, p. 36. Cf. L. Ge. 7/11/70). *The Birth of Tragedy* already contains a hint of the theory of the genesis of good out of evil (I 66, 70 f.). Nietzsche also recognizes the converse process: things once considered good may later be considered evil; for example, the violent criminal of today is a kind of moral atavism (II 66 f.; VII 106; XII 91; XIII 122 f.).
[78] VII 419 ff.   [79] XIV 261. Cf. 262, 88; VI 58.

Requirement: the new law must be *capable of fulfilment* — and out of the fulfilment the overcoming and the higher law must grow.

Justice ... ends, as does every good thing on earth, *in superseding [aufhebend] itself.* This self-supersession of justice: one knows by what a beautiful name it is called — *mercy* ....[80]

Nietzsche places himself at just such a critical point in the evolution of morals; his revaluation of values is the self-conquest of the older morality through its virtue of uncompromising sincerity, as this autobiographical sketch shows:

We are illogical and unjust beings from the first — without this there is no life.
All appraisals of the value of life false.
Final aimlessness. Waste.
Universal resignation: knowing better and better, hovering over the valuations, sole solace.

Result: I need believe in nothing.
Things are unknowable.
I need not suffer from my injustice.
Despair driven away by scepticism.

I gained the right to *create*, the right to *approve* [*gutzuheissen*], the right to attach myself to the past.
At last: in the whole movement I discovered *living morality, driving force.* I had only *imagined* myself to be beyond good and evil.
Free-thinking [*Freigeisterei*] *itself* was a *moral action:*

1. as honesty,
2. as courage,
3. as justice,
4. as love.

I had *myself* left over, as one fixing values [*Wertansetzenden*].[81]

[80] XII 365; VII 364. Cf. 481.
[81] XIV 312. Cf. 307 ff.; XIII 114 f., 121, 124 f., 176, 197 f.; IV 8 f.; VII 53, 182 f., 481 f.; XV 118 f.; XI 35; XII 84.

So there is continuity with the old as well as opposition to it. But there is more. Nietzsche intends the new epoch to be in some sense a synthesis of all the past:

We want to be heirs of all previous morality and *not* begin afresh. Our whole activity is only morality which is turning against its previous form.

Zarathustra wishes to *lose* no past of humanity, to throw all into the casting.[82]

The best general formulation of this law of the evolution of values is found in *Thus Spake Zarathustra*. The discourse on "self-overcoming" leads up to it:

... good [*Gutes*] and evil which would be imperishable — that does not exist! Of itself, it must overcome itself again and again.

By your values and words of good and evil you are using force [*Gewalt*], you evaluators . . . .

But a stronger force grows out of your values, and a new overcoming: on it egg and eggshell break.

And he who must be a creator in good and evil: truly, he must first be a destroyer, and smash values.

So supreme evil belongs to supreme goodness [*Güte*]: but this is creative goodness. —[83]

But this dialectic is not inevitable in the sense of Marx's or Hegel's. Nietzsche's language implies that some kind of "self-supersession" must come to "all great things," and this is obviously a necessary preliminary to the establishment of a new ideal — there cannot be two sovereigns. But he does not hold evolution in general to be automatic, and he confronts man in particular with radically different alternatives for the future. Again, he says that Flock Morality, if finally triumphant, would abolish itself,[84] but we know that he thinks the sequel would be stagnation, not

---

[82] XIII 125; XIV 271. Cf. II 111 f.; IV 61; V 258 ff.; XII 85; L.O. 14/4/87.
[83] VI 169. Cf. VII 394.
[84] VII 134.

further evolution. The conclusion seems to be, then, that the dialectic is only hypothetically necessary: every great ideal must transcend itself *if* it attains complete fruition, and every further advance must be the outgrowth of self-transcendence — if there *is* any further advance.

To sum up, Nietzsche envisages his task as the self-overcoming of Christian morality, and, in an extended sense, of the entire Moral Period. Introducing the Extramoral Period will involve destroying the supremacy of the old values, and creating novel ones out of what has hitherto been evil. But it will also grow from previous morality, and will essay a synthesis of all the past which shall preserve what man has accomplished.

CHAPTER VII

Morals in Revolution

*Great enough to turn the despised into gold: spirit-
ual enough to conceive the body as the higher — that
is the future of morals!* (XIII 167)

1. GROUNDS FOR SUSPICION

FROM his history of morals, Nietzsche concludes that
they are in desperate need of criticism. The work of
decadent instincts in the formation of Christian ideals
shows that mankind is not automatically on the right road,[1]
and that we have reason to distrust our present habits and
feelings. He draws a similar conclusion from the fact that
traditional morality depends upon the existence of a "moral
world-order": a God of righteousness whose will establishes
the moral law, who speaks through man's conscience, who
rewards obedience and punishes sin.[2] If "God is dead," conscience can no longer claim to be an oracle of living truth;
and indeed the history of morals makes it probably an oracle
of error.[3]

Nietzsche deduces the last proposition from two others:
that much of man's past has been lived in ignorance and
superstition — "Morality of Mores," for example — and that
feelings embody habitual ancestral judgments. Moral consciousness today is exceedingly complex and derivative:

"Trust your feeling!" — But feelings are nothing ultimate,
original; behind the feelings stand judgments and valuations
which we inherit in the form of feelings (inclinations, disin-

[1] XV 82 f.
[2] VIII 247; IV 78, 367 f.
[3] XV 104; 39 ff., 307; XII 84.

clinations). The inspiration which springs from feeling is the grandchild of a judgment — and often of a false one! [4]

Hence, after describing the Morality of Mores, Nietzsche concludes:

And today we still see the consequence: where a man's feeling is *exalted*, that imaginary world somehow plays a part. It is sad: but for the present *all loftier feelings* must be suspicious to the scientific man, so much are they fused with delusion and nonsense.[5]

And he holds that the formal aspect of conscience, the feeling of a categorical "thou shalt," is an expression of our inherited need for obedience, of the flock instinct, which seeks to master the rest. Instead of saying that an act is wrong because conscience condemns it, we should say that conscience condemns it because it has been condemned.[6]

These are Nietzsche's reasons for rejecting ethical intuitionism — the belief that "the convictions of the plain man" or "the moral consciousness" afford self-evident truth which is beyond criticism. He regards current views of this kind as simply a half-way house between Christianity and ultimate nihilism, soon destined to give place to the latter:

When one gives up the Christian faith one thereby pulls from under one's feet the *right* to the Christian ethic. The latter is by *no* means self-evident.... Christianity is a system, an intellectually connected and *whole* view of things. If one breaks a major notion, the belief in God, out of it, one shatters the whole.... Christianity assumes that man does not know, *can* not know, what is good for him, what evil: he believes in God, who alone knows. The Christian ethic is a command; its origin is transcendent; it is beyond all criticism, all right to criticism; it has truth only in case God is the truth.... If the English actually believe they know of themselves, "intuitively," what

---

[4] IV 40 f. Cf. 95; VI 112 f.; XI 204; XIII 206 f. See the discussion of heredity above, pp. 69 f. IV 40 describes a process whereby feelings are transmitted socially.

[5] IV 39 f.

[6] VII 129; XVI 346 f., 359. Cf. III 226 f.; V 254 ff.

is good and evil . . . this itself is merely the *result* of the authority of the Christian value judgment and an expression of the *strength* and *depth* of this authority . . . .⁷

Here as everywhere men have ceased to be Christian without having the courage to be anything else.

2. MORALITY AS MISUNDERSTANDING

Granted the necessity for a critical examination of existing morality, we may conveniently consider first those phases of Nietzsche's critique which appeal primarily to judgments of fact, later those which are based on judgments of value. With regard to the former he writes:

So I deny morality [*Sittlichkeit*] as I deny alchemy, that means, I deny its assumptions: but *not* that there have been alchemists who believed in these assumptions and acted on them. — I also deny immorality: *not* that countless men *feel* themselves immoral, but that there is a basis in *truth* for feeling oneself so. I do *not* deny — as goes without saying, supposing that I am no fool — that many actions which are called immoral are to be avoided and combatted; likewise that many which are called moral are to be done and encouraged — but I mean: the one as well as the other *on other grounds than hitherto*. We have *to learn differently* [*umzulernen*] — in order finally, perhaps very late, to attain still more: *to feel differently.*⁸

Nietzsche sums up his position with the paradox that there are no moral phenomena but only moral *interpretations* of phenomena — which are therefore false. He singles out certain essential features of "Absolute Morality," namely free will, responsibility, guilt, and selflessness: if an act must be unegoistic if it is to be moral, and if it must be free if it is to be either moral or immoral, then no such act has existed or can exist. Morality is based on a misunderstanding, or — to use stronger language — on a "psychological forgery." It refers to a fictitious world, and therefore

⁷ VIII 120. Cf. XV 331 ff.; XVI 406; XIII 141; XI 165; II 138 f.; V 201.
⁸ IV 97 f. Cf. 307; XII 84; XIV 319.

has no claim on us. This is another meaning of "beyond
good and evil" — having "the illusion of moral judgment
beneath oneself." [9]

The ideas of sin and guilt presuppose moral responsibility, and this in turn rests upon freedom of will and conscious
motivation, both of which Nietzsche denies.[10] And since the
Moral Period rested on the belief that conscious motives
cause actions, he introduces a new era, the "Extra-moral,"
by teaching that the main sources of action are unconscious.[11] This is the reason for most of his psychological
critique of consciousness. We never know the real motives
of our acts. Therefore, "We are learning to *think less*
[*geringer*] of all that is conscious: we are learning not to
make ourselves responsible for our self, since *we*, as conscious, purposing beings, are only the smallest part of it." [12]

In so far as "will" means "conscious will," its freedom is
irrelevant to the moral judgment of conduct, because consciousness is not the cause of actions. Nietzsche ascribes the
origin of belief in free will to the isolated, apparently spontaneous character of conscious states.[13] He denies the fact,
but not the feeling, of freedom — "He who *feels* that the
will is unfree, is psychopathic: he who *denies* it, is stupid." [14]
Psychologically, it is the feeling of heightened energies
which might be released in several directions, or the "affect
of command," the feeling of obeying oneself.[15] But he denies the reality of free will on four grounds. There is no
will at all in the sense usually meant — neither a "faculty"
nor a magically efficacious conscious process.[16] Strict determinism holds everywhere: a man's nature, the source of

[9] VIII 102; XV 335; XVI 216 ff.; VII 100; IV 151 f. Cf. XIII 127, 136; XIV 313.
[10] XVI 201; VIII 99 f. Cf. III 209–12, 214 f.
[11] VII 52 f.
[12] XVI 139. Cf. 129 ff.; IV 115 ff., 128 f.; V 310 f.; VIII 93 f.; XIII 119, 127 f.,
132 ff., 157 ff., 215, 241, 246, 263 ff.; XI 199 f., 204 f., 287 ff.
[13] II 35 f. Cf. III 197 f.
[14] XII 303.   [15] XIII 137, 157, 262 f., 265; VII 30. Cf. III 195 f.
[16] XIII 263; above, pp. 91 ff.

his motives, is a necessary resultant which "concresces out of the elements and influences of past and present things." [17] Schopenhauer's argument for a supernatural "intelligible freedom" assumes, fallaciously, that the feeling of guilt is justified because it exists.[18] And the very idea of free will is self-contradictory: it implies self-causation, the wish "to pull oneself by the hair, with a more than Münchhausenian daring, out of the swamp of nothingness into existence." [19]

Nietzsche suggests that the sense of guilt is a misinterpretation of unpleasant states of mind which are really due to physiological disorders. Moral feeling and judgment generally are best regarded as a kind of clumsy sign language by which bodily conditions express themselves.[20]

With regard to selflessness as the criterion of moral worth, Nietzsche speaks of it in six senses, of which four are relevant here. One of them involves the notion of a "soul" or "substantial ego" separate from the *process* of living. Nietzsche denies that there is such a thing; so for him the whole antithesis of egoistic and altruistic, thus understood, is nonsense.[21]

In another sense, unegoistic action is impossible, and all actions are necessarily egoistic. Since the self is a system of urges, every act is the work of one or more of them, and "unselfish urge" is a contradiction in terms:

A good author, who really has his heart in his subject, desires that someone come and annihilate him by presenting the same subject more plainly, and by answering without remainder the questions contained in it.... The soldier desires to fall on the battlefield for his victorious fatherland: for in the victory of the fatherland his supreme desire is victorious too. The mother gives the child what she deprives herself of, sleep,

---

[17] II 63 f. On Nietzsche's determinism see below, pp. 282 ff.
[18] II 64 f. Cf. VIII 100; XVI 90.
[19] VII 32.
[20] IV 82 f., 122 f.; VII 442; VIII 97 f.; XIII 163 f.; XIV 317 f. See above, p. 88, for the special meaning of "body."
[21] XV 57, 407; XVI 217 f.; VIII 94 f.; XIII 148; XII 128 f.

the best food, under certain circumstances her health, her fortune. — But are all these unegoistic states? Are these deeds of morality *miracles*, because they are "impossible and yet real," according to Schopenhauer's expression? Is it not plain that in all these cases man loves *something of his* [*von sich*], a thought, a craving, a production, more than *something else of his*; that he therefore *divides* his being and sacrifices one part for the other? .... The *inclination to something* ... is present in all the above-mentioned cases; to yield to it ... is not "unegoistic" in any case.[22]

Nietzsche believes egoism universal in a subtler sense. We are necessarily self-centered, that is, we perceive and value things in perspective: "Egoism is the *perspectival* law of sensation, whereby that which is nearest appears large and heavy: whereas with distance, all things decrease in size and weight."[23]

Lastly, Nietzsche asserts the universal egoism of will to power: life must exert its force and grow, and growth is at the cost of the environment, including other lives. Nor can we legitimately separate defensive from aggressive egoism, as if only the former were necessary: "There is no egoism which stays at home and does not encroach — consequently that 'justifiable,' 'morally indifferent' egoism, of which you talk, does not exist at all."[24] In a world like this, Schopenhauer's maxim, "Hurt no one," is false sentimentalism.[25]

In the last three senses of "egoism," the ideal of selflessness must condemn all life as immoral. Nietzsche drives the point home with an *ad hominem*: moralities themselves are products of life, therefore they too are "immoral." Would-be reformers of mankind are thoroughly unscrupulous in their choice of means — for example the use of "pious

---

[22] II 78 f. Cf. 137; IV 216, 263; VI 167; XIII 149; XVI 217; VII 53 f. Nietzsche's critique of selflessness is also related to his critique of conscious motivation; we may not *consciously* think of ourselves, yet do so unconsciously at the same time (IV 136).

[23] V 183. Cf. XVI 114 f.; XIII 172; IV 118 f.; below, pp. 259 ff.

[24] XV 407. Cf. XVI 179; VII 326 f.

[25] VII 115.

fraud." Christian morality — the ethic of selflessness — is the creation of priests' will to power and the "mass egoism of the weak." So "in order to *make* morality, one must have an unconditional will to the opposite." [26]

To realize that morality is a form of immorality, that all actions are necessarily egoistic, brings a "great liberation": the antithesis between good and evil is removed from the nature of things, and with it the ground for condemning essential traits of life. Good and evil are "complementary value-concepts," not realities in eternal conflict. Moreover they are interdependent:

... finally one comprehends that altruistic actions are only a species of egoistic ones — and that the degree to which one loves, wastes oneself, is a proof of the degree of individual *power* and *personality*. In short *that, in making man more evil, one makes him better* — and that one is not either without the other . . .[27]

This is what Nietzsche means by "the absolute homogeneity in all becoming." Moral distinctions are "perspectival"; all actions are the same at bottom, being alike expressions of will to power.[28]

The critique of selflessness thus culminates, as did that of conscious motivation and free will, in complete denial of guilt or sin: *all* actions are innocent; repentance is irrational.[29] Nietzsche speaks of the new sense of innocence as a great positive characteristic of the era which he is opening. Here, too, is his dialectical evolution of values: a sense of guilt was necessary before man could become *conscious* of innocence.[30] He believes that it will take generations to purify our spontaneous moral feelings in this way.[31] But

[26] VIII 106 f. Cf. XV 125, 184, 323 f., 345, 365 ff., 410; VII 329 ff.
[27] XVI 221. Cf. II 17 f.; XV 368, 397 f.
[28] XV 343 f. Cf. 314, 368; XVI 221 ff.; XIII 148; II 110.
[29] XV 314; IV 57; XIII 127 f.; XVI 222; VIII 100 f. Cf. III 364; H.K.A. II 143.
[30] II 112. Cf. VII 384, 388.
[31] IV 40, 97, 342 f.; XI 267.

he suggests the importance of that change by saying, "Christianity should have set up the innocence of man as an article of faith — men would have become gods . . . ." [32]

3. MORALITY AS POISON

Nietzsche exposes the errors on which Absolute Morality is based in order to destroy its claims, but he has little objection to error as such. On that ground alone, he would not lift a finger against dogmas a thousand times more absurd. All depends on the purpose behind the lies: Christian morality, he maintains, expresses the desire of decadents for revenge against life; it is anti-natural, poisonous, vampiristic. [33]

With this we turn from the question of fact to the central question in the revaluation of values: what are the old ideals worth? Nietzsche answers in terms of the enhancement of life: Absolute Morality is nihilistic morality. Far from being of unconditional worth, so-called "good" qualities are often harmful, and in the whole vital economy so-called "evil" qualities are worth more than the "good."

The old morality negates life, Nietzsche holds, because it absolutely condemns qualities — those of will to power — which are essential to life, [34] and because any morality which issues categorical commands to all people contradicts life's need of many sets of values for its varying forms and stages. [35] So we face the dilemma of nihilism: "either do away with your venerations or — with yourselves!" [36] This is Nietzsche's deepest reason for breaking with the old values.

Since he diagnoses modern morality as a blend of Flock, Decadence, and Slave Moralities, he brings now one, now another of these to the fore when he criticizes the so-called "good" qualities.

[32] XI 310.
[33] XV 123 ff., 328; XV 439; VIII 88 f., 298, 304.
[34] I 9 f.; VIII 88 f.; XIII 102, 124 f.; XIV 87, 307 f.
[35] XIV 87, 309; VIII 92. Cf. VI 168 f.; IV 161 f.; V 156; VII 174 f.
[36] V 280. Cf. XV 141 f., 147, 155.

He satirizes the conventional ideal of the "good man": he is either a decadent or a flock animal, at best a Pharisee, satisfied, uncreative, conserving life at a given level; therefore a parasite who sacrifices the future to the present, to himself; also a parasite from the point of view of knowledge, for the price of his existence is falsehood, a refusal to see reality as it is. Nietzsche exclaims:

At times I have an enormous contempt for *good* people — their weakness, their wanting to experience nothing, their wanting to see nothing, their arbitrary blindness, their banal revolving in the usual and comfortable, their gratification with their good "qualities," etc.[37]

In short, the "good man" is the most harmful man.[38]

Nietzsche is protesting essentially against the exclusive and unqualified valuation of benevolence in ethics. The *merely* good man in this sense is one who is always good-natured, always well-disposed toward others; therefore he lacks mistrust and hostility, and is, consequently, docile, spiritually obedient, industrious, modest, weak — an ideal slave.[39] He represents — in theory at least — the "hemiplegia of virtue":

The demand is, that man emasculate himself of those instincts with which he can be a foe, can injure, can be angry, can exact revenge . . .

But life requires both friendly and hostile dispositions:

For every kind of man who has remained strong and natural, love and hate, gratitude and revenge, kindliness and wrath, doing "yes" and doing "no," belong with each other. One is good, at the price of knowing how to be evil too; one is evil, because otherwise one would not know how to be good.[40]

[37] XII 221. Cf. XV 119 ff., 339 f.; XVI 440 ff.; XIV 86; XIII 141 f., 145, 147; VI 272 f., 293, 309 ff.; VII 294, 453.
[38] XV 120 f.; XVI 444; XIV 84.
[39] XV 119, 402; XVI 442, 444; XIII 142, 147.
[40] XV 396. Cf. 397, 290 ff.; XIII 146.

So Zarathustra laughs at those whose "goodness" consists in having "lame paws." [41] In practice, to insist on pure benevolence is to trivialize human nature:

... to demand that all should become "good man," gregarious animal, blue-eyed, benevolent, "Beautiful Soul" — or, as Mr. Herbert Spencer wishes, altruistic, would mean to castrate humanity and reduce it to a miserable Chinese existence.[42]

Closely related to the ideal of absolute benevolence is the cult of pity or compassion (*Mitleid*). Nietzsche considers it the only living religion of his day, a residue of softened Christianity.[43] None of the reigning values comes in for more repeated criticism. Here again he is protesting against the view, also represented by Schopenhauer, that pity is *always* good and the *sole* moral motive.[44]

Nietzsche takes pains to unravel the complex psychology of compassion, in order to encourage greater discrimination toward it. He charges that Schopenhauer described it badly for lack of sufficient acquaintance with it — "the cult of pity is *decent* only for men who do not know it from their experience." [45] Pity is not one simple motive but a phenomenon which may involve many, among which are lust, superiority, envy, pleasure, cruelty, and curiosity [46] — sometimes mere hypocrisy or vanity.[47] It does not transcend the separateness of individuality: it is no mystic union, but a more or less inaccurate guesswork based on external signs. Hence it is always egoistic; for the imagined pain, which we seek to relieve, is not the same as the real one. Pity is by no means usually endowed with fine understanding, and actions based on it are often impertinent, tactless, an inva-

[41] VI 173.
[42] XV 120. Cf. VI 245 ff.
[43] VII 75, 421; IV 133 ff.
[44] VII 292 f.; IV 137 f.; L.M. 8/83.
[45] XII 297. Cf. IV 137 f.; XV 405; L.O. 14/9/84.
[46] VI 79, 318; XI 225 f., 229; III 175; IV 136 f., 142; XII 90; XIV 90; XV 199.
[47] III 40 f.; V 335 f.; VII 75.

sion of personal privacy, and humiliating to the recipient.[48]

Nietzsche remarks that, save for a few exquisite souls who know no excess, the giving vent to *any* feeling without reserve — so fashionable since Rousseau — is repulsive: pity included.[49] Modern compassion is an expression of decadence, of morbid over-sensitiveness: in short, weakness. Hence it is not a virtue today, but a vice, harmful both to ourselves and to others.[50] It is contagious, a useless duplication of misery, and tends rather to cripple effective beneficence.[51] The call to pity others often tempts a man away from the severity of his own task in life; Zarathustra meets it as his last sin.[52] Pity would lead us to sacrifice the future we might create to the relief of present misery — against this, Zarathustra commands, "Be hard" — and it *has* led us to preserve the wretched mistakes of life who should have been allowed to perish. It has frustrated "the law of selection" and deteriorated the race; and comprehensive compassion for the misery compassion has created is leading straight to a total disgust with humanity — to nihilism.[53]

Behind both the religion of pity and the religion of comfort stands a kind of negative hedonism, the belief that suffering is absolutely evil, something to be destroyed at all costs. Nietzsche attacks this assumption also as an expression of weakness and decadence. Happiness and unhappiness are twins; to seek to avoid the latter is to make the former petty.[54] Healthy men live for purposes for which they are ready to make both themselves and others suffer.[55]

[48] IV 136 f., 144 ff.; XI 226 f., 229; XIII 180, 182; II 105 f.; XV 16, 406; V 260 f.; VI 127 f., 384 ff. Cf. IV 148, 263.
[49] XI 270.
[50] XV 16, 170 f., 180; VIII 146 ff.; VII 175, 270; II 70; VI 130, 248; X 495; XII 297. Cf. XVI 322; III 226, 228.
[51] IV 138 f., 141; VIII 221; XV 406.
[52] V 262 f.; VI 351, 475 f.; XV 17. Cf. L.M. 8/83.
[53] VI 130, 312; VIII 221 f.; VII 88 f., 293, 432 ff.; XV 180 f. Cf. II 72. The unrestricted Christian ethic of love for those who merely happen to be living now has the same effect on the race (XV 323 f.).
[54] V 261; VII 64. See above, p. 117, note 8.   [55] XV 158; IV 149 f.

You wish if possible — and there is no madder "if possible" — to *abolish suffering*; and we? — it quite seems that *we* had rather have it greater and worse than it ever was! Well-being, as you understand it — that is no aim, that seems to us an *end*! A condition which soon makes man ridiculous and contemptible — which makes his downfall *desired*! The discipline of suffering, of *great* suffering — know you not that only *this* discipline has produced all enhancements of man hitherto? That tension of the soul in misfortune, which breeds strength into it . . . .[56]

Finally there are the ascetic ideals of Christianity in its prime. Nietzsche has more respect for them than for the softer and more dishonest contemporary values,[57] but they are decadence ideals *par excellence*: the body despised, the sense of sin an instrument of torture turned against all natural impulses, sex unclean, selfishness evil, even the highest values of the intellect considered temptations; self-denial, self-crucifixion good — these are the values by which decadents have poisoned life for the healthy. Christianity is a "capital crime against life," and never more so than in its cruelty to the noblest men:

What we combat in Christianity? That it wants to break the strong, that it wants to discourage their courage, to exploit their bad hours and wearinesses, to pervert their proud certainty into unrest and distress of conscience; that it knows how to make noble instincts poisonous and sick, until their force, their will to power, turns backwards, turns against itself — until the strong go to ruin from debauches of self-contempt and self-maltreatment: that frightful way of going to ruin, of which Pascal furnishes the most famous example.[58]

4. SACRED SELFISHNESS

Nietzsche has demoted the "good" qualities; he completes his revaluation by elevating the "evil" ones. So he illus-

---

[56] VII 180. Cf. 64 f., 90; XVI 299.
[57] VII 478.
[58] XV 329. Cf. 327, 59, 124 ff., 420 f.; VII 89, 187, 384 f., 388 ff., 394, 455 ff.; VIII 219 f., 298 f.; IV 44, 62 f., 74, 161.

trates the transmutation of "evil" into "good" in the dialectical evolution of values. He seems to regard this as his most genuinely creative work, comparable to making gold out of base metals, a positive *addition* to human values: "My task this time is quite curious: I have asked myself what has been most hated, feared, despised by men so far — and of exactly that I have made my 'gold' . . ." [59]

Accordingly Zarathustra discourses "Of the Three Evils": *"Lust, thirst for mastery, self-seeking:* these three have been best cursed and worst defamed and slandered till now — these three I intend to consider with human decency." His conclusions are: lust is the bridge between present and future, "innocent and free for free hearts . . . all the future's exuberance of thanks to the present"; thirst for mastery drives the lofty from self-sufficient solitude to exercise power upon lower humanity; self-seeking distinguishes what is good from what is worthless, "bids even the highest — grow upwards." [60]

Cruelty is a fourth evil which Nietzsche revalues as a kind of antithesis to the ethic of pity. He contrasts modern squeamishness with the lustier vitality of older times, when men counted cruelty among their chief holiday diversions — an execution, a torture, a fight — and laughed themselves half to death over the mishaps of Don Quixote. Gods, too, were called in to enjoy human suffering. Life was much gayer then, when men were unashamed of their cruelty, than in our timid, hypersensitive, and pessimistic age. But we have not really banished cruelty:

Almost everything we call "higher culture" rests upon the spiritualization and deepening of *cruelty* — this is my thesis; that "wild animal" has by no means been killed off; it lives, it flourishes, it has only — deified itself. What constitutes the agonizing voluptuousness of tragedy, is cruelty; what makes pleasurable effect . . . . even in all the sublime, up to the loftiest and most delicate thrills of metaphysics, derives its sweetness from the commingled ingredient of cruelty alone.

Cruelty, the passage continues, can be the enjoyment of our own as well as others' suffering: witness the religious ascetic, and the scientist who forces his mind to cut beneath appearances and recognize truths which hurt.[61]

The crux of revaluation is Nietzsche's view of egoism, in contrast to the ethic of self-denial or altruism. Of the six meanings of "egoism" which he employs, two are relevant here: self-development and self-expression.

Every urge is of course an urge *of* a self, but it need not act *for* the self. It simply strives to spend energy in its own way, often sacrificing the health, or even life, of the whole:

> Therefore: the "unegoistic," sacrificial, imprudent is nothing special — it is common to all urges — they do not think of the advantage of the whole *ego* (*because they do not think!*); they act against our advantage, against the *ego*: and often *for* the *ego* — innocent in both! [62]

Such intelligent adaptation as our impulses now have has been bred into them under conditions of group life; hence "clannishness [*Gemeinsucht*] is older than selfishness," and social impulses outweigh individual ones.[63]

From this point of view Nietzsche complains of the weakness and stupidity of ordinary egoism, especially in his own day:

> When an age, a people, a city stands out, it is always the case that its *egoism* becomes self-conscious and no longer shrinks from any means (is *no longer ashamed* of itself).... On the other hand to glorify selflessness! And admit, as Kant does, that

[61] VII 186 f. Cf. 355 ff., 380 f., 384; IV 25 f., 36 f., 75 ff., 110 ff.; VIII 136; XII 87 ff.; XVI 228 f., 268 f. Nietzsche's attitude to cruelty cannot be understood apart from his belief, in opposition to hedonistic assumptions, that suffering may be a positive constituent of intrinsic value as well as a means to it — an index of force and a condition of heightened experience: see below, pp. 308 ff., and above, p. 117, note 8.
[62] XV 407. Cf. XVI 323 f.
[63] XIII 213 f., 187; XII 114 ff.

a deed of it has probably *never* been done! So merely in order
to disparage the opposite principle, to depress its value, to pre-
dispose men to be cold and contemptuous, therefore *intellectually lazy*, about egoism! — For so far it has been the *lack* of fine,
carefully planned egoism which keeps men, on the whole, at
such a low level! [64]

Therefore Nietzsche approves both the lofty self-esteem of
the Greek philosophers and the egoism of the aristocrat
who accepts the sacrifices of others without question.[65] He
wishes to free men of the bad conscience about egoism in-
duced by the old morality; to encourage them to undertake
that "rigorous selfishness" which is the most fundamental
condition of thriving life.[66]

However, Nietzsche does not favor such selfishness for
everyone, at least not to the same degree. All depends on
the kind of ego:

Egoism is worth as much as he who has it is worth physiologically.

Every individual is the entire line of evolution to date (and
not merely, as morality conceives him, something that begins
with birth). If he represents the *ascent* of the line "Man," his
value is in fact extraordinary; and care for the preservation and
encouragement of his growth may legitimately be extreme. (It
is the care for the future promised in him, which gives the
well bred [*wohlgeratnen*] individual such an extraordinary
right to egoism.) If he represents the *declining* line . . . then he
has little value: and the first demand of justice is that he take
as little room, force and sunshine from the well bred as possible.
In this case society has the duty of *suppressing egoism* . . . .

For such purposes, the passage continues, a religion of love
may be useful.[67]

<hr/>

[64] XII 118. Cf. IV 99; XV 405; L. Ge. 6/4/67; L.S. 11/83. During his enthusiasm
for Schopenhauer, Nietzsche occasionally espouses the ideal of selflessness, but
in the same period he expresses the view destined to remain his own (L.D.
2/6/68; L.Ge. 6/4/67).

[65] X 45; VII 251 f.

[66] IV 152; XV 124; XIII 111; VIII 142 f.; V 132. Cf. V 248. Nietzsche illustrates the "casuistry of selfishness," in this sense, in his autobiography (XV 43 f.,
46).   [67] XV 408. Cf. 405; XVI 145, 151, 216; VIII 140 f.; XI 231; XIV 63.

The rhythm of the will to power gives us a clue to the two forms of egoism which Nietzsche approves. Self-development — "getting" — leads to "spending":

> You force all things to you and into you, in order that they shall flow back from your spring as the gifts of your love.
> Truly, such lavishing love must become a robber of all values; but I call this selfishness sound and sacred.

At the same time, he regards *Katzen-Egoismus*, a desire for petty self-enjoyment, as the most repulsive of human traits. So he discriminates between *kinds* of acquisitive egoism:

> There is another selfishness, a too poor, a hungry one which wants to steal forever, that selfishness of the sick, the sickly selfishness.

> Tell me, my brothers: what do we consider bad [*Schlechtes*] and worst? Is it not *degeneracy*? — And we always suspect degeneracy where a lavishing soul is lacking.
> Upwards goes our road, from the species across to the super-species. But the degenerating heart which says, "Everything for me," is abhorrent to us.[68]

On similar grounds he condemns the usual love of one's neighbor as bad love of self, which sacrifices the future to the present, and he enjoins love of the most distant possibilities of man (*Fernstenliebe*) instead.[69]

He finds in pregnancy the type of his ideal selfishness: self-nurture for the sake of something growing within, which we hope will be greater than we are.[70] This leads to the second pulse in the rhythm of life. In some kinds of love, in creative work, in heroism, there is no self-*seeking*: rather there is self-giving, "lavish virtue [*schenkende Tugend*]." [71]

---

[68] VI 110 f. Cf. I 446 f.; drafts of letters to Lou Salomé and Paul Reé, *Ges. Briefe* V 502 f., 506.

[69] VI 88 f. Cf. XV 323 f.

[70] IV 361 f. Cf. VI 236.

[71] XV 361; XIII 178; XVI 245; VI 94, 109 ff., 278; *Ges. Briefe* V 506. Cf. XII 252. In view of certain remarks which contrast those who merely *produce* and those who *are*, and a similar distinction between the "hero" and the "god"

But this is egoistic in the sense that we are *using* power, are impressing *our* shape, our ideal on men and things. So Zarathustra's conception of virtue is "that *your* self be in the action, as the mother is in the child." [72] We may give in the most tactful, secret, and least coercive manner, but it is none the less power.[73] Common people misinterpret the egoism of great men as unselfishness, because they do not understand "the urge of the artist toward his material." [74] Moreover this second form of egoism presupposes the first — "only the *most entire* persons can love":

> "Selflessness" has no value in heaven or earth; the great problems all demand *great love*, and of this only strong, round, secure minds, which are firmly seated in themselves, are capable.[75]

As in the case of acquisitive selfishness, here too Nietzsche distinguishes between good and bad types. Good love comes from self-abundance; bad love expresses inner misery — we run to others in order to escape from ourselves. So Nietzsche concludes that we cannot love others rightly unless we love ourselves, and he adds that the converse is also true.[76]

5. THE VALUE OF EVIL

We are now prepared to consider his defense of evil in more general terms. His praise of the "evil man" is the counterpart of his satire on the "good man." He finds "The good people almost worthless now. The *evil ones with religious will* are those who count! And it was ever so!" [77]

To interpret this paradox, let us recall that Nietzsche recognizes two important types of negative value: "evil,"

(XVI 331, 328), Nietzsche probably has in mind a yet loftier egoism than the heroic, namely the godlike (cf. XIV 147; L.S. 11/83).

[72] VI 139. Cf. XIII 177; XVI 203, 376; L.S. 11/83; L.M. 8/83.

[73] IV 304 f. Cf. 313.

[74] XVI 292, 343. Cf. VII 173 f.

[75] XV 361; V 276. Cf. XV 57; XVI 324, 446.

[76] IV 336, 358; VI 282; L.G. 18/7/80. Cf. IV 170 f.

[77] XIV 316. Cf. 100.

the slaves' valuation of fearful traits, and "worthless," the aristocrats' valuation of things that call for contempt. He insists that the two notions be kept distinct: "You shall not couple the contemptible man together with the fearful man, by a word." [78] Now it is precisely the fearful qualities of man, previously called "evil," which Nietzsche intends to revalue. He believes them far more important than those hitherto held up as the ideal of goodness.[79]

He explains this position in part by his theory of sublimation, as his remarks about cruelty hinted. To try to extirpate man's wild passions is unnecessary and wasteful; they can be mastered and used: everything fearful can be made fruitful.[80] Indeed, they are absolutely essential to high achievement because they are the greatest sources of energy, and because they alone can give force to the more amiable or spiritual qualities:

In the most lauded actions and characters, murder, theft, cruelty, dissimulation are present as necessary elements of force.

Even for knowing, I need all my impulses, the good as well as the bad, and should soon be at an end, were I not willing to be hostile, distrustful, cruel, treacherous, vengeful and feigning, etc., toward things.[81]

Nietzsche applies the same principle on a historic scale. All higher cultures begin with barbarism, which releases the frightful energy of "evil" passions, and when they become tired with over-cultivation they must again resort to barbarism to stir up fresh forces.[82] A society in which rivalry and strong passions are rife, rather than a tame one, is most apt to kindle the spark of genius.[83] And the dialectical evolution of values requires the "evil" man as an innovator.

[78] XII 262.
[79] XV 63 f., 120. Cf. VI 212 f.
[80] XV 418 f.; XVI 375 f.; IV 365 f.; VI 50. Cf. III 223, 231, 239.
[81] XII 87, 86 f. Cf. 266; VI 319, 420; XIII 146 f.; XVI 222, 310.
[82] II 227 f., 231, 355 f.; III 295. Cf. V 41; XVI 148.
[83] II 219 ff.

Nietzsche goes even further. He extols dangerous urges not only for their effects on the "good" qualities, "but for their own sake, as the mightier, more fertile, *truer* aspects of existence, in which its will is more plainly expressed."[84]

Having rejected absolute antitheses in ethics, Nietzsche does not fall into the trap of substituting a new absolute for an old one. He does not call "evil" unconditionally good, nor does he hold that "good" qualities should be abolished. Rather he distinguishes between "the evil of weakness" and "the evil of power" — only the latter is now to be called good.[85] And instead of renouncing "goodness," man should become better *and* more evil[86] — possibly an allusion to the Apollinian and Dionysian dimensions of power. The greatest evil goes with the greatest goodness:

> The mightiest man, the creator, would have to be the most evil, inasmuch as he carries through his ideal in all men *against* all their ideals, and remoulds them to his own image. "Evil" here means "hard," "painful," "coercive."[87]

The whole position culminates in Nietzsche's conception of "the Great Economy" which uses all the forces in nature.[88] Even weakness has its place.[89] Nietzsche does not wish to destroy the Christian ideal and its kin, but only to end their tyranny and make room for more robust ideals; he will need their rivalry to maintain his own strength:

> We do not easily deny, we seek our honor in being affirmers. More and more we have come to perceive that economy which uses, and knows how to turn to advantage, all that which the holy insanity of the priest, of the *diseased* reason in the priest, condemns; for that economy in the law of life which derives its profit even from the repulsive species of bigot, priest, virtuous

[84] XVI 383. Cf. XV 63 f.; I 57 f.
[85] XII 92. Cf. IV 274. Compare the similar distinction between kinds of cruelty (XIV 82).
[86] XVI 221, 296, 344 f., 368 f., 377; VI 59, 319, 420. Cf. XIII 147.
[87] XVI 376. Cf. VI 169.
[88] V 33 f.; XII 86 f.; XV 63, 357; XVI 324.
[89] XV 433.

person — *what* profit? — But we ourselves, we immoralists, are the answer here . . .[90]

Pity too has its value; to be altogether without it is to be "sick in mind and body." Not pity as such but the excess of it, and on the part of weaklings who cannot restrain themselves, is the object of Nietzsche's attack. He says that the pity of hard, warrior souls has worth, and that his own compassion is for lost human capacities, above all for those future possibilities of man threatened today by the very religion of pity.[91]

6. MORALITY FOR VITALITY

The idea of "the Great Economy" is not intended to obliterate all distinctions of value. Nietzsche simply protests against *unconditional* valuations: "Morality, in so far as it *condemns* absolutely [*an sich*], *not* out of regards, considerations, intentions of life, is an idiosyncrasy of degenerates . . . ." [92] His denial of Absolute Morality is, then, by implication an affirmation of morality that is relative — to life. With this we pass to the positive phase of his ethics, for his relativism is constructive, not sceptical merely: he holds it just as childish to infer the invalidity (*Unverbindlichkeit*) of all morals from the necessary diversity of moral judgments, as to argue for the absolute validity of a single morality from an alleged consensus of all the "tame" peoples.[93]

Of the five essential features of Absolute Morality, he has now disposed of guilt, pity and selflessness, and absolute antitheses of value. He rejects the other two — unconditional status and universal validity — by asserting that morals should serve life, and that various moralities are required to fit its varied forms. This is the meaning of his

[90] VIII 90. Cf. 86; XV 120, 403 f.; IV 183.
[91] XII 296 f.; VII 180 f., 269 f.; VI 82; IV 168 f.; II 165; XV 406.
[92] VIII 90. Cf. XV 358 f., 362 f.; XVI 222 f.
[93] V 277 f.

"moralistic naturalism" or "restoration of nature in morals";
moral values are to be dethroned: so long sovereign, seemingly emancipated from life, even condemning it, they shall
now be subordinated to its enhancement.[94]

In a sense Nietzsche's "return to nature" reverses the trend
toward "denaturalization." Yet he means not a literal "return," but a "rise" to a kind of naturalness which has never
existed in the past — notably a recognition that life is naturally "immoral" and makes free use of moralities for its own
ends, as did Napoleon.[95]

Here Nietzsche addresses his philosophy, not to all, but
to the few who have become free from the shackles of the
old morality, and are no longer afraid or ashamed of their
own instincts. Such freedom, however, has to be won, not
just taken, and is therefore only for heirs of the old discipline: "freedom of spirit" is for "ennobled men only." [96]
Contrary to popular impression, this is no ethics for liber-
tines: "The *blind disposition to yield* to a passion, quite
indifferently whether it is a generous and compassionate
or a hostile one, is the cause of the *greatest mischiefs*
[*Übel*]." [97]

In this respect, Nietzsche gives much credit to Christian
morality. It over-tamed man, but it tamed him. Its fundamental "errors" mitigated the destructiveness of his passions; "the beast in us has to be *lied to* — morality is an
emergency fib." Also, the "errors" have ennobled man and
raised him above the animal level, by causing him to think
of himself as a creature of another order, and to impose on
himself, therefore, more rigorous laws.[98]

So Nietzsche's attack on Christian values asserts, not that

[94] XV 363, 249, 291; XVI 363, 458.
[95] VIII 161; XIV 310; XV 228 f., 363, 379.
[96] III 372; XIV 419 f.; V 205. Cf. VI 61. See note 68. Here also, Nietzsche's
"naturalism" is not so much a "return" as a "rise" (cf. X 279).
[97] XVI 323.
[98] XIII 204; II 65 f.; III 198 f., 371; IV 293; V 155 f.; XI 238; XV 316 ff., 340;
XVI 288 f. Cf. VIII 84.

they have been an utter misfortune, but that we have outgrown them, and that further submission would be disastrous:

Deepest gratitude for what morality has done hitherto: but
now only a burden which would become a catastrophe!

. . . all moralities till now were useful for giving the species
absolute stability [*Haltbarkeit*] *first: when* this is achieved the
goal can be taken higher.[99]

Thus the most adequate perspective of Nietzsche's ethics
is historical; he is destroying the old to initiate a new stage
in the dialectical evolution of values, but the new stage
grows out of the old and builds upon it.

By subordinating morals to life, he gives his ethics a
frankly purposive basis: moral rules are to be justified only
in terms of the vital values they produce. The "only meaning of virtue" is "means for the preservation and enhancement of a particular kind of man." [100] So moral imperatives
are not "categorical" but "hypothetical":

I consider *all* moralities till now as built upon *hypotheses*
about means for preserving a *type* — but the temper of the
mind, till now, was still too weak and uncertain of itself to take
a hypothesis *as* hypothesis and yet as regulative — there was need
of *faith*.[101]

For faith, Nietzsche substitutes will, which sets a goal
and holds fast to self-dictated laws as a means of attaining
it.[102] He believes that the moral discipline of past ages has
trained such a will in a few individuals — a dependability
and self-control which enables them to keep a firm resolve.
Such is the meaning which he adopts for "responsibility"

[99] XV 434; XIV 261 f. See above, p. 147, note 27.
[100] XV 271. On the dependence of moral principles upon ends see further:
V 158 f.; XII 124 f.; XI 45, 192, 213, 373; III 213; IV 103.
[101] XIII 139. Cf. VII 118.
[102] XIV 319, 333, 209; XVI 295. Cf. XIII 54 f.; VII 137 f.; XVI 342.

and "conscience." Of the "autonomous supermoral individual" he says:

> The proud knowledge about the extraordinary privilege of
> *responsibility*, the consciousness of this rare freedom, this power
> over self and fate, has sunk down in him to his lowest depth
> and become instinct, the commanding instinct . . . . This sover-
> eign man calls it his *conscience* . . .[103]

Conscience in the new sense, then, is strength — "length" —
of will.

He reinterprets moral obligation likewise. "There are
no objective obligations . . . . There are commands of individuals: an unconscious slavery." [104] "Duty," for the elite
at least, consists in self-dictated means for the attainment of
self-chosen ends:

> Such as we are — we become rebellious under a "thou shalt."
> Our morality must be called, "I will."

> It is the time of the vow-takers: — *free* pledges of fidelity in
> favor of some virtue: not because this virtue commands, but
> because I command it to myself.[105]

Having described "responsibility" or moral autonomy as a
rare privilege, Nietzsche probably expects that duty will
continue to mean "thou shalt" for the masses, and will be
in fact the "command" of some external authority.[106]

7. ETHICAL PLURALISM

Nietzsche challenges the old morality most radically with
his principle of gradation (*Rangordnung*). He roundly
denies that all men are equal: they form a vast scale of
differences in degree and kind of power (therefore value),

---

[103] VII 347. Cf. 345 f.; XV 469 f.; XVI 409. For similar uses of "responsibility"
or "conscience" cf. III 8; IV 155, 248; VII 85, 138, 163, 180; XV 47. There is a
kindred notion in his demand for integrity in art; see below, pp. 218, 226 ff.
[104] XIV 309. Cf. XIII 150.
[105] XIII 217. Cf. XVI 313; XIV 320, 333; IV 103; XV 337; XII 393 f., 404, 411.
[106] Cf. VII 85 ff., 129 f.; XIII 216, 221 f.; XII 273; XV 236 f.

with corresponding differences in rights and duties. Therefore no single morality is valid for all. Against utilitarianism he maintains:

... that the "general welfare" is no ideal, no goal, no concept intelligible in any manner, but only an emetic — that what is fair for one by no means *can* be fair for another, that the requirement of one morality for all is an injury precisely to the superior men; in short that there is a *gradation* between man and man, hence also between morality and morality.[107]

From this position he opposes collectivism *and* individualism, for both these forms of Flock Morality treat all men as equals:

My philosophy is aimed at *gradation*: *not* at an individualistic ethic. Let the will [*Sinn*] of the flock rule in the flock — but not grasp out beyond it: the leaders of the flock need a fundamentally different valuation of their own actions; likewise the independents, or the "beasts of prey," etc.[108]

Nietzsche holds, therefore, that duties should vary according to the sort of life concerned, and that this is not a merely quantitative difference of more and less, but one of kind. To the Kantian theory of universalized duty he replies:

The reverse is commanded by the profoundest laws of conservation and growth: that each invent *his* virtue, *his* categorical imperative. A people perishes if it confuses *its* duty with the concept of duty in general. Nothing ruins more deeply, inwardly, than every "impersonal" duty, every sacrifice to the Moloch of abstraction.[109]

He advocates, instead, that each human type be allowed that philosophy which suits it best:

If one considers how a philosophic total justification of his manner of living and thinking affects every individual — namely

[107] VII 185. Cf. 50, 135 f., 174 f., 260; XVI 277 f., 375; VIII 162; XIV 57 f.; IV 161 f., 185; L.G. 3/8/83. For early hints cf. H.K.A. II 23, 129, 167.
[108] XV 354. Cf. 232; XIV 68; XVI 195, 213 ff., 278, 298 f.; XI 141; VII 135 f.
[109] VIII 226. Cf. 48; V 158 f.; XV 377; VI 49, 136 f.; VII 413 f.; IV 362 f.

like a warming, blessing, fructifying sun, shining expressly for him; how it makes independent of praise and blame, self-sufficient, rich, generous with happiness and good will; how it unceasingly recreates evil into good, brings all forces to blossoming and ripening, and does not allow the little and big weeds of grief and vexation to take root at all: — then at last one cries out with longing: "Oh, that many more such new suns were created! Even the evil, even the unfortunate, even the exceptional man shall have his philosophy, his good right, his sunshine! . . . ." [110]

Rights are likewise unequal and different in kind, according to the human nature involved:

The order of castes, the *order of rank*, merely formulates the chief law of life itself . . . for the preservation of society, for making possible higher and highest types — the *inequality* of rights is the condition for the existence of rights at all. — A right is a prerogative. In his manner of being [*seiner Art Sein*] each person has his prerogative as well. [111]

And since, for Nietzsche, both rights and responsibilities are related to a man's human "size," they increase together. [112]

Apparently Nietzsche means the foregoing doctrine to apply only within some limited society, for he denies that there are any "natural" rights or "rights of man." He defines rights as "recognized and guaranteed grades of power." They arise by agreement, either as contracts between approximate equals or as the grant of a higher power; so they presuppose a certain equilibrium of power, tend to maintain it, and change or dissolve as it does. [113] He insists that a legal order is not an end but a means in the service of life's will to power — creating larger power-units and sparing fruitless strife. Outside such a contractual order, the aggres-

[110] V 218 f. Cf. IV 161 f., 166, 314 f.
[111] VIII 302 f. Cf. VII 136. For other passages which base rights on the nature of the possessor cf. XV 408; IV 238; V 314; VII 63, 165 f.; XIV 58 f., 411; XVI 278; XIII 143.
[112] Cf. VIII 303; XVI 291; XI 119.
[113] IV 107 ff., 264, 301; III 208, 213, 217, 224, 328, 390 f.; XI 143; II 93 ff., 331; XVI 179; XII 105.

sion of the strong and the self-defense of the weak are neither
rights nor wrongs but simply facts; and the dream of a universal order which shall abolish *all* conflict is hostile to
life, "a sign of weariness, a hidden path to nothingness." [114]
A man, *merely* as such, has no more "right" to work, happiness or existence than a worm.[115]

Correspondingly, by "wrong" Nietzsche means "breach
of contract," an action "unworthy of the presupposed
equality of sentiments." [116] Having rejected the traditional
notion of guilt, he retains praise and blame, reward and
punishment only as means for moulding human nature
toward an ideal.[117] Since all actions are innocent, he would
cleanse punishment of the ideas of purification and retribu-
tion, with their accompanying emotions, shame and contempt. One should not punish single actions by themselves,
for they are seldom typical of the person behind them, but
once a man has proved himself unworthy of his rights, he
should be punished by demotion to a lower social grade.
Criminals who are not hopeless parasites should be given
opportunity to make up for their misdeeds by some noble
actions, perhaps self-dictated, such as submitting to a risky
medical experiment; by being socially useful, they could
regain self-respect.[118]

8. MEANS TO MIGHT

Since moralities are to enhance life, Nietzsche employs
his own theories of life and human nature for a better un-

[114] VII 368 f., 237 f.; III 213, 216; XVI 179; XIII 198; XII 273. Nietzsche's
language in the passages cited in note 111 sometimes suggests a non-contractual
theory which would base rights on the intrinsic value of the individual concerned. From this point of view the contract theory would have either to be
condemned as inconsistent or regarded merely as a theory of positive law. The
link between the two is the power standard of value, which makes it difficult
to be sure when Nietzsche is describing and when he is prescribing.
[115] XVI 197, 291 f.; IX 164.
[116] XIII 189. Cf. XVI 186.　　　　　　[117] XIII 137, 143, 193, 197 f., 221 f.
[118] XVI 187 ff.; XIII 189 ff., 200 f.; XV 315 f.; VI 52 ff., 100; XI 40 f.; XII
368; IV 176 f., 195 ff. Cf. III 292 f., 295.

derstanding of ends and means. Against the traditional moralist's exclusive concern with mind, reason, and consciousness, he emphasizes the body, instinct, and heredity — a further revaluation of values. If consciousness has little to do with the origins of action, if unconscious urges are the prime movers of man, and if these become efficient in proportion to the accumulation of instinctive skills, then clearly it is with them and for them that one must work, if life is to ascend to its highest goals.

Much of his criticism of Socratic rationalism and Lutheran protestantism follows from this position. He calls Luther's insistence upon faith instead of works "Christian dilettantism." Works produce faith — i.e. disposition, valuation, *Gesinnung* — not conversely. "One must practise, *not* the intensification of value-feelings, but doing; one must first *be able to do* something . . ."[119] Socrates' doctrine, "Virtue is knowledge," is no better. By itself, right knowledge cannot produce right action; nor can it transform our nature: our nature decides what we shall accept as "knowledge." [120]

Nietzsche further argues that since consciousness expresses maladjustment and interferes with instinct, unconsciousness is necessary for perfection in life.[121] To adopt consciousness as the basis of conduct is to condemn life to pretense (*Schauspielerei*) — this explains why plain people have outdone philosophers in practice.[122] Socrates' demand for "rationality at any price" is both a symptom and an instrument of decadence: the need to make a tyrant of reason indicates disintegration of instinct, and the ruthless use of dialectical analysis — putting our dark impulses in a "perpetual daylight of consciousness" — increases disintegration. Asking for reasons upsets the unconscious sureness of instinct, and awareness of alternatives causes hesitation; any stable pros-

[119] XV 282 f. Cf. IV 29 f.; XII 137 f.
[120] IV 30, 117; XVI 129; XIII 98, 307; L.D. 2/70.
[121] XV 194, 356, 458, 464, 469 f.; VIII 301.
[122] XV 463 f., 193 f., 356, 412.

perity of life requires that some things be undiscussable; analysis kills; abstraction ignores historic individuality; knowledge exposes the inevitable illusions and injustices of any life whatsoever: these are Nietzsche's objections to radical rationalism in ethics.[123]

Therefore "the desire for a *reasoning virtue* is not reasonable," he concludes; [124] so he reverses the Socratic relation of virtue and happiness:

> ... *first* example of my "revaluation of all values": a well bred [*wohlgeratener*] man, a "happy" one, *must* do certain acts and instinctively shrinks from other acts; he carries the order which he represents physiologically into his relations with men and things. In formula: his virtue is the *result* of his happiness .... Every mistake in every sense is the result of degeneration of instinct, of disintegration of will: that almost defines the *worthless* [*Schlechte*]. Everything *good* is instinct — and therefore easy, inevitable, free.[125]

For Nietzsche, virtue means not good intention but power, ability (*Tüchtigkeit*), Renaissance *virtù*.[126]

This explains why the Extra-moral Period will place decisive value on the unintentional and unconscious origins of actions.[127] Since it will judge particular actions neither by their conscious motives nor by their consequences, it will break with "formalism" and utilitarianism in ethics. Nietzsche objects to utilitarianism in the sense of basing conduct upon a *conscious calculation* of results, partly because we cannot know all the possibly important results, and partly on the grounds just urged against rationalism

---

[123] VIII 72 ff., 38 f., 153, 226, 246; II 211, 215, 218, 364; VII 121; XV 235, 343, 412, 449, 458 f., 461 f.; I 93 ff., 160 f., 293 f., 339, 341 f. Cf. X 22, 183; H.K.A. III 321 or L.F.N. I 332. On abstraction see also note 153. The dominance of "reason" in the seventeenth century (Descartes) had a different meaning (XV 209). The destructiveness of reason is no ground for renouncing it altogether (cf. VI 151 f.; VII 186 f.): Nietzsche is protesting against reason as tyrant.

[124] XV 469.

[125] VIII 92 f. Cf. XVI 164; XV 382 f.

[126] XV 373 f., 378; VIII 218; XVI 188.

[127] VII 52 f.

generally: true virtue is instinctive, a "noble madness," and has a fine scorn for reasons and opportunism; prudence (*Klugheit*) is Slave Morality.[128]

Nietzsche would regard actions as symptoms of "physiological values," i.e. of a grade of life. Because heredity is cumulative, the individual is not merely something that begins with birth, but an entire strand of life with the tasks of all the future before it:

> The decisive factor lies *behind* "intentionality" [*Absichtlichkeit*]. One will never be justified in isolating the individual. "Here," one must say, "is a growth with such and such a previous history." [129]

Nietzsche holds that actions are ambiguous and unfathomable; some are "epidermal," others deep; some are unworthy of us, and of some we are unworthy. Hence we cannot know enough of their vital sources to estimate their worth, and he discourages brooding about their "moral value." [130] He urges instead that we revise our opinions and valuations and live for a long time according to one morality, by way of experiment.[131]

This experimental phase of his ethics grants something to reason and utility; one might call it "long range utilitarianism." We are deeply ignorant of the best means for enhancing life, he believes. In fact, morality has discouraged inquiry concerning natural causes.[132] Man has yet unexhausted possibilities. He must ransack history for light on the conditions under which he grows best, frame hy-

[128] XV 357, 373 f., 449, 461; XII 95; VII 319; XVI 285 f., 320; VIII 63; XIII 152. Cf. VII 121; XIII 135; XI 204; XV 27.
[129] XIII 133. Cf. XV 357 f., 408, 414; XVI 145, 151, 216; VIII 141.
[130] VII 266; XIII 214, 281; XV 315 f., 359; XVI 188; V 257. Cf. IV 117, 124, 127; V 204; XI 287 f., 290 f.; XII 124.
[131] V 257; XIII 97.
[132] IV 28, 39; XV 249 f. Cf. VI 295; VII 294, 338 n.; XIII 118. Nietzsche welcomes the use of the natural and social sciences for the solution of this problem — they alone can supply "building stones" for the construction of the new ideal — but he believes that they are not yet ready to give conclusive results (IV 307).

potheses accordingly, and live long enough under each to
test it adequately by its fruits:

Instead of faith, which is no longer possible for us, let us set
above us, as heuristic principle, a strong *will*, which adheres to
a provisional series of basic valuations [*Grundschätzungen*]:
in order to see *how far* one can get with it. Like the mariner
on an unknown sea. In truth all that "faith" was nothing else:
only the *discipline of the spirit* was too slight, formerly, to be
able to endure our *magnificent foresight*.[133]

This resolute continuity distinguishes Nietzsche's view from
ordinary "experimentalism" in morals. And he does not
believe that such research should last indefinitely. With the
breakdown of the old morality we are living in a kind of
moral interregnum when experiment is necessary and appropriate.[134] But after a great variety of experiments, the results can be harvested only if we cease experimenting. Then,
under an authoritative code, the ways of living which experience has proved best can be converted into instinct.[135]

In order to think more justly about morals, Nietzsche
would substitute for it "two zoological concepts": "*taming*
the beast and *training a definite species*." [136] Christian
morality, we have seen, had value as a means of taming,
but it threatens to tame too much. Moreover only barbarians and decadents need such extreme measures. For
us, it is stupid to try to kill the wilder passions root and
branch; we can afford to try giving them freer rein. Nietzsche says:

I measure by the extent to which a man, a people, can un-
chain the most fearful urges in itself and, instead of perishing
from them, turn them to its welfare: to fruitfulness in deed
and work.[137]

[133] XIV 319. Cf. VII 64 f., 137 ff.; IV 162; XV 337; XIII 54 f., 139, 175 f.; XII
191.
[134] IV 307 f.   [135] VIII 299 ff. Cf. 150 f.; V 296 ff.
[136] XV 428. Cf. VIII 103; XIII 204; XIV 90 f.
[137] XIII 122. Cf. 123 f.; VIII 85; XVI 289, 324 f., 375 f.; XV 316 f., 418 f.;
III 223.

Accordingly he advocates moralities which *train* — too often confused with those which tame. Taming means weakening, often sickening; training is strengthening:

> Training is . . . a means to the tremendous storage of power in humanity, so that the generations can build further on the work of their forefathers — not only externally but inwardly, growing organically out of them, into *greater strength* . . .[138]

Master Morality is Nietzsche's prime illustration of training technique: a severe discipline, self-imposed, enduring for ages. Hence his general support of the master type: "Beyond good and evil" "means at least *not* 'Beyond good and worthless.' "[139] This insistence upon the value of stiff discipline is a further difference from ordinary utilitarianism:

> Every morality, in contrast to *laisser aller*, is a piece of tyranny against "nature," also against "reason" . . . . The essential and invaluable thing in every morality is that it is a long restraint [*Zwang*]: in order to understand Stoicism or Port-Royal or Puritanism, let one remember the restraint under which every language so far has attained strength and freedom — the restraint of metre . . . . — "For the sake of foolishness," as utilitarian boors say, who think themselves clever for it . . . . But the strange facts of the case are, that all there is on earth of freedom, subtlety, daring, dance and masterly sureness . . . has first developed by reason of the "tyranny of such arbitrary laws" . . . . Let one examine every morality on the point: it is the "nature" therein . . . which teaches the *narrowing of perspectives*, and hence, in a certain sense, stupidity, as a condition of life and growth. "Thou shalt obey, someone, and for long: else thou wilt go to ruin and lose the last respect for thyself" — this seems to me to be the moral imperative of nature, which to be sure is neither "categorical" . . . nor addressed to the individual . . . but rather to peoples, races, epochs . . . .[140]

---

[138] XV 429. Cf. XVI 358; VIII 103 ff.
[139] VII 338. Cf. 246 f.; XIV 76 f.; VIII 218.
[140] VII 116 ff. Cf. XVI 312; IV 24; XIII 310 f.

An effective discipline, of course, must concern bodily action:

Good things are immoderately expensive: and the law always holds, that he who *has* them is other than he who *earns* them. All good is a heritage: what is not inherited is imperfect, is a beginning.... Now let us make no mistake here about methodology: a mere cultivation [*Zucht*] of feelings and thoughts is almost nil....: one must persuade the *body* first. The strict maintenance of significant and choice demeanor, an obligation to live only with men who do not "indulge themselves," is perfectly sufficient for becoming significant and choice: in two, three generations everything is already *made inward* [*verinnerlicht*].[141]

Of a piece with this is Nietzsche's demand that we again become "good neighbors of the nearest things," i.e. take matters of diet and bodily health more seriously than the hollow "idealism" which has so long taught us to despise the physical.[142]

Since he regards all moralities as a "sign-language of the affects," he hardly claims to start a new one by argument:

Do *not* make men "better," do *not* talk morals to them in any manner, as if "absolute [*an sich*] morality," or an ideal type of man in general, were given: but *produce conditions* under which *stronger men are necessary*, who in turn will need, and therefore *have*, a morality (plainer: a *bodily and mental discipline*) *which strengthens!* [143]

No revaluation of values can take effect unless it finds energies clamoring for release.[144] So we meet the ultimate irrationality of moral judgments: "With regard to the strongest urge, which ultimately regulates our morality, we must give up the question 'Why?' " [145]

---

[141] VIII 160 f. Cf. XV 445.

[142] III 191 ff., 202 f. 359; XV 26 ff., 46. On the superior importance of body over mind in morals, see further: XIII 167, 175 f.; XIV 317 f.; VI 46 f.

[143] XVI 352. Cf. 335. Danger is "the mother of morals" (VII 248, 246; XIV 76 f.).

[144] XVI 363.   [145] XI 201. Cf. 200, 220 f.; VII 121 f.; XII 95 f.

9. MORALS FOR INDIVIDUALS

Since Nietzsche contrasts his principle of gradation with both individualistic and collectivist philosophies, the individualism in his thought is rather special. He objects to ordinary democratic individualism because of the *quality* of *men* it produces: it is converting humanity into "sand" — smooth, equalized, sterile pebbles, "individuals without individuality": a petty vanity of each, which is opposed alike to the development of strong individuality and to the submerging of it in a great type, like the Jesuits or the Greek city-state.[146]

His power standard implies that *genuine* individuals are the supreme ends:

...it would be extraordinarily dangerous to believe that humanity as a *whole* would continue to grow and become stronger while the individuals become flabby, equal, average . . . Humanity is an abstraction . . . .

Herds and states are the highest organisms familiar to us — very imperfect. *After* [*hinter*] the state there at last arises the human individual, the highest and *most imperfect* being, who perishes *as a rule* and ruins the organizations out of which he arises. The entire *curriculum* [*Pensum*] of the urges of herd and state is concentrated in his core. He can live alone, by laws of his own — he is *not* a lawgiver and *does not want* to rule. His *feeling of power* strikes *inward*. The Socratic *virtues!* [147]

So for Nietzsche, these select individuals alone can give meaning to life: societies are at best means to these, not superior ends in themselves.[148] For this reason he opposes nationalism and socialism:

[146] XVI 213 f.; IV 170 f.; XI 237; XIX 388. Cf. I 422 f.; X 277 ff. Nietzsche objects to the ethic of altruism because it tends to pale and blur individuality (IV 135, 169 ff.; XI 230, 233 f., 237). He proposes that we substitute "joy in others" for "love of others," i.e. that we encourage them to develop their own natures, not force a common nature upon them in the guise of altruism (XI 247, 240, 242, 244; XII 125).   [147] XV 429; XII 113. Cf. XVI 171; XI 251.
[148] XVI 203, 127; XV 341 f.; X 230 f., 276, 309 f., 323, 384 f.; XI 142; I 364, 367 f., 411 f., 439 f., 442 ff., 464; V 65.

In the functional spirit, philosophers are now considering how to turn humanity into *one* organism — it is the opposite of *my* tendency: *as many, changing, diversified* organisms *as possible*, which, having come to their *maturity and corruption*, drop their fruit: the individuals — of whom indeed the majority perish — but it is a question of the few.[149]

But during the Pre-Moral Period man was submerged in his group, and he has remained for the most part a group animal in whom the social urges preponderate, a carrier of one or more types rather than a *person*.[150] True "individuals" arise in the autumn of a people, when the rigor of group morals relaxes and the energy stored up through generations of discipline can explode in a riot of variation — "the individual dares to be individual and to detach himself." These men are an "extract of the folk," inheriting the experiences, judgments, and urges of the parental society within which they grew. For this reason Nietzsche calls them the "fruit" or "eggs" of the social organism: they are both the product for the sake of which the people existed, and "seed carriers of the future," from which new societies may grow.[151] His individualism, then, is limited in several ways: it is for a select few; for ripe products of a tradition, not savages; and only for those who can be a law unto themselves and achieve a personal goal which justifies emancipation from the flock.[152]

When an "individual" drops from his parent tree, he faces a new problem: his instinctive equipment, developed by group life, is ill-adapted to individual living; he must re-shape it to perform the essential functions of life in and

---

[149] XII 204 f. The passage continues to the effect that socialism is really a ferment which will lead to a multitude of state organisms and "eggs" (in other words socialism will produce results opposite to its intentions).

[150] XII 113 ff.; X 348; XVI 298 f.; V 156 f., 174 f.; XIII 187, 213 f.; XV 375. Nietzsche commonly uses *Individuum* for this distinctive sense (cf. VII 247 f.; II 261, 348; V 56 f.; XI 240; XVI 204), but not always (cf. X 194 f.; IV 198; XVI 173, 213).

[151] V 64 ff., 178; VII 247 f.; IX 243; XI 235 ff.; XII 110 ff.; XVI 206. Cf. XI 251. XVIII 191 f. gives an early hint.

[152] On the last point: VI 91 ff.

for himself, or else perish. Most do perish. And at this point moral philosophers usually arise to preach a conceptualized version of the old group morality. That spells mediocrity: abstract patterns of virtue teach men to neglect what is most individual — therefore, in this case, most valuable — in themselves.[153]

In opposition to all past moral philosophy and moral codes, which he regards as variants of group morality, Nietzsche devotes his best energies to the problem nearest his heart: *Individual* Moralities. Each is to enable one man to attain "stylized individuality" by creating and realizing a strictly personal ideal.[154]

Solitude is painful, and it kills those it does not heal, but an individual must endure it for a time if he is to learn independence.[155] Through it he can readapt his group urges to fit his peculiar needs:

> ... in himself he has to *suffer to the end* the after-effects of the social organism; he has to do penance for the unsuitableness of existence conditions, judgments and experiences that were fitted *for a whole*, and finally he gets so far as to create in himself the *possibility of his existence as an individual*, by reorganization and assimilation, and by excretion, of urges.[156]

Nietzsche hopes that the sciences will help novel individuals to discover their own conditions of survival.[157]

To become himself, the individual must find himself, but not too soon. Nietzsche believes that premature self-

[153] XII 110 ff.; VII 128, 248; IV 102; XI 238; XIII 38; XIV 77 f. Cf. VIII 155. Nietzsche's love of individuality partly explains his disparagement of abstractions (cf. I 317, 324; X 194 f.; XII 44 f.; and note 109 above). On individuality vs. commonness as a standard of value see further: IV 339 f.; V 257; VII 63; XI 367; XIII 214; XVI 320 ff.

[154] XI 62, 244, 247; XII 119; V 134, 174, 205, 256 f.; I 387 ff. Cf. IV 185, 215; X 13 f.; I 393 f.; L.R. 15/7/82. The motto *Become what you are* or some variation of it is to be found in II 247; V 205, 257; VI 346; XI 62; XII 177; XV xliii, 43, 382. See above, pp. 102 ff.

[155] VI 91 ff., 236 f.; XII 368; XIV 394; XVI 299; XI 390 f.; IV 325, 329.

[156] XII 112. Cf. I 383.

[157] XII 5; V 257 f.; XI 243, 246.

knowledge, in the case of exceptional men, is dangerous to integrity, likely to produce ridiculous self-admiration and self-imitation, and to distract attention from necessary preliminary training.[158] Yet he would not have them work for a "phantom ego." [159] His recipe is: to live through a series of temporary "selves," each of which is effective because believed permanent at the time, under the unconscious guidance of the ultimate self which finally makes itself known and uses the previous selves as functions.[160]

Finding oneself means attaining one's own standard of good and evil, a personal "legislation" derived from the ideal self.[161] This is Individual Morality proper. It demands the minutest care: "So look about yourself! Examine the least detail! Whither does it tend? Does it belong to *your* nature [*Art*], to *your* goal?" [162]

Nietzsche wants each "individual" to adopt that discipline which will bring him wholeness and ripeness. "We must learn from the animal and from the plant, what *thriving* [*Blühen*] is": "one can manage one's urges as a gardener," bringing each to flower and fruit.[163] And this must be done so that one does not blight another. His psychology attacks the problem as one of integration. He regards Cellini as a model, and thus describes Goethe's self-formation:

What he wanted was *totality*; he fought the separation of reason, sense, feeling, will (— preached in the most intimidating scholasticism by *Kant*, the antipode of Goethe); he disciplined himself to wholeness, he *made* himself . . .[164]

Perhaps as the final perfection of wholeness, "one must learn to love oneself" — of all arts "the finest, craftiest, last

[158] XI 297; XV 43 f. Cf. XII 215.
[159] IV 99; III 365 f.
[160] XV 44, 73; V 5, 8, 202; XII 14, 121 f., 369; II 12 f.; VII 161; XIV 148, 387. Cf. VI 125; VII 190 f.
[161] VI 284; V 174, 257; VII 248. Cf. VI 49.
[162] XII 121. Cf. IV 188 f.; XVII 344 f.
[163] XI 245; IV 365 f. Cf. XI 250; IV 183; I 444.
[164] VIII 163. Cf. I 393 f.; X 279 f.

and most patient" — not with blind or sickly love, not with vanity or self-adoration, but "with a whole and healthy love: that one may endure staying with oneself and not rove about." [165] Nietzsche illumines this imperative from many angles: the need for belief in self, for a "good conscience" in living one's own life, and, above all, for the cardinal virtue of self-reverence. Most of the ugliness in human life comes, he thinks, from men's bad relations to themselves; "one who is dissatisfied with himself is continually ready to avenge himself for it." [166] Writing ostensibly of Wagner, he states the problem of achieving personal integrity through mutual "loyalty" of the several urges, and gives this happy solution:

Every further stage in Wagner's development is marked by the fact that the two fundamental forces of his being unite more and more closely: the dread of one for the other subsides; thenceforth the higher self no longer patronizes its rude, earthlier brother with its service: it *loves* him and has to serve him. Finally, at the goal of development, the most delicate and pure is also contained in the most powerful; the impetuous urge runs its course as before, but on other roads, thither where the higher self is at home; and the latter in turn lovingly descends to earth and recognizes its likeness in everything earthly.[167]

Individual Morality culminates beyond morality. For the "sovereign individual" discipline issues in freedom; the "lion" turns into the "child," heroism into play. The self he has learned to love is no longer a burden, and he has learned to "fly" — a symbol of victory over "the spirit of heaviness." No longer ashamed of himself and his divergence from group patterns, he is free because there is nothing he is too weak to use rightly. His life has the divine union of ease and necessity known to artists in their supreme moments. He has risen from "I will" to "I am." [168]

[165] VI 282 f. Cf. XVI 317; XI 246 f., 297, 389.
[166] V 220. Cf. IV 215, 242, 336; VII 147, 261, 267; XIV 165; X 45; L.G. 10/12/85.
[167] I 548. Cf. 506 f., 514; XV 66 f., 72.
[168] Cf. VI 35, 282 f.; V 134, 205; VIII 163; XIV 268, 419 f.; XVI 164, 204, 328.

Since Apollo is the god of individuation and limitation, the sovereign individual might be called an Apollinian culmination of a Dionysian world.[169] But these twin principles warn us that even he is not utterly self-contained. He is relatively, apparently such, but if taken absolutely he is an illusion. He lives "in and for" himself, but "in truth something flows on and on *beneath* the individuals," and their feeling of isolation spurs them toward creating the future.[170] Nietzsche also balances his passion for individuality with its opposite: "And how narrow this everlasting meditation on the *ego* makes us! One would have no time for knowledge of the world!" [171]

So his individualism appears, in a wider perspective, as one phase in the rhythm of life, illustrating his belief that "opposites" exist only in relation to each other:

> . . . for us to be able to live individually, society must first be highly advanced and be advanced on and on — [as our] opposite [*Gegensatz*]: in alliance with it, individuality first gets some force. — At last there comes a point when we wish to go beyond the individual and idiosyncratic: but only in alliance with the individual, with the opposite, can we lend force to this endeavor.[172]

Even the godlike man will create beyond himself and, in so doing, perish.[173]

[169] Cf. XVI 387; I 22 f.

[170] VIII 141; XII 45, 128 f.; XVI 151, 386 f.; V 66. Cf. X 148. In Nietzsche's early period, at least, there is also the conviction that the great individual is somehow not *complete* apart from some cultural solidarity within which he lives and which responds to his deeds: cf. I 318, 497 f.; X 14 f.; XVII 335; XVIII 145.

[171] XI 244. Cf. VII 149; XVI 212.

[172] XII 47. Cf. XIII 124 f.

[173] VI 94; XII 392, 394.

CHAPTER VIII

Art and Artist

Place small, good, perfect things about you, ye higher men! Their golden ripeness heals the heart. Perfection teaches hope. (VI 426)

1. EX VITA

NIETZSCHE sees in art a natural antagonist of morals — of Christian morals, that is — and for this reason he would make it an ally in his war against the philosophies of negation.[1] Art may be tinged with pessimism or asceticism occasionally, but it must needs cling to life on earth for both means and effects. After all, it requires a sensuous medium; so he says:

In the main, I consider that artists have been more nearly right than all philosophers so far: they did not lose the great trail on which life marches; they loved the things "of this world" — they loved their senses.[2]

And art is by nature anti-pessimistic:

The essential thing in art remains its *consummation* of existence, its production of perfection and abundance; art is essentially *affirmation, benediction, deification of existence* . . . What does a *pessimistic* art mean? Is it not a contradiction? — Yes.... Art affirms. Job affirms. — But Zola? But the Goncourts? — The things they show are ugly: but *that* they show them, is from *pleasure in this ugliness* . . .[3]

In his romantic days Nietzsche made art a god rather than a mere ally. *The Birth of Tragedy* is a rhapsody at once on

[1] XVI 225, 272 f. Cf. I 8 ff., 18, 168.
[2] XVI 246.
[3] XVI 247. Cf. I 22, 30, 32, 116 f., 167 ff.; III 241; VIII 124, 136; VII 473.

the artist god of nature and the artist god Wagner. But
when these deities died together he outgrew romanticism.
As late as 1873 he said, "Culture can never start except from
the centralizing significance of an art or a work of art." [4]
But a few years later he gave the artist a subordinate place:

The work of art is *not* one of the necessities, pure air in head
and character *is* one of the necessities of life. Let us free ourselves from an art which sells its fruits too dearly. . . . An artist
is not leader of life — as I formerly said.[5]

So, though much of his philosophy grows out of art, he
does not remain an aesthete. He rejects "art for art's sake"
equally with "morals for morals' sake": both are but means
to the "enhancement of life." [6] Artists simply have the
advantage of working on a small scale which enables them
to round out their creations: "they are permitted to en-
gender something perfect, as a *whole,* and even frequently:
whereas the others are always working only on small parts
of a whole." [7]

Nietzsche therefore tries to understand and to evaluate
art in terms of its vital setting. That is his meaning when
he asserts that "aesthetics is nothing but applied physiology,"
its foundation being the fact "that the aesthetic values rest
upon biological values." [8] As in his general value theory,
he excludes both transcendental or Platonic theories and
those which isolate art from the whole of life.

Previous aesthetics, he holds, made a capital mistake: it
began from the point of view of the contemplator, and so
mistook certain superficial characteristics of contemplation

[4] X 188.
[5] XI 333 (italics mine). Cf. 118, 381; I 522 f.; XIV 147 f.
[6] VIII 135; XV 362 f. On the relationship of art and morals see further
XII 75; XIV 148. Some passages in *The Birth of Tragedy* already generalize
the term "art" to include religion and science (I 107, 109).
[7] XI 77. Cf. XVI 225.
[8] VIII 187; XIV 165. Cf. the earlier statement that aesthetics is a natural
science, and that Apollinian and Dionysian are natural forces (IX 286, 144;
I 25, 46).

for the essence of aesthetic experience. Kant and Schopenhauer, to be specific, attributed to it a peculiar passive objectivity and freedom from interest; in short, they assimilated
art to cognition — theories false in fact and decadent in significance.[9]

In the artist at work, Nietzsche finds a process which is
intensely active, interested, and personal. " 'Being free from
interest and *ego*' is nonsense, and inaccurate observation: —
it is rather the enchantment of being now in *our* world, of
being released from the dread of the strange!" The artist
does not passively register external fact; he exerts a "will
which *underscores* all features of an object that help him
to be content and harmonious with himself (and eliminates
the rest)." His function is "the *invention and arrangement*
of a world in which we *affirm ourselves* in our inmost
needs." [10] His essential deed — although it may not be
consciously intended — is communication of himself through
his work to his audience: for art is a kind of language. He
"builds himself into" his material; like the conqueror and
the lawgiver, he exercises formative will to power.[11]

Nietzsche interprets the enjoyment of art in the same
terms, which imply that contemplation is never pure passivity and disinterestedness. The artist makes artists of
all who can appreciate his message; "works of art *arouse the
condition which creates art*." [12]

The difference between artist and contemplator is simply
that "the latter has his acme of sensitiveness in receiving,
the former in giving." An appropriate receptive attitude
suspends our usual resistances and distrusts and "grants a
conquest" — "first assimilation to the work, later *assimila-*

---

[9] VII 407 ff.; XIII 100; XIV 134 f.; XVI 240 f. Cf. XVII 324. *The Birth of
Tragedy* echoes the Schopenhauerian view verbally (I 39, 44. Cf. XVII 311 f.)
but in practice it concentrates on the nature of artistic creation, in opposition
to Schopenhauer (XIV 365).

[10] XIV 134 f. Cf. 94.

[11] XVI 237 f.; XIV 134, 136; XIII 177; VIII 136. Cf. XVIII 145.

[12] XVI 247, 229, 236; IX 286. Cf. XV 56; III 181.

tion to its creator, who was only speaking in signs." It is often preceded by a preparatory stillness. "Becoming quiet in the presence of beauty is a profound *expectancy*, a wanting to *listen* for the finest, farthest tones . . . ." [13] The older theories misinterpreted all this as pure objectivity. But contemplation is none the less action, though of a subtle kind:

In it, a very *equable outflow of our energy* evidently takes place: by it we adapt ourselves, as it were, to the tall colonnades in which we walk, and give our soul motions which, through repose and loveliness, are *imitations* of what we see. [14]

2. FRENZY

Nietzsche's account of artistic creation includes all dimensions of his power standard. He says that the "physiological prerequisite" of art is a state of intoxicated vitality called "*Rausch*" or "frenzy." This supplies the "Dionysian" dimensions of artistic power:

Rausch must first have heightened the excitability of the whole machine: no art is forthcoming before. . . . The essence of *Rausch* is the feeling of enhanced power [*Kraftsteigerung*] and abundance. With this feeling one gives to things; one *compels* them to take from us; one violates them: — this process is called *idealizing*. [15]

Nietzsche discovers many kinds of *Rausch*, fed by as many sources; for example:

. . . the *Rausch* which attends all great desires, all strong passions; the *Rausch* of the festival, of the contest, of bravura, of victory, of all extreme movement; the *Rausch* of cruelty; . . . the *Rausch* of an overloaded and swollen will.

There is also religious ecstasy, and oldest and most important of all, of course, is erotic *Rausch*, a source of art extending down into the animal kingdom:

[13] XVI 239; XIV 131, 135 f.
[14] XIV 131.
[15] VIII 122 f. Cf. XVI 227, 238, 432 f.

Artists, if they are good for anything, are ... strongly built, excessive, forceful brutes, sensual; no Raphael is conceivable without a certain overheating of the sexual system . . . Making music is also a kind of making children; chastity is merely an artist's economy ... .[16]

But these are secret springs. They do not enter consciousness with usual directness. The aesthetic *Rausch* sublimates them.[17]

Nietzsche makes *Rausch* the first differentiation of the artist from other human types. Art is not for mediocre people — dry, serious, humdrum — still less for the physiologically exhausted. The latter are the very opposite of artists; instead of enriching things they impoverish them:

... history abounds in such anti-artists, such men, starved of life, who inevitably have to appropriate things, consume them, make them *leaner*. For example, this is the case with the genuine Christian, with Pascal ... .[18]

Rausch also distinguishes artist from scientist. The power of the second, though exceptional, is clear-headed rather than intoxicant; it abstracts from the senses.[19] But artistic frenzy is sensuous, imaginative, and muscular. An artist has unusually vivid perceptions and imagery which he has to express by bodily movement. On the receptive side he is deaf to all else, but within the range of his inspiration his awareness becomes extremely distinct and capacious. It surveys immense distances, catches fleeting details, and divines the meaning of the slightest hint. And his responses have a correspondingly enhanced vigor, suppleness, and precision of movement, which becomes articulated with perception in an imperious urge to communicate:

... a need as if to get rid of oneself through signs and gestures; ability to speak of oneself in a hundred linguistic media

---

[16] VIII 123; XVI 228. Cf. 227 ff., 232 ff., 243.

[17] VII 418; XVI 141, 229, 235.   [18] VIII 124; XVI 229, 433.

[19] XVI 244, 433. Cf. the antithesis between artistic and Socratic man in *The Birth of Tragedy* (I 86 f., 104 ff.).

— an *explosive* state. One must imagine this condition, first, as a compulsion and craving to get rid of the exuberance of inner tension by muscular work and liveliness of all kinds: then as involuntary *coordination of this movement* with the inward processes (images, thoughts, desires) — as a kind of automatism of the entire muscular system . . . .

The artist imitates his vivid experience, not sober "reality"; he undergoes a

. . . *having-to-imitate:* an extreme irritability, during which a given model is contagiously communicated —; from mere symptoms, a state is guessed and *portrayed* . . . An image, arising within, operates immediately as movement of the limbs . . . .[20]

Rausch, in sum, is heightened sensitivity and heightened communicativeness.

3. THE EVOLUTION OF THE ARTS

Nietzsche explains the affinities and antagonisms between the several arts, as we know them today, by an evolutionary hypothesis akin to the progressive differentiation of will to power. "The fuller phenomenon is always the beginning: our faculties are subtilized from fuller faculties." [21] *The Birth of Tragedy* identifies these pregnant capacities with the Apollinian and Dionysian urges or "art forces of nature": they give rise to aesthetic type phenomena (*Urphänomene*) from which in turn the special arts unfold.[22] *The Will to Power* speaks in essentially the same terms:

Apollinian — Dionysian. — There are two conditions in which art itself appears as a force of nature in man, disposing of him whether he will or no: now as compulsion to vision, now as compulsion to orgy. Both conditions are preluded in normal life too, but more weakly: in dream and intoxication [*Rausch*].[23]

[20] XVI 227, 239. Cf. 237; XI 330; I 25 f., 88, 120 ff.; VIII 122.
[21] XVI 237. Cf. 152.
[22] I 19 f., 25 f., 60 f., 157.
[23] XVI 226. Cf. I 20.

But in his last period, Nietzsche regards both conditions as forms of *Rausch* in the more general sense.[24]

The Apollinian type pauses in the illusion of a timeless beauty, based on a desire for measure, order, and repose:

The word *"Apollinian"* expresses: the urge [*Drang*] toward perfect separate existence [*Für-sich-sein*], toward the typical "individual," toward all that simplifies, throws into relief, makes strong, clear, unambiguous, typical: freedom under law.[25]

Psychologically, it is heightened visualization, the common origin of one group of arts:

The Apollinian *Rausch* above all keeps the eye excited, so that it gets power of vision. The painter, the sculptor, the epic poet are visionaries *par excellence*.[26]

The Dionysian type plunges into the flux of things; as a power big with future, it revels in creation and destruction; it is a principle of excess, an urge toward reunion with nature which breaks through the limits of order and individuality:

The word "Dionysian" expresses: an urge toward unity, a reaching out beyond person, commonplace, society, reality, beyond the abyss of perishing: the passionately painful overflowing into darker, fuller, more suspended states; an ecstatic assent to the total character of life . . .; the everlasting will to generation, to fertility, to recurrence . . . .[27]

This form of *Rausch* is primarily emotional and suggestible:

In the Dionysian state . . . the entire affective system is stimulated and heightened: so that it at once discharges all its means of expression, and the power of representing, imitating, transfiguring, transforming, forces out all kinds of mimicry and acting simultaneously. . . .[28]

[24] VIII 124. *The Birth of Tragedy* describes the Dionysian as the original art force, the Apollinian being in some sense secondary (I 171. Cf. 35 ff., 61 f.).
[25] XVI 387. Cf. 386, 263, 226; XIV 364; I 22 f., 35 f., 65, 116, 171.
[26] VIII 124. Cf. I 20, 60.
[27] XVI 386 f. Cf. 263; XIV 364 f.; I 23 f., 37, 110, 116 f.
[28] VIII 124 f. Cf. I 60 ff.; VII 271 f.

The Dionysian phenomenon is the source of another group of arts, and Nietzsche suggests the course of their evolution:

The actor, the mime, the dancer, the musician, the lyrist are fundamentally akin in their instincts and one in themselves, but gradually specialized and separated from each other — even to the point of contradiction. The lyrist remained longest united with the musician; the actor with the dancer.[29]

Nietzsche's general theory of *Rausch* also enables him to fit into his scheme the one important art conspicuous by its absence from his early aesthetics — architecture.[30] The *Rausch* of will corresponds to that of vision and emotion:

The architect presents neither a Dionysian nor an Apollinian state: here it is the great act of will, the will that moves mountains, the *Rausch* of the great will, which demands access to art. The mightiest men have always inspired architects.... Pride, victory over gravity, the will to power are to be made visible in the building; architecture is a kind of power eloquence in forms, now persuading, even flattering, now merely commanding.[31]

The Apollinian and Dionysian forces do not remain in simple opposition. Nietzsche says that their mutual antagonism is the basis of the continued evolution of the arts, just as the hostility of the sexes makes for the continuation of life.[32] The antagonists provoke one another to fresh creation, and occasionally become reconciled to produce an art inexplicable in terms of either alone — tragic drama.[33]

[29] VIII 125. Cf. I 24, 28 f., 41.
[30] I 28 gives a very slight hint that architecture might be classed as Apollinian. II 198 f. might imply a combination of Apollinian and Dionysian. XVI 433 asks where architecture belongs.
[31] VIII 125 f. Cf. the allusions to the Palazzo Pitti (XIV 94; XVI 260) and to Gothic (VI 147 f.).   [32] I 18; XVI 387.
[33] I 19 f., 38, 50, 116; IX 176 ff. Nietzsche does not develop a complete theory of drama in all its forms. For example he makes only passing allusions to comedy (e.g. I 56, 78). Hence it is difficult to say how far the "dramatic *Urphäno-men*" — an Apollinian vision projected by a Dionysian group enchantment (I 60 f.) — is intended to reveal the essence of all drama, how far only the germ of tragic drama.

In Nietzsche's account of Greek tragedy, the noble characters, their eloquent language and statuesque gestures, the articulation of scenes — the stage world in short — are Apollinian in nature, like the beautiful dream of an epic; but through the music and the chants of the chorus, the Dionysian madness speaks of its "everlasting lust for becoming," which unites joy and horror, creation and annihilation. Nor are the two sides of tragedy merely juxtaposed: the beautiful vision both symbolizes and veils the full import of the orgiastic music, and the latter lends its clairvoyant powers, as if illuminating the stage figures from within. Then in the tragic catastrophe the Dionysian fury rends the veil, shatters the lovely dream world and triumphs in cruel gladness of destruction.[34]

Nietzsche directs his view of tragedy against Aristotle's theory that it purges our emotions of pity and fear, Schopenhauer's doctrine that it teaches resignation, and the common philistinism which interprets the hero's fate as a vindication of "the moral world order." [35] Tragedy is a

[34] I 61 f., 116 f., 149 f., 153 ff., 165 ff.; VIII 173 f.; XIV 365 f.; XV 64 f. This account obviously applies in its full detail only to Greek tragedy. Nietzsche does not offer a correspondingly specific analysis of later forms, although he does sketch at some length the contrasts between the development of classic and modern drama (XVII 296 ff., 302–8, 314 f.). He often has Shakespeare in mind during the composition of *The Birth of Tragedy*, but recognizes that Shakespearean and Greek tragedy are very different (I 55, 118, 157; IX 33 f., 57, 177, 183, 251). In later writings, he regards Shakespeare as a "great barbarian" rather than a finished artist (II 203; III 84 f.; XIII 311; VII 178; XV 34; XVII 308 f.), but he describes the essential tragic effect in Shakespeare in much the same terms as he does that in Sophocles (IV 226 f. Cf. I 55 f., 157; XVII 298). In his early period Nietzsche also recognizes, besides Apollinian and Dionysian, a third "force of nature," the logical, which, though initially destructive of the indispensable "music" in tragedy, must end in the "tragic knowledge" of its own illusions and may thereby provoke a re-birth of music. He says this last is the "Germanic mission," and mentions Shakespeare in relation to it — perhaps an allusion to Hamlet (IX 177, 179 ff.; I 55 f., 85 ff., 95 f., 101 ff., 108 f., 125, 127 ff.).

[35] In *The Birth of Tragedy* Nietzsche, under the spell of Schopenhauer, speaks occasionally in terms of pity, resignation, and "metaphysical consolation" (I 63, 90, 99, 107 f., 123, 129, 150), but his own Dionysian doctrine is clearly one of overwhelming joy in existence (I 116 f., 168 f.). In later writings he makes it quite plain that Schopenhauerian renunciation is the exact opposite of tragic affirmation. If Schopenhauer were right, tragedy would be a symptom of nihilism

tonic, an exultation in the face of the terrible, not a depressing emotion like pity or fear. It attains "a supreme
state of affirmation of existence ... from which even the
greatest pain cannot be excepted":

> The bravery and freedom of feeling before a mighty enemy,
> before a sublime hardship, before a problem that wakens hor-
> ror — it is this *victorious* state which the tragic artist chooses,
> which he glorifies. In the presence of tragedy the warlike ele-
> ment in our souls celebrates its saturnalia; he who is accustomed
> to sorrow [*Leid*], he who seeks out sorrow, the *heroic* man
> praises his existence with tragedy — to him alone the tragedian
> presents this draught of sweetest cruelty. — [36]

4. INSTINCT AND DISCIPLINE

We now turn to an account of the "Apollinian dimensions" of artistic power — the organization and sublimation
of the free energies of *Rausch* at progressively higher levels
of complexity and integration. Among these, Nietzsche
mentions a group of instincts — urges with accumulated
skills — which are active both in the evolution and in the
present functioning of the artist.

Notably, he stresses the play instincts. Art begins when
men learn to make an agreeable use of leisure by activity
freed from ordinary utilitarian ends.[37] And art is also akin
to play in its harmless use of impulses which cause harm in

and decadence, but in fact it appears in ages of maximum vitality (XVI 267,
269, 377; XIV 365; VIII 173; I 11 ff.). Against Aristotle, Nietzsche says that the
Greeks were psychologically superficial, and that Aristotle formulated the decadent tragedy of a later day, not that of Aeschylus (V 323 f.; I 118; IX 44 f.).
The doctrine of "catharsis" is moral or medical, not aesthetic, and false to boot:
pity and fear are depressing and weakening emotions; arousing them does not
bring release from them; the Greeks in fact made every effort to counteract
their direct effect. Pity and fear may be ingredients of the tragic experience,
but they do not dominate it. The essence of tragedy is victory *over* fearfulness.
(I 117, 156 f., 168; II 192 f.; V 110; VIII 173; XVI 267, 269, 377. Cf. *Ges. Briefe*
III 45 n.) On Nietzsche's rejection of moral interpretations of tragedy cf. I 50 f.,
156 f., 168; XVI 269; XVII 293 f., 314 f. In contrast to these, Nietzsche's view
of Aeschylean tragedy is that it justifies human evil, including sin (I 70 ff.).
So he is an "immoralist" from the first.

[36] XVI 273; VIII 136. Cf. XVI 268 f.; VII 186; XIV 370; IV 168 f.
[37] XI 70 f.; XIV 164; XVI 141, 226.

serious circumstances, such as self-assertion and deception. Part of the enjoyment of art rests on this paradox.[38] The element of deception — "falsehood with a good conscience" — is what Nietzsche has in mind when he says that there is an actor in the make-up of every artist. In this case art feeds on another complex of instinctive skills as well — mimicry and disguise.[39]

Nietzsche gives great scope to falsehood in art. There is a necessary chasm between what the artist is and what he creates:

> Actually the matter stands thus, that *if* he were exactly that, he would positively not picture, contrive, express it; a Homer would have invented no Achilles, Goethe no Faust, if Homer had been an Achilles and Goethe a Faust. A perfect and whole artist is separated from the "real," the actual, to all eternity . . . .[40]

There is also falsification, rather than literal imitation, of "nature" in the work of art: "Nature, artistically appraised, is no model. She exaggerates, she distorts, she leaves gaps. Nature is *accident*." [41] So Nietzsche asserts a fundamental antagonism between the scientific mind, which endeavors to penetrate appearances and "see what is," and the artistic, which naturally dwells on the surface of things, and seriously believes "that what a thing is worth is that shadow-like residue which one gains from colors, shape, sound, thoughts." [42] The artist is more than a passive mirror of "surfaces"; he gives his own *Rausch* to things and re-shapes them "until they are reflections of his perfection." [43] Hence "falsification" is not a mere defect of art but belongs to its positive essense, as "the *good* will to appearance [*Schein*]." [44]

But of course Nietzsche does not hold art to be false in

[38] XII 175; XIV 132, 135 f.; XI 329; XVI 141.
[39] V 311 f.; XIV 132, 164; X 190 ff.; XV 411.
[40] VII 404. Cf. II 192.
[41] VIII 122. Cf. I 22; XVII 301 f.; XVIII 260; III 65.
[42] XVI 70. Cf. VIII 122; VII 84 f.; V 11; I 104; X 206.
[43] VIII 123; XVI 232.   [44] V 142; VII 472.

every respect, for he believes that art is communication, and asserts that "every style is *good* which really communicates an inner state."[45] Just as *Rausch* is the source of languages, so the artist proper, when he emerges in history, becomes the heir and exploiter of the linguistic instincts accumulated by the race.[46]

Nietzsche is far from leaving art at the level of a comparative spontaneity based on the older instincts. We now pass to higher stages in the organization of artistic power, to the disciplines applied by the cultural tradition, the artistic school, and finally the individual will.

Convinced that artists are not "leaders of life," the later Nietzsche regards them as necessarily dependent on some cultural milieu, such as church or court, for guidance, limitation, and inspiring values:

In all ages they were valets of a morality or philosophy or religion . . . . They always need at least a safeguard, a support, an already established authority: artists never stand by themselves [*für sich*]; standing alone goes against their deepest instincts. So, for example, Richard Wagner took the philosopher Schopenhauer . . . for his safeguard . . . .[47]

Even in *The Birth of Tragedy* Nietzsche says that without religious myth the productive imagination cannot be saved from indiscriminate vagabondage (*Herumschweifen*).[48]

In art as in morals, Nietzsche attaches the greatest importance to rigorous discipline. A hard schooling is good because it is definite: it hammers lumpy, slack human material into determinate shape, and turns clumsiness into grace, stiffness into plasticity, vagueness into precision, heaviness into lightness: in the word which he loads with all this meaning, it teaches one to *dance*.[49] Nor is he think-

[45] XV 56.
[46] XVI 237; V 291 f.
[47] VII 405; XV 489; V 117 f.; XIV 146 ff. Cf. XVIII 145 ff.; IV 233.
[48] I 160. Cf. XVII 312 f.
[49] VII 116 f.; XVI 312; VIII 115 f. Cf. I 65.

ing merely of one person — "as an individual one can never make up for the school" — but rather of the cumulative practice of generations, the outcome of which is perfect mastery:

> The essential, "in heaven and on earth," as it seems, is . . . that there be *obedience*, long and in one direction: from that issues, and in time always did issue, something which makes it worth while to live on earth, for example virtue, art, music, dance, reason, spirituality — something transfiguring, exquisite, mad and divine.[50]

Nothing, not even genius, can take the place of "absolute probity" of training and the artistic conscience it produces.[51]

Nietzsche's praise of schooling is akin to his defense of convention. Art must have form, but there is no absolute form: all form is convention.[52] Moreover language depends on conventions, and art as a kind of language must have an abundance of them. Therefore "convention is the condition of great art, *not* its hindrance." [53] For a time a convention may seem arbitrary and require compulsion; "all the same there is no other means to get away from naturalizing than first to limit oneself most strongly (perhaps most arbitrarily)." [54] Artistic freedom does not reject convention; it masters it.[55]

Hence Nietzsche approves the imitation of models, when it is pursued steadily as a means of self-discipline. In that case it is no blight upon talent:

> The Germans, in proof that their originality is not a thing of nature but of ambition, believe it lies in complete and exaggerated *difference*: but Greeks did not think so toward the

---

[50] XV 194; VII 117. Cf. II 201 f.

[51] V 320; VIII 40. Cf. XVI 249.

[52] XI 76. This does not mean that all conventions are equally good; they may be used as shams (cf. I 383 f., 526).

[53] XVI 237 f. Cf. III 262.

[54] II 201; VII 116 f. For the meaning of "naturalizing" in this sense cf. XVII 335; XVIII 89 n. On conventions in life cf. X 279.

[55] II 201 ff.; VII 117; XVI 164.

Orient, nor Romans toward Greeks, nor French toward Romans and Renaissance — and *became* original (for one *is* not so at first; rather one is raw!).[56]

But he condemns imitation which restlessly copies one style after another, for that prevents even the beginning of a sound school or tradition.[57]

Finally there is the discipline of self-formation, in which the powers of the individual artist become developed and integrated around the leadership of his master instinct. He is presumably describing this instinct when he writes of:

> ... the passionate indifference of the genuine artist ... who grants more importance to a sound, a breath ... than to himself. Who grasps at his most secret and innermost things with all five fingers. Who grants a value to nothing unless it can become form (— gives itself up, makes itself public —).[58]

The artist's will — his "inner tyrant" — learns strength by the cultural disciplines already discussed.[59] As it, in turn, shapes the individual personality to final perfection, it follows the typical rhythm of the organization of power: growth followed by maturity, becoming by being. Nietzsche describes what he may have regarded the ideal case in an early passage ostensibly about Wagner:

> ... what severity and uniformity of will, what self-conquest the artist needed in the time of his growth, in order finally, in maturity, to do the necessary thing in every moment of creation, with joyous freedom ....[60]

Such perfected integrity is the source of beauty "as the expression of a *victorious* will, an enhanced coordination, a harmonization of all strong desires, an unerringly perpendicular weight." [61] The "artistic deed proper" consists not

---

[56] XI 362. Cf. X 169.   [58] XVI 245. Cf. 242 f.
[57] II 203. Cf. I 130; VII 176.   [59] XV 489.
[60] I 573. II 170 f. describes a process of self-training for the novelist. XVI 243 alludes to the artist's "dominating instinct."
[61] XVI 227.

in venting elementary urges but "in *restraining* [*Bändigung*] the representative power, in the organizing subjugation of all artistic media." [62]

5. APPRECIATION

Since, for Nietzsche, the enjoyment of art and its creation are essentially the same, his analysis of the one applies to the other, *mutatis mutandis*. The "aesthetic state" is of course primarily a *Rausch*, a blend of "very delicate nuances of agreeable animal feelings and desires"; and bodily vigor capable of such a response is the prerequisite of proper aesthetic appreciation. So the capacity for *Rausch* distinguishes the aesthetic from the unaesthetic human types on the receptive side too — "one who cannot give, receives nothing either." [63] Nietzsche says that the contemporary public, lacking robust vitality, perverts art to unartistic purposes, such as morals or amusement:

The weary and slow-breathing worker, who looks good-naturedly, who lets things go as they go: this typical figure which one meets now, in the age of work (*and* of the "Reich"! —), in all classes of society, is claiming *art* in particular for himself today . . . . In such ages art has a right to *pure foolishness* — as a kind of vacation for mind, wit and heart. Wagner understood that.[64]

By Nietzsche's standards, on the contrary, art should be not taste but a hunger.[65]

He has an additional explanation to make concerning the *Rausch* in the contemplator. How do particular sensory stimuli come to be associated with it? And how account for the aesthetic enjoyment of nature as well as of art?

What instinctively repels us, aesthetically, has been proven by the very longest experience to be harmful to man, dangerous, deserving distrust: the suddenly speaking aesthetic instinct (e.g.

in disgust) contains a *judgment*. So far the *beautiful* stands within the general category of the biological values of the useful, beneficent, life enhancing: yet in this manner, that a multitude of stimuli, which quite remotely remind us of, and connect with, useful things and conditions, give us the feeling of beauty, i.e. of increase of feeling of power . . . .[66]

These utilitarian judgments are distinguished from ordinary ones by their "short-sightedness" and profusion. A judgment of beauty "overloads the object which excites it, with a *magic* . . . which is *quite alien to the essential nature of that object*." [67]

Nietzsche believes that all our sense perceptions contain such inherited value judgments, which account for the aesthetic effect of simple colors and patterns.[68] They also explain more abstract qualities:

. . . e.g. pleasure in the ordered, perspicuous, limited, in repetition — they are the feelings of ease and comfort [*Wohlgefühle*] on the part of all organic beings in relation to the dangerousness of their situation, or to the difficulty of their feeding. . . . The logical, arithmetical and geometrical feelings of ease form the capital [*Grundstock*] of aesthetic valuations . . . .[69]

And our delight in complex qualities of landscape is based on past associations, individual or racial, which enable the scene to symbolize types of human happiness, and give it such qualities as nobility, grandeur or charm.[70]

Nietzsche accordingly bases his theory of beauty and ugliness upon "biological" values: he makes aesthetic values relative to the prosperity or decay of some kind of life, therefore to its increase or decrease in power:

Nothing is beautiful, only man is beautiful: all aesthetics is based on this naïveté; that is its *first* truth. Let us immediately

[66] XVI 230 f. Cf. 236 f., 247; IV 32, 335. This does not mean that Nietzsche holds an ordinary utilitarian view of the worth of art: cf. XVI 294.
[67] XVI 232. Cf. 231.
[68] XIII 81, 270 f.; XVI 22 f.; XII 37.
[69] XIV 133. Cf. III 259.   [70] XII 37, 175 f.

add its second: nothing is ugly except the *degenerating* man —
therewith the realm of aesthetic judgment is circumscribed. —
Calculated physiologically, everything ugly weakens and dejects
man. It reminds him of decay, danger, impotence; he actually
loses force thereby.... His feeling of power, his will to power,
his courage, his pride — they fall with the ugly, they rise with
the beautiful . . .[71]

Nietzsche asserts a wide variation of aesthetic judgment
among men, because they differ so much in power:

It is a question of force (of an individual or of a people),
whether and *where* the judgment "beautiful" is applied. The
feeling of fulness, of dammed-up force (through which one is
allowed to accept courageously and cheerfully much at which
the weakling *shudders*) ... pronounces the judgment "beautiful" even over things and conditions which the instinct of impotence can only rate as *hateful*, as "ugly." The scent for what
we should approximately manage if it faced us in the flesh, as
danger, problem, temptation — this scent determines our aesthetic "yes" too.[72]

And since Nietzsche divides men first of all into healthy and
decadent, he holds that there is a corresponding distinction
between "Classical Aesthetics" and "Decadence Aesthetics"
— an ultimate difference of perspective about which there
is no common ground for argument.[73]

Nietzsche values art according to the grade of life it expresses, and therefore he adopts "Classical Aesthetics" as
his own. His first question about a work of art is:

... has *hatred* for life or *wealth* of life become creative here?
In Goethe, for example, wealth became creative, in Flaubert
hatred: Flaubert, a new edition of Pascal, but as an artist, with
the instinctive judgment underneath: "Flaubert is always hateful, man is nothing, the work is all" . . . He tortured himself
when he wrote, exactly as Pascal tortured himself when he
thought — both felt unegoistically . . . "Selflessness" — the decadence principle, the will to cease, in art as well as in morals. —[74]

[71] VIII 131 f. Cf. XVI 227, 237.   [73] VIII 48 f. Cf. 89; XVI 278; XV 174 f.
[72] XVI 268. Cf. 231.   [74] VIII 194 f. Cf. V 325 f.; XVI 261 ff.

Nietzsche shows a similar contrast in the contemplation of art. The healthy rejoice in themselves and their happiness; the decadent seek escape from self, and therefore demand narcotics or opiates, anything to numb pain or drown the feeling of inner dissatisfaction. Of the modern public he asks:

And what do they really desire of art? It is to banish their discontent, their boredom, their half-bad conscience for hours and moments, and if possible to re-interpret grandiosely the faults of their life and character as faults of world-destiny — very differently from the Greeks, who felt their art the outflowing and overflowing of their own well-being and good health, and liked to see their perfection *once more* outside themselves: — they were led to art by self-enjoyment; these our contemporaries — by self-dissatisfaction.[75]

Nietzsche employs this basic contrast to define Romanticism, and to distinguish it from his own ideals. "A romanticist is an artist whom great self-discontent makes creative — who looks away, looks back from himself and his contemporaries." [76] Romanticism can express itself in two ways which parody the Dionysian and Apollinian moods but have opposite meaning:

The craving for *destruction*, change, becoming, can be the expression of superabundant power [*Kraft*] big with future (.... "Dionysian"), but it can also be the hatred of the misfit [*Missratenen*], the destitute, unsuccessful.... The will to *eternize* likewise needs a twofold interpretation. Sometimes it can come from gratitude and love: — an art of this origin will always be an art of apotheosis, dithyrambic with Rubens, perhaps, blessedly mocking with Hafiz, clear and kind with Goethe.... But it can also be that tyrannical will of a severe sufferer... which would like to stamp... the peculiar idiosyncrasy of his suffering into a binding law and coercion, and which takes revenge on all things, as it were, by... branding

[75] III 88. Cf. 87, 174; IV 181 f.; V 118 f., 122, 325; VIII 133 f.; XIV 367; XV 77; XVII 303.
[76] XVI 261. Cf. 252; XIV 367; III 317.

them with *his* image, the image of *his* torture. The latter is *romantic pessimism* in its most expressive form, be it as Schopenhauerian philosophy of will, be it as Wagnerian music . . . .[77]

Similarly, the love of tragedy characteristic of strong ages must be distinguished from the romantic cult of horror which is only a stimulant for morbid nerves.[78]

The fulness or starvation of life in the artist calls forth a corresponding elevation or depression of vitality in the contemplator. "The perfect cures, the sickly sickens," and Nietzsche sometimes enjoys making the test physiologically specific:

> . . . what does my whole body really *want* from music after all? . . . . Its alleviation, I believe: as if all animal functions should be accelerated by light, audacious, wanton, self-assured rhythms; as if brazen, leaden life should lose its heaviness through golden, tender, oily melodies. My melancholy wants to rest in the hiding places and abysses of *perfection*: for that I need music.[79]

Decadent art, being a product of "physiological distress," also produces it. For example, Nietzsche's feet, stomach, and viscera protest against Wagner's music; it makes him hoarse, causes "irregular breathing, disturbance of circulation, extreme irritability with sudden coma" — certainly enough to condemn it.[80]

Nietzsche judges a work of art in two ways. He estimates its success in carrying out its intention, and he evaluates the quality of life behind that intention. So he denies absolute beauty and says that every style is good if it really communicates an inner state, and yet adds that this presupposes the existence of someone *worthy* of the state to be communicated.[81] More vividly, he praises *Parsifal* to the skies for its

[77] V 326 f. Cf. XVI 261 ff.
[78] XVI 269. Cf. I 6 f., 167.
[79] XIV 165; VIII 187. Cf. V 321; L.G. 21/4/86, 15/1/88.
[80] XIV 165, 367; VIII 8 f., 187; V 321.
[81] XV 56.

adaptation of means to ends, — yet condemns the ends as decadent.[82]

6. EXCELLENCE

Since Nietzsche's account of artistic creation and appreciation follows the dimensions of his power standard, we may infer many of the features by which he would judge artists and their works — for instance, the abundance of *Rausch*, the number, strength, and skill of the contributory instincts, schooling, power of will. And he states the ideal of combining the maximum of Apollinian and Dionysian dimensions very clearly: "In order to be a *classic*, one must have *all* strong, apparently contradictory, gifts and desires: but in such manner, that they go together under one yoke . . . ." [83]

In his judgments of art and artists, he applies aspects of his standard which we called "the Apollinian virtues." But we must be careful to distinguish his rating of the artist as a human type from his comparative valuation of types of artists. He says that he thinks both better and worse of the artist type than have previous thinkers, who handled that concept with "unforgivable good-nature." He wishes to see it plainly, not through rose-colored glasses, but also to think out its loftiest possibilities.[84]

With respect to "nobility," he holds that the type has many defects. An artist is often childish, vain and ambitious, undignified, shameless in exploiting personal experience for artistic purposes; as we have seen, he has to lean upon church or court, religion or philosophy; often he is a servile flatterer of wealth and fashion.[85]

But artists differ greatly in "nobility" among themselves. Van Dyck, for example, is nobler than Rubens because he

---

[82] VIII 41; L.G. 21/1/87. Cf. VIII 186 f.
[83] XVI 264. Cf. 297; IX 19; XVIII 222.
[84] V 311; XIV 147, 164.
[85] XIV 146, 374; V 120; VII 405; XVI 242 ff. Cf. III 110.

followed his own standards more than those of fashionable society.[86] In terms of the relation between artist and audience, Nietzsche divides artists into makers of "monologue art" and producers of "art before witnesses":

I know no profounder distinction in the total perspective [*Optik*] of an artist than this: whether he looks at his growing work of art (at "himself" —) from the eye of the witness, or else "has forgotten the world": as is the essence of every monologic art . . . .[87]

Of "art before witnesses" there are several descending grades: that of the pious artist, a "dialogue with God"; "social art," which presupposes a cultivated society as Mozart presupposes Rococo aristocracy; and finally "demagogic art," plebeian, histrionic, aiming at effects on the masses — the art of Hugo and Wagner.[88]

The case of Wagner, as usual, is ambiguous. Nietzsche admires him as a miniaturist of the soul, and says that he has written "the loneliest music there is," but side by side with this he finds a pretentiously theatrical Wagner:

No one brings the finest senses of his art with him to the theater, least of all the artist who works for the theater — loneliness is lacking; all that is perfect suffers no witnesses . . . In the theater one becomes people, herd, woman, Pharisee, vote-cattle, patron, idiot — *Wagnerian*: there even the most personal conscience succumbs to the levelling magic of great numbers; there the neighbor reigns, there one *becomes* neighbor . . .[89]

Nietzsche does not rank the artist, as a type, very high in "integrity" either: every artist has something of the actor in him. Yet he is capable of a kind of integrity which, to Nietzsche, is very important: probity of artistic conscience which comes of sound schooling, contempt for mere appear-

[86] XIV 146.
[87] V 320 f. Cf. VIII 126; IV 233.
[88] V 320; XIV 137, 141, 164; VIII 35, 190; XV 213. Cf. XVII 324. XIV 137 classes pious art with the monologic type; V 320 distinguishes them.
[89] VIII 188 f. Cf. 40, 185 ff.

ance or effect, passionate devotion to perfection of work-manship: [90]

Honesty in art — nothing to do with realism! Essentially honesty of artists toward their powers: they wish neither to deceive nor to intoxicate themselves — not to make effect on themselves, but to *imitate* the experience (the real effect).[91]

A sincere artist will not attempt something beyond his size: "What can be well done, masterly done today, is only the small. Here alone is integrity still possible." "If a man is not rich, let him be proud enough for poverty!" [92]

This explains why Nietzsche can reproach contemporary art with falsity, despite the fact that he considers a certain amount of it essential to art. He makes a long list of the ways in which artists try to conceal defects of talent and training — for example: demagogic appeals to the masses and to non-artistic interests such as church or race; mixing the different arts so as to conceal deficiencies in one by bor-rowing from another — "as musician Wagner belongs among the painters, as poet among the musicians, as artist in gen-eral among the actors"; the choice of spicy and erotic or pathological materials to stimulate jaded nerves; the effort to tyrannize, to get "emotion at any price" by massive and brutal effects; the *mise-en-scène* of some literary or philo-sophical program.[93] In such matters modern artists are either conscious actors, like Wagner, who are "false toward us" yet do not deceive themselves, or half-hearted decadents, like Brahms, who are dishonest with themselves — much the worse sort, to Nietzsche's taste.[94]

Nietzsche regards the romantic cult of passion and the

[90] XIV 164; V 319 f.; II 224.
[91] XI 330. On the relation of honesty to purity of style cf. XVIII 168; III 269 f.
[92] VIII 47, 45. Cf. XI 76, 335; XII 182. Nietzsche praises Bizet's *Carmen* because it does perfectly what it sets out to do, without pretending to "the great style" (VIII 7 f.).
[93] VII 229 f.; XVI 248 ff., 255, 259; VIII 45; XIV 153; XV 219. Cf. III 75.
[94] VIII 46. Cf. XI 261 f., 379.

exotic as a form of the prevalent falsity in the arts; he says
that striving for such effects betrays a lack of power, not
abundance.[95] By contrast, he values nineteenth-century realism or naturalism in so far as it is an effort at sincerity, in
revolt against romantic lies. But in its attempt to "be objective" after the fashion of Flaubert or the Goncourts it
expresses weakness, fatalism, self-contempt, and indeed it
fails to understand the sort of sincerity which is appropriate
to art: [96]

> Realism in art an illusion. You reproduce what delights,
> attracts, you in an object — but these sensations are quite cer-
> tainly *not* caused by the realities [*realia*]! .... Every good art
> has *fancied* itself realistic! [97]

With respect to the closely related criteria of "style,"
"form," "measure," and "limitation" Nietzsche probably
would not regard the artist as the best of human types, but
he also uses those criteria as standards in comparing artists
among themselves.[98] Not that he champions one eternal
model for all style: "To demand great form absolutely [*an
sich*] is silly, and ruins art; it means wanting to tempt the
artist to hypocrisy or to re-stamp the great and rare into
convention coin." [99] Nietzsche himself is proud to be master
of many styles, and he judges any particular style first by
its adequacy of expression.[100] But there is a deeper sense of
form, in which it is a quality of the life behind the work of
art: "The *great form of a work of art* will appear, if the
artist has the great form in *his essential nature!*" "Let us

---

[95] XVI 374, 250 f., 264; VIII 121; XV 210.
[96] XV 195, 210 f., VIII 122; XIV 197 f. See above, pp. 206, 216.
[97] XI 329. V 109 ff. even stresses the value of a certain unnaturalness of artistic
conventions, such as the expression of passion by eloquent speech or song. This
point of view may help to explain Nietzsche's preference for the typical and
allegorical rather than individual character in art (II 205 f.; I 122 f.; XVII 305).
Cf. the criticism of naturalistic imitation in *The Birth of Tragedy* (I 78 f., 88,
120 f.; also XVII 310, 312).
[98] Cf. II 192, 201 ff.; IV 270, 335.
[99] XII 182.   [100] XV 56.

not play with artistic formulas: let us regenerate life, so that afterwards it *must* formulate itself." [101]

Nietzsche finds his idea of organized and organizing power — central in these notions of nobility, integrity, and style — expressed at a maximum in what he calls "the classic style" or "the great style," a type which he describes in deliberate antithesis to romanticism:

... a quantum of coldness, lucidity, severity, belongs to every "classic" taste: logic above all, joy in intellectuality, "three unities," concentration; hatred for feeling, heart [*Gemüt*], *esprit*; hatred for the various, uncertain, rambling, foreboding, as well as for the short, pointed, pretty, kindly.

In it the profusion of life is subdued; *measure* becomes master; beneath lies that *repose* of the strong soul which moves slowly and finds the over-lively repugnant. The universal case, the law, is *honored* and *thrown into relief*; the exception, conversely, is put aside, the nuance sponged away. The firm, mighty, solid, the life that rests, broad and powerful, and hides its force . . . . [102]

Nietzsche again places Wagner at the other extreme. He created not a new form but "formlessness"; his so-called dramatic style in music is really "the renunciation of style altogether." In his music, art is dissolved into its elements — "sound, motion, color" —, and although he invented a wealth of new means of expression, he sacrificed the end

[101] XII 182; XVI 265. Cf. XIV 197; above, p. 199. On "necessity" of form cf. II 201 f.; XIV 145; XVII 308; XVIII 167, 224.

[102] XVI 264 f., 245 f. Cf. 226 f., 260; XIV 145, 148; VIII 126; XV 389; III 97. Although Nietzsche uses the term "logic" he does not mean conceptual logic. There is a marked anti-conceptualism in his aesthetics, beginning with the contrast between Apollinian image and Socratic concept in *The Birth of Tragedy* (I 60, 112, 114, 118, 120, 151. Cf. IX 19; below, p. 248, note 30). II 202 f. distinguishes art which is controlled by "artistic measure" from that controlled by — presumably conceptual — logic. Perhaps the most enlightening comment on this distinction is to be found in VII 117, to the effect that concepts are much vaguer than the severely definite laws an artist obeys in his most inspired work. But deeper, hence less capable of explanation, lies the antagonism between logic and instinct, rationalism and mysticism, which is best expressed in *The Birth of Tragedy* (I 83 f., 89, 95, 99 ff.).

worth expressing, the essential artistic act of organizing the means. Victor Hugo similarly sacrificed style to sensuousness in language.[103]

"Perfection" is also one of Nietzsche's standards for the judgment of art. It is that culmination of artistic power which combines accuracy and effortlessness in a kind of divine play:

"The good is easy, everything divine runs on delicate feet": first principle of my aesthetics.

Artists ... know only too well that precisely when they do nothing "arbitrarily" any more, and everything inevitably, their feeling of freedom, acuteness, authority, of creative composing, disposing, shaping, comes to its peak — in short that, for them, necessity and "freedom of will" are then one.[104]

It is important to emphasize that this is not an ideal of just any sort of ease; it means "lightness in what is most difficult." [105]

Nietzsche correspondingly condemns art which has signs of uncertainty, clumsiness, and strain. "Wagner is heavy, awkward: nothing is more foreign to him than moments of the gayest perfection ..." His music shows "complete degeneration of the feeling for rhythm." He always troubles Nietzsche by his incapacity for walking, still more for dancing: he can only swim.[106] This is part of the meaning behind Nietzsche's demand that music be "Mediterraneanized":

.... what *we halcyon men* miss in Wagner — *la gaya scienza*; light feet; wit, fire, loveliness; the great logic; the dance of stars; exuberant intellectuality; the light-tremors of the South; *calm* sea — perfection . . .[107]

---

[103] XVI 254, 256 f.; VIII 26 f. Cf. II 204; III 73, 79.
[104] VIII 7; VII 165. Cf. IV 344; XV 47, 90 f.; VIII 93; XVI 164; VI 58.
[105] XVI 254.
[106] *Ibid.* and VIII 189 f., 42, 187; XIV 163. Cf. XVI 265.
[107] VIII 34. Cf. 10; VII 227 f.

But there are higher and lower perfections, and when Nietzsche compares the imperfection of Wagner with the perfections of Bizet and Offenbach he does not mean that the latter are even nearly as great as Wagner.[108]

Nietzsche's use of "beauty" in a superlative sense is evidently akin to the notion of perfection in art:

"Beauty" is something beyond all gradation for the artist, because in beauty opposites are subdued — the supreme sign of power, namely over conflicting things; moreover without strain: — that no more violence is needful, that everything *follows*, *obeys* so easily, and in obedience wears the most amiable mien — that delights the artist's will to power.[109]

Nietzsche contrasts this meaning of "beauty" with "the sublime" — "the cloak of the ugly." [110] Of the "hero," "the sublime man," Zarathustra says:

He must yet unlearn his hero's will too: for me he shall be an exalted one [*Gehobener*] and not merely a sublime one . . . .

But precisely for the hero is the beautiful the hardest of all things. Unattainable is beauty for all vehement willing.

When power becomes gracious and descends into the visible sphere: beauty call I such descending.[111]

Thus there can be no doubt that the later Nietzsche regards beauty as a higher category than sublimity, just as he ranks "the god" higher than "the hero," "being" higher than striving.[112] But the hero and the sublime are associated with Nietzsche's conception of tragedy as a triumph over ugliness.[113] Therefore he probably does not continue to consider tragedy the highest form of art, as he appears to do in *The Birth of Tragedy*,[114] and his later aesthetic ideal

---

[108] VIII 7 ff.; XVI 254. Cf. VIII 1 ff.; L.F. 27/12/88.
[109] XVI 230.
[110] VI 67, 458.
[111] VI 172. Cf. 170 ff.; XII 311; XIII 104; XI 344; XIV 147; III 165.
[112] See above, pp. 138 f.
[113] Cf. IX 87; I 6, 167 f.; XVI 230; L.St. early 12/82.   [114] I 154 f., 165.

culminates, not in the tragic union of Apollo and Dionysos, but rather in the perfect Apollinian transfiguration of Dionysian energies: "The great style arises when beauty carries off the victory over monstrosity." [115]

7. ART, CULTURE, LIFE

Nietzsche's philosophy of art is not complete without a picture of its historical and cultural setting. He does not apply his standards in static fashion, as if every type of achievement were equally possible under all conditions. His stress upon schooling and upon the social and intellectual milieu imply the contrary; and his theory of cumulative heredity implies that the greatest art can come only as the flowering of a stable tradition. His rhythmic conception of life also suggests flowering must in turn give place to decline.

So Nietzsche attributes a kind of life cycle to arts and artistic styles in general, in which rise, climax, and fall are alike the work of an immanent necessity:

If one pursues the history of an art, that of Greek oratory, for example, then, proceeding from master to master, in view of this ever-increased circumspection in order to obey the old and newly added laws and self-limitations together, one finally gets into a painful suspense: one apprehends that the bow *must* break, and that the so-called inorganic composition, covered and masked with the most marvellous means of expression — in this case, the Asiatic baroque style — was one day a necessity, and almost a *kindness*.[116]

These self-limitations or conventions are necessary for the development of strength and freedom — for example, the Gorgian figures in Greek rhetoric, the rules of French drama or of counterpoint. The ideal is a "happy, gradual self-

---

[115] III 253. Cf. II 482; VII 49; XVI 387 f.; L.St. early 12/82. "Beauty" is an Apollinian category (cf. I 65, 110 f., 116; XVI 386 ff.).

[116] III 72. Cf. 69, 258 f.; XVIII 199 ff. This is far from being a necessity which orders every detail (cf. XVIII 163 ff.).

extrication [*Herauswicklung*] from the self-imposed fetters" until they *seem* to have dropped away: "this *appearance* is the supreme result of a necessary evolution in art." [117]
But the fortunate case does not always occur. Sometimes, as
in Lessing's break with the French tradition, continuity
of development is cut, and premature decadence sets in;
for "even the most talented man attains only a perpetual
experimentation, if the thread of development is once
broken off" — Goethe, for instance.[118] In this sense the cycle
is not completely inevitable.

A cycle culminates in a period of classic masterpieces in
"the great style":

> To be a *classic*, one must . . . come at the *right* time, to bring
> a *genus* of literature or art or politics to its pinnacle (not *after*
> this has already happened . . .): reflect in one's deepest and
> inmost soul a *collective condition* [*Gesamtzustand*] (be it of a
> people, be it of a culture), at a time when it still endures and is
> not yet painted over with imitation of the foreign (or is still
> dependent . . .); be not a reactive but a *concluding* and forward
> leading spirit, saying "yes" in all cases, even with one's hate.[119]

Nietzsche describes the classic period as one of repose, of
"power in equilibrium":

> . . . in a classic era, ebb and flow make a very delicate differ-
> ence, and a cosy [*wohliges*] feeling of power is the norm: that
> which generates the profoundest agitations is always *absent*:
> their production belongs in periods of decay.[120]

A little too late, and the same artist, with the same talent
and effort, becomes baroque instead of classic:

> The baroque style arises, at the fading of every great art
> when the demands in the art of classic expression have become

---

[117] II 201 f. Cf. III 271, 278; VII 116 ff. The limitations imposed by a long
development under stable socio-political conditions are also important (cf.
XVIII 150).

[118] II 202 ff. Cf. XVIII 323, 335.

[119] XVI 264. Cf. 227; XI 76; III 266.

[120] XI 332. Cf. XVI 264, 226, 245 f.; III 70 f.; VII 179.

too great, as a natural event which one will doubtless watch with melancholy — because it is a forerunner of night — but at the same time with admiration for the compensatory arts peculiar to it . . . .[121]

With its superabundant means and purposes and its weak power of organization, baroque style becomes overladen, deficient in logic, addicted to all the grandiose effects and extremes of feeling previously forbidden by the severity of classic standards.[122] In art as everywhere, decadence means disintegration, the emancipation of the parts from the whole.[123]

Nietzsche also indicates many connections between cycles of art and other cultural changes. For example: the tearing apart of Apollinian and Dionysian principles, which killed Greek tragedy, meant the death of religious myth also, as well as fundamental social and political changes; [124] love of tragedy typifies strong ages and rationalistic optimism is a sign of oncoming fatigue, as in Epicurus; [125] an age of democracy brings actor and charlatan to the fore in the arts; [126] no schooling can avoid decadence in an age of chaotic values rooted in "physiological contradiction." [127]

This is Nietzsche's most brilliant vision of the dependence of an art upon the course of civilization as a whole:

Of all arts which manage to grow up on the ground of a particular culture, music emerges as the last of all plants, perhaps because it is the most inward and therefore arrives latest — in the autumn and fading of the culture belonging to it in each case. The soul of the Christian Middle Ages died away only in the art of the Netherland masters — their tone architecture

[121] III 77. Cf. XI 76.
[122] III 77 f., 66, 70. Of course decadence brings many kinds of relapse from the classic standard: some artists become restless imitators, some coarsen, some over-refine, some become reactionaries, etc. (cf. XVIII 166 ff., 224 ff.; II 203 ff.).
[123] VIII 23; L.F. winter/84–85, 26/8/88. Cf. XVII 308, 310, 324; XVIII 226.
[124] I 162 f.
[125] I 7 f.; XIV 369 f. Cf. I 123 f., 132 ff.
[126] VIII 35, 27; XIV 164.
[127] VIII 47, 51.

is the younger but legitimate sister and peer of Gothic. In Handel's music first resounded the best from the soul of Luther and his kin, the Jewish-heroic trait which gave the Reformation a touch of greatness — the Old Testament become music, *not* the New. Mozart first gave out the age of Louis XIV, and the art of Racine and Claude Lorrain, in *ringing* gold; not until Beethoven's and Rossini's music did the eighteenth century sing itself out — the century of enthusiasm, shattered ideals, and *fleeting* happiness. Every genuine, every original music is a swan-song. — Perhaps our latest music, too, however much it rules and is bent on ruling, has barely a short span of time yet before it: for it sprang from a culture whose ground is rapidly sinking away — a culture forthwith *sunk*.[128]

Thus the arts are not exactly synchronous: each has its own time-relations to the rest of civilization.

Nietzsche rejects, as we have seen, the doctrine of "art for art's sake." His biocentric aesthetics naturally culminates in a conception of the significance of art for the entirety of life. Art is not always beneficial. By showing perfection detached from the labor which bore it, artists teach dissatisfaction with the necessary change and imperfection of real life.[129] When they preserve ideas of dead or dying epochs they tend to enslave men to the past.[130] *Rausch* is akin to pathological states, and artists are peculiarly liable to corruption, the worst form of which is the service of ascetic, other-worldly ideals, as in Wagner's later music.[131] Artists are apt to tire of the everlasting unreality of their work and attempt to become direct leaders and educators of men — that "typical velleity of the artist" to which the aged Wagner succumbed.[132]

Nevertheless, Nietzsche gives art a very positive vital function: it can be "the great stimulant to life," healing, refreshing, urging to renewed creation.[133] In it he obtains

[128] VIII 191. Cf. III 90 f.; XIV 144; XVI 260 f.
[129] II 157, 170; XI 77.   [131] XVI 238, 433; VII 400, 473. Cf. IV 53 f.
[130] X 416 f.   [132] VII 404; I 522; X 460 f.
[133] VIII 135; XIV 370 f.; XIII 166; I 32, 522 f.

support for his struggle with the tragic antithesis of life and truth:

Our last gratitude to art. — Had we not approved the arts and invented this kind of cult of the untrue: then the insight into the universal untruth and mendacity, which is now given to us by science — the insight into delusion and error as conditions of cognitive and sentient existence — would not be endurable at all. *Honesty* would have disgust and suicide in its train. But now our honesty has an opposing force which helps us to avoid such consequences: art, as the *good* will to appearance. We do not always forbid our eye to round out, to compose to an end . . . . As an aesthetic phenomenon, existence is still *bearable* for us, and through art we are given eye and hand, and above all, good conscience, to be *able* to make such a phenomenon out of ourselves.[134]

As his thought matures, Nietzsche distinguishes more emphatically between the glorification of reality in art and the flight from reality in religious illusions. The artist does, in a sense, value appearance more than reality, but " 'appearance' here means reality *once more,* only in a selection, intensification, correction." [135] Great art is fundamentally affirmative in nature:

The overpowering artists, who make a *consonance tone* ring out of every conflict, are those who give the benefit of their own mightiness and self-redemption to things as well: they proclaim their inmost experience in the symbolism of every work of art — their creating is gratitude for their being.[136]

In the future Nietzsche would have art look forward instead of backward for its inspiration, consciously realizing what it is in essence, "the innermost hopes and wishes becoming visible": [137]

I have my goal and my passion: I desire nothing of art except that it show me my goal *transfigured,* or amuse, cheer, tempo-

[134] V 142 f. Cf. 10 f.; VII 472; I 168; XVI 248.
[135] VIII 81. Cf. I 12 ff., 137, 167; XI 332; XVI 272.
[136] XVI 270.   [137] XVI 335; X 456; III 56 ff. Cf. VI 180.

rarily divert me. The *first* is my kind of religion: I see my ideal loved and transfigured and carried up into the clouds by others. I worship *with* them! [138]

Evidently with this function of art in mind, he also writes: "Where is beauty? Where I *must will* with all my will; where I want to love and perish, that an image remain not merely an image." [139] Thus does Nietzsche overcome the isolation, and idolatry, of art and artist.

[138] XI 332. Cf. X 418. XI 74 states that knowledge rather than art is the proper substitute for religion, art being at best only an aid. This probably means only what has already been made clear, that art cannot originate leading values.

[139] VI 180.

PART THREE

FIRST AND LAST THINGS

CHAPTER IX

The Revaluation of Truth

*Only by adaptation to living error can the truth,
always dead at first, be brought to life.* (XII 47)

1. TRUTH AS A VALUE

NIETZSCHE'S thought is a living whole, and the whole is not complete until he settles matters with the principles of knowledge, the universe, and the place of values in the universe. His philosophy of life demands a total world view. Unless there is valid knowledge in some sense, what becomes of the entire theory of will to power? What in turn becomes of the charge that the old values are false or hostile to life? Indeed, among the problems leading to nihilism we found a complicated scepticism involving relations between life, truth and the will to know the truth, and this tangle is now before us.

Truth, according to Nietzsche, is but the last, austere embodiment of those values — the "ascetic ideal" — which he would revalue. Agent destroying the others, it is itself the last to fall, in the dénouement of the *self*-overcoming of Christian morals. To enact this catastrophe is Nietzsche's special pride, for he finds that even the most radical of contemporary freethinkers still believe in "Truth." [1]

Here we have a further explanation of his dictum that the moral problem is more fundamental than the problem of knowledge. Not only have philosophies been dictated by ulterior moral ideals: the supreme ideal has been "Truth" itself. Why was it fundamentally a *moral* phenomenon? Be

[1] VII 468 ff., 480 ff.

cause philosophers — and scientists too — were dominated by a belief that truth is unconditionally good, that to seek it at any cost, therefore, is man's inexorable duty. Hence the moral imperative, "I will not deceive, not even myself." [2]

Nietzsche holds that the traditional ideal of Truth had a content, also, which alone could justify the conviction that it absolutely must be sought. Behind the will *to* truth lay the belief that Truth is something rational, eternal, divine — in short that "God is Truth." The universe itself was supposed to be trustworthy, ultimate Reality to consist of True Being — something which never changes, therefore never deceives.[3] But when the last subterfuge of this belief is blown aside by the ever-sharpening will-to-truth itself, the result is intellectual nihilism. Man sees only the changing, false, immoral realm of nature and history, utterly condemned by the old standard of Truth, and the value of knowing the truth about *this* world is dubious.[4]

Nietzsche gives more reasons for making the question of values prior to that of knowledge. Both our senses and our intellect are instinct with valuations: acceptance by either expresses some sort of preference, and both idealize — compose, supplement, round out — their data.[5] Even logic, as applied to reality, is not a formulation of what we have perceived to be true but our criterion of what we will take to be real, "an *imperative* about what *shall* count as true." [6] Alleged knowledge, in short, depends upon a standard of truth, and that implies a valuation.

So Nietzsche believes that he has opened a deeper issue:

People have always *forgotten* the main question — : *why* does the philosopher want to *know* [*erkennen*]? Why does he prize "truth" above appearance [*Schein*]? This valuation is older

[2] V 273 f.; VII 469 f. Cf. III 226 f.; IV 32 f.; XVII 338.
[3] V 275; VII 471; IV 8; XIII 57 f.; XV 431, 466; XVI 5, 69–90; VIII 82. Cf. XIII 26.
[4] V 275 f.; VII 481 f.; IV 7; XIV 307 f. See above, pp. 50 ff.
[5] XVI 22 f.; XIV 18, 50 f., 327; XII 35 f.; XIII 172.
[6] XVI 28 f. Cf. XIV 328; XIII 54; XVI 91.

than any *cogito, ergo sum*: even granted logical procedure, there is something in us which *affirms* it and *denies* its opposite. Whence the preference? All philosophers have forgotten to explain *why* they *value* the true and the good, and no one has tried to experiment with the opposite.[7]

Accordingly Nietzsche completes his revaluation of all values by approaching Truth much as he did morals.

2. THE BIOLOGY OF ERROR

As Nietzsche precedes his critique of morals by a natural history of morals, so he writes a historical preface to his theory of knowledge — a "historical critique of pure reason," it might be called. Here too he differs consciously from earlier thinkers: they mistook man's mind in its present form for something fixed and absolute, neglecting the fact that it has had a long evolution and may be changing still:

What separates us most thoroughly from all Platonic and Leibnizian ways of thinking is: we believe in no eternal concepts, eternal values, eternal forms, eternal souls: and philosophy, so far as it is science and not legislation, to us means only the broadest extension of the concept "history." From etymology and the history of language we take the view that all concepts have evolved [*geworden*], many are still evolving: and moreover in such fashion, that the most general concepts, being the *falsest*, must also be the oldest. "Being," "substance," "absolute" [*Unbedingtes*], "sameness," "thing" — : at the first and earliest period, thought devised for itself these schemata, which in fact contradict the world of becoming most thoroughly, but which *seemed* to correspond to it as a matter of course, given the obtuseness and all-the-sameness [*Einerleiheit*] of consciousness as it began in the lower animals ....[8]

These are the main features in Nietzsche's genealogy of mind: the crude beginnings, the contrast between concept and flux.

[7] XIV 12.
[8] XIII 21. Cf. 10, 23; XII 46; XIV 13, 32; VIII 76; II 18 f., 432; XV 438; X 159.

As in the case of morals, he is aware that the question of validity is distinct from that of origins.[9] But here also the two are closely related. Mental structure is rooted in valuations which are mostly unconscious. We cannot criticize them unless we know them; so the historical approach must supply an inventory of the factors which, in varying degree, have become part of our intellect:

> Even today, the proper critique of concepts, . . . a real "genetic history of thought," is not even *dimly conceived* by most philosophers. The *valuations* which surround logic ought to be discovered and evaluated afresh: e.g. "the certain is worth more than the uncertain," . . . the consciousness of triumph in every inference, the imperativeness in judgment, the innocence of the belief, implied in concepts, that things are intelligible.[10]

The earliest of these valuations, Nietzsche assures us, did not come from a disinterested desire for Truth. The primitive situation consisted of organisms striving to flourish at the expense of an environment. They needed, not to "know" the environment as accurately as possible, but to *interpret* it with reference to basic necessities, to ignore the flux of detail and go straight for what might satisfy appetite. "The chief need of organic life is *simplification* . . . ." Accordingly "error" was "father of living things." Not the truest beliefs but those most favoring survival won out. An organism which developed unseasonably discriminating perceptions fell behind in the race for food. A fantastic variety of interpretations appeared, no doubt, in the welter of organic effort, but most were eliminated.[11]

Nietzsche calls the fundamental ways of thinking and perceiving, thus developed, "errors" or even "fictions," because he believes that everything is really a process of change. Modern science, he notes, reveals a world which is a flux

---

[9] XIV 48 f. Cf. XIII 131, 277 f.; VII 369 f.
[10] XIV 23. Cf. II 32 f.; XIII 22.
[11] XII 46, 25 ff., 38 ff.; XIII 69, 80 ff.; XIV 34 f., 51, 322; XVI 19 ff., 80; V 152 f.; X 190 f.

of energies down to its smallest detail, and if some things seem fixed, some forms definite, to us, it is only due to the coarseness of our senses.[12] But life could not survive with utterly fluid perceptions: it had to treat the changing as permanent, the different as identical, the continuous as isolated, the related as absolute, the complex as simple. Not truth but happy fiction came first, and our mind produced nothing else throughout the greater part of its history. These figments of organic will-to-power-over-an-environment are the basic categories of thought today — "thing," "substance," "identity," "quality," "agent and act," "cause and effect." [13] Nor is it likely that we can ever learn to live with naked flux alone: error is not only father of life, it is the permanent basis of living.[14]

Nietzsche observes that man's conscious thinking shares the functions of all organic existence — interpretation, assimilation, elimination. Of course the "fictions" necessary for these functions did not begin as abstract concepts, but rather as rudimentary total responses of protoplasm, becoming refined and differentiated as higher organisms evolved. The primary, fiction-producing impulse was always the tendency to treat things as the same, for purposes of assimilation; but in the struggle for survival it was countered by an increasing sensitivity to difference, fostered by disastrous experiences. Higher forms combined greater responsiveness with greater self-control, yielding a more subtle adaptation to environment.[15]

In man, Nietzsche finds several levels of "simplification." Our senses respond to only a limited range of physical

[12] XIX 174 ff. Cf. III 197; V 154; XII 22 f., 29–34, 48; XIV 14, 19; XI 72 f., 180 f.

[13] XII 25 ff., 29 f., 46; XIII 21 (quoted above), 69; XIV 34, 322; V 149. The space which these entities inhabit is likewise artificial (XII 31, 54; XIII 48).

[14] XII 23 f., 48 f., 24; XIII 235; XIV 16, 19, 34 f.; XVI 19, 31 f.; II 5; VII 12 f. Cf. L.F.N. I 363 or H.K.A. III 387.

[15] VII 187 f.; XIV 32, 46, 50 ff.; XII 25 f., 38 ff., 46; XIII 21 f.; XVI 25, 100; II 34 ff.

influences, present the world in perspectives with finite horizons, neglect countless details, exaggerate others, have strange gaps, and are shot through with inherited valuations — witness the emotional tone of qualities like red, blue, hard, soft. It is superficial to speak of sense *impressions*: we do not merely receive them, but *give* them shape [*Gestalt*] and rhythm.[16] "Experience is possible only with the aid of memory," and memory makes another simplification — "a reduction [*Abkürzung*] of a mental process to a sign."[17] Becoming conscious of sensations or thoughts is a third process of active simplification and arrangement — contrast the complexity of physiological process and the simplicity of conscious states; also there is introspective evidence: "We are aware of *the work*, when we wish to grasp a thought, a feeling, sharply — by aid of *comparison (memory)*."[18] Finally, concepts are applied to the raw materials of sense and memory for the sake, not of "truth" to these data, but of mastery over them; here again there is simplification: the "world of thought" is "only a second degree of the phenomenal world."[19]

In agreement with his belief in the inheritance of acquired characters, Nietzsche thinks of our present mental structure as a solidification of transmitted experience. In this sense we — an entire line of life down to the present — have created "the world which concerns us." The world in which we consciously live, with its colors, lines, shapes, things, causes and effects, is part product of our mental activities. And since it was built with creative "errors," "the world which *concerns us* is false."[20] Its various levels

[16] XIV 18, 50 f.; XVI 22 f., 44; XIII 81, 265; XI 72, 278 f.; XII 35 ff.; IV 118 f.; X 134.
[17] XIV 47. Cf. XVI 44; XII 36. Compare the simplification in organic memory, above, p. 69.
[18] XIV 42. Cf. 41, 44, 35 ff., 328; XIII 235; V 293 f.; above, pp. 108 f.
[19] XIV 52, 26, 133. Cf. XVI 44.
[20] II 31 ff.; V 93 f.; XII 170; XIII 50 f., 76; XVI 100; XIV 15, 36; VII 55 f. Cf. XIII 80.

of simplification are rooted to various depths in our past. For example the "judgments" involved in sensori-motor coordination belong to the stage, chiefly pre-human, before the invention of language.[21] The oldest "errors" are now so deeply "assimilated" that we cannot think differently and live. Such are the so-called *a priori* judgments: being oldest, they are unusually false, "necessary" *for us now* but not for all life or for the nature of things. They shape all incoming experience and require that new "knowledge" be adapted to fit them.[22]

But man has survived with his fictitious world: does that not prove it true? Not at all, in Nietzsche's opinion. Man, indeed, has been an incorrigible pragmatist, like other animals, ever maintaining the truth of those beliefs which seemed to help him live. Because of the age-long selective process, surviving modes of interpretation probably do stand in some favorable relation to real conditions — just favorable enough for survival. "We are 'knowing' [*erkennend*] to the extent that we can satisfy our needs." [23] That truth is always best for life, however, is a moral prejudice. Falsification has been shown to be essential; truth is often ruinous, and sheer illusion helpful, as experience testifies.[24] And of course there is no certainty about even the pragmatic value of our beliefs; there is merely the fact that we have survived so far. Beliefs not immediately harmful may yet be fatal in the long run.[25]

The historical critique concludes that "*pure* reason" is a contradiction in terms: [26] reason is conceived in error, born of animal need.

[21] XII 36 f.
[22] XII 40 f.; XVI 20, 46; VII 12 f.; XIV 320.
[23] XIV 37. Cf. XII 33, 39 f.; XIII 81; XVI 10 f., 19 f.
[24] VII 55; XIV 27, 32 f.; II 369; XII 40; XV 479; XVI 12, 80; V 274; IV 292 f. Cf. VIII 213.
[25] XI 186; XII 46, 193; V 294. Cf. XV 478.
[26] XIII 10; VII 429; XIV 396.

3. THE SOCIOLOGY OF SCIENCE

So far we have considered man simply as a biological being, but he became a social one, and this introduced new factors in his mental development.

The earliest of these is language. It now dominates our *conscious* thinking, Nietzsche holds — so much so that we tend to observe and think only what we have words for, and if we rebel altogether against this linguistic tyranny we cease to think.[27] But we believe language adequate to experience only if we forget its origin, which must have occurred for the sake of ready social intercourse in a primitive world. A word, once mistaken for knowledge, is really a sound used as a sign for an experience, and it becomes a concept as soon as it is used for more than the one original experience. Words serve only to denote (*Bezeichnen*), not to comprehend (*begreifen*).[28] True to its social origin, language expresses only what is shared by the "flock" — "the word dilutes and blunts; the word de-personalizes; the word makes the uncommon common." [29] "A concept is an invention to which nothing corresponds *entirely*, but many things a little," and so provides a "sign apparatus" for the mastery of great masses of facts. But it disregards the individuality of fact.[30] And after all, "the demand for an *adequate mode of expression* is *nonsensical*: it lies in the essence of a language, of a medium of expression, to express a mere *relation* . . ." [31]

[27] XVI 35; IV 115, 234; V 292 f.; XIX 385. VII 416 possibly contradicts the last point.

[28] X 192 ff.; V 292 ff.; II 25; III 198; IV 51; VII 253; VIII 79; XIII 66 f., 267; XIV 22, 50; XVI 23; XVIII 249 f.

[29] XVI 238; V 293 f.; VIII 137; VII 253 ff., 274; VI 49. Cf. VI 316 f.

[30] XIV 46; X 195; III 197 f. Cf. V 293. The assumption that reality is utterly individual is akin to the assumption of universal flux. The resulting theory of the concept probably accounts for much of the anti-conceptualism in Nietzsche's aesthetics (cf. I 60, 112, 114, 151; VII 117; above, p. 229 n.). For further insight into his position see the discussion of similarity below, p. 281. VII 373 suggests an interestingly Bergsonian idea of concepts which condense a historical process into an indefinable unity. [31] XVI 106. Cf. X 60, 193 f.

Language, moreover, has become the shrine of the ancient biological "errors." The primitive men who formed it believed in souls possessing free will as a faculty of capricious action. They projected this notion into things, and came to interpret their own sensations as the "actions" of other "agents," later as the "qualities" of those "agents." These superstitions became grammar — subject and predicate, active and passive, etc. Since that time, grammar has been a "folk metaphysic" dominating even the greatest philosophers. Hence false separations and hypostases: of substance and changing qualities, of cause as distinct from effect, of the "subject" which worries epistemologists about its "object."[32]

Nietzsche also has a social explanation of the passion for truth as such. He considers such a passion rather a puzzle, for, as a biological weapon, intellect is primarily an instrument of cunning, getting the better of stupider beasts by deceit. But social life creates a common interest in the truthful use of language within the group. Group moralities therefore enjoin the duty of telling the truth — i.e. of expressing the conventional "falsehoods" in a conventional manner, the liar being one who violates linguistic custom. So to begin with, and to a great extent ever since, man has valued truth for utilitarian reasons, and has detested, not deception as such, but its bad consequences.[33]

The introduction of morality finally turned development toward a *non*-utilitarian concern for truth. As in the Morality of Mores generally, the original grounds for the duty to speak honestly were forgotten. An urge toward honesty as such grew up with the practice of pragmatic honesty, and its domain expanded to include thoughts and things. Thus the genuine urge for knowledge arose: a demand for the abolition of all illusions.[34]

[32] XVI 43, 50 f., 112 f.; VII 31 f., 56, 327; XIII 47 f., 51, 61; XIV 21 f.; II 35 f.; V 294; VIII 80, 93 ff.; XIX 385.

[33] X 190 ff., 196, 208 f.; III 25; XIV 12 f.; V 161 f.

[34] X 161 f., 196; III 25 f.; V 274. Cf. XI 35; VII 93.

The rise of Absolute Morality gave the conception of truth a corresponding absoluteness which imparted tremendous impetus to the truth impulse. This ideal of Truth shared most of the features of Absolute Morality. Nietzsche takes Plato as the type: (1) Since there is a perfect antithesis between positive and negative moral values, truth cannot have arisen from this world of error and illusion: therefore it must have come from (2) a world of heavenly and eternal Truth, something not merely true for us but true in itself, true Being, absolute in status and universality. Naïvely trusting in "reason" — the crude metaphysic in language — and expecting the universe to be moral in the same way, philosophers indeed noticed that their elementary concepts did not match experience, but concluded that they must therefore have come from a higher world — instead of a more primitive one, as was the case. They projected social values into the cosmos. Corresponding to the realm of Truth, the philosophers added, there is (3) an absolutely certain and immaculate knowledge, pure passionless reason contemplating impassive Being. (4) It is categorically imperative that we shun all illusions which stand between us and this Truth. Such, Nietzsche maintains, is the nihilistic ideal which has dominated the history of philosophy; like Absolute Morality in general, this heaven of perfect security expresses the yearnings of decadents, who at the same time took revenge on life by degrading its world into "mere appearance." [35]

But the passion for truth had not yet reached its height. The philosophers, at bottom, wanted a kind of belief, conviction, faith — not truth regardless of what it might be. The Greeks still thought of knowledge as a means to virtue, and Christianity made it subordinate to the salvation of

[35] II 17; VII 10; VIII 78 ff.; XV 431, 437 f., 458 f., 466; XVI 5, 24, 34, 72 ff., 80 ff., 87, 422, 435; XIII 27, 47 f., 57; XIV 87; IV 8; V 275. On trustfulness as a moral quality cf. VII 54 f.

the soul.[36] But age-long Christian examination of conscience bred an ever-increasing demand for scrupulous truthfulness, and the conflict of passionately held convictions brought about an appeal to more objective standards of evidence, until finally the "scientific conscience" appeared — a demand for "intellectual cleanliness at any price" — which scrutinizes every conviction and shatters every illusion, no matter how sacred.[37]

It would be difficult to exaggerate Nietzsche's esteem for the essentials of scientific method — as distinguished from *concepts* of science. He declares that methods are the most valuable of all insights, and that scientific method is what *he* calls "truth." [38] By it he means such things as: inexorable examination of all beliefs; imaginative formation of hypotheses which are then subjected to unremitting criticism and testing; weighing probabilities; concern for problems regardless of personal danger.[39] He also attests his belief in scientific method by condemning unscientific criteria of truth, for instance: the various *effects* of believing something, such as happiness, ecstasy, security, familiarity, inspiration, passion, elevation; moral or aesthetic qualities of the belief or of its advocates, such as martyrdom, sincerity, strength of conviction, simplicity, picturesqueness.[40] On scientific method thus conceived, Nietzsche takes his stand for the revaluation of the old ideal of Truth.

[36] XIII 26; V 161 f.

[37] V 302, 150 f., 37 f.; II 409; X 125; XV 479 f.; XVI 4. Cf. IV 296 f.; II 252; XII 6.

[38] XVI 3; VIII 228 f.; XV 480. Cf. II 409; XV 63. — Or "the method of truth" (XV 479). Nietzsche's valuation of the method, which of course is not limited to official "science" — he adopts it as part of his philosophic method —, should be distinguished from his valuation of the scientific specialist as a human type: see above, p. 34. X 132 f., 157 f. show that the methods of science and philosophy have much in common.

[39] XVI 3 f.; XV 481 f.; II 247, 408 ff.; IV 273; V 272 f.; VIII 307 f.; XVII 16 f. On esteem for scientific method, see also II 19 f.; VII 57; XV 111; XVII 337 ff.

[40] II 22 f.; IV 72 f., 351 f.; VI 134; VII 467; XI 162, 326; XIV 15, 21, 311, 325; XV 479 ff.; XVI 4, 45 f.; VIII 61, 227 ff., 241, 286 f.

4. THE DEATH OF THE ABSOLUTE

As in his treatment of morals, Nietzsche denies absolute, but affirms relative, truth. And here again, as we have seen, he has several aspects of absoluteness in mind: certainty and finality of knowledge, absolute status and universality of truth, unconditional value of truth.

In defending his own position Nietzsche argues against several representative attempts to establish some perfectly certain knowledge. To the Kantian school, which maintains that a criticism of the mind's capacities will provide a secure foundation, he replies: if we doubt the veracity of our intellect, how can we trust it to tell the truth about its own shortcomings? We could decide how much truth our minds can know only if we had another mind whose knowledge was absolute. We do not even have access to other finite minds so as to make a *comparative* valuation. Kant merely begs the question, assumes we do in fact have some universally valid knowledge.[41] Further, self-knowledge, far from being the bedrock of scientific certainty, is the most precarious of all modes of knowledge.[42] Passion usually beclouds both mind and object, and the passion for knowledge is no exception.[43]

Alleged "immediate certainties" fare no better at Nietzsche's hands. They are really just so many beliefs, and to call them "immediate" is self-contradictory: claim always outruns possession. For instance the Cartesian "I think, therefore I am" involves a number of bold assumptions — that I know what "thinking" and "existence" are, that thinking implies a thinker, that I am the thinker in this case, that the inference indicated by "therefore" is logically valid. Thus it involves judgment, interpretation, and therefore

[41] XV 438; XVI 5, 14, 40 f.; XIV 3; XIII 47; IV 5 f.; V 332; VII 20, 54.
[42] V 254, 295 f.; VII 263, 287 f. Cf. XV 452 f.
[43] XII 6.

refers to something beyond the "immediate." And changing the proposition to "it thinks" is no escape.[44] So for
"facts of consciousness" generally: as in his discussion of
psychological method, Nietzsche holds the "inner world"
to be as "phenomenal" as the outer.[45] He even says that there
are no "facts":

Against positivism, which stops with phenomena — "there are
only *facts*" — I should say: no, precisely facts do not exist, only
interpretations. We can establish no "absolute" fact ["*an
sich*"]: perhaps it is absurd to wish such a thing.[46]

If it is nonsense to seek non-interpretative knowledge, perhaps the whole notion of absolute knowledge is absurd.

Mathematics and logic have also been favorite sources of
infallibility. Nietzsche regards mathematics as applied logic,
and both as a "sign convention" or "theory of signs" which,
in themselves, have no concern with reality at all.[47] As applied to experience, they are animal contrivances of great
utility for mastering the environment, but, far from revealing a structure of eternal Being, they positively falsify
reality by using such fictitious entities as straight lines,
points, and enduringly self-identical things. There is no
reason, therefore, to take our human logic as more than
one of many possible kinds.[48] So in any case neither logic
nor mathematics can give certainty about the world.

Why cling to the craving for dogmatic certainties in
philosophy? Nietzsche considers it a product of religious
habit and of fear-ridden existence in primitive times. Life
is comparatively secure today; it no longer needs fixed hori-

[44] XIV 4 ff., 42; VII 26 f., 54 f.; XIII 52 f.; XVI 13 f. XII 22 f. gives an
earlier, less radical form of the argument. This and VII 56 f. use the "given"
experience of psychic process as the basis for hypothetical metaphysical generalization (cf. VI 43).
[45] XVI 6 ff. See above, pp. 86 f.
[46] XVI 11. Cf. 60; XV 195.
[47] VIII 78. Cf. XIII 60; XIV 320.
[48] XIV 22, 33 f., 37, 43 f., 48 f., 320; XIII 88 f.; XVI 28 ff.; VII 12 f.; XII 33 f.;
II 26; V 301. Cf. IX 187.

zons. In keeping with his conception of method, Nietzsche adopts a thorough-going experimental attitude in philosophy generally, as he did in ethics. He prophesies the rise of new "philosophers of the dangerous Perhaps": "In place of fundamental truths I put fundamental probabilities — provisionally assumed *guides* [*Richtschnuren*] by which one lives and thinks." [49]

He believes that some men are strong enough to live on hypotheses without becoming weak or indecisive: they have that "German" scepticism [50] which unites doubt and purpose, as he himself combines powerful assertion with agile scepticism. We misread him if we forget the "dangerous perhaps" behind his seemingly dogmatic passages. Even with regard to that most cherished of all his ideas, the eternal recurrence, he remarks, "Perhaps it is not true: — let others wrestle with it." [51] And he includes himself when he says to philosophers:

> After all, you know well enough that it cannot matter whether precisely *you* are right in the end, — likewise that no philosopher has been right yet; and that a more praiseworthy sincerity may lie in each little question mark that you put after your favorite sayings and pet theories (and occasionally after yourselves), than in all solemn gestures and trump playing before prosecutors and courts! [52]

Besides certainty, the traditional conception of truth involved an Absolute, or True Being, and a correspondingly quintessential knowledge. For Nietzsche, the two are closely connected: there can be no absolute knowledge if there is no absolute Being for it to be *about*; if reality is a flux of relations, knowledge must be a flux of relativities, and can never hope to fathom or *exhaust* the nature of things. That

[49] XIII 72. Cf. 73, 56; III 201 f.; VI 439 f.; VII 11, 62; XIV 319, 353; XVI 383.
[50] VII 157 f.; XIII 54 f., 59 f.; XVI 342.
[51] XII 398; XIV 295. XIV 331 describes it as a *vorläufige Conception*.
[52] VII 42 f.

is what he means when he says, "There is no Truth." [53] He writes quite early that scientists now content themselves with "a conscious relativity of knowledge," and toward the end he insists more and more that science can only indicate (*Bezeichnen*), not comprehend (*Begreifen*); only describe, not explain.[54]

Since they are connected in this manner, absolute Being and quintessential knowledge must be attacked together. Nietzsche argues as follows. It would be baseless and superfluous to assume an unconditioned Being, because the world, as we encounter it, is everywhere change and interdependence. The assumption would also be useless: an Absolute would be sterile, for "only the conditioned can condition." [55] Moreover, the very notion of an absolute existent is self-contradictory:

There is no "state of fact by itself" ["*Tatbestand an sich*"], but *a meaning* [*Sinn*] *must always be put in first, in order that there may be a state of fact.*

The "what is that" is an *assignment of meaning* [*Sinn-Setzung*], as seen from something else. The "essence," the "entity," is something perspectival and already presupposes a plurality. At bottom there always lies "What is that for *me*?" (for us, for all that lives, etc.)

The properties of a thing are effects upon other "things": if one imagines other "things" absent, a thing has no properties,

i.e. *there is no thing without other things,*
i.e. there is no "thing by itself." [56]

Similarly for knowledge: if there were an unconditioned Being it would be unknowable, since to be known is to be

[53] XVI 5, 98, 100, 106 f.; XV 152 f.; XIV 28 f., 40, 329; XIII 23; II 19; L.D. 5/68. Cf. I 105, 107, 120.
[54] L.D. 5/68; V 153; XIII 66, 83 ff.; XIV 48; XVI 27, 59, 98, 106. Cf. XIII 22 f.
[55] XIV 29; XIII 76. Nietzsche's criticism of the *Ding an sich* begins, well before he wrote *The Birth of Tragedy*, in a searching examination of Schopenhauer's position: L.F.N. I 344 f. or H.K.A. III 354 ff.
[56] XVI 60 f. Cf. 61 f., 77 f.; XIII 23, 64, 76; XIV 28.

related or conditioned in some manner.[57] "Absolute knowledge" is a self-contradictory expression because knowledge is relational:

> To know [*erkennen*] means "to put oneself in mutual dependence with something": to feel oneself conditioned by something and likewise condition it in turn — — thus under all circumstances it is a *determining* [*Feststellen*], *indicating* [*Bezeichnen*], *making-conscious*, of conditions (not a *fathoming* of essences, things, "absolutes" ["*An-sichs*"]).

> "To comprehend everything" — that would be to abolish all perspectival relations: that would be to comprehend nothing, to fail to recognize the essential nature of knowledge.[58]

If knowledge is perspectival, there is no standard perspective either: "There are many kinds of eyes. Even the Sphinx has eyes — : and therefore there are many kinds of 'truths,' and therefore there is no Truth." [59]

5. APPEARANCE IS REALITY

The denial of absolute truth is not an absolute denial of truth. Nietzsche devotes so much energy to polemics that he is apt to obscure this point for his readers, and it is all the more important, therefore, to insist that he really does believe in some kind of knowledge — probable, not certain; [60] comparatively and partially, not absolutely and exhaustively true. His stand on scientific method implies as much, and his admission that our "errors" have some adaptive adequacy points in the same direction. He acknowledges that, despite the necessity of using a medium of "error," "a kind of truth" is possible: [61] the tested results of science *endure*, survive criticism, hang solidly together,

[57] XVI 59 f.
[58] XVI 60; XIII 64. Cf. XI 177 f., 186, 258 f.; VII 429; XIV 28. Another approach to the same conclusion: *complete* knowledge of things would involve the complete absorption of the knower by the things, therefore the self-abolition of knowledge (cf. XII 6; XIII 125; H.K.A. III 211).
[59] XVI 47. Cf. XIII 69; L.F. 26/8/88; above, p. 253.
[60] III 190; XI 178; XIII 72.   [61] XII 24; XIV 48 f. Cf. XVI 10 f.

enable us to build further on them, and afford comparatively reliable calculation and control of events.[62] Moreover, the development of more rigorous thinking has revealed the *truth* about the old "errors" — that they are fictions used to navigate a world of flux.[63] In a similar vein Nietzsche refers to the discoveries of science, e.g. in physiology, as "knowledge," in contrast to the "errors" of earlier times.[64] At a deeper level, his belief that sincere communication is possible, though imperfect, implies the same view.[65]

There is no reason to condemn human experience for failing to conform to a non-existent standard, once the idea of absolute Truth has become meaningless. The philosophic tradition, spellbound by that idea, usually degraded the world of life to "mere appearance," or even illusion. Nietzsche's revaluation of values, with its re-emphasis on *this* world, reverses the situation. If there is no Absolute, there is no "mere" relativity: so-called appearance *is* reality.[66]

For traditional modes of thought, this position would mean a collapse into some form of subjectivism, for they assume that experience is primarily located in some mind — thinking substance, "subject" — and that if it is not in touch with an absolute standard, it is "mental" or "subjective." But Nietzsche rejects all these assumptions: the "thinking subject" is part of the same grammatical mythology which led to the notion of an absolute object or *Ding an sich*. In both cases an "agent" is separated from the process of acting and then hypostatized into an enduring entity. There is no valid ground for supposing a mysterious something which "does" the thinking or makes the fictions and interpretations.[67]

[62] II 20, 36 f., 40, 46; V 81 f.; XII 4, 33, 47; XIII 59.
[63] V 149 ff.; II 35; XII 47 f.
[64] II 409; V 49; XII 4 f., 12, 74. Cf. X 153; II 120 ff., XIX 4 ff.
[65] See above, pp. 14–20, 217.
[66] VIII 82 f.; XVI 55, 66 f., 77 f.; XIII 49 f.; V 88.
[67] XVI 12 ff., 55, 61; XV 407; XIII 23, VII 56. Nietzsche challenges the self-evidence of several idealistic assumptions: The world need not *necessarily* exist

The world of our acquaintance thus ceases to be a thin veil of illusion between mind and ultimate Being; it takes on depth and becomes indeed a "labyrinth" for endless exploration. Nietzsche replaces the old simple-minded contrast between appearance and reality or subjective and objective with a conception of numerous "gradations" of "being" or "appearance" — the choice of terms is now indifferent.[68] Nietzsche speaks of the world constructed by science as a "second degree" of appearance in comparison to the world of ordinary experience; and in a different way the artist too creates a world of glorified semblance.[69] Consciousness itself is a superficial "appearance" of our actions and their environment;[70] and so are the other levels of human "simplification." Nietzsche recognizes that continued use of the old language exposes him to the charge of perpetual self-contradiction,[71] but he retains the term "appearance" in his own philosophy to mean, not a contrast with "reality," but that reality is inaccessible to logic.[72]

Nietzsche believes that some modes of simplification are probably too deeply ingrained in our hereditary mental structure to be changed — our types of sensation, for example, and, for some purposes at least, the logical fictions: we cannot divest ourselves of a need for the static in this world of change.[73] Yet he also claims to transcend, in a

only as object for a subject (XI 184 f.; XVI 77 — an earlier passage, X 152, calls the belief true but trivial). Our sense organs are part of the external world, therefore cannot be the causes of it (VII 25; XIV 54. Cf. XIII 47). Leaves may after all be really green; in any case the emergence of a color-forming sense in a colorless world is unintelligible (XIV 53. Cf. XIII 229; XI 184. XI 72 takes the old position). Raw experience does not separate inner and outer worlds: "*Gefühle* sind uns gegeben, *und die äussere Welt*: und selbst die Gefühle *localisirt in dieser*" (XIII 47). In this connection see also Nietzsche's preference for "external phenomenology" and his theory of consciousness.

[68] VII 55; XVI 13, 55, 62; XIII 52. Cf. H.K.A. III 324 or L.F.N. I 334. In nihilism, these appeared as levels of illusion: see above, pp. 49 ff.

[69] XIV 52; XVI 68; VIII 81. Cf. VIII 122 f.

[70] V 293 f.

[71] XIII 52.

[72] XIII 50. Cf. I 105, 107.

[73] XIV 16, 18; XII 48. See above, p. 101.

measure, the fictions and other simplifications of "the world
which concerns us," and to see these as part of a larger world
whose attributes are flux, strife, and perspectivity. This is
Nietzsche's "ultimate reality" — something very different
from absolute Being. Nor would he claim that his knowledge of it is absolute, for he admits vast tracts of ignorance.
But he does assert that certain traits belong to all existence.[74]

Finding active interpretation in all knowledge, and no
reason to suppose a substantial agent to "do" the interpreting, Nietzsche begins constructing, without the aid of the
old fictions, a picture of reality as a whole. This is his ultimate revision of the notions of truth and reality. He gives
it only in a few late notes which, because of their importance,
will be quoted at length:

"Appearance" ["*Scheinbarkeit*"] itself belongs to reality: it
is a form of its being . . .
: "appearance" is an arranged and simplified world, on which
our *practical* instincts have worked: for *us* it is perfectly true:
namely we *live*, we can live in it: *proof* of its truth for us . . .

The question is, whether there could not be many more ways
of producing such an *apparent* world — and whether this producing, logicalizing, arranging, fabricating, is not itself the best
authenticated *reality* . . . . The other "beings" act upon us; our
arranged [*zurechtgemachte*] world of appearance is an arrangement and *overpowering* of their actions: a kind of *defense*
measure . . . .

The *measure of power* determines what nature the other
measure of power has: under what form, constraint, compulsion,
it acts or resists.

As if there would be any world remaining, if one subtracted
the perspectival! By that indeed one would have subtracted
relativity!

Every center of force has its *perspective* for all the rest, i.e. its
quite definite *valuation* [*Werthung*], its mode of action, its

mode of resistance. The "apparent world" is thus reduced to a specific kind of action upon the world, going out from a center.

Now there is no other kind of action at all: and the "world" is only a word for the total play of these actions. *Reality* consists exactly in this particular action and reaction of each individual against the whole . . .

There is not a shadow of *right* left any more, to speak of appearance here . . .

The *specific mode of reacting* is the sole mode of reacting: we know not how many and what kind of modes there are.

But there is no *"other,"* no "true," no essential being; — by that a world *without* action and reaction would be expressed . . .[75]

Here Nietzsche is integrating his theory of knowledge and existence as a whole with his will-to-power theory: the perspectives themselves are *constituted* by tensions between power-urges. He therefore intends the will-to-power hypothesis to cut beneath the fictional level of thought and to give us, in some sense, the world as it *is.* Moreover, any center's "perspective" of its world is not a mere hallucination, not created *ex nihilo,* but is a *joint* product of "center" and environing forces: through our perspectives we are in commerce with a real external world. So it is more accurate here to call a perspective a simplification or reduction than to call it fiction.[76] The heart of any perspective is a valuation — magnifying what is "nearest" to us [77] — for the sake of living; the test of a perspective is our ability to live with it; [78] and valuation expresses power: our perspectives are functions of our degree of power. There is no absolute

[75] XVI 67, 69, 68, 66 f. Cf. 60 f., 112 ff.; V 332; XI 178, 185; XII 21, 71; XIII 80, 227 f.; above, pp. 68 f.

[76] "Der Gegensatz ist nicht 'falsch' und 'wahr,' sondern *'Abkürzungen der Zeichen'* im Gegensatz zu den Zeichen selber" (XIII 69. Cf. 60). Simplification is indicated as the essential feature of perspectives in XIV 47; XV 153; XVI 18. Cf. XIV 28. On perspective as joint product cf. XIV 51, 133.

[77] Cf. V 183, 200; XVI 114 f.; II 11.

[78] XVI 143; I 482. "Woran *ich* zu Grunde gehe, das ist *für mich* nicht wahr, das heisst es ist eine falsche Relation meines Wesens zu anderen Dinger" (XI 186. Cf. 258 f.).

Truth or Being, in the sense of something upon which all perspectives tend to converge. Knowledge is perspectival, because reality is.

6. TRUTH WITHIN LIFE

Nietzsche holds not only that there are countless varieties of perspectives for countless forms of living process, but also that we human beings inhabit, not one, but a veritable nest of perspectives. The "gradations of appearance" previously mentioned are such. The sciences, working with sensations and concepts created by the life history of the species, are building what might be called an all-human perspective,[79] but there is a possible "individual knowledge" which would be the perspective not of group or race but of some particular person.[80] Also we live through different perspectives in succession: each condition of health has its peculiar philosophy, and so has every period of life — childhood, youth, manhood, old age.[81]

Is one perspective as good as any? Is there no ground for comparison, argument; no standard of objectivity in knowledge? Is there no such thing as error in the ordinary sense? Why do we discard one perspective and adopt another?

Nietzsche answers in psychological language which restates in other terms the point of view of the "biology of error." The human self, he has said, is a society of urges, passions, or instincts. It has no separate faculty of reason which dispassionately apprehends truth: thinking *is* an interplay of passions. Each passion has its bias, its perspective, which it endeavors to make dominant.[82] How can there be such a thing as objectivity of thought, intellectual justice? It is impossible, if by it we mean utter absence of interest. But objectivity is a matter of degree, and relative

[79] XII 42 ff.; XVI 143; V 154; II 36 f.
[80] II 218; V 5; XII 5, 44 f. Cf. XI 186; X 55 ff.; XIX 266.
[81] V 7 f.; II 226 f., 392 f.; III 139 f.; XIV 380.
[82] V 252 f.; VII 15; XIII 64 f., 70; XV 419; XVI 12. Cf. XIV 327; XVI 142.

objectivity comes as the passions learn to live together in a kind of constitutional order, in which each point of view is given a hearing. Not absence but sublimation and organization of passion are the clue to fairness of mind,[83] which increases with the variety, intensity, and control of available perspectives. The ideal is not negation but comprehensiveness of perspective:

> . . . "objectivity" . . . not understood as "uninterested intuition" (which is an absurdity and contradiction), but as the capacity of *having under control*, and turning off and on, one's "pro" and "con": so that one can make precisely the *difference* of perspectives and affect-interpretations serviceable for knowledge. . . . There is *only* a perspectival seeing, *only* a perspectival "knowing"; and *the more* passions we allow to speak about a subject . . . the more complete will be our "concept" of this subject, our "objectivity." [84]

This conception of intellectual objectivity follows the dimensions of the power-standard. Our power determines our perspectives. Therefore some perspectives are better than others. So Nietzsche has a criterion of *relative* truth:

> How much truth does a mind *endure*, how much does it *dare*? For me that became more and more the real standard of value. Error . . . is not blindness; error is *cowardice* . . . Every achievement, every step forward in knowledge, *results* from courage, from severity with oneself, from cleanliness with oneself . . .[85]

The same idea explains why we change from one perspective to another: life compels us. Growth in power brings about the self-overcoming of the old "truth," and opens wider perspectives.[86] Even Nietzsche's theory of truth rests finally on this ground: it claims to be the perspective

---

[83] XI 260 ff. Cf. III 26; V 155; VI 178 ff., 293; XV 487; below, pp. 366 ff.

[84] VII 428 f. Cf. XV 11, 44; XVI 60; XI 284 f.; XII 7, 9, 11, 13 f.; IV 298, 345 f.; I 332.

[85] XV 3. Cf. 64, 110, 119, 121 f., 158; VII 84; VIII 61, 169, 296; XIV 60, 370; XVI 383; L.O. 12/2/87; L.B. 2/12/87.

[86] XVI 11, 100. Cf. X 153.

we — some of us — are now ready to grow into, life itself having forced us to outgrow the old.[87]

And what of the relentless will to truth which has been the instrument of this revaluation? It too must at last be revalued. Nietzsche holds that the absolute value of truth falls with its absolute status. We are under no obligation to go on unmasking illusions without cease, at no matter what cost. On the contrary, since error is a necessary condition of life, the urge to know, not restrained by service to life, "is one of the most dangerous excesses": [88]

Absolute knowledge is an insanity of the Period of Virtue; life would perish from it. We must *sanctify* falsehood, delusion and belief, injustice. We must emancipate ourselves from morality *in order to be able to live morally.*[89]

As a foretaste of this position, Nietzsche justified art as "the good will to appearance." Science too builds a world with man-made errors, and commendably so: the falsity of its static concepts is now no objection as long as they enhance life.[90] It is too late to change some of our "assimilated illusions" even if we would: "One must sanction and accept much that is false and bad [*Schlimmes*]." [91] Nietzsche's last word on science is not to expose its fictions. We have to measure things with man-made units; in this sense truth is not *there* to be found, but something to be progressively created.[92] So let us carry onward this "humanization of things" with maximum fidelity:

1) Let us hold fast our senses and the belief in them — and think them through [*zu Ende*]! The anti-sensualism [*Wider-*

---

[87] XIV 16 f., 31. Cf. XII 42 f.
[88] XIII 27 f.; XIV 307 f. Cf. VIII 61.
[89] XIII 124. Cf. 102; XIV 87; IV 333; V 10 f.
[90] VII 12 f.; XIV 16.
[91] XIV 13.
[92] XVI 56; XI 177 f., 258 f.; IV 118 f.; XV 438. "Aber diess bedeute euch Wille zur Wahrheit, dass Alles verwandelt werde in Menschen-Denkbares, Menschen-Sichtbares, Menschen-Fühlbares!" (VI 124. Cf. 126, 165.) XV 94 says that Zarathustra creates truth.

sinnlichkeit] of philosophy hitherto is man's biggest nonsense.

2) Let us build *further* the existing world, which all earthly life has built so that it appears as it does (enduring and *slowly* moved) — but not criticize it away as false! [93]

Nietzsche hopes that in time the scientific knowledge of life will become "assimilated" and function instinctively, replacing many of the "errors" inherited from darker ages.[94] "Whether the truth is useful and hurtful to you or me — what do I care? Let us create men to whom the truth is useful." [95]

The Birth of Tragedy not only formulates the antinomy between knowledge and life: it presages Nietzsche's solution with the symbol of "Socrates studying music," suggesting that the antagonism between Socraticism and art may not be necessary.[96] Just as the revaluation of morals concluded that, since "evil" is necessary for "goodness," the radical contrast between "good" and "evil" impulses is false, so Nietzsche abolishes the absolute antithesis between truth and falsehood.[97] There could be no knowledge at all without perspectives, without some initially arbitrary choice of scale and point of view, some ingredient of distortion; and the objectivity of mind lives on the subjectivity of passion.[98] So knowledge learns that it can survive only by cherishing error: as man must become "better" and "worse," so must he enhance truth and illusion together:

Love and further life for the sake of knowing, love and further erring, illusion, for the sake of life.... So we discover, here also, a night and a day as condition of life for *us*: wanting

[93] XVI 385. Cf. VI 124; XIV 44 f., 320; IV 359; V 154; X 114, 199; VIII 77; XIX 265 f.

[94] V 49, 149 ff.; VI 112 f., 187; XII 4 f., 12, 74. The final truth of the universal flux does not permit of "assimilation" (XII 48).

[95] XII 245.

[96] I 101 f.

[97] Cf. VII 10 f., 41 f., 55; XIV 73, 308. Hence the statement that truth is not the opposite of error but a certain relation between errors (XIII 81; XVI 46. Cf. X 196; XIV 322).

[98] XI 177 f., 258 f.; II 36 f.; XII 11 f., 24, 72.

to know and wanting to err are ebb and flow. If *one* reigns absolute, man will perish, and *the capacity with him*.[99]

The stern duty to seek truth is overcome, but not the passion. This is becoming the strongest urge in some men, Nietzsche believes, and will one day flower in the lives of supermen. Perhaps it will destroy humanity, but "if humanity does not perish from a *passion*, then it will perish from a *weakness*: which does one prefer? This is the main question. Do we desire an end for it in fire and light, or in sand?" [100]

[99] XII 49. Cf. 47 f.; XIII 125; II 5; IX 113.
[100] IV 297. Cf. V 214 f.; XII 6, 157, 397; below, pp. 374 f.

CHAPTER X

The Music of Chaos

*Even in the wisest, reason is still the exception:
chaos and necessity and whirl of stars — that is the
rule.* (XII 243)

1. A NEW INTERPRETATION OF ALL HAPPENING

NIETZSCHE develops his theories of perspectivity and will to power into a general account of the universe. His theory of knowledge leads us to expect that his cosmology will also be a perspective — a simplifying interpretation — but a perspective which has greater claim to objectivity, is more genuinely in touch with reality, than the usual human vistas. Perhaps the essence of this claim appears in a remark about the superman:

> . . . this kind of man . . . conceives reality *as it is*: he is not estranged, removed, from it; he is *reality itself*; he has, even in himself, all its fearful and dubious qualities, *without which man cannot have greatness* . . .[1]

Nietzsche is a philosopher of life, but he does not ignore the setting in which life occurs. From his earliest years he ponders the ultimate questions of existence and destiny.[2] *The Birth of Tragedy* rests on an "artist's metaphysics" — a Primordial One, suffering from inward Dionysian abundance, finds redemption through perpetually creating and destroying a world of Apollinian semblance, of "becom-

---

[1] XV 122. Nietzsche recognizes that his own theory of existence is an *interpretation* (VII 35; XIV 418; XVI 415) — so much is implied by his rejection of immediate certainty of knowledge. He also implies *simplification* when he calls "the will to power" a *verkleinerte Formel* (XVI 101).

[2] XIV 347; H.K.A. I 48, 277 f.: L.F.N. I 315 ff.

ing." [3] *Things Human*, the first work of Nietzsche's middle period, begins by renouncing "metaphysics" for the methods of history and natural science,[4] but by "metaphysics" he means explanation in terms of absolute entities transcending the temporal world. The idea of eternal recurrence, the central inspiration of his final period, concerns the entire universe, and one subtitle planned for his great systematic work is "Essay at a new interpretation of all happening." [5] So he retains metaphysics in the sense of ascribing some completely general traits to reality. "God's shadows" fell upon many aspects of the physical world as well as on man.[6] Nihilism is a feeling of the meaninglessness of *all* existence. Therefore nature as a whole must be redeemed before Nietzsche's task is complete.[7]

Like the Pre-Socratics whom he so admired, Nietzsche includes in his philosophy a picture of reality done with a few broad strokes, giving the heart of things with vast simplicity. A true understanding of his thought should distinguish this from the complicated structure of argument and specialized application. Here are his ultimate intuitions of the nature of things. Underneath the last ground of logic, they become audible like great pedal-tones of being — the roar of universal surf.

These intuitions pervade his thought. Everywhere we have found change supreme, everywhere flux, everywhere becoming and perishing of forms, nowhere perfect con-

---

[3] I 8, 18, 24 f., 34 ff., 40, 44 f., 116 f. Cf. VI 41 f.; IX 193 f., 198 f., 203 f., 206; XII 169 f.; XVII 296, 298, 336 f.; XIX 237 f. Traces of this metaphysics continue as late as the third of the *Untimely Views* (1874), e.g. I 428, 431, 435 ff. Nietzsche's later ideas are already in germ in *The Birth of Tragedy*: cf. I 8 ff.; XIV 364 ff. His only essential change is to drop the transcendent One and its contrast with Appearance, leaving a flux of "perspectives" as sole reality.

[4] II 17 ff. Nietzsche had already reached substantially this point of view some years before *The Birth of Tragedy* (L.F.N. I 313 f., or H.K.A. II 54 f.). In this respect his romantic period seems a temporary deflection of his compass toward Schopenhauer and Wagner.

[5] XIV 418. Cf. XVI 415.

[6] V 147 ff.

[7] XVI 164 f.

stancy — except in the specious fixity of fictions. Life indeed is given to relative "fixation," but that is only a slower kind of perishing. Here is one "absolute" which Nietzsche does not reject — the "presumably *absolute flow of happening*." [8] As evidence, he points out that all our experience (*Vorstellen*) is continually flowing, and that the world as science describes it is a flux of energies.[9] But he never really questions it: for him it is supremely obvious.[10]

The same ultimacy of conviction holds to the irreducible manyness of things. Nietzsche is a pluralist of the first water. He is inclined to suspect and uncover differences beneath every alleged sameness, and puts the burden of proof upon the other side: usually it is we who read sameness into things because we have an initial animal bias toward it.[11] He does attribute a few traits to all existence — multiplicity, for instance — but these very traits exclude the more honorific forms of cosmic unity. He denies all identities incompatible with the universal flux: every moment of change is unique.[12] So he is not an atomist but a kind of infinite pluralist: there are no ultimate separate units because everything is perpetually flowing into something else.[13] Even the notion of an "instant" of change — "a flash-image from the everlasting flux" — has falsely static connotations, though it is nearer the truth than is the concept of an enduring individual.[14]

Multiplicity rather than unity is evident in the total aspect of things as well. Existence is illogical; reason the exception, not the rule; and even human reason — the only

[8] XII 30. It is also called absolute in XII 32, 48; XIV 19.

[9] XII 22 f.; XIX 174 ff. Cf. XI 182.

[10] Cf. I 366 f.; II 19; III 197; V 154; VI 124 f.; VIII 77; X 159; XII 12, 29, 45; XIII 10, 21, 23; XVI 31 ff.; L.F.N. I 315 or H.K.A. II 56.

[11] V 152. Cf. XI 178; above, p. 245.

[12] XII 26, 28 ff., 45; XIII 242; XVI 33. See above, p. 248, note 30. On uniqueness see also I 387; V 293; X 194 f.; XVI 203.

[13] III 197 f.; XIII 169; XIV 37, 325; XVI 32, 57, 151, 163 f., 171 f., 216; XIX 176.

[14] XII 45.

case we know — is none too rational; its very origin was irrational — an accident.[15] Nor is there any over-arching wholeness or purpose:

> On the contrary, the total character of the world is chaos to all eternity, not in the sense of lacking necessity, but of lacking order, articulation, form, beauty, wisdom, and whatever the names of our aesthetic anthropomorphisms may be. Judged from the viewpoint of our reason, unlucky throws are by far the rule, the exceptions are not the secret goal, and the whole music box everlastingly repeats its tune, which can never be called a melody — and finally, even the expression "unlucky throw" is an anthropomorphism itself....[16]

Again, the perspectival character of experience implies the possibility of countless perspectives other than our own. The world may be endless in a new dimension: endlessly ambiguous, multi-interpretable.[17]

A third trait of reality Nietzsche calls "the antithesis [Gegensatz] character of existence." [18] The flux is not an equable flow, the many not a jolly company: the properties which constitute the world are "change, becoming, multiplicity, antithesis, contradiction, war." [19] Antagonism, the strife of opposites, goes deep in Nietzsche's universe. We have encountered it in the general nature of life, the structure of the organism, the psychology of conflict, the extensive dimensions of power, the valuation of barbarism and war, the tensions in an aristocratic society, and the dialectical evolution of values. But it is not only something that must increase with the intensity of life; Nietzsche thinks opposition in some way essential to any existence whatever: "Re-

[15] III 190; IV 125; XII 215, 243.
[16] V 148. Cf. 147; VII 16 f.; XII 52, 60 f.; XVI 169 f.; H.K.A. III 322, 372, 385 f., or L.F.N. I 332 f., 353. Professor Jaspers (op. cit. pp. 261 f., 330, 350 f.), I think mistakenly, infers that a denial of cosmic order, system, wholeness, is a denial of all strictly universal propositions about existence. But Nietzsche says nothing so sweeping: he denies that there is a Gesammtprocess (diesen als System gedacht —) (XVI 169).
[17] V 331 f.; XVI 12, 95.   [18] XVI 296. Cf. XIII 50; XII 240.
[19] XVI 81. Cf. I 35; IX 98; H.K.A. I 44.

sistance is the form of *force*," and "only contrast [*Gegensatz*] makes a quality [*Eigenschaft*]." [20]

"All happening," therefore, is a fight [21] — "*Esse est pugnare*," he might have said. Though never finished, it moves through stages of relatively decisive victory or "overcoming": "Nature must be conceived [*vorgestellt*] by analogy to man, as erring, experimenting, good and evil — as struggling and overcoming itself." [22] This suggests extending the pattern of "dialectical evolution" to all nature: the "antitheses" not only fight each other but succeed one another through "self-overcomings," and are forged into novel unities — "conciliation of inner opposites into something new, *birth of a third*." [23] In any case, Nietzsche says that the flowing struggle of events is perpetually creative, for "*creation* is one of the inalienable and constant properties of the world itself": "I discerned the *active* force, the creative amid the accidental: — chance itself is only the *collision of productive impulses*." [24] By the same token, the struggle is destructive: the old does not merely fade out, it is demolished and swept away by the storm of being. Creation implies annihilation.[25]

[20] XII 119; L.F.N. I 317 or H.K.A. II 59. Cf. XIV 347; XII 47 f. On the necessity of *Gegensätze*, tension between opposites, for maintaining or increasing power cf. XIII 125; VIII 86, 148 ff.; XV 404; VII 180 f., 196; XVI 204, 299, 326 f., 344 f., 387; I 19; L.F.N. I 324 or H.K.A. II 408. As usual Nietzsche uses the term *Gegensatz* in at least two senses, one which he denies and one which he affirms. The sense denied has been explained in connection with "Absolute Morality": he rejects absolute, irreconcilable antitheses, of the sort which exclude the possibility of degrees, of synthesis, and of one developing from the other — for example evil-good, egoistic-unegoistic, false-true, changing-permanent, material-immaterial — cf. II 11, 432, 17 f.; III 237; VI 10 f., 41, 55, 73; XII 71; XIV 20, 354; XV 165 f.; XVI 55 f. At the same time, though holding that the popular mind has often imagined antitheses where there are none, he claims to have discovered underlying antitheses generally ignored, e.g. between decadent and Dionysian, and he scolds the Germans for their good-natured hospitality to such opposite values (XV 63, 108 f.; VIII 48 ff.). The antitheses he favors do not seem to have the objectionable features listed above; they are dynamic rather than logical: witness the dialectical evolution of values.

[21] XIII 62; XVI 57, 111.
[22] XII 240. Cf. VI 167 ff.; XVI 101.
[23] XIV 139. Cf. 44 f.; XIII 277; XV 95; XVI 230, 296, 344 f.; VI 336.
[24] XIII 77; XVI 136. Cf. H.K.A. II 56 f. or L.F.N. I 315.
[25] VI 169; XV 65, 442 f.; XVI 386 f. Cf. H.K.A. III 386.

Reality — fluid, many, clashing and overcoming, shaping and breaking — is this not the will to power once more? So Nietzsche intends it. Beyond life, the will to power comes at last to include all nature, droning the utmost music of chaos.[26]

2. BEYOND MECHANISM

Nietzsche clothes his "Pre-Socratic" cosmology with an intricate structure of evidence and application. When he decides to extend the will-to-power hypothesis from life to the inorganic world, he naturally turns to contemporary scientific theory as the reigning view which he must somehow "overcome." Considering his wretched health and lack of scientific training, one can only admire his insight into the trends of recent physics.

The nineteenth-century universe consisted of solid particles of matter in motion. This was generally called the "mechanistic" conception of nature, and Nietzsche develops his own position out of a running criticism of mechanism in this sense. He also sees much good in mechanism: it has practical applications; it is a severe mental discipline, an unsentimental view of the world, a foe of supernatural teleology; and in many respects it is a valuable working hypothesis which we should continue to use and test out.[27]

But when dogmatists assert it to be the last word about the universe, Nietzsche has ready an arsenal of arguments. Mechanics is really applied mathematics, yet mathematics depends upon fictitious identities for its application; mechanics is therefore similarly entangled with fictions.[28] Scientists themselves are coming to realize that it is a description, not an explanation. It substitutes reversible equations for causation, leaves out the inner reality and driving force behind the motions of "matter," and "will

[26] XVI 401 f.   [27] XIII 82 f.; XIV 353.
[28] V 330 f.; XIII 88; XIV 22. See above, p. 253.

end by producing a system of symbols [*Zeichen*]." [29] It is nonsense to reduce *everything* to quantity; a purely quantitative world would be rigid, unmoving.[30] To accept the mechanistic view as final is like mistaking a musical score for the music itself.[31]

Of all the inherited categories of the human mind, as Nietzsche exposed them in the "historical critique," none is more fundamental than "substance," rooted in the structure of grammar itself — the belief that "all that happens is related as a predicate to some subject or other." He holds that, though we may continue to use it for practical purposes, this notion of a separate bearer of qualities and agent of actions is sheer fiction and must be discarded if we want to grasp reality.[32] Now the material atom used by the mechanists is only a special case of "substance"; however useful for calculations, it renders mechanics fictitious.[33]

In his opposition to materialism Nietzsche takes pleasure in appealing to revolutionary tendencies in physical theory developing along lines suggested a century earlier by Boscovich, whose work he considers as revolutionary as that of Copernicus: "solid" matter is becoming a structure of energies, mechanics yielding place to dynamics. In short, he says, "We have got rid of *materiality* [*Stofflichkeit*]." [34] (We should never have had the ordinary idea of matter, he remarks, if our sense of touch were not so crude and our eyes did not portray reflecting surfaces as continuous planes.[35])

The other fundamental concept of mechanics is motion. But what is motion? he asks. Something we perceive by sight and touch. And sensations are ingrained human per-

[29] XIII 85. Cf. 83 ff.; XVI 53, 59, 112 f., 152; XIX 197.
[30] XV 65, 127.
[31] V 331; XIII 60; XVI 106.
[32] XVI 50 f., 13 f., 26, 29, 31, 35, 43, 55 f., 109, 113.
[33] XVI 55, 105 f., 112 ff.
[34] XVI 56, 104; XIII 84, 86; XIV 353; VII 22; L.G. 20/3/82. Cf. II 37; XI 73.
[35] XI 72 f.

spectives, highly simplified grades of appearance. The motions which are the subject matter of mechanics are not the inner flow of nature but "symptoms," "translations" of it into the "language of the senses." [36]

And how are motions produced? The materialist would like to explain them in terms of the jostling and crowding of atoms, but that will not do. The billiard-ball effect presupposes forces of cohesion and elasticity, otherwise no particle could hold together or exert and resist pressure. And finally even the mechanist is unable to get rid of some "action at a distance," namely gravitation, and so has to admit something that is unintelligible in terms of material contact.[37]

To sum up the argument:

So these are *phenomenal*: the intermingling of the number concept, the thing concept (subject concept), the agency concept (separation between being-a-cause and acting), the motion concept (eye and touch): we still have our *eye*, our *psychology* therein.

If we eliminate these additions, then no things are left, but dynamic quanta [*dynamische Quanta*] in a relation of tension with all other dynamic quanta, whose essence consists in their relation to all other quanta, in their "action" upon them.[38]

Thus we come back to Nietzsche's perspectivism: the world is a complex of interacting processes of interpretation; existence is through and through relational; nothing is distinct from its relations.

3. PHYSICS AND THE WILL TO POWER

But how shall we conceive the "dynamic quanta" which are the residue from the critique of mechanism? Nietzsche evidently demands that we go beyond mere shorthand de-

[36] XVI 18, 104, 106, 111 ff.; XIII 60, 64, 66, 69; XIV 45 f. Cf. XIV 365.
[37] XVI 104 f., 153; XIII 81, 230; XII 72 f.; L.G. 20/3/82. Cf. XVI 107.
[38] XVI 113.

scription with symbols. He prefers the idea of force or energy to that of matter, but finds it also inadequate:

A force which we cannot picture [*vorstellen*] to ourselves is an empty word and can have no civil rights in science — like the so-called purely mechanical power of attraction and repulsion, which is *intended to make* the world *conceivable* [*vorstellbar*] for us, nothing more! [39]

We can comprehend (*Begreifen*) only a force analogous to the one in ourselves — the energy of will, of life.[40] Hence the hypothesis that will to power is the nature of all energies in the universe.

Nietzsche's fullest development of the hypothesis is worth quoting at some length:

Suppose that nothing else is "given" as real than our world of desires and passions, that we can get down or up to no other "reality" than precisely to the reality of our urges — for thinking is only a behavior [*Verhalten*] of these urges toward one another —: is it not allowable . . . to ask the question, whether this "given" does not *suffice* for understanding, in terms of something like it, the so-called mechanistic (or "material") world too? I mean not as an illusion, an "appearance," an "idea" (in the sense of Berkeley and Schopenhauer), but as of the same grade of reality which our passion [*Affekt*] itself has — as a more primitive form of the world of passions, in which everything still lies shut in mighty unity, which then branches out in the organic process . . . — as a *pre-form* of life? — After all, it is not only permissible to make this experiment: it is commanded by the conscience of *method*. Do not assume several kinds of causality as long as the attempt to do with one has not been driven to its utmost limit. . . . Ultimately the question is . . . whether we believe in the causality of will: if we do — and at bottom our belief *in that* is exactly our belief in causality itself — then we *must* make the attempt to suppose causality of will hypothetically as the sole causality. . . . Suppose, last of all, that we should succeed in explaining our whole impulsive life as the metamorphosis and branching-off of one basic form of will —

[39] XVI 105. Nietzsche uses the terms *Kraft* and *Energie* without apparent distinction.   [40] XII 304; XIII 83; XVI 77, 107 f.

namely of will to power, as *my* principle runs — suppose that one could trace back all organic functions to this will to power, and that one found in it the solution to the problem of generation and nutrition ... then one would have obtained the right to define *all* efficacious force univocally as: *will to power*. The world seen from within ... would be precisely *will to power* and nothing besides. — [41]

If we expand this highly condensed reasoning and supplement it with other passages we obtain the following argument:

1) The mechanistic world is a superficial world. Beneath the surface of bodily motions we infer energies or forces at work. But the only forces in our acquaintance, therefore the only inner content we can assign to forces generally, are our own urges, whose integrated activity we call our "will." Therefore we might try interpreting all energies of nature by analogy to those of human nature.[42] In so doing we apply to the physical world the combination of "internal and external phenomenology" already used in Nietzsche's biology and psychology:

Everything material is a kind of motion-symptom for an unknown [*unbekanntes*] happening: everything conscious and felt is likewise a symptom. The world, which gives us intimations about itself from these two sides, could have yet many other symptoms. ...

Motions are symptoms, thoughts are likewise symptoms: desires are manifest to us behind both, and the fundamental desire is will to power.[43]

But we must beware falling into the old duality of appearance and reality: the "symptoms" are not separate from the processes of striving for power; "motions are not '*effected*' by a '*cause*' (that would be the old soul idea again!) — they are the will *itself*, but not wholly and completely! "[44]

[41] VII 56 ff. Cf. VI 43, 46 f.; XII 22 f.   [42] XIII 228; XVI 104.
[43] XIII 64. Cf. 69; XII 304; XIV 327; XVI 415.
[44] XIII 60. Cf. 69 (quoted above, p. 260 n.). Compare the comparison of consciousness to a "skin" (above, p. 109).

2) Nietzsche admits that this procedure is hypothetical for a second reason, for we cannot be certain that our "willing" is really a causal process. But at any rate it is the ultimate source of our belief in causality, projected thence into the outer world; so why not translate "the concept 'cause' back again into the only sphere with which we are acquainted, from which we have derived it?" [45] If we are going to use it at all, this is its most likely form, which we are bound, by the principle of parsimony, to use as far as it will go. Accordingly Nietzsche frames the hypothesis: "The sole *force* that exists is of the same kind as force of will: a commanding to other subjects, which thereupon change." [46]

3) Nietzsche justifies his theory, in part, by our intimate connections with the rest of nature. Interaction suggests similarity of kind — "of course 'will' can act only upon 'will' — and not upon 'materials.' " [47] And if all life is a development of will to power, it is plausible to suppose that the inorganic world is but a more primitive stage of the same evolution. [48]

4) Nietzsche claims that perspectivity of will to power renders more intelligible the "action at a distance" which confounds the mechanist, and the selectiveness of natural processes — of chemical reactions, for example. Action at a distance implies something like perception. If the world consists of strivings-for-power, each makes its *specific* perspective of the others: "every center of force" "construes, *from itself outward*, all the rest of the world, i.e. measures by its own power, handles, shapes...." [49] It involves *all* the rest, because it is striving to master all space: "every atom works out into the whole of being — it is thought

[45] XVI 153. Cf. 51; IV 132; VII 28 ff.; X 165; XIII 261–67; above, pp. 92 ff.
[46] XVI 17. "Subject" is here used not in the old sense of "substance" but in Nietzsche's sense of "center of willing-to-power": cf. XVI 16 ff., 61 f., 66, 69.
[47] VII 57. Cf. XVI 18; XI 188.
[48] XVI 101, 152, 154 ff.; XIII 66, 228 f.
[49] XVI 114 f. Cf. 66 f., 117 f., 122 f.; XI 187 f.; XIII 82, 227 f., 230; V 183; X 150 f.

away, if one thinks away this radiation of will to power." [50]
So everything is constituted by its relations *to* everything.
This persuasion of the internal connectedness of all exist-
ence is another of Nietzsche's primary intuitions of reality.[51]

5) Nietzsche also uses will to power to explain why natural
processes "take time," and why they never cease:

> *All struggle* — all occurrence is a struggle — requires *duration*.
> What we call "cause" and "effect" leaves out the struggle, and
> therefore does not correspond to the occurrence. It is consistent
> to deny time in cause and effect.[52] That change does not cease
> is a fact of experience. Why? —

> ... an *attained condition* would seem to have to maintain
> itself, if there were not in it a capacity to will precisely *not*
> to maintain itself . . . Spinoza's principle of "self-preserva-
> tion" would really have to put a stop to change . . . .[53]

Accordingly we must supplement the conservation of energy
with another principle which accounts for the restlessness
of nature — "Not merely constancy of energy, but maximum economy of consumption: so that the *willing-to-
become-stronger from each center of force outward* is the
only reality . . . ." [54]

So will to power explains even change. Being the reason
for "becoming," it cannot itself "become," yet it is not a
"substance." It is neither a "being" nor a "becoming,"
"but a *passion [Pathos]* . . . the most elementary fact, from
which a becoming, an acting, then results" [55] — reality "indicated from within, and not from its incomprehensible,
fluid Proteus-nature." [56]

[50] XVI 114, 111.
[51] See further: XII 29, 71; XIII 74; XV 358; XVI 82, 115, 378; above, p. 255.
[52] XIII 62.
[53] XVI 152 f.
[54] XVI 154. Cf. 111, 115.
[55] XVI 113. Cf. 115, 61.
[56] XIII 50. Cf. XIV 45 f., 365; XVI 104, 156; VII 58. Contrast II 31 for the
sense of "inside" which is *not* meant.

If will to power is extended to include all nature, what accounts for the distinctive features of life? The question is less critical for Nietzsche than for the mechanist, because extending will to power to both lessons the gap between them.[57]

Nietzsche's "error as father of living things" gives a clue to the differentia of life. We have seen that will to power implies a sort of perception in the physical world too. The difference comes with the kind of perception; life introduces "simplification":

> The transition from the world of the inorganic to that of the organic is one from fixed perceptions of force values and power relations into a world of *uncertain, indefinite* ones (because a multiplicity of mutually struggling beings ((= protoplasm)) feels itself over against the external world).[58]

His central idea seems to be that life has a certain cumulative unity and persistence which distinguishes it from the brutal instantaneity of inorganic forces. A protracted "fight" comes to feel itself as an enduring "thing," and to feel the environment as made up of other "enduring things" which it can assimilate or of which it can become a function. Here Nietzsche finds the original "error" which makes living possible, and he believes that the whole process may have originated as an accident.[59] In any case, relation to a persisting process accounts for the egocentric, therefore "falsifying," perspectivity of life: "laws of preservation for enduring processes [*Dauer-Processe*] presuppose perspectival *illusion*." [60] The

[57] Cf. XVI 122 f., 117. At times Nietzsche suggests that life has always existed (XIII 231 f.; XIV 35), but on the whole he holds that it evolved from the inorganic, as stated above. This is supported by his astronomical picture of nature (V 147 f.; III 200; X 189; XV 364 f.). Also, if life were eternal, its organic memory would make eternal recurrence impossible (XII 60).

[58] XIII 227. Cf. 228; XIV 45; XI 187 f.

[59] XII 25 f., 156; XIII 62 f., 69, 71; XVI 117. Cf. XI 187 f. Connecting the last passage with X 150 f., I infer that Nietzsche once attributed *Empfindung* (therefore error), and memory too, to all existents. XIII 243 still does so, as far as memory is concerned, but only casually.

[60] XIII 88. Cf. 243, 271.

fundamental capacity of life is its "faculty for creating (shaping, inventing, fabricating)" — hence for assimilation and reproduction.[61] The idea that life is distinctively an *enduring* process may be connected with three other differentiae which Nietzsche suggests: organic memory or retention of the past, differentiation of functions, and self-regulation.[62]

4. UNITY, ENDURANCE, ORDER

So far Nietzsche has emphasized the chaos, change, and interrelatedness of nature. But in some sense there obviously is' at least transient order, relative endurance, and partial separateness of things — he has spoken of "dynamic quanta" and "centers of force." What is his account of these?

The problems of endurance and separateness are bound up, in Nietzsche's treatment, with the question whether despite the indefinite plurality of things there are unities of some kind in nature. Otherwise there would be nothing to endure, and unity *within* the universe implies a contrast which marks it off from the rest of nature.

He denies any absolute unity, i.e. simplicity, unity that is not also complexity:

Everything that is simple is merely imaginary, is not "true." But what is real, what is true, is neither one nor even reducible to one.

All unity is unity *only* as *organization and ensemble*: not otherwise than as a human community is a unity: *consequently* the *opposite* of atomistic *anarchy*, accordingly a *power structure* [*Herrschafts-Gebilde*] which *signifies* one, but *is* not one.[63]

This is consonant with Nietzsche's picture of the unity of the living organism and of the human self. Despite the second passage, it is not certain that he believes that every

[61] XIII 80, 238. See above, pp. 60 f., 73 ff.
[62] Cf. VII 57; XIII 172, 228 f., 231 ff.; XII 110.
[63] XVI 46, 63. Cf. 62 f. For other instances of the term *Herrschaftsgebilde* cf. VII 382; XV 486; XVI 171.

complex is in turn composed of complexes, and so on to infinity. But if everything is constituted by its relations, it must be *relationally* complex, and therefore constantly liable to change. This is Nietzsche's main contention:

There are no permanent, ultimate unities, no atoms, no monads . . . .

We may speak relatively of atoms and monads: and it is certain that *in duration* the smallest world is *the most durable* . . . There is no will: there are will-points [-*Punktationen*] which constantly increase or lose their power.[64]

In what sense are there "relative" unities? In the case of living organisms we found that there is a measure of internal organization for the sake of aggression and defense against the outer world. This seems to be Nietzsche's general account of such separateness as exists in nature. At bottom lies the principle of "opposites," the antagonism essential to the struggle for power:

But *who* desires power? . . . Absurd question, when the essence itself is will to power . . . .! Nevertheless: there is need of antitheses [*Gegensätze*], of resistances, therefore of *encroaching unities*, relatively speaking . . .[65]

The resistances between aggressive powers, then, keep them in a measure distinct, though related.

"Relative" unities evidently have a temporal dimension: they last for a while. How so, in a world of ceaseless flux, different at every instant? Nietzsche's key to this, and to

[64] XVI 171 f. Cf. 16 ff., 163 f.; XIII 169; XIV 325; above, pp. 268 f. The passages which support the view that nature is "infinite downward" are XVI 63 (as quoted); X 148 f.; XIX 176. Those which support the contrary are XVI 163 f., 171 f. (quoted in part); XIII 84. A comparison of these shows that Nietzsche's ground for the first view is the continuity of change, and the second view is certainly not intended to deny this. Therefore he probably means that the processes in nature are infinitely divisible in time but perhaps not in space. One passage (XII 32) suggests that there may be an ultimate unit of time but not of space — but the language indicates that "becoming" would still be going on *during* the unit of time (cf. XII 57).

[65] XVI 156. Cf. 117, 122 f.; above, pp. 72 ff.

the uniformities in nature, is *similarity*. Having denied all identity, he says, "Similarity is not a degree of sameness, but something completely different from sameness." "We should say 'similar qualities' instead of 'the same' — even in chemistry. And 'similar' for us. Nothing occurs twice . . . ." [66]

Therefore he defines "relative" endurance as a comparatively slow tempo of change, such that for the observer in question the successive differences are negligible. In other words, we call a process of change an enduring thing — a star, an animal species — when the successive moments, as we observe them, are very similar. Such "endurance" is relative to an observer, because similarity and tempo of change are relative matters: if our perceptions were much more rapid and acute, we should perceive a slumbering cliff as a dancing chaos.[67]

Like connectedness and change, the relative permanence, separateness, and unity in things are explained by aspects of the will to power. Will to power organizes, limits, therefore makes for duration — as in the special case of life. But also it reaches out for more, and this we have seen to be the cause of perpetual change. So it has a double aspect which, in most rudimentary form, appears as the forces of attraction and repulsion. More generally, it might be described as the combination of limitation and transcendence, of Apollinian and Dionysian traits.[68]

The source of cosmic emotion for a nineteenth-century scientist was Natural Law — eternal, invincible, exact. Nietzsche pokes fun at the idea: it petticoats the universe with middle class morality, as if cyclones and nebulae must really be respectable citizens enjoying democratic equality before

---

[66] XII 28. Except for eternal recurrence, that is.

[67] XVI 33, 55, 171 f.; XII 28 f.; XIX 174 ff. See above, pp. 278 f.

[68] Cf. XVI 117, 122 f., 386 f.; I 22 ff.; IX 289; XIX 199 f.; above, pp. 60–65, 73 ff., 163 ff., 205. II 211 ff. and V 148 testify that order is the condition of endurance.

the law. More seriously, it is another "shadow of God," a relic of ages which thought the world obedient to decrees of omnipotent deity.[69]

Nietzsche admits of course that we do recognize certain approximate regularities — recurrent *similarities* — in the course of events, but the practical success of science in calculating these proves neither that they are perfectly exact, nor that they are eternal, nor that some "necessity" is hovering over the process and compelling it to run a definite way.[70] We have seen that he retains some kind of causation for the will to power, but he rejects the grammatical mythology of a *separate* "cause" which "compels" the "effect" to happen: there is no such separation or universal compulsion in the nature of things.[71]

Since the total aspect of the universe is chaos and flux, Nietzsche holds that the rough uniformities described by science are local and temporary; the "laws" of nature have come to be, are changing, will perish:

I believe that even our chemical affinity and coherence are perhaps late-evolved phenomena, belonging to definite epochs in particular systems. Let us believe in absolute necessity in the All, but let us beware asserting of any law, be it even a primitive mechanical one in our experience, that it reigns in the All and is an eternal property.... Innumerable "properties" may have evolved, the observation of which is not possible for us, from our corner of space and time. The *alteration* of a chemical quality is perhaps taking place even now, only in so fine a degree that it escapes our subtlest calculation.[72]

And of course the development of these transient bits of order implies no intelligent purpose at work in nature: the play of chances and the will to power are enough.[73]

[69] XVI 33, 108 f.; V 148 f.; VII 33 ff.
[70] XVI 33, 53 f., 104 f., 108 ff., 154; XII 28, 30 f.; XIII 63; VII 35; H.K.A. III 323.
[71] VII 33; XVI 50–4, 109; XIII 60 f.
[72] XII 60. Cf. 58 f., 30 f.; V 148; XVI 105; X 151.
[73] IV 132, 125. Cf. XIX 197 f.; H.K.A. III 372, 385 f. Nietzsche has described

It is a special feature of Nietzsche's position that he completely separates the questions of universal law and universal determinism. He is an absolute determinist. Yet
his determinism is of a sort very different from the kind
held by believers in cause and effect as defined above. In
fact he holds that the usual belief in, and denial of, free will
rest alike on the fallacy of separating segments from the
continuous flux:

> Cause and effect: such a duality probably never exists — in
> truth a continuum confronts us, of which we isolate a few pieces,
> just as we always perceive a movement only as isolated points....
> An intellect which saw cause and effect as a continuum...
> which saw the flux of occurrence — would reject the conception
> of cause and effect and deny all conditionality [Bedingtheit].[74]

The fact that everything must happen as it does is

> ...not a determinism above the happening, but merely the
> expression of the fact that the impossible is not possible; that
> a definite force can be nothing else than just this definite force;
> that it does not discharge itself against a quantum of force-
> resistance otherwise than according to its strength; — happening
> and happening necessarily is a tautology.[75]

In this sense every man is indeed "a piece of fate." [76]

In place of docile obedience to "law," Nietzsche describes
the process — of inorganic nature at least — as "an absolute
settlement of power relations" in which "every power draws
its ultimate consequence at every instant. Precisely that
there is no ability to do othewise [Anderskönnen], on that
rests the calculability." [77] Traditional determinism was a
foe of novelty in nature because the effect was supposed to
be somehow "pre-existent" in the cause, but Nietzsche sub-

---

all happening as a *Feststellen* of power relations: perhaps the regularities we
call "laws" are simply cases where the power relations have been relatively
settled for a time (cf. XVI 57; XII 43; XIV 39).

[74] V 154. Cf. III 197 f.; VII 32 f., 327; XII 32; XVI 132.
[75] XVI 116. Cf. 54, 58, 109 ff.; VII 326 ff.
[76] III 235; VIII 89 f. Cf. XV 424.
[77] XVI 108, 111. Cf. 154; VII 35; XIII 62, 82.

stitutes for the atomic succession of causes and effects the notion that reality is a "tangle," an *Ineinander*, of wills to power, in which a new constellation of powers is continually arising — "the second state is something fundamentally different from the first (*not* its effect)." [78] Strictly speaking, the universal flux implies that every instant is something new.[79] And Nietzsche recognizes significant novelties, like the emergence of new qualities, which are not deducible from their origins.[80] The human spirit is a source of such novelties at present:

> Chaos still operates incessantly in our mind: concepts, images, sensations are *accidentally* brought together, jumbled up. . . . Here is the last bit of world, at least as far as the human eye reaches, where something new is being combined.[81]

5. A FINITE UNIVERSE

We are now ready to approach the idea which Nietzsche considered *the* supreme glory of his philosophy: eternal recurrence. He describes how the thought suddenly came to him in the summer of 1881,[82] and there can be no doubt that it made a decisive turning-point in his development. To understand his attitude toward it several facts must be considered. Being a Greek scholar, he knew of course that something *more or less* like this idea, as a bare factual belief, had been current in Antiquity.[83] Yet in 1881 something about it struck him with such force that it produced the overwhelming inspiration of *Thus Spake Zarathustra*, and gave him a permanent mission in life. *What* struck him? Surely not the mere bones of the doctrine, but some sig-

---

[78] XVI 110. Cf. 109, 102, 152; XII 72.
[79] XIII 242; XVI 33; XII 30 f.
[80] XIII 131, 277 ff.; XIV 44 f.
[81] XII 27 f. Cf. VII 223.
[82] XV 85. There are earlier traces of lines of thought which lead in the direction of the idea, but no evidence of serious concern with it (I 74, 169, 291, 298 f.; H.K.A. II 56, 68, 129).
[83] XV 65; I 298.

nificance that clothed it with fresh meaning, made it in effect
a startlingly *new* idea. Three years later he wrote to Overbeck:

> . . . it is possible that there has come to me for *the first time*
> the idea which will cleave the history of mankind into two
> halves. . . . *If it is true*, or rather: if it is believed true — then
> *everything* changes and revolves and *all* previous values are
> devalued.[84]

This gives the clue, abundantly verified elsewhere: eternal
recurrence appealed to Nietzsche not primarily as a cosmological theory, but as a way to transform humanity and
escape nihilism: [85] in short, it came as a new religion, and
certainly no one had made it the *basis* of a religion before.

But the idea just as a suggestion would be powerless. It
had to be established, at least as a probability, before it
would be taken seriously. Accordingly, part of Nietzsche's
inspiration must have been an intuition that his theory
could be supported by the rigorous standards of modern
thought — he later described it as "the *most scientific* of
all possible hypotheses." [86] In any case, he set about gather-
ing evidence for it, and connecting it with the rest of his
philosophical principles — many of which were already
fairly well matured.

In following Nietzsche's argument, we should remember
several things. He does not claim to prove his thesis beyond
doubt: on the contrary, he leaves open the possibility that
it is false, and tries to think up objections to it.[87] Nor does
he expect quick acceptance, or want uncritical "faith" at
all; rather he asks that his readers apply the most relentless
scepticism; only that will tell whether the idea deserves to
survive:

[84] L.O. c. 10/3/84. Cf. XV 125. Zarathustra is described as the first to teach
eternal recurrence (VI 321).

[85] See below, pp. 303 ff., 356 f.

[86] XV 182. Cf. 63. I 298 f. evidently holds the idea unlikely to be proved.

[87] XII 58 f. See above, p. 254.

Let us beware teaching such a theory as a sudden religion! It must infiltrate slowly; whole generations must build on it and become fruitful . . . .

You must have lived through every degree of scepticism . . . else you have no right to this idea; I wish to *defend* myself against the credulous and fanatical! [88]

But Nietzsche does sincerely believe in it; he stakes his life on it and keeps alive for it, though he is able to question it, and has black moods when all seems lost.[89] He is confident that it will be substantiated in the end:

An inevitable hypothesis, which humanity must hit upon again and again, is *more powerful* in the long run than the best believed belief in something untrue (like the Christian faith).[90]

Why is this a hypothesis to be taken seriously, why perhaps inevitable in the long run? That is our present problem.

Nietzsche has stressed the perpetual flux of things — the reality of time. Will there ever be an end to it? Certainly not, he argues. There has been endless time already: *if* the world were capable of coming to an end it must already have done so — whether the end be realization of an intelligent purpose or merely the final equilibrium of evenly dispersed energies implied by the Second Law of Thermodynamics. If it had ever found complete equilibrium once, it could never have got out of it again, and change would not now be going on. But change *is* going on. And for the same reason the flux could not have begun at a finite time in the past; if the world were previously in equilibrium it could never have begun to change. Nietzsche considers this fact one of the most certain we can grasp, and he proposes it as a criterion of possible world-hypotheses: since contem-

---

[88] XII 68 f. Cf. XIV 295; XV 116; VIII 126, 293 ff.; VI 114 f., 187. *Ecce Homo* is such a self-defense (XV 116).

[89] On the black moods and the sustaining power of his mission cf. L.O. c. 11/2/83, summer/83, c. 8/12/83, 14/4/87, 3/2/88; L.G. 15/1/88.

[90] V 169. See Abel Rey, *Retour éternel et la philosophie de la physique*, Paris: Flammarion, 1927.

porary mechanistic science predicts a final equilibrium at a finite time in the future, mechanism is to that extent *refuted*.[91]

Although time is infinite, he holds that space is not. If it were, energy would long ago have dispersed into triviality and the universe have run down — which is contrary to fact. For a similar reason space cannot be spherical: that too would have brought about a final equilibrium of forces. So the finitude and peculiar configuration [*Gestalt*] of space must account for the fact that change is ceaseless.[92] This is intelligible because there is no such thing as empty space, space *an sich* — that is an abstraction associated with such fictions as "matter" and "motion." [93] The world is everywhere a play of energies, and " 'energy' [*Kraft*] and 'space' are only two expressions for . . . the same thing." [94]

Nietzsche maintains that the energy of the world is finite too, for the very notion of indefinite or infinite energy is nonsense.[95] Now a finite energy can have only a finite number of possible states and combinations.[96] What will become of it in endless time? Either there is some infinite being outside it — in other words, a Divine Creator — who supplies it everlastingly with novelties and intentionally prevents the recurrence of an identical world situation, or it sooner or

[91] XVI 400 f., 396, 49, 116, 167; XII 53–57, 62; XV 182. Cf. VI 294. XVI 399 and XII 370 reply to the Kantian argument against the infinity of past time: such infinity means simply that if we should count backward from the present we never could reach an end. The creationist hypothesis is of course rejected (XVI 399).

[92] XII 54; XIII 86; XIV 325; XVI 49, 398; L.G. 23/7/85. H.K.A. II 69 contains a startling anticipation of the theory of the finite universe, although it includes time as well.

[93] XII 31 f., 54; XIII 86 f.; XIV 325; XVI 32. Cf. X 202; XII 33 f.; XIII 48; XIV 48 f.; L.M. 2/1/75.

[94] XIII 87; XVI 49, 401. This makes the finitude of space presuppose that of energy.

[95] XVI 397 f., 400 f.; XII 51, 53, 57, 61; XI 178 f.; XIII 87; VI 274.

[96] XVI 400; XII 52 ff. XII 55 argues that *Kraft*, being an attribute of *Lage*, cannot be absolutely divisible. This, together with the hint of an atomic theory of time (note 64, above), is apparently as near as Nietzsche comes to realizing that two additional assumptions are necessary to prove his case, namely that neither space nor time are continuous.

later exhausts its possibilities and must repeat itself. The
first alternative is excluded by Nietzsche's entire philosophical position; he regards such beliefs as moribund, incompatible with the modern scientific mentality; he condemns
the notion of creation out of nothing as utterly unintelligible, a mere word that explains nothing. So, although he
believes in novelties, he rejects the hypothesis of *eternal*
novelty.[97] The only conclusion therefore is, *"An infinite
process can* not be thought at all otherwise than as
periodic."[98]

We arrive, then, at the theory of eternal recurrence. If
the universe ever reaches a total state exactly identical with
a previous state, the principle of determinism implies that
the whole process must then repeat exactly the same course
previously followed between the two states, so that every
event recurs identically in every detail, and so on to all
eternity. As previously argued, a finite universe must sooner
or later repeat itself; therefore it is in fact always repeating
itself, always has, always will.[99]

So Nietzsche replies to the present theory of an inevitable
"running-down" of the universe:

The *last* physical state of energy [*Kraft*] which we infer must
also necessarily be the *first*. The dissipation of energy into latent
energy must be the cause of generation of the *most living* energy.
For a state of *highest* affirmation must follow a state of negation.[100]

Accordingly he pictures the world cycle as an alternate integration and disintegration of forces:

Mechanistically considered, the energy of total becoming
remains constant; economically considered, it rises to a peak
and sinks down from it again in an eternal revolution. This

[97] XVI 396 f., 399; XII 52 f., 56 f.; V. 149. He also appeals to the principle
of conservation of energy (XVI 398. Cf. 401).
[98] XII 370.
[99] XVI 400 f.; XII 51, 53, 56.
[100] XII 54.

"will to power" expresses itself in the *interpretation,* in the *manner of consuming energy* ....

"God" as moment of culmination: existence an everlasting deification and undeification.

The *recession from the peak in the becoming* (from the highest spiritualization of power on the most slavish foundation) [is] to be pictured as a *result* of this highest power, which, turning *against itself* after it has nothing more to organize, employs its power to *disorganize* . . .[101]

The end came before Nietzsche had completed his statement of his cosmology, and he did not fully clarify the relation of the eternal recurrence to the rest of his theories. But on several points he is explicit. The recurrence is a strictly universal and eternal law, thus an exception to the previous denial of eternal regularities in nature; the total aggregate of energy is likewise eternal, therefore both are exceptions to the universality of change — as was the will to power itself.[102] But total recurrence does not imply comprehensive order in nature:

The "chaos of the All" as exclusion of every purposiveness [*Zwecktätigkeit*] does *not* stand in contradiction to the idea of periodic return: the latter is precisely an *irrational necessity,* without any formal, ethical, aesthetic consideration.[103]

The recurrence is identical, and Nietzsche has otherwise denied identities in nature: but he bases that denial on the improbability of any two things being exactly alike — which would imply identical histories — and this he continues to maintain except for eternal recurrence, where of course the histories *are* identical.[104]

In these and other respects, eternal recurrence contrasts

[101] XVI 115, 170. Cf. I 169; XIX 199 f.
[102] XII 61. See above, p. 277.
[103] *Ibid.* See above, p. 269.
[104] XII 51 f. Cf. 29. VI 122 makes it very explicit that the recurrence is identical, not merely similar.

sharply with the tendency of his other cosmological views. He feels this not as lame qualification but as triumphant synthesis — union of opposites is the spirit of his entire thinking. Here, he says, is a philosophy which, without any dishonest escapes from the real world, finds a kind of eternity *within* time:

To *imprint* upon becoming the character of being — that is the *highest will to power.*

That *everything returns,* is the extremest *approximation of a world of becoming to that of being: — pinnacle of speculation* [*der Betrachtung*].[105]

[105] XVI 101. XVI 396 states that eternal recurrence unites the two extremest modes of thought — mechanism and Platonism.

CHAPTER XI

Dionysos

*Now I am light, now I fly, now I see me beneath my-
self, now a god dances through me.* (VI 58)

1. REALITY AND VALUE

THE anatomy of the universe is not enough. A
complete philosophy must clothe it with the flesh
and blood of emotion. Less than anyone would
Nietzsche be satisfied with a bare statement of fact about
the nature of things. What *sense* can we make of this world?
What can it mean for us, and what attitude shall we adopt
toward it? The pinnacle of Nietzsche's philosophy is a
poetic world view which re-unites reality and value.

As a prelude to that finale we must face a question which
underlies his entire revaluation of values: what *is* value?
We have seen the concrete patterns of worth which Nietzsche offers in place of the old, and also the standard which
defines the new scale of values. But so far they have simply
been asserted and applied. Is the revaluation finally nothing
more than a bold declaration? Can it be justified? The
answer depends on the nature of value.

In the relevant passages, Nietzsche uses not only this but
a variety of kindred terms — for example "disvalue," "valuation" (*Schätzung*), "esteem" or "estimation of value"
(*Wertschätzung*), "value feeling," "value judgment," "good
and evil," "yes and no" — and though they sometimes have
important differences of meaning they appear to a great
extent to be used interchangeably. What is the fundamental
idea behind these words?

The chief traditional view of values is that they are qualities which have a sort of timeless existence by themselves, and may be realized "in" things; they are absolute and universally valid. "Valuation" is accordingly an appreciation of independently existing "values," which is either true or false to them. Nietzsche rejects this view: values are not absolute; they exist neither by themselves *(an sich)* nor "in things," and none are eternal. Value is either the same as valuation or inextricably bound up with it:

> Verily, men gave themselves all their good and evil. Verily, they did not take it, they did not find it, it fell not as a voice from heaven.
>
> Man first put values into things to preserve himself....
>
> Valuing [*Schätzen*] is creating: listen, ye creators! Valuing is itself the treasure and jewel of all valued things.
>
> Only through valuing does value exist: and without valuing the nut of existence would be hollow.[1]

[1] VI 85 f. Cf. 43, 288, 293 f.; V 231; IV 213 f.; XII 357 f., 405; XIII 148; XIV 58 f.; XV 56, 151 f., 333 f., 336, 446; XVI 66 f., 92, 100, 231; I 497; L.Ge. 2/67; above, pp. 162 f., 187 f. Nietzsche sometimes seems to contradict this view, but careful reading shows that he means something else. For instance he demands an "objective" measure of value, but the context indicates that he is rejecting modes of *consciousness* as a standard: "objective" means "not a subjective state," not "independent of human preferences" (XIII 135; XVI 137, 165. See above, pp. 116, 125). On the contrary he ridicules affected "objectivity" of valuation in the latter sense (XV 451). Sometimes he speaks of "false values," but by "false" he again does not mean to imply an independent standard; rather he means "presupposing false judgments of fact" or "false to the nature of life," i.e. "unrealizable," "inapplicable"; or he means "hostile to the instincts and needs of life generally or of some particular life," i.e. false to Nietzsche's standard of value; or he means a case of valuational "lag" — inherited values false to new conditions and new aims, especially to those just emerging (XV 119 f., 151, 222, 338, 389, 397 f.; XVI 363, 431, 439; XIV 103, 319; XII 357; XI 373; VIII 88 f.; VI 69 f., 132, 423 f.; above, pp. 170 ff., 175, 360). He protests against overlooking the value of a man *an sich*, but means that we should value him for what he *is* and not merely for his effects on others: how we value him is still a matter of taste (XVI 294 f.; XV 399 f.), and Nietzsche of course does so primarily in terms of promise for the future of life (XV 408). In general, the dependence of value on valuation does not make it impossible to prize things for their own sake (cf. VIII 140; XVI 324, 383). Nietzsche comes nearest to contradicting his explicit theory of the status of value when he speaks of *Rangordnung* as something inborn, according to which we act whether we know it or not, and as obvious in the case of healthy vs. decadent lives (VII 165 f., 249; XIV 59; XVI 92, 278). The most plausible interpretation is: for Nietzsche, *Rangordnung* is *Machtordnung* (XVI 277 f.), and of course power is inborn (XVI 280) and

Values, therefore, can be created because they depend on valuations. For Nietzsche, revaluation of values means not a mere revision of opinions with respect to norms that are eternally fixed, but a re-making of values themselves.[2]

In his own language, values are *vital perspectives*. Each presupposes a point of view: "If one does not have a definite standpoint, nothing can be said about the value of anything: i.e. a definite *affirmation* of a definite life is the presupposition of every *valuation*."[3] He uses this relativity to a living process to explain the peculiar polarity of positive and negative values: good and evil, value and disvalue, are not a mysterious dualism in the nature of things but expressions of the fact that life must discriminate, must be "for" and "against," has "yes" and "no" in all its instincts. Good and evil are "complementary value concepts": to posit a good is *ipso facto* to posit an evil.[4]

The affinity between will to power and the power standard of value at times suggests that Nietzsche inconsistently claims a kind of absolute status for his own values — because life is an urge for power, power is universally good. But that does not seem to be the case:

> Whence shall we *take* valuations [*Wertschätzungen*]? From "life"? But "higher, lower, simpler, more complex" — are valuations [*Schätzungen*] which *we put* into life first. "*Evolution*" in every sense is always also a loss, an injury; even the specialization of every organ [is such].[5]

determines conduct; but that the degree of power constitutes the degree of value is finally *his* valuation. XIII 114, 172, make *Rangordnung* an expression of *Wertschätzung*, and imply that it changes as morals change in the course of history. Sometimes Nietzsche writes that only a few have the *right* to set up a new scale of values, but by "right" he evidently means "power," thus again presupposing his own standard (VI 35, 91; XIII 30 f. Cf. II 11 ff.). He seems to claim the superiority of his standard without transcending the principle of perspectivity in so far as his perspective is more comprehensive (cf. II 11 ff.; XI 371; above, pp. 261 f., below, pp. 366 ff.).

[2] Cf. V 94 f., 231; VI 288; VII 161; XVI 351, 363; above, p. 180.
[3] XIII 139. Cf. 172, 256; VII 55, 346; II 11; V 158 f.; XV 335; XVI 66; L.O. c. 25/7/84; above, p. 173.
[4] XV 396 f., 359, 363; VII 17; II 11; XII 264.
[5] XIII 138. Cf. 228; VII 17, 339; XII 359; XVI 310 f.; IV 103. It is possible

To one who thinks non-existence better than existence, or sickness better than health, all appeals to the nature of life are vain.[6]

Nietzsche calls the central valuation, around which a set of values crystallizes, an aim or "why" (*Ziel, warum, wozu*): everything else is valued with reference to it. His fundamental question is always, what shall be our goals?[7] And he charges that men have thought very foolishly and carelessly about ultimate "desirabilities" (*Wünschbarkeiten*) — they have been naïve and unrealistic, have confused means and ends, ignored incompatibilities, and tried to impose ends of a particular type as a law for all.[8]

By definition, supreme aims cannot be chosen for the sake of other aims. So Nietzsche makes ultimate valuations frankly a matter of "taste" (*Geschmack*).[9] But what is taste? What governs valuations? They are not arbitrary whims or mere states of consciousness. We do not say, "Go to, I will now like supermen." Values go as deep as life itself; they are perspectival, therefore many and changing; but *valuing* is an indestructible part of living. Indeed we cannot *take* our values from life: they spring from it. "When we speak of values, we speak under the inspiration, from the perspective, of life: life itself compels us to set [*anzusetzen*] values; life itself is valuing through us, *when* we set values . . ."[10] Valuing, in short, *is* will to power;

---

even to value inorganic existence higher than life (XII 229, 359; XIII 228). For passages which, if read without this warning, suggest that Nietzsche is "taking" his values from the nature of life, cf. XI 204; XV 169, 184, 232, 249, 363, 401; VIII 88 f.

[6] XI 220 f. Cf. VIII 49.

[7] VI 87, 288; VII 399, 482 ff.; VIII 217 f.; XV 82, 155 f., 321, 337, 423; XVI 223, 337. Cf. VII 338 f.; XII 95 f., 124 f.; XIII 150 f.; XV 158, 164, 336, 341 f.; XVI 97, 171, 177, 295, 342, 446. Hence the statement that we must take the future as *massgebend* for our valuations (XVI 359. Cf. VI 294 f.). Nietzsche expressly confines the term *gut* to the class of instrumental values (XI 251; XIII 148) and his usage generally conforms to this (e.g. VI 84 f.; VIII 9, 218; XI 373; XII 357).

[8] XV 384, 421 ff.; XVI 166, 170; VIII 139 f. Cf. XV 380 ff., 400.

[9] XII 95 f., 189; XIII 257; XV 400.

[10] VIII 89. Cf. XII 264; XIII 172; above, pp. 68 f.

this prime mover of reality prompts all our values.[11] Therefore taste "is weight and scale and weigher together."[12]

The discovery that values are not furnished us by the eternal nature of things is at first a phase of nihilism, but Nietzsche answers it by his revaluation of "appearance" generally. That values are perspectival does not desolate us, if we understand that reality is perspectival too: with the death of the Absolute goes its disparaging contrast with the relative. Values are woven into the texture of perspectives which make up the world; they are "appearances," but appearance is "the very thing which acts and lives."[13]

At the same time, Nietzsche believes in many levels of "appearance," and holds that values belong chiefly to the higher levels; aesthetic values, for instance, dwell in the humanized world of colors, tones, and shapes; and in general

... the more superficially and coarsely we comprehend, the more *valuable*, definite, beautiful, significant the world *appears*. The deeper one looks in, the more our esteem [*Wertschätzung*] vanishes — *unmeaningness draws near!*[14]

That is why he praises Greeks and artists for living wisely on the surface of things. "Inverted Platonism" he calls this view, because value varies inversely with truth: not truth but falsehood is divine.[15]

We have made "the world which concerns us" — but "we" in this case are an entire line of evolution; the life which values through us is instinct with all the past. So our values are not creations of the moment, nor can they be sloughed off quickly. They are inherited value judgments which in the course of generations have sunk deeper and

[11] VI 43, 84, 168; XIII 219; XIV 327; XV 333 f.; XVI 92, 100, 138, 415. See above, p. 118. Our particular valuations, including our ultimate aims, are a function of our degree of power (XIII 256; XV 152; XVI 177, 358. Cf. 363, 375).
[12] VI 171.
[13] V 88; XV 152, 155; XVI 66. See above, pp. 256–61.
[14] XVI 96. Cf. 65; IV 50; XI 72; XIX 176.
[15] V 10 f.; IX 190; XVI 70, 78 f., 365. Cf. I 34 f.; XIII 28 f.; XIV 366.

deeper into human nature until they have become part of our flesh and blood.[16] But we can participate in this process, Nietzsche says: by learning to see things as beautiful we *make* them beautiful.[17]

Though, racially speaking, "we" have made the values of things, we have long since forgotten it, believing that they were not created but simply "there." The discovery of this fact comes as a disillusion, because we, as individuals, are accustomed to having aims dictated by external authority. Let us learn instead to take pride in being artists of the value world:

All the beauty and sublimity we have lent to real and imaginary things, I intend to reclaim as property and production of man: as his most beautiful justification. Man as poet, as thinker, as god, as love, as power —: O, the royal munificence which he has bestowed upon things, to *impoverish* himself and feel wretched! That was his greatest selflessness hitherto, that he admired and worshipped, and was able to conceal from himself that *he* it was, who made that which he admired.[18]

And not only pride in past and present, but hope for the future: we have lent things their value predicates; let us take care that we do not lose the faculty of lending.[19]

2. THE BIRTH OF VALUE

In a minor way at least, every individual is a creator of values, Nietzsche believes,[20] but significant innovations — the great well-springs on which humanity lives — are born in the lives of a few supreme individuals who quietly mould history:

The world revolves — invisibly revolves — about the inventor of new values.

[16] V 94 f., 339; XIII 76, 173, 220, 256. Cf. II 207; XII 37; above, pp. 69 f., 101 f., 220 f., 246.

[17] V 209. Cf. 228 f., 230 f., 253, 263 f., 94 f.; IV 332, 359; VIII 123 f.; XV 175.

[18] XV 241. Cf. 155 f., 335, 381; VIII 131; XII 170 f., 358 f.; XIII 51; XIV 15; XVI 395; V 231; H.K.B. I 181.

[19] IV 214. Cf. XVI 97, 365.   [20] XVI 203.

All names of good and evil are similes: they do not express fully, they only hint. . . .

Give heed, my brothers, to every hour when your mind desires to speak in similes: then is the origin of your virtue.

Then is your body exalted and risen from the dead; with its ecstasy it transports the mind, so that it becomes a creator and valuer and lover and a benefactor of all things.[21]

The great beginnings occur when the spirit speaks a new language, but the language springs from the depths of man's being, not the surface of consciousness. Such are the decisive moments in the dialectical evolution of values; with them life takes another step.

Therefore, although Nietzsche speaks of the "lawgiver" who "commands" new values, he does not mean an act of frivolous caprice. He says rather that a great man feels his ideal *above* himself — "because he *sees* the higher, he is compelled to *carry it into effect* and enforce it." [22] Nietzsche describes his own experience of inspiration as a kind of involuntary compulsion,[23] and confesses:

I believe I have *guessed* something of the soul of the highest man; — perhaps everyone who guesses him will perish; but whoever has seen him is constrained to help make him *possible*.[24]

The first stirrings of new values manifest themselves as a change of "taste" — something deeper than a change of opinion. A new taste expresses a transformation of the "body," and he in whom a value is being born should have the courage to "profess" his nature and "to give ear to its demands even in their subtlest tones": then the value can live and become general.[25] So the motto of the creator of

[21] VI 73, 111. Cf. VI 112, 278; XII 141, 263; XIV 65, 361; XVI 171; above, p. 155.
[22] XIV 103. Cf. 374; I 413.
[23] XV 90 f. Cf. VII 138, 269.
[24] XVI 359. Cf. VI 180.
[25] V 76. A sudden change of "taste" preceded the inspiration of *Zarathustra* (XV 86. Cf. VIII 207).

values is not "I will" but finally "I am." In the symbolism
of *Zarathustra*, the lion — "I will" — can win freedom from
the old; but to make the new he must become a child: "The
child is innocence and oblivion, a fresh beginning, a play,
a wheel rolling of itself, a first motion, a sacred affirmation." [26]

With expressions like "command" and "lawgiver," Nietzsche seems to indicate rather the element of violence done
to existing preferences by the spread of the novel valuation
to others. Most people copy the tastes, enact the rôles, of
the great originators, like putting on so many clothes. But
in time rôle becomes character. So values, born in one,
come to live in many.[27] But here also the violence is not
purely arbitrary; it makes an appeal to energies, blind as
yet, stirring in others: "Morality can do nothing but erect
images of man, as art does: perhaps they may affect such
and such persons. Strictly speaking, it cannot prove them." [28]

Although Nietzsche makes ultimate values a matter of
"taste," he does not agree that we should not dispute about
them: life *is* a fight about tastes. The budding of new values
rives the old, and there is rivalry for power among the new.
That is but the inevitable expression of the struggling, ven-
turing, self-overcoming will to power. All "commanding"
involves risk, and society is an experiment to see who *can*
command. Nietzsche would call out many "lawgivers" to
contest the future of humanity — may the best poet win! [29]

To return to the present crisis, how does he justify his
own revaluation of values? First, because *some* new aims

[26] VI 35. Cf. 91; XVI 328.
[27] V 76, 230 f.; IV 332; VI 169; XIV 60. On "command" and "lawgiver" see
VI 111, 166 f.; VII 161 f.; XII 365; XIII 150, 177, 197 f.; XIV 103, 309; XVI 351.
[28] XI 216 (italics omitted). Cf. 220, 373; XIV 351; XVI 363, 375; below, pp.
360 f. Nietzsche speaks of the thinker as a poet and of ideals as *Dichtungen*
(V 230 f.; XII 122, 124, 170 f.), thus suggesting an important function for imagination in the formation of new values.
[29] VI 86 f., 111 f., 147, 166 ff., 171, 309; XII 256, 363, 365. So, though he
admits no standards *external* to taste, he believes that a taste should evolve
its justifying theory (cf. L.G. 19/11/86; XI 80 f.; XVI 255 f.).

are imperative. The old ones are falling about our heads: they are a chaos of ideals derived from narrower circumstances, contradicting each other and incompatible with reality.[30] That is nihilism. Amid the general debacle, we can only appeal to the creative vital instincts whence all values spring: perhaps our scepticism is a sign that new life is stirring.[31]

Nietzsche offers his values as a new language in which life has spoken through him, hoping that mankind can be persuaded to speak it with him. He is *recommending* a goal for humanity.[32] And his values claim this advantage: they fit the nature of things, both justifying the inevitable and glorifying the possible. They will help man, now tragically at odds with himself, to feel his ideals identical with his strongest urges, and teach him to set as his goal the making of divine individuals — supermen — who will be a transfigured image and justification of all existence: [33]

To create a being, higher than we ourselves are, is *our* being. *Create beyond ourselves!* That is the urge to procreation, that is the urge for the deed and the handiwork. — As all volition presupposes a goal, *so does man presuppose a being* which does not exist, but which serves as the goal of his existence.[34]

3. FOR THE STRONG

The completed theory of value provides the basis for a final settlement with nihilism. Nietzsche says that the familiar controversy between optimism and pessimism is based on a misunderstanding, as if the universe had a total value about which estimates must be either true or false.

[30] XII 357 f., 362; XIV 335; XV 337. See above, p. 160.
[31] XIV 17; XII 264, 358.
[32] IV 103; VI 13, 87, 111 f., 115. Cf. XV 337.
[33] XVI 166, 296, 365, 451; XIV 335; VI 43, 112 f. Cf. XV 122. The most valuable aspects of existence, in Nietzsche's estimation, are those which express it (i.e. the will to power) most plainly (XVI 383. Cf. XV 389). Nietzsche seems finally not to claim to deduce his values *from* life, but to shape them so as to harmonize *with* life.
[34] XIV 262 f. Cf. 267; XII 359; VI 94, 125 f., 168, 236; above, pp. 183 f.

Since valuations are perspectival, assertions about the value of all existence are meaningless. It is not only ridiculous that man, one small part, should set up as judge of the whole: it is impossible. He would have to assume a point of view outside the all, and have something else than it in terms of which to judge — both excluded by definition. Moreover, when a pessimist condemns living, he is *doing* what he condemns, in that very act.[35]

Nietzsche sees no more sense in arguing with him than with a color-blind person. The only significance of such blanket assertions about the world is that they are symptoms of a kind of life — in this case, decadence. Life's will to power speaks even through the values of decadents, for life needs death. But the old morality lied when it taught them to generalize their case: instead of saying truly, "I am no longer worth anything," they have said, "Life is worthless." [36] The real issue reads: Is *our* life worth living? "Where do *we* belong?" To the healthy or the decadent? "It is absolutely not a question of the best or the worst world: — No or Yes, *that* is the question." [37]

Nietzsche writes for men who mean to say Yes. His philosophy is emphatically not for everybody; it is only for the healthy, the strong, who are able to *make* life worth living.[38] By "health" he means "great health" or "plastic force" which is able to overcome the diseases of modernity:

It is finally a question of power [*Kraft*]: this whole romantic art could be bent around entirely into anti-romanticism or — to use my formula — into the *Dionysian*, by an exuberant artist, mighty of will: just as every kind of pessimism and nihilism, in the hand of the strongest, only becomes one more hammer and instrument with which a new stairway to happiness is built.[39]

[35] XVI 138, 167 f., 170, 202, 406 f.; V 7, 148, 279 f.; VIII 69, 88 f., 101; XV 63. Cf. VI 274.
[36] VIII 143, 49, 69, 88 f.; XV 63, 166 f., 174 f., 184 f.; V 7; XVI 138.
[37] XIV 221; XVI 406 f.
[38] See above, pp. 35 f., below, pp. 356 f.
[39] XIV 162. Cf. III 11; V 342 ff.; VI 395 f.; XVI 366.

Nihilism makes existence seem meaningless: the world is certainly not worth what we once thought. But, since values are created, what is to prevent us from making new ones in terms of which life will be supremely good? Instead of condemning reality with the old ideals, Nietzsche urges that we "contrive a new perfection" which will justify it. "Suppose our usual conception of the world were a *misunderstanding*: could a *perfection* be conceived, within which even such *misunderstandings* would be *sanctioned*?" [40] Perhaps so, if we are strong enough: "It is a measure of *will power*, how far one can do without *meaning* in things, how far one can endure living in a meaningless world: *because one organizes a little bit of it himself*." [41]

Nietzsche's recipe for the "new perfection" is the superman: he is to be "the meaning of the earth," the aim of humanity.[42] We have caught sight of this ideal from many angles: Nietzsche's intuition of value, the potentialities of human evolution, the perfection of integrated and spiritualized power, individualities as the ultimate ends, the "sovereign individual" as the ideal outcome of "individual morality," superlative beauty in art, maximum objectivity in knowledge. The superman would be a fulfilment of all these promises: the "whole man," the "synthetic," "complementary," "redeeming" man, "in whom the *rest* of existence justifies itself"; a "type of highest successfulness [*Wohlgeratenheit*]" in whom life really "comes off" to perfection; an epitome of nature, uniting all her antitheses — highest and lowest — in serene freedom: a transfiguration of existence.[43]

[40] XVI 365. Cf. 95, 450; XV 163; V 279 f.
[41] XVI 84 f. Cf. 97; XV 152 f., 155 f., 186 f.; XIII 78; X 275.
[42] VI 13, 24, 43, 112 f., 123 ff., 418.
[43] VII 152, 325; XII 255; XIV 335, 340; XV 51, 122; XVI 246, 287, 296 f., 344 f., 379, 387, 391; X 276; L.G. 3/8/83. Cf. I 32, 440 f., 443; II 50; IX 203 f.; XIII 167; XV 12 f.; XVI 361; above, pp. 123, 128, 131 f., 138 f. Though Nietzsche had a period of romanticism, he later wished to mark off his position very distinctly from the nineteenth-century genius and hero cult (cf. IV 248 f.).

Nietzsche draws his fullest portrait of a superman in a comment on *Thus Spake Zarathustra*:

He contradicts with every word, this most affirmative of all spirits; in him all opposites [*Gegensätze*] are bound into a new unity. The highest and the nethermost forces of human nature, the sweetest, wantonest and fearfullest, flow out from one spring with immortal sureness.... Here man is overcome at every moment; the idea "superman" became supreme reality here .... The halcyon quality, the light feet, the ubiquity of mischievousness and exuberant gaiety, and all else typical of the type Zarathustra, have never been dreamed of as essential to greatness. Precisely in this amplitude of space, in this accessibility to the diametrically opposed, Zarathustra feels himself to be the *highest species of all existence* ...

> — the soul which has the longest ladder and can descend lowest,
> the amplest soul, which can run and stray and roam farthest in itself,
> the most necessary, which plunges with zest into chance,
> the "being" soul, which *rushes* into "becoming," the possessing one, which *rushes* into willing and craving —
> the self-fleeing one, which overtakes itself in widest circles,
> the wisest soul, to which folly speaks most sweetly,
> the most self-loving, in which all things have their current and counter-current and ebb and flow — —

But that is the idea of Dionysos himself.[44]

Dionysos is Nietzsche's symbol for the deification of life, and its highest formula is the attainment of just that unqualified Yes to existence which is the goal of his philosophy. He describes how, by thinking out pessimism to its extreme, his eyes were opened to the opposite ideal "of the most exultant, alive, world-affirming man" who has not merely reconciled himself to reality but calls for the whole piece over and over again, to all eternity.[45] Zarathustra, although he is one who

... has the most fearful insight into reality, who has thought the "most abysmal thought," nevertheless finds therein no ob-

[44] XV 95 f. Cf. VI 304.   [45] VII 80. Cf. V 343 f.

jection to existence, not even to its eternal recurrence — rather
an additional reason *for being himself* the eternal Yes to all
things, "the enormous and unbounded yea-and-amen-saying"
.... *But that is the idea of Dionysos again.*[46]

Such a "Dionysian world view" is, properly speaking, a
superhuman perspective of the world.[47] How can it concern
even the strong among us, who after all are not supermen?
Nietzsche believes that one who can thus affirm life justifies
it vicariously for us who will work to make him possible.
A note, written perhaps in a time of despondency, runs:
"I do not want life *again.* How have I borne it? Creating.
What makes me endure the spectacle? The glimpse of the
superman, who *affirms* life. I *myself* have tried to affirm it —
ach!" [48] It remains to trace the steps by which the supreme
Dionysian experience is obtained.[49]

4. ETERNAL RECURRENCE

Nietzsche's problem is how to say Yes to reality; and his
description of reality has culminated in the idea of eternal
recurrence. What is the human significance of this theory?
In his mind, it is first of all a means to extremes. If the
reader has felt a deep repugnance to it, that is exactly what
Nietzsche expects and wants, and undoubtedly what he
himself often felt. By present standards it would be the
greatest conceivable senselessness — "the extremest form
of nihilism: nothingness ('meaninglessness') everlasting!" [50]
— a tale told by an idiot, idiotically repeated *ad infinitum.*

[46] XV 96 f. Cf. VI 231 f., 334 ff.; VIII 163 f., 172 ff.
[47] XII 413.
[48] XII 359. Cf. 397, 399 f.; XIV 294; I 417 f.; X 420; XI 13; above, pp. 42 f.
Nietzsche seems to have attained the Dionysian experience repeatedly but not
continuously or perhaps for very long — most so during the composition of *The
Birth of Tragedy* and *Zarathustra,* and toward the end. He says that *Zarathustra*
contains a picture of his nature when he has thrown off his "whole burden"
(L.O. c. 11/2/83. Cf. XV 86, 90 f., 94 ff.).
[49] That Nietzsche may have considered it a type of mystic experience is suggested by XIV 322, 331; XIII 297; XII 259. Cf. I 95.
[50] XV 182. Cf. VI 197 ff., 314 f., 319 f.

On the other hand *if* one attained an unreserved love of this world as it is, its everlasting return would raise affirmation to ecstasy: nothing would ever be lost; there would be no last farewells. "Courage . . . strikes even death dead, for it says, 'Was *that* life? Well then, once again!' " [51]

The moral import of eternal recurrence, therefore, places an infinite weight on every moment of life, forcing us toward one extreme or the other: either the weight will crush us or we shall overcome "the spirit of heaviness." Hitherto mankind has faced an unsolved dilemma: either this life is all, and in that case the last word is vanity of vanities, for nothing abides; or there is a Beyond which indeed makes life a serious business, but at the cost of condemning it as illusory and evil — ultimately, nihilism:

> How can we give weight to the inner life without making it angry [*böse*] and fanatical toward those who think differently? Religious faith is decreasing and man is learning to conceive himself as ephemeral and unimportant; he is finally becoming weak thereby; he no longer practises endeavor and endurance, he wants present enjoyment, he takes it easy . . . .[52]

Nietzsche offers the eternal recurrence as a view which solves the dilemma, and without the fanaticism of the older religions — its sole punishment for unbelief will be the consciousness that one's life is utterly transient: [53]

> My teaching says: the task is, so to live that you must *wish* to live again — you are going to *in any case!* Let him strive, to whom striving gives the highest feeling; let him be tranquil [*ruhen*], to whom tranquility gives the highest feeling; let him obey, to whom orderly arrangement, following, obedience gives the highest feeling. Only *let him become conscious of what it is* that gives him the highest feeling, and shrink from *no means!* *Eternity* is at stake!

[51] VI 230. Cf. XII 66, 369, 409; XV 85, 443; XVI 398.
[52] XII 63. Cf. 64, 66 ff.; I 422 f.
[53] XII 68. He calls it a religion or a substitute for religion in XII 69, 415; XV 487.

In all that you want to do, the question, "Is it such, that I want to do it innumerable times?" is the *greatest* weightiness [*Schwergewicht*].[54]

Nietzsche deliberately devises the theory as the extremest form of fatalism, in order to generate the greatest possible degree of energy [55] — as indeed fatalistic beliefs have sometimes done.

These beneficent effects, one should remember, will come only to men strong enough to learn to endure, and if possible to love, the idea of recurrence. Nietzsche shapes the rest of his philosophy as a kind of counterpoise to enable some men to sustain this "most abysmal thought." [56]

Fatalism can arouse several responses: it can make us open-hearted and release our energies, but it can also make us cowardly, resigned, indifferent or reckless. How we take it depends ultimately of course on ourselves. But Nietzsche's theory of determinism at least eliminates a misunderstanding: fate is not something external that compels us against our wills; it partly acts through our willing, and therefore gives no reason for resignation or passivity. What we do is part of the process: "*Ego fatum*" — "I myself am fate and *condition existence from all eternity*," [57] — all existence, even past and present, since time is circular. And belief in eternal recurrence, as it becomes "assimilated," will shape our lives.[58]

Effort, therefore, does make a difference. But the whole drama has been acted out an infinite number of times before: are we really accomplishing anything by our efforts? Against the feeling that "all is the same, all was" [59] Nietzsche

[54] XII 64 f. Cf. 67; V 265 f.; above, pp. 191 f.
[55] XIV 331. Cf. XVI 396. He calls eternal recurrence his "completion of fatalism" because it involves a kind of eternal pre-existence as well as future repetition (XIII 75). On the relation to freedom of will cf. XIII 262 f.
[56] XVI 295 f.
[57] XII 399; XIII 74, 40; XIV 99, 294; III 172, 235; XVI 396. Cf. VIII 217; H.K.B. I 180 f. On weak fatalism see further XV 18 f., 320; VIII 122.
[58] XII 64.   [59] VI 197, 319.

summons all the uncertainty, infinite perspectivity, chance, and creativity of his universe. Eternal recurrence involves a finite universe, but it leaves plenty of "infinity" for *us*. Its total character is chaos; no mechanical uniformities run through it. Its flux of perspectives, its multi-interpretability, give to existence what Nietzsche calls its "enigmatic character." The inexhaustible riddles and dangers of life, her seductive sphinx-nature, are what make him love her most.[60] And since the determinism in nature works through the chance encounters of formative energies, the "extremest fatalism" is "identical with chance and creativity." The inevitable course of events is not, so to speak, there already; there is "no repetition in things, but rather it is first to be created." [61]

Again, eternal recurrence would be unbearable if the old moral values survived — if there were such things as guilt, sin, absolute evil. Therefore it constrains those who would say Yes to revalue the old values.[62] The result of discarding those cardinal points of "absolute morality" is, as we have seen, a kind of second innocence. Accordingly "the innocence of becoming" forms part of Nietzsche's joyous affirmation. He finds it "a great restorative" that there is no God, no cosmic purpose to which we are responsible, and that nothing whatsoever is to blame for things being as they are; our world is cleansed of all resentment, revenge, punishment. He symbolizes this novel world-feeling by Heracli-

[60] XVI 395 f., 5 f., 95, 370 f.; XIV 354; VI 157 ff., 228 f., 275, 328 ff. Cf. VII 9, 358; VIII 416; XIV 178; XVI 73; above, pp. 268 ff. This appreciation of uncertainty instead of certainty is part of the revaluation of values; see above, pp. 252 ff. It is possible that *one* meaning of the symbol *Ariadne* is "seductive, labyrinthine life": she is the labyrinth in which the "hero" perishes; but she in turn is hunted by the "god" (Dionysos), and is the answer to his dithyramb of solitude: Dionysos is the victorious, philosophic lover of life (cf. XIV 253; VI 328 ff.; VIII 429, 432, 131; VII 273; XV 100). He is also the creative "sun" and life the "deep ocean" which he draws up to himself (VI 182. Cf. 153 ff.; XV 97, 100).

[61] XIV 301. Cf. XII 405; XVI 101, 395 f. Compare the creation of truth: XV 94; XVI 56.

[62] XII 68; XIV 331; XVI 395.

tus' image of the Child Zeus whose innocent play is the flux of nature. Such, in part, is Nietzsche's "aesthetic justification of existence": the world as a whole transcends moral distinctions, is beyond good and evil.[63] Zarathustra's dithyramb, "Before Sunrise," is a song of innocence:

This freedom and celestial serenity I put like an azure bell over all things, when I taught that above them and through them no "eternal will" — wills.

This boisterous gaiety and this folly I put in the place of that will, when I taught, "In everything, one thing is impossible — rationality!"

A little wisdom is possible, no doubt; but this blessed certainty I found in all things: that on feet of chance they prefer to — *dance*.[64]

5. THE TRAGIC MEANING OF PAIN

Being beyond good and evil, the Dionysian world view escapes the problem of moral evil which bedevils theologians, but it has to face the disgusting, ugly, and painful features of existence. How can we bear the everlasting recurrence of these?[65]

Nietzsche feels it a great relief that there is no cosmic consciousness, no God who feels and knows of all suffering in the world, yet does not prevent it. Such a "summation of pain and illogicality" would be "the greatest objection to existence."[66]

But Nietzsche despises the "pessimism of sensibility"

[63] XVI 166 f., 201 f., 222 f., 225 f.; XIII 75, 127; VII 381, 388; VIII 99 ff.; I 8, 45, 168 f.; X 41; XIX 177 ff., 184, 187. On "child" and "play" see further III 139; V 344; VI 35, 108, 218; VII 98; XI 71; XV 47; XVI 73; L.F.N. I 317 or H.K.A. II 59. On life as an aesthetic spectacle see also IV 329, 334; V 142 f.; XIII 90.
[64] VI 243. Cf. 240 ff.; above pp. 174 f. For sinfulness Nietzsche would substitute a feeling of the general *Missratensein* of man, with resulting self-dissatisfaction and self-contempt, producing an urge to create men who are not contemptible (XIV 330. Cf. VI 13 ff., 52, 60, 94, 261, 277 f., 388, 425 f.; XIII 77).
[65] Cf. XVI 395; VI 298 f., 319 f.; XV 442.
[66] XVI 167 f. (italics omitted). Cf. 166, 395; II 51.

which despairs of life because it thinks the total sum of misery greater than the sum of pleasure. That is for weaklings. A strong will might still affirm life, finding the excess pain necessary for its goal.[67] The real problem is one of meaning:

> Man, the bravest animal and most accustomed to grief, does *not* deny suffering absolutely: he *wants* it, he even seeks it out, provided one show him a *meaning* for it . . . . The meaninglessness of suffering, *not* suffering, was the curse which hitherto lay spread over mankind . . . .[68]

Hence the fascination which the ascetic ideal has exercised in history: God's delight in human pain was at least *a* meaning for it.[69] That solution is no longer possible or desirable for Nietzsche, but he hopes that we shall remain heirs of Christianity to the extent of utilizing, instead of condemning, suffering as such.[70]

He finds the Dionysian meaning of pain in tragedy. This is a world of everlasting becoming, and will to power makes it an active process of creating and destroying. "The affirmation of perishing *and annihilating*" is therefore "the decisive feature of a Dionysian philosophy." [71] Only so can one say Yes without reservation:

> The psychology of the orgy as a feeling of overflowing life and energy [*Kraft*], within which even pain operates as a stimulant, gave me the key to the notion of the *tragic* feeling . . . . The assent to life even in its most alien and hardest problems, the will to life, rejoicing at its own inexhaustibleness in the *sacrifice* of its highest types — *that* I called Dionysian . . . . Not in order to get rid of terror and pity . . . but rather, out beyond terror and pity, *to be oneself* the eternal joy of becoming . . . .[72]

---

[67] XV 164; XVI 161. See above, p. 117, note 8.
[68] VII 483. Cf. I 434 f.
[69] VII 482 f.; 358 f.
[70] XIII 90.
[71] XV 65. Cf. V 326; XIV 366; XVI 386 f., 402.
[72] VIII 173 f. Cf. XIV 78, 331; XV 62 f., 86, 443; XVI 268, 272, 377; I 116 f.; above, pp. 214 f.

Nietzsche believes that pain and ugliness are inextricably involved in the becoming of the best. Ugliness is the condition of things antecedent to the creation of beauty.[73] Pain is inevitable in the destruction of what has been — even the noblest must die in order to be born again in the great circle of time. "Grief says, 'Perish!'" But it is also an instrument of transmutation. Like dissonance in music, it spurs man onward, beyond the present moment, and only the discipline of sorrow brings him to his full height. The more future a man has in him, the more he must suffer — "this is the profoundest conception of *suffering*: the formative forces collide."[74] Moreover pain is "father of joy": they increase and diminish together. To increase sensitiveness in variety and depth is to enhance pleasure *and* pain, and the zealots who want to abolish suffering are really tending to make man callous and mediocre.[75] In the most exquisite pleasures, pain is a subtle ingredient. Nietzsche describes the glow of inspiration in which he wrote *Zarathustra* as "a depth of happiness, in which the most painful and dismal does not act as opposite [*Gegensatz*], but rather as conditioned, as demanded, as a *necessary* color within such an excess of light."[76]

In contrast to "pessimism of sensibility," he calls his own view "pessimism of strength": "With this will in one's breast, one does not fear the fearfulness and dubiousness which belong to all existence; one even seeks for that. Behind such a will stands valor, pride, the desire for a *great* enemy."[77] The tragic artist affirms "the Great Economy," glorifies the fact that both evil and good are necessary.[78]

---

[73] XV 442. Cf. 100 f.; I 6; VII 384.
[74] VI 468 ff.; XVI 151. Cf. V 8 f.; VI 125, 333, 426; VII 64 f., 180 f.; XIII 362 f.; XIV 301; I 168 f.
[75] XVI 395; V 49 f.; VII 64 f., 180 f., 258; XII 195. Cf. V 230; XIII 37; XIV 99, 292, 302.
[76] XV 90. Cf. XVI 373; XIII 274; above, p. 117, note 8.
[77] III 12. Cf. 8; I 2, 6 f.; V 326 f.; XIV 219, 370 ff.
[78] XVI 270. Cf. 383; VIII 90, 206; XV 63 f., 119 f.; above, pp. 185 f.

Man must grow "better and more evil," and the supreme evil coincides with the supreme good. Nietzsche does not reproach life for its cruelties; he would have life more cruel that it might attain its highest form — the "victor." [79] In fact we must cultivate a certain taste for cruelty if we are thoroughly to like this world.[80] Existence reveals its best only to men who fearlessly hunt out its worst:

> The ancient thinkers sought happiness and truth with all their might — and one shall never find what he is obliged to seek, runs Nature's wicked rule. But whoever seeks untruth in everything and voluntarily consorts with unhappiness, for him perhaps another miracle of disillusionment is being prepared: something ineffable, of which happiness and truth are only idolatrous imitations, draws near him; earth loses its heaviness . . . .[81]

Pain is not the last word, therefore. Nietzsche does not say that there is *more* joy than pain; he says joy is *prior* and *deeper*. Prior, because pain is "only the *consequence* of the will to joy [*Lust*] (— to creating, shaping, destroying, demolishing) and, in the supreme form, a variety of joy." [82] More profound than pain, because

> . . . all joy wants eternity —,
> — wants deep, deep eternity! [83]

Sorrow brings the morrow, but joy lives in the magic moment, which eternally returns: it reaches beyond death to immortality. "Love for life is almost the opposite of love for living long. All love thinks of the moment and eternity — but *never* of 'length.' " [84]

[79] XIV 81, 331; VI 169; VII 64 f., 181; XV 416; XVI 311, 344 f.
[80] XIII 43. Cf. VII 356 ff.; XII 295; XIV 78.
[81] I 432. Cf. III 10; XII 285; XVI 382 f.
[82] XIV 369. Cf. XVI 273; XIII 274.
[83] VI 471. Cf. 333, 468 ff.
[84] XII 308. Cf. III 183. On *Augenblick* see further: I 523; II 343; V 265; VI 160 ff., 231, 289, 402, 469; VII 179; XII 371; XIV 306; XV 81. Compare the earlier contrast of the "historical" with the "unhistorical" and "over-historical" points of view (I 283–94, 379).

Nietzsche agrees with Christianity that suffering must be given a meaning; he disagrees about the kind of meaning:

Dionysos versus the "Crucified": there you have the contrast [*Gegensatz*]. It is *not* a difference with respect to the martyrdom — this only has a different meaning. Life itself, its everlasting fertility and recurrence, stipulate agony, destruction, the will to annihilation. In the other case, suffering, the "Crucified as the innocent one," counts as an objection against this life, as a formula for its condemnation. — One divines: the problem is that of the meaning of suffering: whether a Christian meaning, or a tragic meaning. In the first case it is supposed to be the path to a sacred existence [*Sein*]; in the latter case, *existence* is accounted *sacred enough* to justify immensely greater sorrow. The tragic man affirms even the bitterest suffering: he is strong, full, deifying enough for that; the Christian disavows even the happiest lot on earth: he is weak, poor, disinherited enough to suffer from life in any form. The God on the cross is a curse upon life, a warning to deliver oneself from it; — Dionysos cut to pieces is a *promise* of life: it will be everlastingly reborn and return home out of destruction.[85]

6. AMOR FATI

In the crisis of values Nietzsche's final position is: instead of condemning reality as not to our "taste," let us cultivate a taste for reality. The supreme achievement of this goal is the Dionysian relationship to existence, Nietzsche's formula for which is *amor fati* — love of the fate which returns everlastingly.[86]

Learning to love fate — particularly the fate that is oneself — is the hardest and longest of the arts, but because values are plastic we *can* learn it, in our distant grandchildren at least. The illumination which begins Nietzsche's third period, casting a serene light on everything, is based

[85] XVI 391 f. Cf. VIII 172 f.; XIII 218; I 74; above, pp. 42 f. Among the first symptoms of his insanity were some notes which Nietzsche signed, "The Crucified": cf. Podach, *op. cit.*, pp. 136 ff.
[86] XVI 383; XII 225; XV 48. Cf. VIII 163 f.

on the perception that evil as well as good, and sorrow as well as joy, serve in the total economy of life, and that an alchemy of valuation is possible which will make all dross gold — there is no accident, no misfortune which we cannot turn to gain:

Amor fati: may that be my love from now on! I intend to fight no war against the ugly. I do not intend to accuse, I do not even intend to accuse the accusers. Let *looking away* be my only negation! And, all in all, and in the large: I want some day to be only an affirmer [*Ja-sagender*]! [87]

This knowledge is Nietzsche's "gay science."

Perfect love of fate will come only with the superman — in fact that is his very essence. With deepest knowledge and sensitiveness, he loves eternal recurrence without reserve, and so becomes an "everlasting Yes to all things." [88] Anticipation of him alone makes belief in recurrence tolerable for *us*.[89]

Nietzsche symbolizes all the burdens of life by "the spirit of heaviness." Completed love of fate means a victory over this spirit, which he symbolizes by dancing, flying, laughing, and singing — when the world has become *light*, that will be the divine culmination of existence for man.[90] Pity for the sufferings of the world hangs heavily upon a sensitive man. He must take courage. "Courage is the best killer: courage kills even pity. But pity is the deepest abyss: as deep as man sees into life, so deep he sees also into suffering." [91] Compassion for "higher men" is accordingly the last temptation which Zarathustra has to overcome.[92] And the ultimate, blessed victory over all heaviness is foretold in the allegory

---

[87] V 209. Cf. 210, 33 f.; VI 162, 223, 250, 282 f.; VIII 206; XII 141; XIV 226; XV 45; L.Ge. 2/67; L.Mu. 18/10/75; L.O. c. 25/12/82, summer/83; L.B. 23/5/88; H.K.A. III 344.

[88] XV 96 f.   [89] XIV 265, 306; XII 399 ff.

[90] VI 58, 156 ff., 281 ff., 289, 326 f., 338 f., 427 ff.; V 339 f., 342; I 13 f. Cf. XIX 190. Earlier terms of the series are "standing, walking, running, jumping and climbing" (VI 285).

[91] VI 230.   [92] VI 475 f. Cf. XII 310; XIV 147.

of the shepherd and the snake: the shepherd, waking to find
the "most abysmal thought" — eternal recurrence of "all
that is heaviest and blackest" — caught fast like a snake in
his throat, is almost suffocated with horror and loathing;
but he courageously bites off the head of the snake and
leaps up:

No longer shepherd, no longer man — one transformed, shone
about with light, who *laughed*! Never yet on earth did ever a
man laugh as *he* laughed!

Oh my brothers, I heard a laughter that was no man's laughter
— — and now a thirst consumes me, a longing which never grows
still.[93]

It is the laughter of the superman for which Nietzsche longs,
the laughter of one who is beyond tragedy.[94]

In a cyclic world the past cannot be simply dismissed
forever, for it is also the future. And of all life's burdens,
the past is most inexorable — we can never change it. But
a Dionysian man must love this fate too. Nietzsche would
redeem the past itself by creating a future which justifies
it after the fact:

We must take upon us and affirm *all* suffering that has been
suffered, by men and animals, *and have a goal in which it gets
reason.*

We justify all the dead subsequently and give their life a
meaning, when we form the superman out of *this* material and
give the entire past a *goal*.[95]

It is as if Bach, given a half-written and chaotic piece of
music, should carry it to a close for which every note had
become an inevitable preparation.

[93] VI 234. Cf. 126; 317 ff. I 56 describes comedy as a release of *Ekel*.

[94] Cf. V 34 ff.; VI 428; VII 270 f.; XII 310; XVI 357; L.St. 12/82. "Wer von
euch kann zugleich lachen und erhoben sein?" (VI 57). On laughter in general
see also XVI 356, 382. The Primordial One in *The Birth of Tragedy* appears to
see the world as a comedy (I 44 f.).

[95] XIV 266; XII 360. Cf. VI 206 ff., 290, 297; XV 100; XII 65; V 73; L.F.N.
I 317 or H.K.A. II 58 f.

Nietzsche's world view thus ends, when "the world has become perfect," in a pantheistic benediction of all existence:

This very *pessimism of strength* ends with a *theodicy*, i.e. with an absolute *assent* [*Ja-sagen*] to the world — but on the grounds formerly given for saying No to it —: and, in such fashion, to the conception of this world as the actually *attained highest possible ideal*.[96]

But does this not again present a problem analogous to that of fatalism: why should we discriminate values and try to make things better, if everything is perfect? Nietzsche is careful to guard himself against this interpretation. In *Zarathustra* he satirizes the complacency (*Allgenügsamkeit*) of "asses" who say "*I-A*" (yes) to everything that comes along. Distinctions of value are perspectival. But to affirm everything is to affirm *them* too, thereby saying Yes to all the actual No's. Thus Zarathustra can be at once the most "Yes-saying" and the most "No-doing" of minds.[97]

But affirmation, not negation, is the last word. For things are so connected that to negate anything unconditionally is to negate all — including that negation — and to say Yes to one instant is to say Yes to eternal recurrence. Therefore:

If becoming is a great ring, then everything is of the same worth, eternal, necessary. — In all correlations of Yes and No, of preference and rejection, loving and hating, only a perspective, an interest, of definite types of life is expressed: in itself, everything that is says Yes.[98]

To him who has married "the ring of rings," all moments of time are bound together in a mystic unity of shared value. Nothing is merely for the sake of something to come.[99] His Dionysian rapture beholds the universe as a divine dance:

[96] XVI 372. Cf. 362; VI 401 f.; VIII 302; XV 183, 442.
[97] VI 279, 284, 453 f.; XII 67; XV 95 f., 102, 117 ff., 358 f.
[98] XV 359. Cf. 358, 183, 343 f., 380 f.; XVI 82, 378; XIII 74; VIII 90, 163 f.; VI 241 ff., 469 f.
[99] XVI 167 f., XV 183. Cf. I 291 f.; VI 334 ff.

And do you know too, what "the world" is for me? ... a
sea of forces storming and streaming in itself, eternally wandering, eternally flowing back; with vast years of recurrence, with
an ebb and flow of its formations, driving out from the simplest
into the most complex, from the stillest, rigidest, coldest out
into the hottest, wildest, most self-contradictory; and then returning home again from abundance to simplicity, from the
play of contradictions back unto the joy of unison; affirming
itself even in this sameness of its courses and years, blessing
itself as that which must come again everlastingly, as a becoming
that knows no satiety, no boredom, no weariness —: this my
Dionysian world ... this mystery world of the two-fold lusts
... — will you have a *name* for this world? A *solution* for all
its riddles? .... *This world is the will to power — and nothing
else!* [100]

[100] XVI 401 f. Cf. 515; VI 289; X 30–47; XIX 182.

PART FOUR

HISTORY AND PROPHECY

CHAPTER XII

The Rise and Fall of Cultures

The verdict of the past is always an oracle: only as architects of the future, as knowers of the present, will you understand it. (I 337)

1. A PHILOSOPHY OF HISTORY

WE HAVE seen how thoroughly Nietzsche's thought is saturated with the historical point of view. Though a critic of its excesses, he takes pride in sharing the famed German "historical sense" — "we are historical through and through," he declares; "we are the self-consciousness of history in general." [1] He feels himself an heir of all the ages, and writes an appeal for them which now reads like a prophecy:

Have you no pity for the past? Do you not see how it is abandoned, and depends, like a poor little woman, upon the mercy, the spirit, the fairness of each generation? Could not a great fiend come at any moment who would force us not to recognize it at all, who would make our ears deaf to it, or even put in our hands a whip for maltreating it? [2]

Indeed, history is more than an intellectual spectacle for Nietzsche: he thinks, and lives, consciously within it, and a historical setting and mission is at the heart of his philosophy.

From the beginning, he insists that historical studies be based upon philosophic assumptions. Only by relating particulars to general ideas can we understand them. Sheer photographic objectivity is an illusion: there are no "pure

---

[1] XIII 10; XV 303. Cf. II 18 f., 40 f., 432 f.; VII 176 ff.; VIII 76; H.K.A. II 353 f.; above, p. 243, note 8.
[2] XII 193 f. Cf. VI 295; XII 216 f.; III 183; above, p. 166, note 82.

facts" within reach, and to search history for them is simply
to get lost in detail — or to be an unconscious victim of
the commonplace assumptions of "common sense." Nor will
mere universal sensitiveness suffice. Our historians are indeed learning to vibrate sympathetically with the most
varied tones of the past — but only the overtones. Utter
receptiveness is too soft for the "coarseness and might" of the
fundamentals. Renan, for instance, is not just; he is effemi-
nate. This widespread refusal to interpret and judge the
past is a symptom of nihilism.[3]

But Nietzsche does not favor a dogmatic use of philosophy
in history. His aphoristic sketches of men and epochs show
how he approaches broader conclusions by patient, detailed
observation, based on his brilliantly intuitive psychology:

My way of reporting something historical is really to tell
my own *experiences* [*Erlebnisse*], with past times and people as
my occasion. Nothing discursive: some things I have perceived,
others not. Our historians of literature are tedious because
they force themselves to speak about everything, and to judge
even where they have *experienced* nothing.[4]

Nietzsche interprets history, like art, as an expression of
life. Commonplace, petty or indifferent thinkers find triviality in history. Men of freshness and nobility alone can grasp
what is worth knowing in the past:

History will make you only those confessions which are
worthy of you!

Only out of the highest power [*Kraft*] *of the present is it
permissible for you to interpret the past:* only in the most intense exertion of your noblest qualities will you divine what in

[3] I 330 ff.; IV 251 f.; VII 469, 476 ff.; IX 1, 14, 24, 246; XIII 321 f.; XV 446;
XVII 329, 336. Cf. L.O. 23/2/87; L.F.N. I 334 or H.K.A. III 324; above, pp. 252 f.,
255, 257 f., 261 f. Nietzsche does not disparage methods of exact scholarship. He
admires and was trained in them, and only insists that they are means, not ends
(XVII 337 ff.; VII 157 f.; XV 447; XVI 390).
[4] XI 114. Studies like literary history "must become a natural outcome of
countless particular observations" (XVII 349. Cf. I 335).

the past is worth knowing and preserving. Equals by equals! Else you drag the past down to yourselves.[5]

Each new life, therefore, adds a different perspective to history: "Every great man has a retroactive force," and "history is always speaking *new truths*." [6]

Nietzsche also demands that history serve vital needs. He protests against excesses of historical erudition which seem to him both cause and symptom of modern cultural disintegration — "the historical disease," he calls them. The effort to make history a science has promoted indiscriminate accumulation of more knowledge than our age can digest.[7] As a guide to sanity, he suggests three ways in which history can serve life, when there is a corresponding need. "Monumental history" is an exemplary portrayal of great events which omits minute inquiry into their causes. It can supply able men of action with models and companions, proving that great things are possible. "Antiquarian history" is piety toward the past; it preserves the sources of our own being, for those who come after. "Critical history," conversely, breaks the grip of the past by revealing its unsavory features. That is legitimate when the past oppresses the present; but it is dangerous, because it destroys part of ourselves.[8] Nietzsche himself writes both critical and monumental history: his work on Christianity is critical, on pre-Socratic Greece, monumental. And in general he studies the past with a threefold purpose: to destroy what is decadent, preserve what has been positively accomplished, and find models for building the future.

He denies comprehensive order in history, as in the universe, whether it be purpose, rational necessity or linear progress. He objects particularly to the Hegelian influence, because it has led men to "naked admiration of success" and

[5] IX 443; I 336. Cf. I 302, 306, 335 ff.; L.F.N. I 335 or H.K.A. III 330.
[6] V 73; XVI 350. Cf. XIII 287.
[7] I 293 f., 310 ff., 319 ff., 378. Cf. XVII 344 f., 349.
[8] I 294–310. Cf. X 127; H.K.A. II 336 ff.; H.K.A. III 321, 336 ff.

"idolatry of the actual." History is not the work of immanent reason; it is full of accident and irrationality, and "whoever does not comprehend how brutal and meaningless history is, will also not understand at all the impulse to make history meaningful." On similar grounds he attacks history written in terms of mass movements, as if the masses were the real creators. Such history expresses a debased sense of values: the finest things do not affect the masses.[9]

Nietzsche denies perfect order, but he does not assert perfect chaos. The comprehensive fact is lawlessness, but within it are bits of local and conditional order, floating islands appearing and disappearing in the sea of chance — "a *little* reason . . . scattered from star to star." But none are everlasting; "chance breaks everything up again."[10] There is purposive order, for example, in the plans of a leader or the desires of a class, but in detail these are indefinitely serrated by blind circumstance. In the small as in the large, chaos has the last word.[11]

The ultimate tendency of the historical mind, according to Nietzsche, is to establish continuity between human and animal, moral and physical, uniting all in a "cosmic self-consciousness."[12] His conception of man maintains such a

[9] X 401 f., 273 ff.; I 353 ff., 367 f., 513; VII 138, 256 f., 454; VIII 203 f.; XII 190 ff.; XIII 321 f.; XVI 293 f., 355. Cf. II 225 f.; H.K.A. III 319–25. More weight is attached to success by I 497 f. and H.K.A. II 23. IX 14 f. gives a more favorable view of the rôle of the masses in history, but the fundamental criterion of value is evidently still the same as in I 367 f. Also the two passages refer to different types of historiography, the former to the German Romantic School, the latter to writers like Buckle (cf. XVI 393; VII 307). Nietzsche reverses the current "neurotic's theory" that the great man is a product of his milieu (VIII 155 f. Cf. XVI 280). In opposition to the philosophy of progress he denies that humanity has moved as a whole in any direction, points out the relativity of the criteria with which "progress" is measured, shows that the usual criterion is only a variant of the Christian moral ideal which he rejects, and maintains that the movement called "progress" is decadence from his point of view (II 51, 226 f.; XV 204 f., 385 ff.; XVI 147 f.; XII 189; VIII 155. Cf. X 270 f.; L.F.N. I 332 or H.K.A. III 322). More specifically, he doubts whether modern science and technology outweigh the deterioration of our artistic, religious, and political powers, and the barbaric formlessness of modern life (XVII 334; IX 3).

[10] VI 243; XIII 323. Cf. L.F.N. I 333 or H.K.A. III 323.

[11] X 401; XIII 321. Cf. XVIII 163 f., 168 f.   [12] III 103.

continuity, and in fact he says that we have learned to see the aimlessness of human history through the study of animal history.[13] But he also derives positive insight into history from his theory of life:

The *powers in history* are doubtless discernible, if one strips off all moral and religious teleology. They must be *those* powers which also operate in the entire phenomenon of organic existence. The plainest declarations [are] in the *vegetable kingdom*.[14]

Previous chapters have already presented aspects of the two chief patterns in Nietzsche's picture of human history. One is the cyclic pattern, first illustrated by the growth and decay of the organism, later by cultural cycles in art and the production of "individuals" as seeds of a social organism. The other is the dialectical pattern of evolution through strife and self-transcendence, illustrated by the evolution of moral values.[15]

The present chapter will trace these patterns through the more familiar parts of the "moral period" or history in the

[13] XIII 322.

[14] XIV 223. Cf. XVI 163 f.

[15] There are also two or three pendular patterns, probably related to the others. *The Birth of Tragedy* suggests a kind of oscillation between Apollinian and Dionysian principles (I 38. Cf. 19, 74 ff., 171 f.; IX 178). *Richard Wagner in Bayreuth* refers the movement from Hellenism to Orientalism and back toward Hellenism to "the pendulum of history" (I 515 f. Cf. 140). Later, Nietzsche describes alternations between master and slave values, symbolized by "Rome vs. Judea" (VII 334 ff.). The last is evidently a kind of indecisive balancing in the dialectical evolution of values. But I 515, II 354, and IX 123 describe Christianity as a form of Orientalism, and several passages (XVII 298; XVI 387 f.; IX 290. Cf. I 26 f., 36 f.) indicate an asiatic origin for the Dionysian movement. Also the rivalry of Apollinian and Dionysian are said to condition all further evolution of the arts, and even to *be* the evolution of man (I 19; IX 178; XVI 387). Hence all three pendular movements are somehow related to the dialectical evolutionary pattern. Further, the Apollinian-Dionysian polarity is also connected with the cyclic pattern: the two principles do not persist in sheer alternation but achieve periodic reconciliation (I 19), notably in tragic drama; their balanced interplay constitutes the upward swing of the Greek culture cycle and their separation brings decline (I 162 f., 171 f.); and we have caught hints of the same relationship in the rhythmic organization of power in the artist and in the "sovereign individual." These facts suggest that the dialectical and cyclic patterns themselves are not wholly disconnected. That is as the will-to-power theory would have it, since it includes both the rhythms of life and the evolution of life.

narrower sense, but we should remember the wider evolutionary setting — the remote formation and stabilization of the species under the duress of mores, introversion producing fresh instability, further intensified during the Moral Period. Nietzsche even speaks of the entire history of man as a cycle, in the vague sense that the highest men arise toward mid-career, and that man will sink back toward the end, perhaps ending even lower than he began.[16] Against this background Nietzsche makes his prophecy of supermen: we are now approaching the mid-point, and he would shoot man to his acme like a rocket, before he sinks again.

2. MODERNITY INDICTED

The principal foci of Nietzsche's historical interests are Ancient Greece and his own century. As his thinking progresses, he expands and clarifies his initial hostility to contemporary culture until it becomes a comprehensive critique of modernity, by which he fulfils the philosopher's duty to be the "bad conscience" of his time. This leads to a study of antecedent history in order to explain why things have gone wrong, and to find out what may be hoped for the future. Of his brilliant observations on the modern age, the following are typical:

In society: mixture of classes, dominance of the middle class, emancipation of the lower classes and of women; disintegration of institutions, including the family, and of the belief in tradition which makes them possible; tyrannical mass-uniformity weakening individuality.[17] *In politics:* the rise of democracy, that is, atomistic disintegration and loss of organizing power; hypocritical leaders who have to flatter

[16] VI 115; XII 209; XIV 263; IV 52; II 221, 232. Nietzsche suggests a law of acceleration and cultural recapitulation which, presumably, applies chiefly to the first half of man's journey (XI 138; XII 190; II 252 ff.). L.F.N. I 315 f. or H.K.A. II 56 f. indicates a very early conception of historical cycles.

[17] XV 177, 189, 197, 208; XVI 281 ff.; VII 154; V 296 ff.; VIII 150 ff.; X 277; IV 134 f.

the masses; state idolatry, prostituting culture to barbarous ends; a system of petty states kept apart by stupid nationalism.[18] *In economic life:* a contemptible money-economy infecting all society with commercialized values, debasing cultural interests for business purposes, and causing senseless waste of nervous energy through over-work; the machine condemning the worker to "anonymous and impersonal slavery." [19]

In science: the undermining of older moral and religious ideas without the power to create a substitute — man no longer the dignified center of creation, but a meaningless accident in a cosmic mechanism, the pawn of environmental forces; the barbarism of increasing specialization in learning, emancipation of specialists from the control of philosophy; science as the last, most subtle form of asceticism in some cases, but generally lacking any sustaining ideal, rather a means to escape inner emptiness or suffering — under the guise of "objectivity" or "knowledge for its own sake"; preponderance of scholarship over creativeness, especially the restless study of remote times and places to compensate for lack of self-assured vitality in the present.[20]

In education: preferment of mediocrity, the chief end being the manufacture of specialized slaves for state and business; universal literacy, journalism and a free press pasting a veneer of motley "historical cultivation" over the masses, thereby degrading the standards of the old education, disguising the ugliness of the modern philistine and making him smug, spoiling folk poetry, folk music, and the integrity of feeling from which they spring — in short our education is the worst obstacle to a purified and re-

[18] XV 111, 194; XVI 192; II 348 f.; IV 173 f.; VI 141, 248, 356 f.; VII 130, 137, 473; I 420, 422 f., 447 f.; VIII 151; XIII 351.

[19] I 421, 446 f.; V 60, 77 f.; IV 169–74, 176, 198; III 305 ff., 317 f., 341 f., 344, 350 f.

[20] XV 142, 160, 194 f., 211, 446; XVI 86; VII 143 f., 148 ff., 154, 176, 465 ff., 473 ff., 476; IX 442; I 229 ff., 313, 421.

juvenated culture.[21] *In art:* romanticism and the disillu-
sioned reaction called naturalism; bizarre combinations of
charlatanism and virtuosity, brutality and over-refinement,
stimulants and opiates; the demand for "effect at any price,"
the cult of passion; preference for exotic and morbid themes,
the fatalistic notation of fact — especially if ugly and horrible; general formlessness, mixture of borrowed forms — all
pandering to the tastes of the mob, the over-worked, the
neurotic.[22]

In religion: a compromised, enfeebled Christianity inwardly losing hold of its dogmatic foundations but still pro-
fessing them outwardly before the populace; now a religion
of comfort instead of fear, little more than sentimental
humanitarianism and cult of pity.[23] *In philosophy:* a pleth-
ora of timid, second-rate minds, devoid of real vocation,
perverted to the service of material ends, who ignore and
are unfit for the royal task of true philosophy, and find a
pitiful occupation as hangers-on to the sciences or as historians of philosophy, but who even at these tasks exhibit
a flabbiness of thought which is an object of ridicule among
their academic colleagues.[24] *In morals:* a confusion of incompatible ideals dominated by humanitarian optimism,
altruism, and pity; a general softening which finds all suffering intolerable and conceives its abolition to be the ultimate end in life; a cowardly and false idealism, blind to
inner and outer realities; the tendency of morality to become
autonomous and to set up makeshift substitutes for its
erstwhile religious foundations.[25]

In addition, Nietzsche observes pervasive traits of the time

[21] I 142, 181, 188 f., 232 f., 312 f., 317 f., 374 f., 421, 446 ff., 452 f., 549; III
156 ff.; IV 303; V 312, 319; VI 56, 174 ff.; VIII 110 ff.; IX 301 f., 323 f., 326, 376 f.;
XI 145; XIV 205 f.; XVI 325.
[22] XV 160, 195, 199 ff., 211, 219 f., 229; XVI 236, 248–61, 266; VIII 7, 35, 138 f.;
V 122; VII 229 ff.
[23] II 128 f.; IV 58, 88, 133 ff.; VI 265 ff., 378 f.; X 289 f., 298; I 396 f., 448, 549;
VII 175; XV 192, 199, 203 f., 318 f.   [24] I 477–92; VII 145 f.
[25] XV 119 f., 155 f., 337; VII 64, 135 ff., 170, 453 f.; VIII 51.

which cut across these fields. Over-work, an effort to escape self, is a typical modern vice: people live in such haste that they receive numerous, therefore superficial, impressions; nothing has a chance to sink deep, take root, mature; man is becoming a marionette of external stimuli.[26] There has been a break with tradition; continuity of development has been destroyed, and men live disconnectedly "by the day." The inward uncertainty of modern life expresses itself in weak tolerance and assorted fanaticisms. All this means a general weakening of will, especially of effective will to build for a distant future.[27] Another aspect of the same trend is the increase of self-consciousness, betokening and accelerating decay of instinct; partly in consequence comes a pestilence of hypocrisy (*Schauspielerei*) and self-deceit.[28] Multiplicity yet fragmentariness are our curse:

What we have is the *manifold* man, the most interesting chaos, perhaps, that has existed to date: but *not* the chaos *before* the creation of the world, but rather after it: — *Goethe* as most beautiful expression of the type (— *absolutely not an Olympian!*).[29]

3.   DECADENCE AND NIHILISM

Nietzsche's indictment ends with a diagnosis: modern civilization is decadent. Although he adopts the term *décadence* quite late, he says that "with respect to German culture" he has "always had a feeling of *decline*." And in fact his earlier writings show much concern for the weakness, sickness, degeneracy of modern life.[30] As his thought

[26] XV 164, 196 f.; I 342 f., 421; V 249 f.; IV 172; VI 65, 271 f.; X 297. This is particularly true of America (V 249; XIII 355, 360).
[27] XV 188, 192 f., 197; V 280 ff., 297 f.; VII 160, 163; II 201 ff.; IV 172.
[28] XV 193 f., 199, 449; V 296 ff.; VIII 46 f., 51, 153; I 311 f., 397 f., 527. Cf. XV 343.   [29] XVI 297. Cf. VIII 111, 154; I 397 f.; VI 204 f.
[30] XV 206; I 195, 294, 316, 378, 396 f., 517; II 41 f., 206 ff.; III 76 ff., 90 ff.; X 9, 337 f. The same feeling is projected into the account of Socrates and Euripides in *The Birth of Tragedy*. The principal change in Nietzsche's views appears to have been that he first hoped that the decline could be overcome, later realized that it must work itself out before a healthy culture could arise (XV 443; III 6 f.; VIII 155, 192 f.).

matures, he unites all problems — even that of morals — in a comprehensive theory of decadence.[31]

He defines decadence as disintegration, conflict, maladjustment, exhaustion. Its most fundamental symptoms are hypersensitiveness, loss of self-control, and consequent *ressentiment*.[32] He claims that the phenomena usually stressed by moral and social critics — scepticism, vice, pessimism, crime, disease, nervous trouble, alcoholism, prostitution — are only more superficial symptoms of decadence; and to the list he adds pacifism, anarchism, optimism, and moral "goodness." To fight these consequences, as if they were the real causes, is delusory, he argues; and the means commonly employed illustrate the rule that decadents choose remedies which only make things worse.[33]

Decadence varies, of course, according to the pattern of life concerned.[34] In his own studies, at times Nietzsche is thinking of decadence in the individual, at times of decadence in society. From his statements we may infer several relations between the two types. They are independent to this extent, that even the healthiest society must produce some decadent men — waste products of the life process, as it were — and that some exceptionally healthy individuals may arise in a time of general decay.[35] But the types are interdependent also: a society becomes decadent if if fails to eliminate its waste products; [36] conversely, if an age is decadent, so are most of the individuals; [37] and social

[31] VIII 1 f.

[32] See above, pp. 76 f., 105, 148 ff.

[33] XV 119 f., 168 ff., 383, 465; VII 441 ff.; VIII 74, 85, 233. He charges that modern sociology, knowing only a decadent society at first hand, has taken decadence instincts for its norm (XV 179; VIII 148. Cf. III 350).

[34] VII 236.

[35] XV 167 f., 443; VIII 47; XII 108. One should distinguish moral and political from cultural decline. Nietzsche places the acme of culture — the finest individualities — in ages of political and moral corruption (VIII 111 f.; V 63 ff.). The proposition in the text seems meant for cultural decline as well, which comes later.

[36] XV 177, 181.

[37] Cf. VIII 1, 47.

decadence is conditioned by the decay of the instincts of solidarity upon which institutions rest.[38]

There are two other types, plainly implied by Nietzsche's language, and very important for his philosophy of history. One might call them "normal" and "pathological" decadence. The first is old age, the inevitable down-swing of the life cycle as a consequence of living:

A society is not at liberty to remain young. . . . The more energetically and boldly it advances, the more it will abound in failures and monstrosities, the nearer it will be to decline . . . One does not abolish old age by institutions.[39]

Of course it is useless to resist growing old, and Nietzsche realizes that the eventide of life has its own poetic values:

A *declining* world is a pleasure, not *only* for the spectator (but also for the destroyer). Death is not merely necessary; "ugly" is inadequate, there is greatness, sublimity of all kinds in declining worlds. Sweetness as well, hopes and sunsets as well. Europe is a declining world.[40]

"Pathological" decadence is due to adventitious causes — class mixture, infection of the healthy parts of the social organism by waste that should have been eliminated, poisoning by alien ideals — and Nietzsche implies that it sometimes *can* be resisted.[41]

We have seen earlier that he has another diagnosis of the ills of modernity: the rise of nihilism. Most, perhaps all, of his indictments can also be taken as its harbingers — occasions for disillusion or expressions of it. "The whole European system of human endeavors *feels itself* partly

[38] VIII 150 ff.; V 298; XV 472.

[39] XV 168. Cf. 386; XVI 281 f. Compare the use of such terms as "age," "fatigue," "late," and "evening" in IV 273, 347 ff.; VIII 239 f.; XI 253; XV 257 ff., 275.

[40] XIII 361 f. Cf. VII 236; L.F. winter/84–85.

[41] XV 168, 177; VII 131, 153 f.; VIII 239 f. Cf. the juxtaposition of disease and age in IV 273, 284; XI 253.

meaningless, partly already 'immoral.' " [42]   Our civilization
is approaching spiritual as well as vital bankruptcy.

How, then, is nihilism related to decadence? Nietzsche
considers nihilism generally an expression of decadence, but
not merely that, because decadence can be "interpreted" in
other ways. The Christian-moral interpretation is the one
now leading decadents to nihilism. [43] But the history of that
interpretation is a partly independent train of events. Originally it protected decadents against nihilism by giving them
a compensatory faith. [44] But recently it has been bringing
about its own destruction: morality first destroys belief in
God and in various secular substitutes (through a sharper
conscience about truth), then collapses for want of support
in reality. [45] At this stage it drives decadents to nihilism —
and others also, for even the strong go through it in sloughing
off the old values. Accordingly nihilism is not proof of decadence; in some cases it may be a sign of increasing
strength. [46]

On the necessities at work in this complex of decadence
and nihilism, Nietzsche bases his predictions for the next
two centuries. [47] But let us first turn to his account of history for a better understanding of the process; there we
shall discover a further relationship: the nihilist values were
originally the creation of decadents or of their leaders, and
the influence of these ideals in Europe has fostered decadence. For Nietzsche, this is a puzzle to be solved. "Problem: how did the exhausted come to make the laws of
values? . . . . How did the instinct of the animal Man come
to stand on its head?" [48] How could life so turn against

[42] XVI 419. Cf. 417 ff.; XV 141 ff., 160. Nihilism is a crisis only for the elite;
the "flock" do not feel the problem (XV 164, 347).
[43] XV 141, 166 f., 170; XVI 423; VIII 143, 145. Cf. VIII 68 f.
[44] XV 145 f.; XVI 199; VII 430.
[45] XVI 417 f., 406; XV 145 ff., 155 f., 161; VII 79.
[46] XV 156, 221 ff.; XVI 85 f.
[47] XV 137 f.; VIII 155.
[48] XV 181. Cf. 82 f., 105, 124 f., 167, 177 f.; VII 424 ff., 429 ff.; VIII 89, 220 f.

itself? In any case the deterioration of the race is a further source of nihilism: it makes us tired and disgusted with man; we see no one whose very existence justifies the human race.[49]

4. THE SECRETS OF GREECE

Nietzsche would be famous, if only for his insight into Greek life, and his own debt to Greece is very great. He acknowledges, "Observation [Kenntnis] of the great Greeks has educated me." [50] His fame as a Greek scholar would be still greater, had he not antagonized the learned guild by the methods which his unique psychological genius employed, and by open contempt for conventional classicism. He believes Greece profoundly different from the modern world, so remote indeed that no amount of learned industry alone could hope to comprehend it. Ordinary classical education and philology are positive barriers to real understanding.[51]

He will not tolerate condescension toward the ancients, as if our culture were superior:

The attitude of the philologist to Antiquity is *palliative* or inspired by the purpose to point out in Antiquity that which our time esteems highly. The correct point of departure is the converse: namely to start with insight into modern perversity and to look back — much that is very shocking in Antiquity then appears as a profound necessity.[52]

Since Nietzsche makes great individualities the supreme end, he considers Greece the pinnacle of history so far, because of its astonishing variety and perfection of geniuses

[49] XV 159, 194 f.; VII 325 f., 432 f.

[50] XIII 8. Cf. I 281. Nietzsche's debt to the Greeks can be exaggerated. He did not advocate a literal revival of Hellenism (X 404 ff.); he criticized the Greeks adversely in some respects, thought European culture superior in some, and prophesied a future superior to both (e.g. IV 191 f.; V 265; VII 420; VI 13; XIII 362; XVIII 163 ff., 168 f.; L.O. 23/2/87). Also his thought consciously retains important Christian elements (see above, pp. 165 ff. below, pp. 349 f.).

[51] IV 185 ff.; I 141 f., 312; IX 345 ff.; X 341 ff., 366 f.; XIV 107; XVII 332.

[52] X 351. Cf. XVII 336.

— a level of humanity not equalled since.[53] So he would have us study the Greeks in order to discover the secret of their success. He searches all sides of their life for clues, and is ready to see a "profound necessity" in such institutions as slavery, the seclusion of women, and even pederasty.[54]

But their secrets must be guessed. Here he finds the typical philologist unimaginative. For he believes that the Greeks were psychologically superficial: their strongest impulses, such as those for simplicity and rationality, led them to give an over-simple picture of themselves, and they achieved their best without reflective awareness.[55] Also they had an instinctive reticence about the mysteries of life:

There is no doubt that the Greeks sought to interpret to themselves, out of their vague experiences and presentiments, the ultimate secrets of the "destiny of the soul" and all they knew about nurture and purification, above all about the immovable *gradation* and inequality of value between man and man: — here is the great profundity, the great silence, for everything Greek — and it is just as certain that one does not know the Greeks as long as the hidden, subterranean entrance here lies buried. Importunate scholars' eyes will never see anything of such things ....[56]

Nietzsche's account of Greek history is at once an illustration and a general statement of his theory of culture cycles. The rise of a culture is not an easy unfolding of an initially pure style, but a conquest of integrity through struggle:

There are probably no pure races, but only ones that have become pure, and these in great rarity. The usual are crossed races, in which, beside the disharmony of bodily forms ... disharmonies of customs and notions of value must also be found.

[53] XIV 111; V 177 f.; XIII 363; XVI 297, 339 f.; X 230 f., 277, 368, 384 ff.; XV 445; XVII 335; XVIII 1°9.
[54] XVII 329, 335 f.; X 385 f.; IX 144, 147, 166 ff., 290; XII 196 f.; I 103 f.; II 240 f.; VIII 134; L.R. 23/5/76.
[55] XIV 107 ff., 116; I 118 f.; V 11, 323 f.; XVII 352; L.O. 23/2/87.
[56] XIV 116. Cf. XVI 389 f.; I 5 f.

... Purity is the final result of innumerable adaptations, absorptions and excretions, and progress toward purity shows itself in this, that the energy [*Kraft*] present in a race *limits* itself more and more to a few chosen functions.... At last ... all that energy, which was previously spent in the struggle of the inharmonious qualities, is at the command of the total organism: for which reason races that have become pure have ever become *stronger* and *more beautiful* as well. — The Greeks give us the model of a purified race and culture: and some day, I trust, a pure European race and culture will also succeed.[57]

The beginning was the pre-Homeric age of the Titans, a time of horror and strife — "only out of an earlier barbarism does a culture arise, and there are times of long wavering and struggling, in which success is doubtful." [58] In this period, presumably, an aristocratic society was formed, as at the start of every higher culture:

Men with a nature still natural, barbarians in every fearful sense of the word, men of prey, still in possession of unbroken powers of will and desires for power, threw themselves upon

[57] IV 239 f. Cf. VIII 160 f.; XVIII 251 f. That Nietzsche does not draw a sharp line between race and culture is a natural consequence of his theory of heredity and instinct: race is essentially the result of ancestral habits (cf. VII 250 f.). His position with regard to current race theories is as follows. He does speak of a conquering blonde Aryan race as having appeared in Europe and India some thousands of years ago, and he admires them for having a religion of affirmation (in contrast to Christianity), but he also blames their influence for having "spoiled everybody" — namely by the model of priestly rule, as in the Laws of Manu (VII 208 f.; VIII 106; XV 251 ff.). He seriously doubts the validity of inferring that peoples who speak the same language are of the same race (X 278, 394). Also he denies, as we have seen, that racial purity is the essential datum for founding a culture: crossed races have rather been the source of great cultures (XIII 356). He recognizes that contemporary Europeans are racially mixed — the Germans, for instance, have hardly any kinship to the ancient Germanic peoples (VII 309, 323) — and therefore has nothing but contempt for German race ideologies — the "race swindle" as he calls them (XIII 356; X 278; XV 109 f.; V 337). He particularly despises anti-semitism (VII 478, 218 f.) and he broke with Wagner, and later with his own sister, partly for this reason (VIII 200; XV 75 f.; L.S. winter/83–84). He criticizes Jews on occasion, and admits that Germany has a serious problem of assimilation on her hands; but he insists upon common decency in the matter, and believes that the Jews will be a valuable ingredient in the future ruling race of Europe which he wishes to see created (VII 218 ff.; XIII 356 f.; II 353 f.).

[58] X 244. Cf. 12; IX 273 f., 282; H.K.A. I 232 ff., 430; H.K.A. II 179.

weaker, more civilized, more peaceful, perhaps trading or cattle raising races, or upon old, mellow cultures .... In the beginning, the noble caste was always the barbarian caste.[59]

And the subsequent fruitfulness of Greek culture depended upon using the raw brutalities of animal man manifested in its beginnings.[60] But utilization meant control, for culture consists not in maximum development of each power but in the right proportion of all.[61]

Far from having an autochthonous culture, the Greeks began with a barbaric mixture of ideas and values. Their real genius showed itself in assimilative learning: they achieved much because they took up the spear of civilization where other peoples had thrown it:

They never lived in proud untouchableness: their "culture" was rather for a long time a chaos of foreign, Semitic, Babylonian, Lydian, Egyptian forms and ideas, and their religion a veritable strife of gods from the entire Orient .... The Greeks gradually learned *to organize the chaos*, by remembering ... their genuine needs, according to the Delphic teaching, and allowing sham needs to die off. In this way they took possession of themselves once more ....[62]

So the Greek development was a series of victories over external as well as internal chaos, and it should be our model, "for the Greek was the first great binding and synthesis of everything Oriental, and precisely thereby the *beginning* of the European soul." [63]

Nietzsche is particularly interested in the Greek reception of the Dionysian religious orgies — already familiar as the background of tragic drama:

This contrariety [*Gegensätzlichkeit*] of the Dionysian and Apollinian within the Greek soul is one of the great riddles by

[59] VII 236. Cf. IX 154 f.
[60] IX 273, 290; X 384 f.; III 116 f. Cf. II 231.
[61] X 124. See above, p. 127.
[62] I 383. Cf. X 11, 390; XIX 4, 15–40, 76, 134 f.
[63] XVI 390.

which I felt myself attracted in the presence of the Greek nature. At bottom I strove to do nothing but divine why precisely the Greek Apollinism had to grow out of a Dionysian subsoil: why the Dionysian Greek needed to become Apollinian: that is, to break his will to the monstrous, manifold, uncertain, dreadful, on a will to measure, to simplicity, to orderly arrangement in rule and concept. The immoderate, disorderly, Asiatic lies. at his base: the valor of the Greek consists in the struggle with his Asiaticism: beauty is not given him as a present, any more than logic, than naturalness of custom — it is conquered, willed, won by fighting — it is his *victory*.[64]

Nietzsche interprets the whole Dionysian phenomenon as a sign of superabundant vitality and youthfulness. In their best days the Greeks showed a will *to* pessimism — very different from instinctive pessimism — which meant strength to face the ugly and terrible aspects of existence, justifying them out of excess health.[65]

For Greek religion, especially for the religious festivals, Nietzsche has great admiration. Theirs was a noble religion because it expressed gratitude rather than fear, and showed a self-respecting attitude toward the gods. They humanized their gods, and idealized human passions in them. There was no sense of sin. The gods were also capable of causing evil, and showed their decency by taking the blame, instead of merely the punishment; they justified human life by living it themselves. Greek religion was a means to enhancement, not denial.[66] Moreover, polytheism encouraged the development of individuality by suggesting a variety of ideals.[67]

The whole of Greek life — its art, its politics — was based

[64] XVI 387 f. Cf. I 26 f., 33, 36 f., 74 f., 124; III 114 ff.; VIII 170; IX 178, 290; XVII 298, 301; XVIII 171 f.

[65] I 2, 6 f.; VIII 170 ff.; IX 79; XIV 270 f. Cf. XIV 219. Yet the Greeks made use of artistic illusions in order to live (I 31 f.; II 162; V 11; X 396).

[66] VII 75, 392 ff.; XIII 299; II 125, 127; I 29 ff., 60; IX 79, 110 f.; X 386, 397; XVI 71.

[67] V 174 f. The mythical heroes formed an intermediate stage in the development of individuality (*ibid.* and IX 287 f., 291).

upon religion in a way difficult to imagine today. Perhaps the most important feature of this dependence was the protective limitation given by mythology:

> . . . without myth every culture forfeits its healthy, creative natural power: only a horizon encompassed by myths locks an entire movement of culture into a unity. All forces of imagination and of Apollinian dream are saved from their indiscriminate vagrancy only by the myth.[68]

Nietzsche says that the strongest Greek impulse was will to power; all their institutions originated as means of self-protection against this "inner explosive." [69] Active first in the Age of the Titans as a "tigerlike joy in destruction," it was eventually organized into the Greek state, the function of which was to be the "iron bracket" that formed and maintained the aristocratic structure of society. In this framework of stable continuity, between terrific discharges of accumulated will to power in warfare, society could bend the energies ignited by strife to the production of culture and men of genius.[70]

Within the state, men converted their wills to power from joy in destruction to rivalry for honor. The institution of the contest (*Agon*, *Wettkampf*) spread through all the phases of Greek culture. Nietzsche considers it a major secret of Greek achievement. It incited the individual to outdo all competitors not only in politics and athletics, but also in poetry, philosophy, and every form of "excellence." The presence of rivals held the tyrannical impulse in check and created the highest pitch of endeavor. Since rivalry

[68] I 160. Cf. IV 82; I 339, 342; X 127, 406 f.; XIX 3, 13, 46 ff., 83. The priesthood was unusually powerless in Greece (XIX 83 f.) — no doubt a favorable point in Nietzsche's eyes.

[69] VIII 169. Cf. IV 270.

[70] IX 273, 154 f., 158 f., 164, 369 f. Nietzsche criticizes Sparta and Rome for what he considers an excessive predominance of the state (X 391 f.; I 145 f.; IX 260 f.). He explains the deep antique reverence for the state as a necessary means to curbing the lust for tyranny which every Greek possessed (IV 192 f. Cf. II 243; X 227).

encouraged each person to develop and glorify his peculiar
gifts, it produced "free individuality." [71] But the impulse
to excel was in turn kept within bounds by the ties of
friendship — so highly developed by the Greeks — and by
the myths, which joined the individual to tradition and
community.[72]

5. GREEK ACME AND DECLINE

Nietzsche places the peak of Greek culture in the age of
Aeschylus and the early philosophers, when stylized indi-
viduality came to greatest abundance and perfection.[73]
Here he finds that purity and integrity which is his ideal
of culture: "unity of artistic style in all the vital functions
[*Lebensäusserungen*] of a people." [74]

"How beautiful they are!" he exclaims at the philosophers:

All those men are entire and hewn of one rock. Strict necessity prevails between their thinking and their character. There
is no convention for them, because there was no profession of
philosophers and scholars at that time.... They all possess the
virtuous energy of the Ancients, by which they surpass all later
men in finding their own form and continuing to shape it out
to the subtlest and the grandest, through metamorphosis.[75]

Individuality notwithstanding, they live in vital communion with a healthily unified culture, circling like planets
in a solar system — "what are exceptions with us, are there
the supreme cases of the rule" — and they are indeed the
noblest, quintessential expression of Hellenic genius.[76] For
this reason they can be helpful as philosophy can never be
in a decadent or barbarous time, acting as "physicians of

[71] IX 290 ff.; X 386 f., 390 f.; XIV 109 ff., 113; XII 196 f.; II 176 f., 351 f.;
III 320; XV 470 f.; VI 85; VIII 134.
[72] IV 68, 331; V 97 f.; IX 287 f.
[73] X 234, 223; II 244.
[74] I 183. Cf. 162, 384, 314; X 15.
[75] X 13, 234. Cf. 233 f.; XV 466 f.; XVII 349 f.; XIX 128 f.
[76] X 13 ff., 221; XVII 335.

culture" by warding off dangerous excesses like those of science, mythology, or cruelty.[77] Some, along with the tragedians, are would-be reformers of Hellas; they seek to provide a substitute for the decaying mythology, and, by modifying the exclusiveness of the city state, to form a Pan-Hellenic union which might have avoided the Persian wars.[78]

This reform, as Nietzsche dreams it, "would have become a marvellous soil for the generation of geniuses: such as never yet existed." In the early philosophers he sees a promise of a still higher type of man, one that has not been achieved — perhaps Plato would have attained it, had he not been spoiled by Socrates.[79] But it was the tragedy of Greek history that all reformers came too late. The Persian wars broke out, followed by the fatal hegemony of Athens. Socrates wrecked the continuity of tradition, and introduced an obsession with abstract concepts and the tyranny of dialectic. The magic thread was cut and decline set in. Greek culture failed to reach its highest possibility.[80]

Although Nietzsche directs most of his criticisms at Socrates and Plato, he is only taking them as outstanding representatives of a decadence that was general, much as he uses Wagner for a guide to modernity. His most complete outline of the Greek cycle shows that decline was bound to come:

One can show by the history of Greek literature through what powers the Greek spirit developed, how it got into different courses, by what it became weak. All that gives a picture of how, at bottom, Greek *morality* has fared too, and how every morality will fare: how at first it was coercion, at first showed severity, then gradually became milder; how pleasure in certain actions, in certain conventions and forms finally ensued, and

[77] X 10 f., 12, 14 ff., 187 f., 219 f., 232 f.
[78] X 236, 223, 227 f., 232, 112; II 242.
[79] X 230, 223, 232; II 244 f.
[80] II 243 ff.; X 220, 222, 224 ff., 230 f. Cf. I 77, 119, 162 f.; XVII 323.

from that in turn a propensity to the exclusive exercise, to the exclusive possession of them: how the road is filled and crowded with rivals; how satiety supervenes, new objects of struggle and ambition are sought out, obsolete ones revived; how the play is repeated, how the spectators grow weary altogether of look-ing on, because the whole circle now seems run through — — and then comes a standstill, an expiring: the brooks are lost in the sand.[81]

Nietzsche also emphasizes the stormy tempo of Greek his-tory. As it nears its climax, tension becomes so great, "the motion of the whole machine is so intensified, that a single stone thrown into its wheels makes it burst asunder. *One* such stone, for example, was Socrates . . . ." [82] A break was therefore inevitable, sooner or later, but untimely accidents produced it a little before the best forces had been spent.

Nietzsche assembles many traits characteristic of Greek decadence: (1) Mixture of styles or fanatical one-sidedness in life, thought, and art — Plato is the first great hybrid (*Mischcharakter*) in Greek philosophy.[83] (2) Hostility to the instinctive foundations of Greek culture: Plato blames them — e.g. the body and the senses, the love of life, the myths, Homer, tragedy, the *agon* — for the decline and, by setting up abstract conceptual patterns of virtue, he de-taches the individual from the concrete traditions of the city-state, and centers attention upon the destiny of the soul in another world.[84] (3) Other philosophical symptoms of decline: the "moral-religious idiosyncrasy" and the tyranny of dialectic, betraying the need of desperate treat-

[81] III 258 f. Cf. II 201 f.

[82] II 244 (italics mine). Cf. X 224 f.; III 72; XVIII 163 f., 168 f. On Socrates and Plato as instruments of a general decadence cf. VII 163 f.; VIII 69, 72, 167 ff.; XV 62; XIX 228 f. The same view is already implied by *The Birth of Tragedy*: Socrates only magnified an anti-Dionysian tendency already present in Sophocles (I 100 f., 122). The relation of Socrates and Plato to Greek decadence did not prevent Nietzsche from expressing great appreciation of the men themselves (e.g. XIX 172; XIII 97). The combination of admiration with hostility is a general characteristic of his thought (XV 22).

[83] X 16; I 98 f.; VIII 167 f.; XIV 91.

[84] XV 453 ff., 458 f., 465; VIII 170. Cf. I 160 f., 170.

ment for inner corruption; [85] optimism, the famous Greek serenity (*Heiterkeit*), a sign of hidden suffering and loss of the older "pessimism of strength"; [86] the logical optimism of science, which believes in the ability of reason to master the secrets of existence and produce happiness; [87] Epicurean hedonism, indicating hypersensitiveness and loss of purpose; [88] Stoicism and Cynicism as renunciations of culture in order to escape suffering; [89] the nihilism of Pyrrho.[90] (4) The belief that all the important things are finished; the predominance of learning instead of doing; the omnivorous scholarship of Alexandria, with its excess of historicism.[91] The rise of democracy and consequent triumph of shams (*Schauspielerei*).[92] — Behind these symptoms Nietzsche sees the essence of all decadence: fatigue and anarchy of instinct.[93]

The signs of ancient decadence tally remarkably with those of recent times, and Nietzsche develops the parallel in his approach to a general theory of cultural decline. Neglecting the influence of extraneous factors ("pathological decadence"), we can elicit from his notes the following elements of a theory of the decay involved in the very processes of culture. (1) Any culture has limited potentialities; when these are exhausted, decline must set in.[94] (2) Culture tends to be destroyed by its own means; these get out of hand and barbarize by setting up as ends in

[85] VIII 73 f., 170; XV 461 f.

[86] I 2 f., 6 f., 99 f.

[87] I 2 f., 7, 100, 104 ff., 124.

[88] VIII 253 f.; XV 307.

[89] XII 131 f., 195 f.; V 235. Cf. XV 454, 465.

[90] XV 467 f.

[91] I 125 f., 130, 163 f.; XVIII 118. But the Alexandrians discovered rigorous scientific method (XVII 351).

[92] I 7, 79 ff., 126 f.; V 297. Nietzsche holds that the Greeks were naturally actors, but that they first became victims of their weakness in the decadent period (IV 251; X 222; XIV 112). As a possible sixth symptom — though referred specifically to the Roman Empire — there was the tendency of the state to become an end in itself (IX 260 f.; I 145).

[93] VIII 73 f.; VII 163.

[94] Cf. X 224 f.; III 258 f. (the latter quoted in this section, above).

themselves — for example science, the state, popular education.[95] (3) Cultivation finally makes men soft, stale, over-specialized; their energies find easier satisfaction in imagination than in action; sublimation of animal drives is achieved at a price — it takes their edge off.[96] (4) Increasing civilization drains more and more nervous forces, inducing more "physiological" wreckage; the demands made, for example, by artistic styles grow until the tension *must* snap.[97] (5) The growth of enlightenment undermines the religious myths on which the culture is based; this emancipates morality, which first turns against the conditions of culture, then destroys itself in nihilism.[98]

6. CHRISTIANITY

Merging with the decadence of Greece and gradually conquering Rome, Christianity arose to be the outstanding fact of the next two thousand years. Its story is Nietzsche's answer to the question of how nihilist values came to dominate the modern world. He traces that story through several stages, each of which reinterpreted the nature of Christianity, so that we now have something very mixed and in fact essentially the opposite of the original. As a typical decadence movement it absorbed morbid elements wherever it went, for example ascetic practices, the agonized conscience, the bloody tastes of the Roman mob, and the torments of Hell. "The fate of Christianity lies in the necessity that its very faith had to become as diseased, as ignoble and vulgar, as the needs which it was to satisfy were diseased, ignoble and vulgar." [99]

Nietzsche believes that the key to the whole movement, its

[95] II 370; VIII 111 f.; IX 260 f.; X 12, 188, 337; XI 145; XV 68.
[96] II 356; VII 199; XI 354; XIV 69. Cf. VII 236.
[97] II 230; III 72; XIV 214.
[98] VII 480 f.; I 76, 120–27, 160 f.; XV 155, 192, 255. Cf. VII 137; X 236; XI 374; II 242. For the oriental parallels see below, pp. 354 ff.
[99] VIII 262 f. Cf. I 368; IV 69 ff.; XV 269 f., 263, 285.

revaluation of values, is really found in both branches of its pre-history — the anti-natural ethics of Platonism and Stoicism, and the change of Jewish theology occasioned by political failure and priestly rule. Not pagan moral corruption but the "moralization" of the ancient world, the "pre-existent Christianity" of Plato's attack on the basic Greek instincts, paved the way for Christian victory — especially for the seduction of the nobler minds. When Christianity arrived, it found the ground well prepared by the supremacy of moral values, hatred of the body, interpretation of natural impulses as vicious, and other-worldly metaphysics.[100]

Nietzsche admires the Jews of the Old Testament as long as they remained free. They were a healthy people, self-confident and prosperous then; their morality corresponded to their natural conditions, and their tribal god was a projection of their gratitude for life and their will to power, potent for good *and* evil.[101] But when political defeat came, they chose existence at any price, and the price was falsification of reality. It is the typical case of the de-naturalization of moral values. The priests, as a means both to their power over the Jews and to the survival of the Jews as a distinct people, changed Jehovah from a tribal god to a universal and merely "good" god expressing the values of the impotent, and substituted for natural causal relations the fictitious sequence of sin and punishment, interpreting the Jewish exile as due to sin. So Jewish priests were the inventors of sin as we have come to know it; their chief deed was the identification of misfortune with guilt and the reduction of all guilt to sin against Jehovah.[102]

This began the great "slave rebellion" in morals. The

---

[100] XV 255, 289, 454, 468 f.; VIII 168; VII 4 f.; L.O. 9/1/87. In this respect Christianity was unoriginal: it merely took over a set of values created by Plato and the Jews (XIII 310; VIII 243).

[101] VII 462; VIII 232, 244 f.

[102] VIII 232 ff., 243 ff.; XV 277 f.; V 169 f. Cf. XV 249 f.

oppressed Jews took revenge on their masters, and shrewdly
devised a means to power, by creating a typical *"ressentiment morality"* which eventually put them at the head of
all decadence movements — the "good" became the poor,
lowly, suffering; the rich, powerful, beautiful became
"worldly" and "evil." [103]

In the midst of this cauldron of resentment, Jesus of
Nazareth instituted a "Buddhistic peace movement." Nietzsche thinks the Gospels hardly worth considering as
historical documents, but he ventures a guess at the psychological *type* of the Redeemer, partly hidden beneath
later accretions. The prophet, miracle worker and messiah, along with the man of anger, are dismissed as cor-
ruptions of the text. The original person was, more
probably, an extreme decadent whose morbid sensitiveness
produced an instinctive hatred of reality, and therefore
of all forms of hostility and exclusiveness. His essential
teaching was not a theological dogma or a cult, but a way
of life which he practised as a means to inward peace:
his "good news" was that sin is abolished, that the "kingdom of heaven" is an inward state, to be realized by renouncing all enmity and resistance and by living utterly
in love and resignation. This *is* eternal life, indifferent to
time and space, indifferent to state and church and culture,
always possible; anyone who lives it is a "child of God." [104]

Nietzsche says that the indifference of Jesus to the worldly
survival of the Jews, to the priestly hierarchy with its apparatus of sin, punishment, and repentance, was only a further

[103] VII 126 f., 312 f.; VIII 243 f. On one point Nietzsche is not clear: in VIII
244 he says that the Jews themselves were not decadents, merely had to pretend
to be; but in XV 124 f. he says that the priests who have set our values *were*
decadents. In VII 437 he says that the ascetic priest had to be decadent enough
to understand decadents, yet strong enough to lead them.

[104] VIII 251–61; XV 259 ff., 298 f.; VII 108. Cf. L.S. early 3/85. VIII 255
gives reasons for eliminating the "Fanatiker des Angriffs" from the reconstructed
portrait of Jesus, though Nietzsche admits that the opposite view is tenable.
VI 107 f., 427; VII 257 f.; XIII 305 f. sketch rather different hypotheses evidently based on the inclusion of the "fanatic."

development of the instinctive hatred of reality which had motivated the Jewish "slave rebellion." But inasmuch as he championed the outcast and denied the last form of Jewish "reality" — the "chosen people" — he was leading a popular uprising against the foundations of Jewish society and the Jewish church, and consequently met his death as a criminal.[105]

Corruption of the gospel began at once. Even his immediate followers, ignorant and simple folk, misunderstood him in terms of the ideas familiar to them. The death on the cross, as Nietzsche views it, was merely the supreme example of the new way of life — freedom from resentment and resistance even under the most shameful abuse. But the disciples could not grasp this; they were shocked instead into the most unevangelical of passions, the desire for revenge. So they interpreted Jesus as a warlike Messiah, bitter opponent of the Pharisees and only Son of God, who would soon return to establish an external Kingdom of Heaven for the glory of his disciples and the judgment of his foes.[106]

St. Paul — that "genius in hatred" — completed this first perversion. Making an arbitrary selection of a few traits from the life of Christ, he improvised around them the doctrines which later ruled Christendom: sin, atonement by the sacrifice of an innocent victim, resurrection, personal immortality. He introduced dogma and cult in place of the way of life, and so prepared the ultimate restoration of the priesthood to power. Step by step his work moved on after him until the Church — linked with the state, sanctioning war, hatred, torture, judgment, punishment, and the whole round of worldly activities — embodied the exact opposite of everything Jesus taught — "at bottom there was only one Christian, and he died on the cross." [107]

[105] VIII 249 f.; XV 278 f., 286.   [106] VIII 254, 267 f.; XV 266.
[107] VIII 265, 269 ff., 273; XV 263 ff., 274, 283 ff., 299.

In this manner Judaism triumphed over primitive Christianity, and Judaized Christianity later conquered Rome. Nietzsche interprets it as a complete perversion of the religion of peace and love into a movement of organized revenge, which merely retained the spirit of Jesus as a camouflage. It was Jesus' fate to be used as a kind of sublime bait by the very tradition which crucified him. St. Paul also enabled the movement to capture the decadent underworld of the whole Empire, for he shaped Christianity to compete as a mystery cult with those of Mithras, Isis, and the rest which were already forming a general anti-pagan movement. At last, only the stimulus of persecution was needed to fan the flames of resentment into aggression and victory.[108]

Nietzsche feels some difficulty in explaining the next stage of Christianity — its conversion of the ruling classes, who naturally represented the opposite values. He suggests that an over-cultivated society found the Christian paradoxes seductive, the adventurous were fascinated by a kind of quixotic heroism in the Christian ideal, Platonism acted as a mediator for the intellectuals, and a movement which controlled the masses appealed to the instincts of rulers — as a great "flock religion," it taught obedience.[109] In any case this transplantation of a lower class movement into the upper classes, and its consequent union with the Empire, injected quite different elements into the Christian tradition — the Church was the last piece of "Roman architecture." [110] Conversely, Christianity in Rome became the

[108] VIII 243 f., 270, 289, 306 f.; XV 263, 270, 274 f., 284 f., 289; VII 314 f.; IV 64 ff., 70 ff. St. Paul also perceived the social reality on which Christianity could build, namely the small Jewish communities of the Dispersion (XV 271).

[109] XV 301 f., 269; XI 317 f.; VIII 168; II 149. Also the old culture was weakened by mixture with barbarian blood (V 178). The most obvious solution of the problem would be to say that the Roman aristocrats were also decadent; several passages suggest this (see above, p. 122, note 27), and if Nietzsche does not say so more plainly, it is probably because he laments so keenly the values which Christianity destroyed (cf. VIII 307 f.).

[110] V 305; I 368. Cf. XIII 326; XV 300 f.

vampire of ancient civilization, destroying achievements which might have served to build the future for thousands of years, notably the beginning of genuine science. "The entire work of the ancient world *in vain!*" Nietzsche exclaims with indignation.[111]

He adds that the conversion of barbarians to Christianity converted Christianity to barbarism, and spoiled the barbarians. For it was a religion evolved by and for the tired population of a late civilization:

An ending, shepherds', evening beatitude preached to barbarians, Teutons! How it all had to be Teutonized, barbarized, beforehand! For *such*, as had dreamed a *Valhalla* —: who found all happiness in war! — A *super*-national religion preached into a chaos where *as yet not even* nations existed —.

It may have suited the jejune Romans, but for the wild peoples of the North it was a poison: Christianity conquered beasts of prey by making them sick. The barbarians absorbed the contagious decadence in all their instincts, and so were cheated of their chance to create an independent culture of their own.[112]

7. EUROPE

Nietzsche's account of the West since the fall of Rome mingles the two chief patterns of his philosophy of history. Despite Christian corruption of the barbarians, a maimed but genuine cycle of culture occurs, and at the same time the dialectical antagonism of value systems continues in a series of indecisive conflicts, now rising to a crisis, now slackening toward mediocrity. There seems also to be some mutual influence between the patterns: the trends of the cycle are sometimes reinforced by a relative dominance of one value system and vice versa, yet the cycle is hampered

[111] VIII 307 f. Nietzsche does not appear always to have blamed Christianity for the fall of Rome: III 122 f. gives a more favorable view.

[112] XV 259; VIII 235 f., 239 f.; III 122 ff.; XIV 366, 372. Cf. VII 70, 73 f.; I 140, 164; H.K.A. I 296 f.

by the presence of alien values, and of course both value systems are somewhat modified by the new culture.

Nietzsche presents a typical outline of the European cycle. In the beginning there was the regular period of barbarism: the conquering "blonde beasts," after much struggle, established feudal aristocracy.[113] Here they laid foundations for long-enduring institutions: fixed classes, guilds, hereditary privilege, and the authoritative church and state, placed men for generations within limits which were unquestioned because felt to be foreordained.[114] Through such limitations European culture evolved toward freedom of movement within a unity of style — in the arts, under the rules of counterpoint or the French drama, for example; in thought, under church dogma; in morals, under aristocratic social tradition.[115]

The culminating epochs were the Italian Renaissance and sixteenth- and seventeenth-century France, as selected by Nietzsche's supreme criteria — high vitality and "free individualities" amid perfected style.[116] He even compares the France of Louis XIV to the culture of Greece:

Decided belief in self. A leisure class who make it hard for themselves and practise much self-conquest. The power of form, will to form *oneself*. "Happiness" admitted as goal. Much force and energy *behind* the formalism. Delight in the spectacle of a life which *seems* so *easy*.[117]

He observes a definite softening in the eighteenth century; the French aristocracy became decadent; and the Revolution, with its concomitants, made the fatal break with tradition which spelled cultural disintegration. The rise of

[113] VII 308 f.; XV 208. Cf. VII 236, 382.
[114] V 296 f. Nietzsche admires the Middle Ages and the Catholic Church for their universality and comparative strength (cf. XVI 298 f.; X 277 f.; III 319; II 354 f.; XI 322; L.O. 23/2/87).
[115] II 201 f.; VII 116 ff.; XIII 310 f.
[116] II 224; XIV 91; VIII 147 f.; VII 177 ff.; XV 206; IV 182 f.; III 315. XIV 91 mentions the Provençal period as another European high point.
[117] XV 208. Cf. 209, 217; IV 181 f.; II 202 f.

humanitarian ideas, of democracy (inevitable, even without the Revolution), of experimentalism and romantic license in the arts — all these were phases of modern decline.[118] In the contrast between Voltaire and Rousseau Nietzsche sees a symbolic confrontation of old and new: Voltaire, the representative of aristocratic civilization, one of the last to combine "the greatest freedom of mind and a positively unrevolutionary disposition, without being inconsistent and cowardly" — against Rousseau, "this doubleness of idealist and *canaille*," weak, moralized, sentimental, the "man of *ressentiment*," whose "return to nature" came of hatred for aristocratic culture, and helped to destroy it.[119]

Here the narrative reaches nineteenth-century decadence, and to some extent the symptoms described earlier may be explained as the "normal decadence" of a culture cycle. Nietzsche says that European culture is now at eventide.[120]

With regard to the dialectical struggle of value systems, Nietzsche sees the high points of our culture cycle as attempts to reinstate pagan values. The Renaissance came very near to a definite triumph for "Rome" — Cesare Borgia as pope would have been its symbol — and the French seventeenth century continued the same effort. But each time a counter-movement restored Christian values: first the Reformation, then the Revolution. Napoleon again embodied the classic ideal, only to be met by the wars of German independence.[121]

But there is a third factor in the dialectical pattern. In the Roman Empire, Christianity attracted the "flock" of ordinary people, as well as the decadent and unfortunate, and in time the "flock" became the preponderant element.[122]

---

[118] XV 189, 191, 204 f., 209; XVI 374; VII 236, 223 f.; II 202 ff., 348; V 324 f.

[119] II 203; VIII 161 f.; XV 213 ff.; XVI 373 f. Hence Nietzsche admires the Enlightenment although he detests the Revolution (III 318 f.; IV 190 f.).

[120] VII 218; XV 179; XIII 362. Cf. II 41 f., 207 f.

[121] VII 335 f.; VIII 310 ff.; III 315; X 277 f., 406. During his Wagner enthusiasm, Nietzsche naturally speaks more favorably of the Reformation (I 162, 165). [122] XV 300 f.

Correspondingly, in modern history Nietzsche observes a recurrent tendency to relax the tension between pagan and Christian values by turning Christianity into a comfortable religion for the "flock." The Jesuits and the democratic movement made such attempts.[123]

He believes that the conflict of values in European history has had both good and ill effects. The unnatural values prevented European man from growing to his full stature, and the mutual inhibition of the two value systems caused a deep-grained falsity and half-heartedness in our civilization.[124] On the other hand, while Asia has grown stagnant under a single code, the fight between two moralities has kept Europe alive and created a "splendid tension of spirit" with which we now can "shoot at the most distant goals." [125] Also there is much to admire in certain types of modern Christian culture: Europeans read many of their nobler feelings *into* Christianity, and for a moment the French created an almost impossible synthesis of values.[126]

Nietzsche acknowledges great indebtedness to the Christian heritage as such. It raised the "temperature" of the soul and sharpened and deepened the mind, especially in psychological insight and moral scepticism. The ascetic ideal made man evil and profound, therefore more interesting; modern science is the fruit of its austere will to truth at any price. Christianity realized that evil can have value, gave suffering a meaning, and spiritualized cruelty. It preserved an access to antiquity for us. Useful for keeping the lower classes contented with their lot, it has also been a valuable discipline for classes rising to power, e.g. the Puritans. And as a hierarchy which gives spiritual men the highest rank, and believes so much in the power of spirit-

[123] VII 5, 149; XV 300 f. Cf. XII 399; XIV 71, 73 f.; XVI 196.
[124] I 396 f.; VIII 51, 265. Cf. X 221.
[125] XIII 327; VII 5; XV 404; V 67.
[126] IV 182 f.; XIII 305 f. Cf. XI 324.

uality as to forbid them the use of force, the Church is a
nobler institution than the state.[127]

But, though we cannot be grateful enough for all this,
the fact remains that Christianity has spoiled the race. Man,
"the still unfixed animal," naturally produces a large proportion of failures, which should be allowed to drop out
for the sake of the fortunate cases. Instead of realizing this,
the Church acted as an antidote to nihilism, preventing the
decadent from suicide, and sought at the same time to break
the self-confidence and happiness of the strong. So "the
Christian resolve to find the world ugly and worthless
[*schlecht*] has made the world ugly and worthless." [128]

European decadence, then, is not altogether "normal."
It is partly "pathological," in so far as it is due to the chaos
of instincts representing the rival value systems, and to the
biological deterioration which one of these has brought to
pass.[129] What does this mean for the future? We shall see.

---

[127] XIV 114 f.; X 225; XIII 90, 151, 317 f.; V 160, 274 f., 308; III 123 f.; VII
85 ff., 311, 467 ff.; XV 271 f.; XVI 219. The best preface to Nietzsche's total
evaluation of Christianity is XII 137.

[128] V 168; VII 88 ff., 430 ff.; XV 324 f.

[129] VIII 50 f.; XV 178, 181. Cf. XV 337. An additional factor has been the
sudden mixture of classes (therefore of instinctive values) which followed the
Revolution (VII 131, 153 f.; XV 177; XVI 282).

CHAPTER XIII

A Philosophy of the Future

Does anyone except me know a way out of this blind alley? . . . A task great enough to bind the peoples again? . . . (XV 111)

1. SIGNS OF STRENGTH

NIETZSCHE does not approach us with the airs of a religious founder — he would rather be clown than saint. He does indeed wish to invoke a world crisis greater than any in history,[1] but he claims no exact knowledge of how the world will move. As we shall see, he predicts certain trends, but he realizes that they may reach their goals — e.g. the unification of Europe — by alternative routes,[2] and that it is uncertain which trends will win out in the end. To accuse him of indecisiveness or hollowness [3] on this score is absurd: he is simply showing good sense.

Nor does he come forward with a neatly imbecile blue-print for Utopia. Among the long-time possibilities there are some which he whole-heartedly supports — he is doing his best to make *his side* win — but these are ultimate goals: about detailed procedure he leaves freedom for experiment and new knowledge:

Men must first learn the new *desire* — and for that there must be someone who excites it in them, a teacher: I trust that they will then become subtle and inventive enough to find for them-

---

[1] XV 1 ff., 116. Cf. VIII 293 ff.; VI 114 f.; XVI 342.
[2] Jaspers, *op. cit.* pp. 234 ff., gives a convenient collection of examples.
[3] As does Jaspers, pp. 223, 246.

selves the ways to satisfy the desire — step by step and experimentally, as they are accustomed. — It does not matter if my
proposals are "impracticable" — they are only meant to tempt
appetite.[4]

Decadence and nihilism are not Nietzsche's last words
about the present age. He holds that many symptoms can
be signs of strength as well as weakness. The dominant
fact is decline; yet modern decadence, in so far as it is
"pathological" rather than senile, is a disease which can
stimulate vitality to a higher pitch, if we "overcome" it with
profounder sources of health. If so, as he says of himself,
the age will turn out to be "at once decadent and a *beginning*."[5] The struggle between value-systems has created
a tension which shows at least that energy is available —
Europe has not simply gone limp. And since unnatural
values have somewhat stunted Western cultural development, by keeping us barbarous they have to that extent
kept us young. Of the Germans in particular Nietzsche says,
"They are of day before yesterday and of day after tomorrow
— *they still have no today*."[6]

So he asks, what are the sound elements in the modern
world — elements strong enough to overcome the diseases
of modernity and outlive nihilism? Technology, natural
science, perhaps history — though the last two with serious
qualification — are expressions of at least *relative* self-confidence.[7] There is a general tendency to "naturalization":
in society, knowledge, morals, politics, and art, men have
an anti-idealistic, anti-revolutionary, anti-enthusiastic disposition, and a greater tolerance of the natural man. They
are coarser, more animal, like strong sensations; they are
also less sentimental and rather enjoy looking at unpleasant
facts. They take the body and its hygiene more seriously

[4] XII 218.
[5] XV 9. Cf. XVI 85 f., 366, 417, 427; III 11.
[6] VII 204. Cf. 5, 231; III 159; V 176; XIII 333, 345, 359; XV 221.
[7] XVI 86, 374, 426; XV 210. Cf. VII 465 f.

than "beautiful feelings." [8] Also one group of philosophers show intellectual rigor — the atheists, sceptics, immoralists, pessimists, and active nihilists who are destroying all the old ideals except their own loyalty to truth.[9]

An added source of crude force will be the nationalistic antagonisms in the twentieth century. Though Nietzsche scorns nationalism, he grants it the temporary value of narrowly concentrated energy. Thanks to Napoleon and the reaction he provoked, we are entering the "classic age of war" in which "the *man* in Europe" will again dominate "the merchant and philistine." Life will be dangerous once more, and will breed stalwart virtues.[10]

Not so for the majority, of course. The violence and confusion will usually produce a hesitant, weakened type of man. But in some cases the same conditions will breed "new barbarians" — born conquerors, men of unbroken desires and wills, no longer softened by over-civilization nor hampered by moral scruples: men who combine superior minds with exuberant vitality. A few of these will be "sovereign individuals" of a yet unknown power and breadth of soul. Where "barbaric aggregations of force" cross with complete emancipation from morality and tradition, where the inner warfare of conflicting streams of heredity stimulates instead of exhausting, and is balanced by tremendous self-mastery, there the great "enigmatic men" emerge — Caesar and Alcibiades, Frederick II and Leonardo da Vinci. Such men get a thousand-fold discipline from inner and outer foes: they are forced to be great. The flock instincts are against them. Many perish, but those who survive are as "strong as the devil." [11] So it is stupid for

[8] XV 210, 221 ff., 226 ff., 234; XVI 366 ff., 456. Cf. XV 445.
[9] VII 157 f., 468, 480; XV 434 f.; L.R. 21/5/87. Cf. VIII 293 f.
[10] V 313; VII 156; XIII 358; XV 233 f.; IV 169. The Russian threat will also be an important factor (VII 155 f.; XI 375; XIII 359).
[11] VII 131 f., 207 f., 322; XV 222, 236, 443; XVI 288, 307; XIV 218. "Barbarian," probably in this sense, is defined in VII 236.

exceptional men to complain of a decadent age: they can perfect themselves now as never before.[12]

2. THE COMING CRISIS

Nietzsche is convinced that decadence must work itself out, that the old order must collapse, before a new one can be built. That is his reply to conservatives, with whom in other respects he has something in common: history cannot be turned backward.[13] This view is supported by his whole philosophy of history, to which he adds Asiatic parallels. In ancient India a decline of culture came with a similar self-destruction of religious foundations — atheism produced by heightened concern for truth, followed by an attempt to make moral values supreme, concluding with renunciation of culture in a nihilist catastrophe. China had an analogous moralistic movement. And both countries ended with cultural stagnation and that lessening of man characteristic of worn-out civilizations.[14]

Correspondingly, Nietzsche predicts *Chineserei* and a "second Buddhism" for Europe.[15] The world economic system and the democratic movement (of which socialism and anarchism are only radical and transient forms) are producing a vast social machine in which individuals are equal and trivial parts — everything a means, nothing an end. The final result would be the flock's dream come true: safety, comfort, and mediocrity for everybody. It would mean slow stagnation.[16]

Nietzsche charges that liberalism defeats its own end. As long as liberal institutions are still being fought for, real freedom is indeed obtained:

[12] XIV 413 f.; XV 443; XVI 300. Cf. XI 242; XII 368.
[13] VIII 155; XV 137 f., 443.
[14] VII 480 f., 137, 253; XV 155, 192, 255, 345; XIV 218; IV 90; V 67. Cf. L.D. 3/1/88.
[15] XV 192, 318 f.; XIV 218; VII 137, 253; XII 203. Cf. IV 90; VI 197 ff.
[16] XVI 286 f., 196, 214 f., 416; VII 135 ff., 180; X 390; IV 134 f.; II 350; V 335. Cf. III 317, 337 ff., 351 f.

Looked at more exactly, war produces these effects, the war *for* liberal institutions, which, as war, makes the *illiberal* instincts endure. And war educates to freedom. For what is freedom? ... becoming more indifferent to hardship, severity, deprivation, even to life; readiness to sacrifice men for one's cause, oneself not excepted.

As soon as liberal institutions are won they become the worst enemies of freedom, undermining will to power, levelling, trivializing — "they make men petty, cowardly and self-indulgent — with them the herd-animal triumphs every time." [17]

Apart from the "new barbarians," therefore, the future European, under industrial democracy, will be an ideal slave, prudent, industrious, modest, complex, weak-willed, "a cosmopolitan chaos of emotion and intelligence." The collapse of old barriers, the increase of communication and mobility, will develop in him a maximum of adaptability. He will be a supernational nomad, inwardly uncertain and therefore needing a master as he needs daily bread. There will be "a kind of European Chinadom, with a meek, Buddhist-Christian faith, and in practice prudently epicurean, as the Chinaman is — reduced men." These mass-men will be the counterpart of the "new barbarians," bred by the same conditions.[18]

Nietzsche predicts that this line of development will be held in check by nationalism in the twentieth century. Socialist and anarchist agitations will contribute to the same effect, their ultimate ideal notwithstanding. But when the last shadows of "the death of God" are falling over Europe, when the old order has collapsed, when the nations have fought themselves out and the inevitable economic unification of Europe has come to pass — then a profound popular reaction against nationalism and war will arise, a "peace

[17] VIII 149 f. Cf. XVI 204, 212; III 339.
[18] XIV 218; XVI 288, 336; VII 207 f.; XV 234 f.; XII 202 f., 205 f.

party" which will really bring the "second Buddhism." Based on universal fraternity, this movement will practice a serious, unsentimental pacifism and renounce conflict in all forms, even the appeal to courts of law, even the very feeling of resentment.[19]

But here the parallel between Orient and Occident ends. Europe has been unique in its struggle between rival value systems; unlike Indian Buddhism it has accumulated tremendous tension on the rack of a fanatical Absolute Morality.[20] Therefore our nihilist catastrophe will involve more than the "passive nihilism" of the "peace party." There will be "active nihilism": the Western habit of action will respond with mass suicide — "Buddhism of deed" — and in stronger cases with the destruction of anything within reach in a kind of blind, illogical rage.[21]

And in this rage lies hope. Because of the residual strength in our era, Nietzsche believes that Europe will not simply fade out in nihilism as Asia has done. Instead, the crisis will weed out decadent elements and compel the healthy to revalue the whole system of values. His own program is for that movement, arising perhaps a century hence from the ashes of the nihilist holocaust, which will affirm the will to power and build life upward.[22] From this point of view nihilism is only an interlude between the death of the old and the birth of the new ideals.[23]

Since the value of that crisis depends upon provoking a sharp reaction, Nietzsche wishes to make it as acute as possible. His weapon for this purpose is the idea of "eternal recurrence." For a typical nihilist, it would be a nightmare. Suppose there is no "other world" to flee to; suppose there

[19] XVI 193; XV 232 f., 192; XI 376; VII 207; V 271. Cf. XV 390; III 341, 343, 345 f.; II 351.
[20] XV 142, 390; VII 5; XIII 327. Cf. XIV 225.
[21] XV 141, 156 ff., 166, 184 ff.; XIV 260; XVI 405. Cf. I 106 f.; VII 152.
[22] XV 138, 166; XVI 279, 286 f., 338 ff.
[23] XVI 85.

is only *this* world, condemned by Christian ideals as cruel, false, purposeless, meaningless; suppose then that it does not happen just once, releasing men forever to a dreamless sleep, but must repeat itself senselessly always, grinding *in* the horror of existence like a cosmic dentist's drill — would that not produce a truly "ecstatic nihilism"? Such is Nietzsche's "philosophy of the hammer," intended to smash what is rotten in humanity and hew out what is sound: [24]

Which will prove themselves the *strongest* thereby? The most moderate, those who have *need* of no extreme articles of faith, those who not only admit but love a good deal of chance, senselessness. Those who can think of man with a considerable reduction of his value, without thereby becoming petty and weak: the richest in health, who are equal to the most misfortunes and therefore are not so afraid of misfortunes — men who *are sure of their power* and who represent the *attained* strength of man with conscious pride.[25]

But the strong will not only be selected; they will be stimulated to a heightened endeavor based on a revaluation of values. For they must adopt ideals which will no longer condemn life root and branch, values which will make them glad to think of *this* world repeated *ad infinitum*.[26]

Nietzsche knows that the outcome of the crisis is by no means certain, and that in wielding his "hammer" he risks destroying humanity altogether. Undaunted, he would "conjure up a fearful decision, make Europe face *consistently* the question whether its will wants to decline." Destruction is better than mediocrity; better perish than "become half-and-half and poisonous." [27]

So humanity will face clear alternatives in the coming age: one the "last man" satirized by Zarathustra and represented by the "peace party"; the other the superman rep-

[24] XV 182, 186 f.; XVI 309, 393 ff.; XIV 260. Cf. XV 100 f.; L.O. c. 10/3/84.
[25] XV 186 f.
[26] XV 166; XVI 395. Cf. XV 182 ff., 187; XVI 417.
[27] XVI 393, 420; XV 435.

resented by the "war party" for which Nietzsche's philosophy is written.[28] Either tameness, or adventure upon the heights — that is the coming decision:

The *one* movement is unconditionally: the levelling of humanity, great ant-hills etc.

The *other* movement, my movement: is conversely the sharpening of all antitheses [*Gegensätze*] and clefts, abolition of equality, the production of supreme men [*Über-Mächtiger*].

The *former* generates the last man, *my* movement the superman.[29]

"Who shall be master of the earth?" is therefore the "refrain" of Nietzsche's practical philosophy.[30]

3. THE BIRTH OF HUMANITY

So far, general predictions. What is Nietzsche's strategy for this eventful period?

He loathes nationalism, despite hoping to make use of its narrow energies:

A little pure air! Let this absurd condition of Europe not last much longer! Is there any idea whatever behind this bull-headed nationalism? What value could it have to stir up these paltry self-conceits now, when everything points to greater and common interests? And that in a condition where the *spiritual dependence* and de-nationalization are obvious, and the real value and meaning of present culture lie in a mutual blending and fertilization! [31]

So Nietzsche welcomes the social and economic forces which are obliterating the old boundaries and will put an end to the petty politics of the nations. For the twentieth century he predicts gigantic wars which will settle the question of world dominion, and he hopes that the danger will force

[28] VI 19 f.; XII 416; XVI 193.
[29] XIV 262. Cf. XVI 335; VII 139; above, p. 114.
[30] XII 406; XIV 320; XVI 337; VI 465, 467.
[31] XVI 192 f. Cf. II 352 f., 359 f.; VI 306; VII 228 f.; XV 111; XIV 374; XIX 388; L.O. 18/10/88, c. 28/12/88.

Europe to unite and become mistress of the earth, completing the work of Napoleon.[32]

When the world is politically as well as economically unified, to what end shall the whole machine be run? The democratic movement, as we have seen, is producing an ideal slavishness in the masses:

> Men who learn easily, accommodate easily, are the rule.... Whoever can command finds those who *have* to obey: I am thinking e.g. of Napoleon and Bismarck. The competition with strong and *un*intelligent wills, which hinders most, is slight.[33]

This increasing docility of the multitude offers an unequalled opportunity for a daring group of men to seize control of the social machinery and make it support a new ruling caste, as a kind of luxury which will exist for its own sake.[34]

That is exactly what Nietzsche wants. The first step, he hopes, will be taken by the "new barbarians": they will set up an aristocracy as the old barbarians did, without scruple about means:

> To fight one's way out of that chaos to this *formation* — for that there is need of a *compulsion*: one must have the alternative of either perishing or *having one's way*. A race fit to be master can spring up only from fearful and violent beginnings. Problem: where are the *barbarians* of the twentieth century? Evidently they will become visible and consolidate themselves only after enormous socialistic crises — they will be those elements which are capable of the *greatest severity with themselves* ˈ ˈan guarantee the *longest will*.[35]

ˈˈˈsche believes that the new aristocracy will not ˈˈne of sheer military force. Later, ideas will ˈˈrs will be fought for philosophies as ˈˈually, the world will fall into the

ˈ 336 f.; V 77, 179.
ff., 351.
ˈ.

hands of the wisest, who will direct its destinies with philosophic foresight.[36]

This expectation implies an ultimately superior power of
ideas upon which Nietzsche is careful to insist: "The gentlest
words bring the storm. Thoughts which come with doves'
feet govern the world." [37] So-called men of action merely
act the rôles — values — which men of thought create:

Those legislative and tyrannical minds who are able to set
fast, to *hold fast*, an idea, men with this spiritual power of will,
who for a long time can petrify and almost eternize what is most
fluid, the mind.... — This species of legislative men has inevitably exercised the strongest influence in all ages: ... they are
the sculptors — and the rest ... are merely *clay*, compared to
them.[38]

Here Nietzsche is thinking of the great prophets and lawgivers of the past — Buddha, Mohammed, and Plato.[39] The
loftiest natures exercise an effortless sway over others. They
alone have self-mastery and belong to themselves rather
than to some social or political function. Unlike the rest of
mankind, who are fragmentary specialists, they inspire con-
fidence by a more balanced use of power. And men willingly submit to a leader if they feel that he ranks above them
in ability and perfection.[40]

Ideas can act only by releasing and directing energies:

Every teaching for which all is not ready in the way of accumulated forces, of explosives, is superfluous. A revaluation of values
is attained only if there exists a tension of new needs, of men
newly needy, who suffer from the old values without becoming
aware of it.[41]

[36] VI 66 f.; XII 207 ff.; V 214 f.; IV 194; XIV 413; XVI 347 ff. Cf. V 155;
XIV 226; XII 412. The "new barbarians" will be men of superior minds, not
dumb brutes (XVI 307).
   [37] VI 217.   [38] XIV 103. Cf. V 230 f.; IV 332; VI 73, 86 f.
   [39] Cf. XIV 92; XV 186; XVI 348; XII 102.
   [40] XII 204 ff.; XI 251; VIII 302; XIII 150; XIV 58, 61, 66; V 77; VII 346, 406.
Cf. I 573.
   [41] XVI 363. Cf. 374 f.; XV 222; V 310; H.K.A. III 319, 324 f. or L.F.N. I
830, 334.

Nietzsche has given his reasons for believing that forces are ripening for his own revaluation of values, and has forged his mighty "hammer" for their control.

Meanwhile it is imperative that the "seeds" of true culture be preserved through the time of barbarism against the day when men of thought shall possess the world. Such are the "good Europeans" whom Nietzsche rallies to his cause. They must stand aside from the petty politics of the age and league together in preparation for ultimate inheritance of power. Their aim, for themselves or their descendants, will be to become "lawgivers of the future" at the head of an international ruling class in which all the European nations and races will be fused. But there is much preliminary work to be done first. Each must realize his own personal ideal, living as a homeless wanderer, steeling his will against inner and outer perils, learning to overcome all the diseases of the modern soul.[42]

"The Great Noon" is Nietzsche's name for that festival, after the struggle for power and the nihilist "earthquake," at which the victorious "party of life" will dedicate humanity to the creation of its highest possible individuals — supermen.[43] This is what he means by saying that man does not matter, and must be "overcome" for the production of a higher type.[44]

The Great Noon will be a

... moment of supreme deliberation on the part of humanity ... when it looks back and looks out, when it steps out from the reign of chance and priests, and puts the question Why? What for? *as a whole* for the first time .....[45]

"As a *whole*" — with this declaration Nietzsche re-affirms his intuition of value, the vision of a solidarity uniting all

---

[42] XV 236 f.; II 353; III 11, 249; V 214 f., 334 ff.; XI 373 ff.; XII 120 ff.; XIV 414; XIX 388; XVI 310 f., 340 f.; VI 113 ff., 296 f. Cf. IV 294 f.; VI 467.

[43] XV 65 f., 238; VI 115, 252, 280, 289, 313, 418; XII 394. In *Ecce Homo* Nietzsche says that he *may* live to see this day (XV 66 f.).

[44] VI 13, 51, 68, 418; XVI 141. Cf. VI 16; VII 371; XIV 74, 275; XVI 127, 144.

[45] XV 82. Cf. VII 137 ff.; XVI 82, 337; II 51; III 297.

men in a tragic but glorious destiny. Humanity, he has argued, *is* not a whole, is not automatically on the right path, not united by providence from the beginning:

> Thus far there were a thousand goals, for there were a thousand peoples. Only the chain of the thousand necks is still lacking, the one goal. . . .
>
> But tell me, my brothers: if the goal for humanity is still lacking, is there not also still lacking — humanity itself? — [46]

Humanity becomes a living thing instead of an abstraction, therefore, when it learns to give itself a purpose.

Such is Nietzsche's final answer to nihilism: though existence be senseless in terms of the old ideal of pre-existent goodness or beauty, we can create a meaning for it by living for a cause great enough to justify all.[47] And his last writings resound with the joy of having found the purpose which will create and redeem humanity — of having found the way out of modern perplexity into clarity of aim: "Love for a work and a child does not need to be commanded. Advantage of the superman." "Formula of our happiness: a yes, a no, a straight line, a *goal* . . ."[48]

4. WORLD CULTURE

"Culture" or "civilization" rather than "society" is Nietzsche's term for the total ordering of human life which most concerns him.[49] A true culture, as he conceives it, has an organic unity of style which is a necessary development of a central integrity — something very different from a pretty veneer or the stereotyped uniformity of modern life. Unity of style implies definite limitation, the exclusion of unas-

---

[46] VI 87. Cf. XIV 335; XV 82; above, pp. 42 f., 77, 321 f.

[47] XVI 365; VI 115, 203 ff.; XIII 78. Cf. X 275 f.; XV 155 f.; VII 482 ff.

[48] XII 359; VIII 218. Cf. III 244; XIV 262 f.; XV 106, 111, 116 f.; XVI 426.

[49] Cf. XV 486. Nietzsche sometimes uses *Zivilisation* in a pejorative contrast to *Cultur* (e.g. XV 230), but he sometimes uses *Cultur* in a similarly pejorative sense (e.g. XVI 148; VII 199, 323 f. Cf. I 57 f.). In English it is advisable to use "civilization" *and* "culture" to suggest the values he has in mind here.

similable elements.[50] A culture rests upon a "synthesis of values and aims"; its function is to nurse individual genius.[51]

Nietzsche is a prophet of cultural renaissance.[52] The future too will follow a cyclic pattern: "Humanity must live in *cycles, sole* form of duration. Not culture as long as possible, but as short and high as possible." [53] So, as his views on order in history imply, he is not a utopian in the sense of believing in a permanent ideal society which will live happily ever afterward.[54] He suggests rather that the "lawgivers of the future" will direct humanity, or parts of it, through several cycles:

... to bring out the form of *multifariousness* of man, to smash him when a variety of type has had its culmination — to be thus creating and annihilating seems to me the supreme delight that men can have.[55]

The "new barbarians" and the resulting formation of a ruling caste will make the characteristic beginning of another culture cycle. Like past aristocracies, this one will perpetuate itself for generations, in a traditional solidarity which gives "duration across thousands of years" "to the will of philosophical men-of-violence and artist tyrants." So, and only so, can life attain that smooth functioning of instinct which is the condition of perfection.[56] And eventually another "tragic age" will appear, bringing that "excess of life" from which the Dionysian *Rausch* must again be born, yielding another springtime of art.[57]

In other respects, Nietzsche anticipates important differences for the future. The change of scale will be immense.

[50] I 183, 186 f., 314, 384; VII 177 ff.; X 15, 116 f., 124, 244 f.; XIV 343. *The Birth of Tragedy* naturally uses somewhat different language (I 57 f., 125).
[51] XV 157; I 439 f., 442 ff.; III 104. Cf. V 177 f.
[52] XV 106, 111.
[53] XIV 260.
[54] I 584. See above, pp. 321 f.
[55] XIII 323.
[56] XVI 341, 338 f.; VIII 300 f. Cf. V 296 ff.; above, pp. 195–99.
[57] XV 66.

Casting aside his earlier belief in city culture and national culture, he opens his middle period with a program of *world* culture — administration of the entire planet for all-human goals.[58] This is his permanent view. The new aristocracy will be international, "an oligarchy *above* the peoples and their interests." [59]

He considers modern scientific mentality both a reason for the impossibility of reviving the old cultures and a support for the new. Former cultures led an unconscious, plantlike existence, subject to ungoverned chance, and they were based on religious ideas of the workings of nature which we are discarding for good.[60] World culture will be conscious, choosing its ends and means deliberately. The course mankind has followed blindly hitherto can now be *willed*. We shall ransack history for the conditions of manhood at its best, but even when we repeat them — for example those that formed the Greeks — we shall do knowingly what history did unawares. And scientists may invent methods which will surpass anything in history. To obtain adequate knowledge of the conditions for world culture will be a task for the great minds of the twentieth century.[61]

Consciousness and change of scale and will concern the past also. Previous cultures were isolated in time as well as in space; they retained unity of style by knowing chiefly their own past, and not too much of that. In this respect nineteenth century historicism is a feature of cultural decadence.[62] But Nietzsche holds that the proper amount of history is a function of the "plastic force" available to digest it, and his final prescription for the "historical disease" is not less knowledge but more force.[63] World

[58] II 41 ff.; III 99, 249; XI 133 f.; XVI 337. Cf. I 161 f., 183, 314; X 186 f., 232; XIII 340; XVIII 118 f. n.
[59] XVI 394. Cf. 340.
[60] II 42; X 404 ff. Cf. XIX 4 ff.
[61] II 42 f., 231; III 99; V 44 f.; VI 43; VII 138; XVI 305 f., 351. Cf. XVI 82, 309 f., 427.
[62] Cf. VII 176 ff.; XVII 313.   [63] I 286 f.; XVI 361, 366. Cf. VI 296.

culture will feed on universal history; it will not have to forget the past in order to be young. Viewed in this light, our "age of comparison" carries a promise. Man will one day feel all history as *his own*. Fusing in one soul all the hopes, losses, victories of humanity, he will know for the first time

. . . a god's happiness, full of power and love, full of tears and full of laughter, a happiness which, like the sun at evening, continually gives away and sheds its inexhaustible wealth into the sea; and, like it, feels richest only then, when even the poorest fisherman rows with golden oar! [64]

But what can replace religion? The older cultures had their backbone, their source of form and limitation, in fictions and myths; [65] and we have seen that when these lapse, decadence follows. Nietzsche must have worried profoundly over this problem, for he well knew the disintegrative effect of scientific analysis and the need for some comprehensive energizing idea. Hence his ecstasy of inspiration when the living answer fell into his hands.

It consisted of the twin "myths" in his Dionysian world view. For faith in divine providence he would substitute a strong will of our own to hold a definite course. But the will needs a goal. The adequate end is to realize the "myth of the future" — the superman:

By looking forward, setting yourselves a great goal, you restrain at the same time that arrogant analytical impulse which now desolates the present for you, and makes all repose, all peaceful growing and ripening almost impossible. Surround yourselves with the hedge of a great and comprehensive hope . . . .[66]

[64] V 260. Cf. 258 f.; II 40 f.; III 99; XII 216 f.; XIV 271; XV 303; H.K.A. II 353 f. This does not mean an indiscriminate muddling of everything — which would certainly be incompatible with unity of style. As in all healthy life there will be selection, digestion, and elimination (cf. II 41; I 287; XVI 361).

[65] I 160 f., 163; II 47, 231; X 127, 404, 406 f.

[66] I 338. Cf. VI 123, 297; XIII 77 f.; XIV 270, 319, 333; XVI 342, 359; XII 400; above, pp. 189 f. The superman is not a myth in the sense of a mirage or fiction. The whole point is that, unlike the myths of old, he is realiza*ble.*

What can compel the will to be so strong? Belief in eternal recurrence: besides inducing the nihilist crisis and the revaluation of values, and weeding out the decadent, it will train the healthy — grading their powers, placing an infinite accent on the decisions of daily life, assuring the immortality of realized values.[67] And this is not a decrepit dogma trembling at each advance of science, but a *true* myth, resting on the fundamental assumptions of science itself.[68] That is why Nietzsche speaks highly of himself.

5. JUSTICE AND THE LAWGIVER

A consciously directed civilization presupposes architects. These will be the "lawgivers of the future," the "wise men," "new philosophers," "Caesars": the "supreme man" "*determines* values and governs the will of thousands of years by governing the highest natures." [69] Zarathustra is a poetic prototype of the lawgiver, and at the same time a herald who summons future lawgivers to compete for the guidance of human destiny.[70]

But why should we obey the Caesarian philosopher? Will his laws be just? And is there not an irreconcilable conflict between his creative purpose and the claims of kindness (*Güte*)? [71]

Nietzsche praises justice as one of the rarest and greatest virtues.[72] Of his own experience with it he says:

It was late when I found out what I still lacked utterly: namely *justice*. "What is justice? And is it possible? And if it should not be possible, how were life then to be endured?" — in such wise I questioned myself unceasingly. It caused me deep

---

[67] XV 166, 487; XVI 393 ff.; XII 63 ff., 399 f., 415; V 265 f. See above, pp. 303 ff. This is a religion for the elect only (cf. XII 69). The lower orders will be given religions appropriate to their stations (XII 418; VII 85 ff.).

[68] Cf. XV 182, 186; XVI 398; above, pp. 285 ff.

[69] XVI 359. Cf. 347, 351, 353, 355; XIV 102, 265, 286.

[70] Cf. VI 287 ff.; XII 365.

[71] Cf. XII 365 f.; II 222.

[72] I 327 f.; II 411 f.; VI 93; VII 172 f., 366.

anguish to find only passions, only narrow perspectives...
wherever I dug into myself....[73]

His answer to the question follows his revaluation of truth,
for the two problems are akin.[74]

The ideal of absolute justice, like other forms of Absolute Morality, is clearly impossible. Life is everywhere
"passions" and "perspectives"; it implies valuation, which
entails "dislocation, distortion and specious teleology of
horizons"; there is "necessary injustice in every 'for' and
'against.'"[75] How can we "give each his own," when life
as such is essentially unjust? "To give each his own: that
would be to will justice and attain chaos."[76] Between life
and justice in this sense there is a hopeless antinomy. Of
the man who tries to be just, Nietzsche writes "that at every
moment he has to atone in himself for his humanity, and
is tragically consumed with an impossible virtue."[77]

To neutralize passion is no escape. If we try to be "liberal" or "broad-minded" in the sense of having *no* perspective, we merely become weak. If justice is more than
magnanimity, it is surely still more than tolerance or indifference. It is at least something positive, active. It *judges*.
It is intolerant. There is nothing charming about it. It is
a "hard and terrible" virtue, capable of passing sentence of
death.[78] Justice requires passion, then, but passion is
unjust!

Nietzsche resolves the paradox by placing the antithesis,
not between justice and passion, but between crudity and
complex subtlety of passion. Forsaking the chimaera of the
absolute, we can at least perceive relative differences of
justice. We can see

[73] XIV 385. Cf. XII 351; XI 386 f.
[74] Cf. II 411; VII 172 f.
[75] II 11. Cf. VII 4, 17; XI 258 f.; XIII 124.
[76] XII 291. Cf. II 108, 411; VI 101.
[77] I 328.
[78] I 327 ff.; VI 15; IV 345; VII 149 ff., 246, 366, 428 f. Cf. VIII 119; XIV 347 f.

... where injustice is always greatest: namely there, where life is least, narrowest, shabbiest, most primitively developed, and yet cannot help taking *itself* as aim and measure of things; ... and how power and right and amplitude of perspective grow up together.[79]

So, with a new meaning, we arrive at an ancient formula: justice is the will of the strongest! The greatest justice available at any given time is the verdict of the most powerful man — in the full sense of "power."

In other words, the comparatively just man can see more sides of a situation — "to see" meaning "to experience intensely." [80] But a mere assortment of perspectives would be vacillating and indefinite. The just man controls, organizes, discriminates; he is "an immense multiplicity which is nevertheless the converse of chaos." [81] He can see things whole — because he *is* a whole. "Do you wish to become a universal, just eye? Then you must do so as one who has gone through *many* individuals and whose last individual *uses* all previous ones as functions." [82]

Nietzsche believes in the "self-demonstrating authority" of the greatest men — "men who are walking legislations." Here, rather than in some Platonic legal norm or democratic assembly, is living justice, the basis of concrete decision.[83] The lawgiver of the future must be an "epitome of the world":

The wisest man would be *the most abundant in contradictions,* who has organs of touch, as it were, for all kinds of man: and in between, his great moments of *grandiose harmony* .... A kind of planetary motion — [84]

Life is more than the present. Nietzsche's justice will not be the "cold justice" intent primarily upon avenging

[79] II 11 f. Cf. VII 366 f.; XIV 80, 89 f.; XVI 358.
[80] XI 260 ff.; XII 7, 13 f.; XV 336; II 12 f.; XIV 347 f.; IV 345. Cf. V 218 f.
[81] XV 44; II 11; VII 428 f.
[82] XII 14. Cf. XIII 143; XIV 80, 385 f.
[83] XIV 66, 103; VII 130.   [84] XV 336. Cf. XVI 351.

infractions of some static code; it will be "justice which is love with seeing eyes." [85] This love for a future object will be the focus around which his just ordering of society will crystallize — *justice* as a building, expelling, annihilating disposition of mind... *supreme representative of life itself.*" [86]

The long view reconciles the demands of kindness and creativity: it is necessary to be merciless with men for the sake of a better future. Nietzsche expresses this reconciliation by the symbol of the lawgiver as "the Roman Caesar with the soul of Christ":

On Zarathustra's *recovery*, there stands *Caesar*, inexorable, kind: *the gulf between being-a-creator, kindness and wisdom is destroyed.*[87]

6. THE CASTE SYSTEM

Presiding at the Great Noon perhaps, the lawgiver will harmonize the fresh forces released by the preceding human earthquake and yoke them to his purpose.[88] That purpose will be to direct thousand-year experiments at training a higher type — the superman — out of existing human material, and therefore he must grade that material into an enduring hierarchy of classes.[89] This will be the work of justice, for justice is gradation, not equality.[90]

In this ideal of future society Nietzsche concludes his defense of aristocracy. His power standard of value implies the principle of gradation — that men vary greatly in value and rights.[91] Evolution through conquest and subordina-

---

[85] VI 100. Cf. XIII 363.

[86] XIII 42. Cf. VI 101; XII 363, 410; I 338. So justice is subordinate to a great goal (cf. V 204; XI 250; above, p. 294).

[87] XIV 286. Cf. XVI 353; XII 366; XIV 80, 102, 265; XV 100 f.; VII 151; II 222. This also is evidently symbolized by the lion with the flock of doves in *Zarathustra* (VI 473 ff.).

[88] XVI 417. Cf. VI 308; X 309 f.

[89] VII 137 ff.; XII 414.

[90] Cf. VII 173; II 11 ff.; VIII 162; VI 146 f.

[91] See above, pp. 190 ff.

tion means that life can rise higher only by favoring a few at the expense of many.[92] Perhaps as a special case of this, he maintains that a high culture can exist only with a privileged class supported by others.[93] He establishes a hereditary basis of excellence by his theory that instincts are accumulations of ancestral experiences.[94] And his psychological analysis of Master Morality reveals two sorts of inner tension, in an aristocracy, which make for strong individuality and progressive elevation of man.[95]

He contemplates a highly differentiated gradation not only of classes but of individuals, consisting of many degrees.[96] But his comments on the *Laws of Manu* indicate that the main division will consist of three castes:

The *order of castes* ... is only the sanction of a *natural order* ... over which no arbitrariness, no "modern idea," has power. In every healthy society three types, differently gravitating physiologically, separate themselves, reciprocally conditioning one another, each of which has its own hygiene, its own realm of work, its own kind of feeling of perfection and mastery. Nature, *not* Manu, divides from one another the ones predominantly intellectual, the ones predominantly strong in muscle and temperament, and the third, distinguished neither in the one nor in the other respect, the mediocre — the latter as the great number, the former as the choice.[97]

Nietzsche says, however, that his aristocracy will not be backward-looking like those of the past: its honor will be placed not in trivialities of court and crusade, but in redeeming the past through the nobility of its children to

[92] See above, pp. 77–83.
[93] II 327; IX 151. Cf. V. 335; XV 487; VII 198, 236 f.
[94] Cf. II 327 f., 337; VII 250 f.; XVI 329; above, pp. 69 ff., 79, 104 ff., 195–99.
[95] See above, pp. 157 ff., 197 f. Also, unlike the masses, an aristocracy preserves our touch with the past (VI 296).
[96] XIV 57 f.; XII 416 f.; XVI 364. Other passages mention single criteria, for example: suffering over man (XIV 266), depth of capacity to suffer and the kind and degree of cleanliness (VII 258 f.), ability to live on hypotheses instead of faith (XIII 54 f.), the amount of truth, happiness or power one can endure without degenerating (XIII 41), the amount of responsibility one can bear (VII 163), the kind of thoughts most readily aroused (XIV 411. Cf. VII 254), and a taste for the Old Testament (VII 77). [97] VIII 301. Cf. XIV 117 f.; L.G. 31/5/88.

come.[98] In fact the hygiene of the whole society will involve careful breeding, selection, and elimination. Though hereditary, the caste system will probably make room for promotion and demotion in exceptional cases.[99] Marriage and childbearing will be a direct concern of the community. Chronic invalids and low-grade neurasthenics will be discouraged from having children; very degenerate individuals secluded or sterilized.[100] When Nietzsche insists that we be inexorable about it he is simply demanding that we do what is best for the future of the race without allowing ourselves to be deflected by false pity. The "weak" or "decadent" are not necessarily the physically delicate or those who merely happen to fall ill, but those wretched lives which poison the air for everybody with their misery. These should be segregated from the rest of society, as we segregate the insane and the contagiously ill. Nietzsche would also permit suicide, and encourage it in some cases by appropriately pessimistic philosophies. But there is no indication that he advocates brutal extermination of such people. And where there is hope of cure — in a criminal, for example — he proposes psychological care far more humane than current practice: "Zarathustra is gentle to the sick." [101]

[98] VI 297.

[99] Cf. II 327; XIV 226.

[100] XVI 183 f. Nietzsche feels the importance of scientific study of heredity, but he does not subscribe to any particular system of eugenics. He simply urges that we take seriously the problem of how to grow men best, making this rather than love the first purpose of marriage (XI 131; II 315; IV 156; VI 102 ff., 307 f.; XVI 182 f.). Though he attacks the nineteenth-century emancipation of women, on the ground that it is based on bad psychology and expresses feminine decadence (VII 191–200; XV 57 ff.; XIV 242 ff.), he has singularly little to say of the desirable future for women. Apparently he wishes to keep them in a subordinate position (VI 97; VII 196; XIV 244 f.), but not literally to restore them to the status of Greek women: II 315 suggests that Aspasia and Pericles' wife change places, in other words that wives in the future should be worthy of intellectual friendship (cf. VI 82; V 101). At any rate Nietzsche was not consciously a woman hater: "One cannot think highly enough of women: but one need not think falsely of them on that account." (XIV 235. Cf. 243; VI 82, 95 ff.; VII 199 f.; L.G. 5/11/79.)

[101] VI 44, 52 ff., 63 ff., 301 ff., 305; VII 88, 432 ff.; XV 66; VIII 218; XII 67; XIV 72, 119; IV 195 ff. See above, p. 193.

Instead of destroying ordinary people, as the popular monster-myth has it, he would use them with great consideration as members of the third caste:

A high culture is a pyramid: it can stand only on a wide bottom; it presupposes a strongly and healthily consolidated mediocrity first of all. . . . If the exceptional man handles precisely the mediocre with tenderer fingers than himself and his peers, this is not merely kindness of heart — it is simply his *duty* . . .[102]

True, their function is instrumental, and they are in this sense "slaves," but there is no injustice in this arrangement:

There is a natural determination for one's being a public utility, a wheel, a function: *not* society but simply the kind of *happiness* of which the great majority are capable makes intelligent machines of them. For the mediocre, being mediocre is a blessing; mastery in one thing, specialty, a natural instinct.[103]

So Nietzsche makes specialization the criterion of mediocrity and "slavery": his lowest caste would include professional and business men as well as farmers and artisans. In short, nearly the whole of modern industrial society would become the foundation of the "culture pyramid" — that is why in the long run he welcomes the development of this society.[104]

But Nietzsche looks forward to a nobler life even for the laboring classes:

From the future of the worker. — Workers should learn to feel like *soldiers*. An honorarium, a salary, but no pay!

No relation between payment and *performance*! But rather so place the individual, *according to his kind*, that he can *do* the *highest* that lies in his reach.[105]

Modern treatment of labor he calls "a short sighted exploitation at the expense of the future." [106]

[102] VIII 303. Cf. XVI 284, 303; XV 197; XI 135; III 104, 349. Here also Nietzsche seems to depart from aristocratic customs of the past: cf. XVI 330.

[103] VIII 303.

[104] *Ibid.*; XVI 286 f.; XII 417. On "slavery" cf. XIV 75; II 261, 337 f.; XVI 410; XII 103 ff., 205 f.; VIII 294 f.; VI 166; L.S. 11/83.

[105] XVI 197. Cf. XV 197.   [106] III 349.

When Nietzsche calls himself "the last anti-political German," he means that he is opposed, as we have seen, to modern state idolatry. In his view culture and state are antagonists, each living on the other, and the state should serve culture, not vice versa.[107] So he places affairs of government in the hands, not of the first caste, but of the second: "they are the guardians of justice, the custodians of order and security; they are the noble warriors; above all it is the *king*, as the supreme formula of warrior, judge and supporter of the law." They are the "executives" of the highest caste, sparing them the coarser part of the work of ruling.[108]

7. THE LORDS OF THE EARTH

Will the first caste be the supermen, or do these rank higher still? Most of Nietzsche's statements imply that the highest caste itself — the "lawgivers," "highest men," "Lords of the Earth" — will train itself to superhuman godlikeness *in the course of time*: "There must be *many* supermen: all goodness [*Güte*] develops only among its peers. *One* god would always be a *devil!* A *ruling race.* — To 'the Lords of the Earth.' "[109] Time is required for the thousand-year

---

[107] VIII 111 f.; VI 69 ff., 194; X 275 f., 308 ff.; I 420. Cf. H.K.A. II 354 f.; above, pp. 325, 336.
[108] VIII 302. Cf. IV 173 f.
[109] XII 414. Cf. 415; XVI 286, 340 f., 359; VI 296; VIII 218 f.; XIV 226, 262; IX 280. Zarathustra says that the self-chosen elect will grow into a "chosen people," and from this will grow the superman (VI 114. Cf. XIV 296). The relationship of Zarathustra to the superman is complex, as one would expect in a poetic figure who goes through a process of transformation. He first appears as an atheist who is the prophet of the superman: no superman has ever yet existed (VI 134 — VIII 218 f. does not strictly contradict this: it only says there have been sporadic instances of a higher type which is "a kind of superman" in comparison to the rest of humanity). Zarathustra is a "bridge to the future," but also "a cripple on this bridge" (VI 205). But after passing through a crisis with the idea of eternal recurrence, he attains the supreme affirmation of this recurrence which transforms him into an embodiment of the superhuman Dionysian ideal (XV 95 f.). He lives out his own prophecy. The poetic language of VI 13 (cf. XII 191, 361 f.) has led some scholars to suppose that Nietzsche first thought of the superman as a new biological species, but later changed his mind (VIII 218 f.). I think they take poetic language too literally. Also Nietzsche's Lamarckian biology makes "new species" a relative matter.

training experiments, back of which stands Nietzsche's theory of how aristocracies have flowered in the past. But that theory, including his "morals for individuals," also places the high point of a culture cycle in the period when the bonds of class discipline relax and sovereign individualities burst forth. He is probably thinking of that when he jots this note:

The order of rank, carried out in a system of world government: finally the Lords of the Earth, a new ruling caste. Originating from them here and there, wholly an Epicurean god, the superman, the transfigurer of existence.[110]

So even if he calls the whole caste, at some future date, supermen, Nietzsche applies the principle of gradation to the individuals within it,[111] and the best of these will be the pinnacles of human history.

The Lords of the Earth have ultimate power, but do not bother with details of government: "Beyond the rulers, detached from all ties, live the highest men: and in the rulers they have their instruments." [112] And not even the exercise of supreme power over society is their main purpose. They are the end to which society is a means; hence they live in detached unconcern like "Epicurean gods." [113] It is their business to represent perfection on earth:

Only the most spiritual men have admittance to beauty, to *the* beautiful: only with them is goodness not weakness. . . . "*The world is perfect*" — so speaks the instinct of the most spiritual, the yes-saying instinct —: "imperfection, the '*beneath us*' of every kind, distance, the passion of distance, the Chandala himself, belong to this perfection too." [114]

These men, be it noted, are the most spiritual, beautiful and kind — how different from the popular notion, which

[110] XII 413. XII 113 supports this more individualistic picture of the superman, describing the highest man as "no lawgiver."
[111] Cf. XII 417.   [112] XVI 359. Cf. IX 424; XII 206.
[113] XIV 262, 285; VI 72; XVI 306 f.; VII 236 f. Cf. VI 296.
[114] VIII 301 f. Cf. III 56 ff.; V,I 172 f.; XVI 306 f.

has mistaken the "barbarian" for the superman! But of course they are not merely spiritual, in the milk-and-water sense. To guard against that, Nietzsche warns that a super-man will resemble Cesare Borgia more than Parsifal.[115] Since man must become "better and worse," a superman will possess the "evil" urges to maximum intensity; his kindness will be terrible; the best of us would call him a devil.[116] This audacity will express itself in his mode of life:

> The most spiritual men, as the *strongest*, find their happiness in that in which others would find their downfall: in the laby-rinth, in severity with self and others, in experiment; their pleasure is in subduing self: asceticism is nature, need, instinct, with them.... They consider the difficult task a privilege; playing with burdens which crush others, a *recreation* . . . Knowledge [*Erkentnis*] — a form of asceticism. — They are the most venerable kind of man: that does not exclude their being the gayest, most amiable. They rule, not because they desire, but because they *are* . . . .[117]

Nietzsche stresses the austerity of their lives. They give to the lower orders the happiness and comfort they renounce for themselves. They suffer most from existence, but also have the strongest antidotes.[118]

In contrast to the fragmentary specialists — "slaves" — the "Lords of the Earth" will be *whole*, complete men, uniting the noblest faculties humanity has attained: " 'I, for the first time, brought the man of justice, the hero, the poet, the scientist [*Erkennenden*], the prophet, the leader together again . . . .' (So shall the superman speak!)" [119] Therefore the education of the aristocracy will be very un-like modern education: it will do everything to prevent

---

[115] XV 51 f. *Not* that he will *be* a Cesare Borgia.
[116] XV 122; V 344; VI 213, 420; XVI 377. Cf. 294; H.K.A. II 129.
[117] VIII 302. Cf. IV 193 f.; VII 420 f.
[118] XII 418; XIII 37.
[119] XIV 264. Cf. 226 f.; XVI 287, 296 f.; VII 152, 325; V 155.

them from succumbing to a single urge, from becoming specialists — and of course it will cultivate the exceptional individual rather than the average.[120]

Suicide is not only for the decadent. The "death of God" is not overcome until man has also settled matters with death. Since there is no providence, Nietzsche says that we ourselves must arrange to "die at the right time." It will be the final dignity of man to meet death by choice instead of chance. He should die when his work is complete, not later. Death in the future shall be a festival:

He who is consummating dies his death victoriously, surrounded with men hoping and vowing.

That your death be no blasphemy upon man and earth, my friends: I beg that from the honey of your soul.
Let your spirit and your virtue still glow in your dying, like an evening glow about the earth . . . .[121]

[120] XII 204; XVI 325; VIII 112 ff.
[121] VI 105, 108; XVI 315; XII 229 f., 351, 394; II 88; III 294, 364. Cf. VI 322, 326 f., 462, 468. So Nietzsche describes the "highest men" as "zuletzt sich zerbrechend" (XIV 58). His occasional remarks about the superiority of inorganic existence are to be understood partly in this connection (cf. XII 228 f., 359; XIII 88, 228).

Epilogue

Having beheld the ultimate vision, we must turn again toward becoming "good neighbors of the nearest things." What are the next steps for one whom this dream has possessed? Nietzsche would not have him broken by the tension between distant ideal and sordid reality; there is no sense in being "insanely impatient for the superman," for "all *actions* have acquired *meaning*, as path and means to that." To one whose life has attained such focus there comes a sense of repose — the "repose of the great stream" — and the immense future spreads out before him like an unrippled sea. There should be no haste, no jumps; every intervening stage must be brought to perfection in due season, every least detail finished with the dedication of a true artist to his task. The abiding mood is "luminousness, peace, *no exaggerated* longing, joy in the *rightly employed, eternized moment!*" [122]

AMOR FATI

---

[122] XIV 286. Cf. 263, 265; XII 66 f., 366 f., 414; III 372; XV 45.

NOTE ON REFERENCES AND ABBREVIATIONS

NOTE ON REFERENCES AND ABBREVIATIONS

It is a great pity that there is not some standard paragraph numbering for all of Nietzsche's works in all editions. As it is, I have found it most convenient to cite by volume and page of the standard *Gross-oktav Ausgabe* in 20 vols. (vols. IX–XII and XV, revised). Roman and Arabic numbers, when unaccompanied by titles or by other symbols, refer to volumes and pages, respectively, of this edition. The material is often scrappy and scattered; sometimes only a short sentence or phrase is relevant to the point in hand, and therefore not everyone will be able to find it even when the page is given. The symbols "f." and "ff." do not imply a continuous passage running from one page to the next one or more; they mean, "Look everywhere on the pages indicated." I have used "cf." to mark citations which bear somewhat less directly on the matter under discussion; if there has been a quotation of some length in the text, "cf." indicates references other than that for the quotation.

Letters are cited by addressee and the day, month, and year (as nearly as possible), as given in *Friedrich Nietzsches Gesammelte Briefe* (Insel-Verlag, Leipzig, 1907 ff.), *Friedrich Nietzsches Briefwechsel mit Franz Overbeck* (Insel-Verlag, Leipzig, 1916), and E. Förster-Nietzsche, *Wagner und Nietzsche zur Zeit ihrer Freundschaft* (Müller, München, 1915). The critical edition now coming out is modifying some of the dates assigned, but I could not adopt its standard because too little has yet appeared.

In citing letters and a few other works, the following abbreviations are used:

H.K.A. — *Friedrich Nietzsche, Werke und Briefe, Historisch-Kritische Gesamtausgabe: Werke.*
H.K.B. — *idem: Briefe.*
L.F.N. — E. Förster-Nietzsche, *Das Leben Friedrich Nietzsches.*
L. B. — Letter to Georg Brandes.
L. Bü. — "   " Hans von Bülow.
L. D. — "   " Paul Deussen.
L. F. — "   " Carl Fuchs.
L. G. — "   " Peter Gast.
L. Ge. — "   " Karl von Gersdorff.
L. K. — "   " Gustav Krug.

L. M. — "   " Malwida von Meysenbug.
L. Mu. — "   " Nietzsche's mother.
L. O. — "   " Franz Overbeck.
L. R. — "   " Erwin Rohde.
L. S. — "   " Nietzsche's sister.
L. St. — "   " Heinrich von Stein.
L. W. — "   " Richard Wagner.

For the convenience of readers who have no access to the *Gross-oktav Ausgabe*, a condensed table of its contents follows:

Vol.	Pages		Approximate Date of Writing
I	1–172	*Die Geburt der Tragödie*	1870–71 (Pref. '86)
	179–589	*Unzeitgemässe Betrachtungen*	1873–76
II	3–418	*Menschliches, Allzumenschliches, I*	1876–78 (Pref. '86)
III	3–183	*Menschl. II: Verm. Meinungen u. Spr.*	1878–79 (Pref. '86)
	187–375	*Menschl. II: Der Wanderer u. s. Sch.*	1879
IV	3–372	*Morgenröte*	1880–81 (Pref. '86)
V	3–362	*Die Fröhliche Wissenschaft*	1881–82, 1886
VI	9–476	*Also Sprach Zarathustra*	1883–85
VII	3–279	*Jenseits von Gut und Böse*	1885–86
	287–484	*Zur Genealogie der Moral*	1887
VIII	1–51	*Der Fall Wagner*	1888
	59–177	*Götzendämmerung*	1888
	183–209	*Nietzsche contra Wagner*	1888
	213–314	*Umwertung aller Werte, Buch I: Der Antichrist*	1888
	315–322	*Disposition und Entwürfe zum dritten Buch*	1888
	333–443	*Dichtungen*	1869–88
IX		*Nachgelassene Werke*	1869–72
	297–430	*Über die Zukunft unserer Bildungsanstalten*	1871–72
X		*Nachgelassene Werke*	1872–76
	5–92	*Die Philosophie im tragischen Zeitalter der Griechen*	1873
	189–207	*Über Wahrheit u. Lüge im aussermoralischen Sinne*	1873

XI		*Nachgelassene Werke*	1875–81
XII		" "	1881–86
XIII, XIV		" "	1882–88
XV	1–127	*Ecce Homo*	1888
	137–489	*Der Wille zur Macht, I & II*	1885–88
XVI	3–402	*Der Wille zur Macht, III & IV*	1885–88
	403–467	*Der Wille zur Macht, Nachträge u. Pläne*	1885–88
XVII–XIX		*Philologica*	1866–77

A little arithmetic will enable the reader to find the approximately corresponding pages in other editions.

SELECT BIBLIOGRAPHY

SELECT BIBLIOGRAPHY

A. BIBLIOGRAPHIES

Bianquis, Geneviève, *Nietzsche en France, l'influence de Nietzsche sur la pensée française*, Alcan, Paris, 1929, pp. 119 ff.

"Friedrich Nietzsches Bibliothek," in *Bücher und Wege zu Büchern*, ed. by Arthur Berthold, Spemann, Berlin, 1900, pp. 427 ff.

Lévy, Albert, *Stirner et Nietzsche*, thèse, Société Nouvelle, Paris, 1904. (Appendix contains list of books borrowed by Nietzsche from the library at Basle, 1869–79.)

Mügge, M. A., *Friedrich Nietzsche, His Life and Work*, 3rd ed., Fisher Unwin, London, 1911 (or later), Part IV.

Tissi, Silvio, *Nietzsche*, Athena, Milano, 1926. (Contains bibliography of many literatures, especially Italian.)

Weichelt, Hans, *Zarathustra-Kommentar*, 2nd ed., Meiner, Leipzig, 1922, pp. 229 ff.

Würzbach, Friedrich, "Nietzsche. Ein Gesamtüberblick über die bisherige Nietzsche-Literatur," in *Literarische Berichte aus dem Gebiete der Philosophie*, ed. by Arthur Hoffman, K. Stenger, Erfurt, Hefte 19/20, 26 (1929, 1932).

(See also bibliographies in works by Andler, Jaspers, Löwith and O'Brien, listed below.)

B. NIETZSCHE'S COLLECTED WORKS AND LETTERS

The long-standard edition of Nietzsche's works is the *Gross-oktav Ausgabe*, published in its final form by the Alfred Kröner Verlag in Leipzig. Its first edition was published by Naumann, Leipzig, 1894 ff., and numbered only fifteen volumes. *Ecce Homo* was not yet allowed to appear, and *Der Wille zur Macht*, in its first guise, filled just one volume. Volumes IX–XII, edited by Fritz Koegel, were deemed unsatisfactory; a second edition, the work of other editors, soon replaced them. When Kröner took over, the old vol. XV gave place to two new ones, which contained *Ecce Homo* and an ampler version of *Der Wille zur Macht* — which had meanwhile appeared in another edition. Then followed three volumes of *philologica*, the last of which appeared in 1912. Finally, in 1926, came Richard Oehler's *Nietzsche-Register*, published as vol. XX. There are several shorter German editions, and the page and volume numbers of some of these are given in parallel columns with those of the *Gross-oktav Ausgabe* in Oehler's *Register*.

The Musarion Verlag in Munich published a de luxe edition of the collected works (1920 ff., 23 vols.). It added little except a volume of juvenilia and an enlargement of Oehler's *Register*.

Strong dissatisfaction with the editing of the *Gross-oktav Ausgabe* appeared early (cf. Ernst Horneffer, *Nietzsches Letztes Schaffen*, Diederichs, Jena, 1907), and the Musarion edition hardly improved matters. At last, in 1933, a really scholarly edition, the *Historisch-Kritische Gesamtausgabe*, began appearing under the direction of a committee of the Board of Directors of the Nietzsche-Archiv; it is published by the C. H. Beck'sche Verlagsbuchhandlung in Munich. It already contains many more of Nietzsche's juvenilia and early letters than had previously been published. For psychological and biographical studies it will be of fundamental importance. How much it will modify our conception of Nietzsche's mature philosophy remains to be seen. When the present volume went to press, the first four volumes of *Werke* and the first two of *Briefe*, in the critical edition, had reached the author.

As indicated, this edition will include letters as well as works. Meantime we must rely on older editions of letters: *Friedrich Nietzsches Gesammelte Briefe* (Insel-Verlag, Leipzig, 1907 ff., 5 vols. — vols. I–III also published earlier by Schuster and Loeffler, Berlin, 1900 ff.), *Friedrich Nietzsches Briefwechsel mit Franz Overbeck* (Insel-Verlag, Leipzig, 1916), and a few letters to Wagner published in E. Förster-Nietzsche, *Wagner und Nietzsche zur Zeit ihrer Freundschaft* (Müller, München, 1915). Other letters have been published here and there: for details, see the first volume of letters in the critical edition.

The Complete Works of Friedrich Nietzsche (ed. by Oscar Levy, Allen and Unwin, London, and The Macmillan Co., New York, 1909 ff. and later printings, 18 vols.) is the fullest edition of Nietzsche in English, and contains all the works which he finished, together with some of the literary remains. There are many English editions of single works, etc. Perhaps the most useful is the Modern Library Giant, which contains several of the best-known works in a single volume. A much shorter but somewhat more varied selection has been edited by Heinrich Mann: *The Living Thoughts of Nietzsche* (Longmans, New York, 1939). Only a fraction of the letters are available in English, chiefly in *Selected Letters of Friedrich Nietzsche*, ed. O. Levy (Doubleday, New York, and Heinemann, London, 1921).

C. Memoirs and Biography

Andler, Charles, *Nietzsche, sa vie et sa pensée*, Éditions Bossard, Paris, 1920 ff., 6 vols., vols. II and IV.

Andreas-Salomé, Lou, *Friedrich Nietzsche in seinen Werken*, Konegen, Wien, 1894; 3rd ed., Reissner, Dresden, 1924.

Bernoulli, Carl Albrecht, *Franz Overbeck und Friedrich Nietzsche, eine Freundschaft*, Diederichs, Jena, 1908, 2 vols.

Brann, Hellmut Walther, *Nietzsche und die Frauen*, Meiner, Leipzig, 1931.

Deussen, Paul, *Erinnerungen an Friedrich Nietzsche*, Brockhaus, Leipzig, 1901.

Förster-Nietzsche, Elizabeth, *Das Leben Friedrich Nietzsche's*, Naumann, Leipzig, 1895–1904, 2 vols. (in 3). (*Anhang* of vol. I gives brief selection of juvenilia.)

——, *The Young Nietzsche*, Heinemann, London, 1912.

——, *The Lonely Nietzsche*, trans. by P. V. Cohn, Heinemann, London, 1915. (These two volumes are translations of a shorter German version of Förster-Nietzsche's biography.)

Hildebrandt, Kurt, *Gesundheit und Krankheit in Nietzsches Leben und Werk*, Karger, Berlin, 1926.

Hofmiller, Josef, *Friedrich Nietzsche*, Coleman, Lübeck, 1934.

O'Brien, Edward J., *Son of the Morning, a Portrait of Friedrich Nietzsche*, Ballou, New York, 1932.

Podach, E. F., *The Madness of Nietzsche*, trans. by F. A. Voigt, Putnam, London and New York, 1931. (The German edition: *Nietzsches Zusammenbruch*, Kampmann, Heidelberg, 1930.)

Salis-Marschlins, Meta von, *Philosoph und Edelmensch, ein Beitrag zur Charakteristik Friedrich Nietzsche's*, Naumann, Leipzig, 1897.

Zweig, Stefan, *Der Kampf mit dem Dämon: Hölderlin, Kleist, Nietzsche*, Insel-Verlag, Leipzig, 1925 and later printings.

D. PHILOSOPHICAL STUDIES

Andler, Charles, *Nietzsche, sa vie et sa pensée*, vols. I, III, V, VI.

Baeumler, Alfred, *Nietzsche der Philosoph und Politiker*, Reclam, Leipzig, 1931 and later printings.

Bauch, Bruno, "Friedrich Nietzsche und das Aristokratische Ideal," in *Den Manen Friedrich Nietzsches*, ed. by Max Oehler, Musarion, München, 1921.

Bertram, Ernst, *Nietzsche, Versuch einer Mythologie*, 7th ed., revised, Bondi, Berlin, 1929. (First ed. 1918. French trans. by Robert Pitrou, Rieder, Paris, 1932.)

Brock, Werner, *Nietzsches Idee der Kultur*, Cohen, Bonn, 1930. (The philosophy of Nietzsche's early period.)

Faguet, Emile, *On Reading Nietzsche*, trans. by George Raffalovich, Moffat, Yard, New York, 1918. (French ed.: Société Française, Paris, 1904.)

Figgis, John Neville, *The Will to Freedom, or the Gospel of Nietzsche and the Gospel of Christ*, Scribner, New York, 1917.

Fischer, Hugo, *Nietzsche Apostata, oder die Philosophie des Ärgernisses,* Stenger, Erfurt, 1931.

Foster, George Burman, *Friedrich Nietzsche,* Macmillan, New York, 1931.

Gaultier, Jules de, *Nietzsche,* Les maitres de la pensée antichrétienne, Éditions du Siècle, Paris, 1926.

Hildebrandt, Kurt, *Nietzsches Wettkampf mit Sokrates und Plato,* Sibyllen-Verlag, Dresden, 1922.

——, *Wagner und Nietzsche, ihr Kampf gegen das neunzehnte Jahrhundert,* Hirt, Breslau, 1924.

Hocks, Erich, *Das Verhältnis der Erkenntnis zur Unendlichkeit der Welt bei Nietzsche, eine Darstellung seiner Erkenntnislehre,* Barth, Leipzig, 1914.

Horneffer, Ernst, *Nietzsche als Vorbote der Gegenwart,* 2nd ed., Bagel, Düsseldorf, 1935.

Jaspers, Karl, *Nietzsche, Einführung in das Verständnis seines Philosophierens,* De Gruyter, Berlin, 1936.

Joel, Karl, *Nietzsche und die Romantik,* Diederichs, Jena, 1905. (Also contains *Nietzsche und die Antike.*)

Kein, Otto, *Das Apollinische und Dionysische bei Nietzsche und Schelling,* Junker und Dünnhaupt, Berlin, 1935.

Klages, Ludwig, *Die Psychologischen Errungenschaften Nietzsches,* Barth, Leipzig, 1926.

Krökel, Fritz, *Europas Selbstbesinnung durch Nietzsche, ihre Vorbereitung bei den Französischen Moralisten,* Nietzsche-Gesellschaft, München, 1929.

Langer, Norbert, *Das Problem der Romantik bei Nietzsche,* Helios-Verlag, Münster i. W., 1929.

Lavrin, Janko, *Nietzsche and Modern Consciousness,* a Psycho-Critical Study, Collins, London, 1922.

Lefebvre, Henri, *Nietzsche,* Éditions Sociales Internationales, Paris, 1939.

Lichtenberger, Henri, *The Gospel of the Superman,* trans. by J. M. Kennedy, Allen and Unwin, London, 1910; reprinted, with a new preface, 1926. (The first French edition: *La Philosophie de Nietzsche,* Alcan, Paris, 1898.)

Löwith, Karl, *Kierkegaard und Nietzsche, oder philosophische und theologische Überwindung des Nihilismus,* Klostermann, Frankfurt a. M., 1933.

——, *Nietzsches Philosophie der Ewigen Wiederkunft des Gleichen,* die Runde, Berlin, 1935. (A suppressed chapter, "Kritik der Bisherigen Darstellungen von Nietzsches Lehre," has been privately printed.)

Mann, Thomas, "Einkehr," in *Den Manen Friedrich Nietzsches*, ed. by Max Oehler, Musarion, München, 1921.

Meyer, Eduard, *Nietzsches Wertphilosophie in ihrem Struktur-psychologischem Zusammenhang*, Winters, Heidelberg, 1932.

Meyer, Richard M., *Nietzsche, sein Leben und seine Werke*, Beck, München, 1913.

Miéville, Henri-L., *Nietzsche et la volonté de puissance, ou l'aventure Nietzschéenne et le temps présent*, Payot, Paris, 1934.

Obenauer, Karl Justus, *Friedrich Nietzsche der Ekstatische Nihilist, eine Studie zur Krise des religiösen Bewusstseins*, Diederichs, Jena, 1924.

Richter, Raoul, *Friedrich Nietzsche, sein Leben und sein Werk*, 4th ed., Meiner, Leipzig, 1922.

Rosenstock, Eugen, and Wittig, Josef, *Das Alter der Kirche, Kapitel und Akten*, Schneider, Berlin, 1927, 3 vols., Vol. I, pp. 21 ff.

Rosenstock, Eugen, *Die Hochzeit des Kriegs und der Revolution*, Arbeitsgemeinschaft, Berlin, 1920, pp. 289 ff.

Salter, William Mackintire, *Nietzsche the Thinker*, Holt, New York, and Palmer and Hayward, London, 1917.

Santayana, George, *Egotism in German Philosophy*, Scribner, New York, and Dent, London, n. d., chapters XI–XIII.

Scheler, Max, "Das Ressentiment im Aufbau der Moralen," in *Vom Umsturz der Werte*, 2nd ed., Neue-Geist, Leipzig, 1923, 2 vols.

Schestow, Leo, *Dostojewski und Nietzsche, Philosophie der Tragödie*, trans. by R. von Walter, Marcan, Köln, 1924.

Seillière, Ernest, *Apollôn ou Dionysos, étude critique sur Frédéric Nietzsche et l'utilitarisme impérialiste*, Plon-Nourrit, Paris, 1905.

Siegel, Carl, *Nietzsches Zarathustra, Gehalt und Gestalt*, Reinhardt, München, 1938.

Simmel, Georg, *Schopenhauer und Nietzsche*, Duncker und Humblot, München und Leipzig, 1907 and later printings.

INDEX

INDEX

Absolute, *see* Antagonism; Becoming; Being; Morals; Truth; Values

Abstraction, 76, 119, 162, 191, 195, 202, 210, 338 f

Abundance, 62, 118, 149, 156, 206, 209, 222 ff, 229, 308, 335

Abysmal thought, 302, 305, 313

Achilles, 216

Acquaintance, 275 f

Actor, *see* Schauspielerei

Adaptation, 60 f

Adventure, *see* Certainty, Danger, Experiment

Aeschylus, 215 n, 337

Aesthetic judgment, 221–32

Aesthetic values, 120, 207, 220 ff

Aesthetic vs moral standpoint, 25, 36 n, 46 f, 50 ff, 120, 206, 216, 236, 295 f, 306 f. *See also* Tragedy

Aesthetics, Chap. VIII; anti-conceptualism in, 248 n; as applied physiology, 207, 209, 220–24, 234; classical, 222–32; creation vs contemplation in, 207 f; decadence, 222 ff

Affekt, *see* Passion; Urge

Affirmation and negation, 27, 116, 119, 155, 159, 173 ff, 176, 186 f, 206, 208, 212, 215, 222, 233, 236, 288, 293, 298, 300, 302 ff, 306, 308 f, 311–15, 333 n, 374

Agent, 90 f, 162, 245, 249, 257, 273

Aim, *see* Goal

Alcibiades, 353

Alexandria, 340

Altruism, 147 f, 154 f, 177, 200 n. *See also* Selflessness

America, 327 n

Anarchism, 151 f, 328, 354 f

Annunzio, d', Gabriele, 6

Antagonism, 23, 31 ff, 51 f, 59, 61 f, 64 f, 67, 74 f, 79, 96–100, 102 f, 110, 114, 117 n, 124, 128, 131 f, 137, 150, 153, 157 f, 163 f, 179, 185 f, 192 f, 205, 213, 216, 229 n, 236, 269 f, 273, 276 f, 280, 309, 332–39, 341, 343 f, 349 f, 352 f, 355 f, 358 f, 368; absolute, 53, 56, 163, 174, 250, 264, 270 n. *See also* Synthesis of opposites

Anti-semitism, 10, 333 n

Antitheses, *see* Antagonism; Synthesis of opposites

Aphorist style, 18, 22

Apollinian-Dionysian, 47 n, 81 n, 99, 100 n, 120, 133, 135, 205, 207 n, 209, 211–15, 223 ff, 229 n, 232, 234, 266, 270 n, 281, 300, 302 f, 307 f, 311, 314 f, 323 n, 334 ff, 363; defined, 212; dimensions of power, 132 f, 225

Appearance, 274 f; gradations of, 109 f, 258, 261; as reality, 257–60, 267 n; value of, 216, 236, 242, 250, 257, 295. *See also* Art

Apperception, 107 f, 110

A priori, 49, 115 f, 247

Architecture, 213

Aristocracy, 81, 333, 347; decadent, 157 n; defense of, 157 ff, 369 f; priestly, 113, 159; temper of, 134, 156 ff. *See also* Caste; Morals; Nobility

Aristotle, 18, 122 n, 214, 215 n

Art, classic, 225, 229, 233; as communication, 208 f, 210 f, 217; and culture, 217 ff, 232–35; cycles of, 232 ff, 338 f; decadence in, 220, 222 ff, 227–30, 232–35; effects in, 226 ff, 234; essentially affirmative, 206, 208, 236; evolution of, 211 ff; and the future, 235 ff, 363; as good will to appearance, 28, 216, 236; integrity in, 137, 219, 226 f; and life, 206, 221 f, 235 ff; and morals, 134, 206 f; naturalizing in, 218; nobility in, 225 f; perfection in, 206 f, 224, 230 ff, 235; and science, 52, 210; standards of, 222–32

Artist, distinguished from other types, 210, 225 f, 228, 235; evaluation of, 35 n, 206 f, 217, 225–32, 235 f; and public, 220, 223, 226; psychology of, 74, 208–20, 222 ff; types of, 222–31; unreality of, 216, 235

Ascetic ideal, 52, 151, 179, 235, 241, 308, 325

Asceticism, 98, 341, 375

Asia, 335, 349, 354

Aspasia, 371 n

Assimilation, 69 f, 101, 104, 110 f

Association, 72 f
Atheism, 36–39, 48, 54, 77, 353 f
Athens, 338
Atomism, 268, 272, 280
Authority, 31, 44, 142, 144, 169 f, 189 f, 197, 217, 296, 368. *See also* Strong; Tradition
Autonomy, 190

Bach, J. S., 313
Barbarian, 121, 157, 197, 346; new, 353, 355, 359, 360 n, 363
Barbarism, 46, 132, 185, 325, 333 f, 340 f, 347
Baroque, 232 ff
Bayreuth, 8
Beast, 98, 188; blonde, 74, 112, 121, 347; of prey, 191, 333 f, 346
Beauty, 219–22, 231 f, 237, 296, 333, 335, 374
Become what you are, 39 f, 103 ff, 138, 202 ff
Becoming, 51, 243 ff, 266–71, 277, 280–84, 286–90, 315; absolute, 268; homogeneity of, 174, 314; joy of, 214, 308
Beethoven, 125, 235
Being, 138 f, 183 n, 231, 290, 302; absolute, 47 ff, 51, 242, 250, 253–57, 260 f
Believe, will to, 38, 48
Benevolence, 176 f
Berdyaev, Nicolas, 6
Bergson, Henri, 6, 248 n
Berkeley, George, 274
Bernard, Claude, 66
Bezeichnen, 248, 255 f. *See also* Symbolism
Bismarck, von, Otto, 359
Bizet, Georges, 227 n, 231
Body, 85, 88 f, 168, 179, 199, 297, 339, 342, 352
Borgia, Cesare, 348, 375
Boscovich, R. G., 272
Brahms, 227
Brain, 68 n
Brutality, 120, 125, 227, 322, 326, 334, 371; sign of weakness, 129
Buckle, Thomas, 322 n
Buddha, 37 f, 150 f, 360
Buddhism, 343; second, 354 ff
Burckhardt, Jakob, 164 n

Caesar, Julius, 353
Caracalla, 122

Caste, 121, 192, 369–73; ruling, 359 fl, 363 f, 373 ff. *See also* Aristocracy
Categories, 243, 245, 249
Catharsis, 215 n
Causation, 245, 249, 271, 274 ff, 277, 282 ff. *See also* Agent; Self-consciousness
Cellini, Benvenuto, 127, 203
Certainty and uncertainty, 21, 23, 50, 86 f, 106 f, 250, 252 ff, 306
Chameleon, 103
Chance, 82, 113, 270, 278, 282, 284, 306 f, 322, 361
Change, *see* Becoming
Chaos, 31, 74 n, 77, 80, 84, 100, 132, 266, 269, 284, 289, 327, 334, 359. *See also* Order
Character, 69 f, 79 f, 102
China, 354
Chineserei, 177, 354 f
Christ, *see* Jesus
Christianity, 6; case against, 37, 116, 151 f, 157, 179, 188 f, 286, 311, 341, 345 f, 350; our debt to, 186 f, 188 f, 308, 349 f; history of, 115 n, 122, 321, 323 n, 341–46, 348 ff; modern, 38, 44 f, 170, 177, 326; morals of, 37, 116, 162 f, 167, 169 f, 173 ff, 206, 210; as Platonism, 51, 141, 342; respect for, 7, 44, 45 n, 179; self-overcoming of, 38 f, 47, 241, 250 f, 330; theology of, 343 f
Church, 127, 344 f, 347, 350; Catholic, 347 n
Civilization, *see* Culture
Class, *see* Caste
Class mixture, 324, 329, 350 n
Classicism, 331 f
Cleanliness, *see* Integrity
Coercion, 74, 101, 184, 186, 338, 359. *See also* Discipline; Restraint
Collectivism, 191
Comedy, 213 n, 313 n
Command and obedience, 27, 33, 65, 72 f, 75, 88, 92, 94, 124, 126, 153, 169, 171, 190, 198, 218, 231, 276, 297 f, 345, 359. *See also* Lawgiver
Commonness, 109, 120, 133 n, 202 n, 248
Communication, 9, 14–20, 98, 108 f, 208–11, 217
Communism, 151 f
Community, 27, 42 f, 205, 314, 361 f
Compassion, *see* Pity

Compensation, psychology of, 37, 97 f, 152, 159 f

Completeness, *see* Wholeness; Perfection

Comprehension, 72, 248, 255 f, 273–77

Concepts, 243 ff, 248

Confessional, 98

Conflict, *see* Antagonism

Conscience, 68, 146, 168 f, 190; artist's, 218, 226 f; good and bad, 34, 43, 111 ff, 152, 161 f, 182, 204; intellectual, 33, 38, 251

Consciousness, *see* Self-consciousness

Conservatism, 354

Contemplation and action, 32 f, 35 f; aesthetic, 207 ff, 220 f, 223 f

Contempt, 41 n, 156, 160

Continuity, 268, 280 n, 283, 287 n; of development, 105, 198 f, 218, 233, 336; of life and nature, 276, 322. *See also* Tradition

Contract, 192, 193 n

Contradictions, alleged, 21, 29, 258; apparent, 19 n, 62 n, 71, 91, 102, 107, 130. *See also* Antagonism; Synthesis of opposites

Contrast, *see* Antagonism; Synthesis of opposites

Convention, 39, 41, 136, 337; in art, 218, 228 n, 232 f, 338 f

Coordination and subordination, 68, 102 f, 127. *See also* Domination; Harmony

Copernicus, 53, 272

Cosmic epochs, 282

Cosmology, Chap. X

Creation and destruction, 27, 60 ff, 84, 139, 166, 186, 212 ff, 223, 266, 270, 279, 299, 303, 306, 308, 310 f, 336, 363, 369. *See also* Self-overcoming; Value; Will to power; World which concerns us

Creation ex nihilo, 287 f

Criminal, 98, 164 n, 193, 371

Crucified, the, 311

Cruelty, 50, 99, 100 n, 125, 147, 151, 180 f, 186 n, 214 f, 310; to self, 112 f, 161 f, 181

Culture, 42, 134, 136, 180 f, 334, 337, 362 ff, 372; and art, 207, 232–35; comparison of, 340 f, 354 ff; decadence of, 327–30, 338–41; seeds of, 201, 361; and state, 373; philistine, 46, 325. *See also* Cycle

Cycle of arts, 232 ff, 338 f; of culture, 185, 323, 332–41, 346 ff, 363, 374; of life, 76 f, 329; of man, 324; of world, 288 f

Cynics, 340

Dance, 18, 158, 198, 217 f, 291, 307, 312

Danger, 32 f, 130, 153 f, 157, 185 f, 254, 353. *See also* Experiment

Dante, 23

Darwin, Charles, 60 ff, 78, 122

Death, 11, 51, 76, 114, 300, 304, 310, 329, 376

Decadence, 63, 65, 77, 81, 105, 149 f, 234, 327 ff, 340; in art, 227–30, 232–35; cultural, 327–30, 338–41, 350, 354; individual, 328 f; moral and political, 328 n; normal and pathological, 76, 329, 346, 348, 350, 352; symptoms of, 117 n, 149–52, 178, 194 f, 300, 328, 339 f. *See also* Exhaustion

Deification, 36 n, 180, 206, 289, 302, 311. *See also* Divine

Democracy, 34, 45, 161, 200, 234, 340, 347 ff, 354 f

Descartes, 106, 195 n, 252 f

Description, 255 f, 271 f

Determinism, 171 f, 283, 305

Devil, 164, 373, 375

Dialectic, 26 ff, 48 n, 163–67, 270, 348 f. *See also* Values

Ding an sich, *see* Being

Discipline, 156 f, 179, 198 f, 217 ff, 353

Disgust, 41, 44, 124, 152, 178, 313, 331

Distance, 31, 34, 133, 134 n; passion of, 155, 157, 374

Divine, 84, 124, 135, 139, 218, 230, 312. *See also* Deification

Domination, excessive and enlightened, 72 ff, 103 f, 122, 127, 334, 336 ff

Don Quixote, 180

Drama, 213 n. *See also* Tragedy

Dreams, 97, 106

Dreiser, Theodore, 6

Duration, 277; as value, 137–40, 310, 363

Duty, 33 f, 72 f, 190 ff, 372. *See also* Conscience; Responsibility; Thou shalt

Earth, 116, 301, 310, 376; lords of, 358, 373 ff

Economic system, 46, 325, 354, 358 f, 372

Economy, the Great, 186 f, 309 f

Education, 325 f, 340 f, 375 f

Egoism, in what senses inevitable, 62, 64, 74, 153, 156, 172 f, 278; in what good or bad, 107 n, 120, 124, 180–84

Eighteenth century, see History

Ends and means, 115 ff, 122 f, 145, 294, 314, 340 f, 354. See also Goal

Endurance, 268, 278–81

Energy, 126, 272, 274–77, 287 ff, 333; source of, 132, 185, 336, 352 f, 356, 360

Enhancement, 115, 117 f, 131

Environment, 60 f, 71, 101 f

Envy, 152, 159

Epictetus, 160 n

Epicurus, Epicurean, 150, 234, 340, 374

Epistemologists, 34 f, 249

Equality, 15, 153 f, 156, 158, 193, 200, 320 f, 358, 373

Error, necessity of life, 236, 241, 264 f, 278; creative, 246; ennobled man, 113, 188. See also Falsity; Fiction; Truth

Eternal recurrence, 288 f; evidence for, 254, 285–88; human significance of, 285 f, 302–7, 310–15, 356 f, 366; as novel inspiration, 284 f; relation to other principles, 281 n, 285, 289 f

Eternity, 304 f; of concepts and values, 166, 243; and joy, 310; within time, 290

Eternization, 223 f, 377

Ethics, comparative, Chap. VI; experiment in, 196 f; formalism in, 195; intuitionism in, 169 f; normative, Chap. VII; pluralism in, 119 f, 163, 187, 190–93, 199, 294; prior to epistemology, 141 f, 241–44; reason and instinct in, 95, 104–7, 110 f, 194–98. See also Conscience; Morals

Eugenics, 371

Euripides, 327 n

Europe, decadence of, 151, 348 ff; history of, 346–50; unification of, 355, 358 f; uniqueness of, 334, 349, 356. See also Future; Modern culture

Europeans, good, 361

Evil, 155, 159 f, 343; made good, 141, 148, 164, 192; problem of, 307–11; revaluation of, 113, 164, 175, 179–87. See also Barbarism; Nihilism; Pessimism

Evolution, 60, 80–84; not automatic,

77 f, 80, 166 f; dialectical, 163–67; of natural laws, 282; as unfolding, 81 n; value of, 293

Excess, 79, 139, 178, 309, 321, 363. See also Abundance; Domination; Measure

Exhaustion, 46, 118, 210, 339 ff

Existence, enigmatic character of, 306; nature of, 21 f, 37, 49 ff, 243, 248 n, 255, 257–61, Chap. X, 315; moralization of, 147, 168, 214, 215 n, 342; vicarious justification of, 40, 132, 301 ff, 312, 374. See also Meaning

Experience, 15, 18 f, 32 ff, 69, 89, 106 f, 246 f, 258 n, 268, 320

Experiment, in art, 219, 233; as mode of life, 375; in morals, 196 f, 351 f, 369; as philosophic method, 254. See also Hypotheses

Explanation, see Comprehension

Exploitation, 61, 372

Extremes, 78, 80, 303–6, 356 f

Facts, 86 f, 253, 319 f

Faculties, 90 f, 95

Faith, 189, 194, 197, 285 f

Falsification, see Simplification

Falsity, 37, 46–51, 54, 119, 175, 342, 349; in art, 216 f, 227 f, 236; necessity of life, 244 f, 247; sanctified, 241, 263 ff, 295; to self and others, 137, 227. See also Error; Fiction

Fanaticism, 286, 304, 339, 343 n

Faraday, Michael, 66

Fascism, 5 f

Fatalism, 228, 305 f

Fate, 62, 64, 105, 283; love of, 311–15, 377. See also Determinism

Faust, 216

Fear, 153 f, 156, 160, 335

Fearfulness, made fruitful, 185, 197

Feeling, as implicit judgment, 91, 147, 168 f; highest, 304; and knowledge, 107. See also Power

Feststellung, see Fixation; Power

Fictions, 90 f, 95, 243 ff, 253, 257, 263, 267 f, 271; transcended, 258 ff, 272 f

Finitude of nature, 287 f

Fixation, 70, 80, 111 f, 114; of error, 247, 258, 263

Flaubert, Gustave, 222, 228

Flock, 46, 114, 122 f, 153; religion, 345, 348 f

Flux, see Becoming

Folk poetry, 325

Force, 74, 105, 126, 166; plastic, 125 f, 130, 300, 364. *See also* Energy; Power

Foregrounds, *see* Masks

Form, 134, 136, 337, 347; in art, 218, 228 f; basic, 69 f, 80; created by life, 199, 228 f

Förster-Nietzsche, Elizabeth, 10, 59, 333 n

France, 347 ff

Fraternity, 356

Frederick II, 353

Free spirit, 19 f, 27, 28 n, 32, 55, 68, 137 n, 165, 188. *See also* Nietzsche, periods

Free will, 92, 170 ff, 230, 249, 283, 305 n

Freedom, 41, 68, 156, 158, 188, 190, 204, 218 f, 230, 232 f, 347, 354 f

Freethinkers, 241

Frenzy, 209–17, 220 f, 225, 363

Frustration, 97 f

Future entails suffering, 309; normative for value, 294 n; possibilities of, 43, 112, 114, 154, 161, 265, 298, 349, 357 f; prediction of, 37, 56, 166 f, 330, 351, 353–58; program for, 201, 299, 333 n, 351 f, 356–66, 368–77. *See also* Morals

Gegensatz, *see* Antagonism; Synthesis of opposites

George, Stefan, 6

Genealogy and evaluation, 144, 244

Generations, continuity between, 105, 198 f, 218, 286, 347

Genius, 28, 42, 64, 78, 185, 218, 301 n, 331, 363

Germans, 125, 218, 254, 270 n, 333 n, 352

Germany, 10, 46, 120, 130, 214 n, 220, 327, 348

Gide, André, 6

Goal, 35, 40, 42 f, 52, 59, 113, 116–19, 126, 189, 191, 236 f, 294, 298 f, 308, 313, 351, 359, 361 f, 365. *See also* Ends and means

God, 18, 27, 64, 138, 161, 164, 175, 180, 183 n f, 206 f, 231, 289, 291, 296, 306 n, 335, 373 f; Christian, 36 n, 37 f, 53 f, 162, 168 f, 242, 287 f, 306 ff, 342 f. *See also* Deification; Divine

God is dead, 36 ff; consequences of, 37 ff, 47, 52, 116, 168, 267, 281 f, 355 f, 376

Goethe, 125, 203, 216, 222 f, 233, 327

Goncourt, de, the brothers, 206, 228

Good, 186 f, 195, 199, 294 n, 342 f; double meaning of, 155 f, 159 f; revaluation of, 175–79

Good and evil, beyond, 141 f, 165, 170 f, 198, 307; complementary and interdependent, 166, 174, 176, 186, 293, 309 f, 342

Good man, 116, 160, 176 f

Goodness, 366, 369, 373 ff; supreme, entails supreme evil, 166, 186

Gospel, 343 f

Gradation, 31 f, 88, 118, 124, 157, 190 ff, 292 n f, 332, 369 f, 374

Grammar as folk metaphysic, 249

Great ages, 64, 107 n, 181, 214 n f, 347. *See also* History

Great men, 64, 120, 184, 266, 322 n, 353

Greatness, 302

Greece, history and culture of, 120, 136, 214 f, 223, 232, 234, 321, 331–42; Nietzsche's debt to, 331

Greeks, 19, 28, 67, 134, 138, 295; psychologically superficial, 215 n, 332

Growth, 61–64, 68, 75, 115, 116 n, 118, 126

Guilt, 74, 146 f, 161 ff, 170 ff, 174 f. *See also* Sin

Guyau, J. M., 131

Habit, *see* Instinct; Memory

Hafiz, 223

Half-heartedness, 30, 38 f, 45, 349, 357

Hamlet, 50

Hammer, philosophy of the, 356 f

Handel, G. F., 235

Happiness, 95, 100 n, 105, 140, 195, 309 f, 362, 375. *See also* Hedonism; Joy

Hardness, 124, 156, 178, 186 f, 347

Harmony, 104, 113, 127, 136 f, 208, 219, 332 ff. *See also* Order

Hartmann, Nicolai, 6

Health, 102 f, 126, 130, 300, 335, 352; mental, 98

Heaviness, 27, 204, 224, 230, 304, 310, 312 f

Hedonism, 116 f, 152, 154, 156, 160, 178 f, 340. *See also* Cruelty

Hegel, 30, 48, 120, 166, 321 f

Heraclitus, 113, 306 f

Herd, *see* Flock

Heredity, 69 f, 80 n, 104 f, 199; inertia of, 70, 80, 102, 111

400 INDEX

Hero, 138, 183 n f, 215, 231, 306 n
Herrschafts-Gebilde, *see* Power structure
Hesiod, 159 n
Hierarchy, *see* Gradation; Rank
Historical sense, 143, 243, 319
History, as disease, 321, 325, 340, 364 f; as field for psychology, 90, 320; governed by creators of values, 30, 296 f, 359 f; and life, 319 ff; method of, 319–23; of mind, 243–51; of morals, Chap. VI; patterns of, 285, 321–24, 346 f; pinnacles of, 331, 337 f, 374; philosophy of, Chaps. XII, XIII;
  periods: Middle Ages, 134, 347; Provençal, 347 n; Renaissance, 64, 137, 347 f; Reformation, 235, 348; seventeenth century, 347 f; eighteenth century, 235, 347 f; French Revolution, 347 f. *See also* China; India; Greece; Jews; Christianity; Modern culture
Hocking, W. E., 6
Homer, 216, 339
Honesty, *see* Integrity
Hope, 39, 113
Hugo, Victor, 226, 230
Humanism, 38, 42 f, 52, 296, 365. *See also* Humanity; Man
Humanitarianism, 45, 161
Humanity, 20, 43, 77, 81, 115, 123, 200 f, 265, 301; birth of, 361 f
Humanization, 129 ff
Hypotheses, 143 n, 189, 196 f, 251, 254, 285 f

I am, 138, 204, 297 f
I will, 138, 190, 204, 297 f
Idealism, 40 n, 85, 199, 257 n f, 326, 352
Idealization, 209, 216
Ideals, 42, 97, 118, 186, 297; personal, 40, 120, 202, 361
Ideas, power of, 30 f, 296 ff, 359 f
Identity, 243, 245, 268, 281, 288 f
Illusion, 47–52, 87, 247, 249 ff, 335 n; levels of, 50 f, 258
Imagination and value, 298 n
Imitation in art, 209, 211, 216, 218, 227, 228 n. *See also* Realism
Immediacy, 86 f, 106 f, 109 f, 252 f
Immoralism, 141, 186 ff, 215 n. *See also* Good and evil
Immortality, 344; substitute for, 304, 310

Imperatives, 110, 154, 162 f, 175, 189, 191, 198, 242
Importance, sense of, 304 f
Impotence poisons, 150, 159 f
Impulse, *see* Urge
In vain, 50, 52 f
Independence, 133, 190 f, 202
India, 333 n, 354
Indication, *see* Bezeichnen; Symbolism
Individual, exceptional, 78, 80; as fate, 105 f, 283, 305; a line of evolution, 182, 196; modern, 200, 354; seed of social organism, 200 f; sovereign, 204 f, 353 f; ultimate end, 123, 129 f, 200, 331
Individual knowledge, 261
Individualism 191, 200 f, 205
Individuality, 119, 134, 136, 202, 212, 228 n, 248, 335 ff, 347. *See also* Freedom
Infinity, 22, 55, 268 f, 306; of time, 286 ff. *See also* Apollinian-Dionysian
Inner world, 32, 86 f, 112
Innocence, 174 f, 180 f, 188, 193, 204, 298, 306 f
Inorganic existence, value of, 294 n
Inspiration, 309
Instant, 268
Instinct, 74, 101, 104 f, 110 f; in art, 215 f; as basis of culture, 339 f; and consciousness, 99, 110 f, 190, 194 f; dominant, 31, 102 ff, 127, 219; in ethics, 104 ff, 107, 110, 194 f, 197, 370. *See also* Urge
Institutions, 324, 329, 336, 347
Integration, 31, 102 ff, 203 f, 219. *See also* Integrity; Organization
Integrity, 38 f, 51, 119, 134–38, 236, 332 f, 337. *See also* Wholeness
Intelligence, 104, 110
Interaction, 259 f, 273, 276 f
Interpretation, 35, 68, 96 f, 106 f, 126, 244 f, 252 f, 259, 266, 289, 319 f, 330
Introspection, 86, 89 f
Introversion, 98, 112, 179
Irrationalism, 49 ff, 110, 229 n, 248 n, 258, 307. *See also* Fiction; Instinct; Logic; Objectivity; Order; Reason; Truth; Unconscious
Isis, 345
Italy, 120

Jaspers, Karl, 21 n, 22 n, 119 n, 269 n, 351 n

Jehovah, 342
Jesuits, 200, 349
Jesus of Nazareth, 150, 343 ff, 369
Jews, 68, 159, 333 n, 342–45
Job, 206
Joy, and pain, 308 ff; wants eternity, 310
Judgment, a priori, 49, 247; and consciousness, 109; implicit in feeling and instinct, 91, 101, 168 f, 220 f, 247, 295 f
Justice, 49, 160, 165, 182, 191, 261 f, 366–70

Kant, 26, 30, 48 ff, 181 f, 191, 203, 207 f, 252, 287 n
Kelvin, William Thompson, Lord, 66
Kierkegaardians, 6
Kleist, von, E. C., 50
Knowledge, as adventure, 28, 54 f, 237 n, 375; biology of, 76, 243–47; and passion, 185, 261 f; is relational, 256; sociology of, 248–51; theory of, Chap. IX; theory of, presupposes theory of value, 141 f, 241–44; tragic, 214 n; and virtue, 194. See also Certainty; Perspective; Truth

Labor, 147, 160, 325, 372
Lamarckian biology, 70, 101, 373 n
Language, 198, 217, 248 f, 333 n; new, 18 f, 26, 297, 299. See also Communication
La Rochefoucauld, 90
Last man, 114 f, 357 f
Laughter, 312 f
Law, 192
Lawgiver, 30 f, 297, 360 f, 363, 366, 368 f
Laws, artistic, 229 n, 232 f; of life, 56, 63, 82 f, 192; of nature, 281 ff, 289; self-overcoming of, 165
Leader, 153 f, 191, 360. See also Command and obedience
Leibniz, 243
Lessing, 233
Levelling, 158 f, 355, 358
Liberalism, 6, 45, 354 f, 367
Life, Chap. III; deepest desire of, 63; differentia of, 69, 278 f; not an ethical imperative, 117 n, 293 f; entails falsity, 50 f, 236, 241, 278; hatred for, 222 ff; healthy and decadent, 76 f, 118, 148 f, 182 f, 300; and justice, 165, 367 ff; perspectival, 68 f, 278, 367;

stages of, 26, 32, 76, 141, 175, 261, 329; as standard of value, 115–18, 162, 187 ff, 206 ff, 221 f, 224, 320 f; as will to power, 59–68, 72–77
Lightness, 217, 230 f, 302. See also Dance; Heaviness
Limitation, 72, 74, 104 f, 126, 218, 228, 232 f, 281, 333, 336 f, 347, 362 f, 365. See also Apollinian-Dionysian
Literature, historians of, 320
Logic, 141, 229 n, 253, 335; artistic, 229 f; implicit valuations in, 242 ff
Lorrain, Claude, 235
Louis XIV, 235
Love, 9, 31 f, 41, 65, 68, 119, 139, 150, 156, 174, 182 ff, 203 f, 237, 310, 343, 362, 369
Lust, 180
Luther, Martin, 194, 235

Man, as animal, 52 f, 85, 322 f; better and more evil, 174, 186, 375; made inward, 112; complementary, 301; creature and creator, 84; different from animals, 111, 113, 132, 146, 188; future of, 114; highest, 132, 139, 297, 366; in evolution, 111–14, 189; plasticity of, 101 f, 105 f, 111 ff; self-overcoming of, 157 f, 302, 361; sickness of, 111 ff; social and individual, 109, 146, 158, 181, 201, 205; sublime, 128; synthetic, 131 f, 301, 368, 375; value of, 182, 292 n; wisest, 368. See also Humanism; Humanity
Mann, Thomas, 6
Manu, 333 n, 370
Marriage, 371
Marx, Karl, 166
Masks, 14 ff, 19 f, 68, 99, 137 n. See also Rôles
Masses, 74 n, 120, 174, 322, 324 ff, 345, 355, 359, 370 n
Materialism, 85, 272 f, 275 f. See also Body
Mathematics, 253
Meaning, of existence, 52–56, 291, 295, 301 ff, 362; of history, 322; of individual life, 40, 42 f; of suffering, 307–11
Measure, 135, 156, 212, 228 f, 233 f, 335
Mechanism, 71 f, 88 f, 93 f, 271–76, 287, 290 n

Mediocrity, 46, 135, 153 f, 157 ff, 309, 325, 354, 357, 370; value of, 78, 80 f, 372

Memory, 246; organic, 69 f, 73 f, 79 f, 101, 104, 278 n, 279

Mencken, H. L., 6

Metaphysics, 36 n, 47 ff, 266 f; as projection of moral values, 21, 48, 141. *See also* Existence

Michelangelo, 23, 138

Mind, 85 n, 106 f, 110 f; ennoblement of, 128 n; genealogy of, 243–51; as instinct, 101 n, 111. *See also* Reason; Thought; Self-consciousness

Mithras, 345

Modern culture, art of, 120, 220, 223, 227–31, 326; description of, 43–47, 124, 324–27, 371 n, 372; diagnosis of, 37, 52–56, 321, 322 n, 327, 329 ff, 348; elements of strength, 30, 352 ff, 358 ff; morals, 141, 160–63, 177 f, 326; philosophy and religion, 33 ff, 37 f, 44 f, 326. *See also* Nihilism

Mohammed, 31, 360

Moment, 140, 310, 377

Monologue art, 226

Moral concepts, 143. *See also* Good; Right; etc.

Moral feelings, 143, 147, 168 ff, 172, 174

Moral judgment, 144 ff, 148, 152, 155 f, 162, 170 ff, 187, 195 f

Moral philosophers, 142, 162, 202

Moral rules, 189. *See also* Imperatives

Moral techniques, 193–99

Morals, consequences in, 145 f, 189, 195–99; contrasts in, 147 ff, 152–55; 157–64; cycles of, 338 f; de-naturalized and re-naturalized, 162, 188, 342, 352 f; dialectical evolution of, 147 f, 163–67; emancipated from religion, 162, 168 ff, 326, 330, 341, 354; not established by argument, 105 f, 199, 298; future of, 145 f, 167 f, 174, 190, 195 ff; hygiene, 149 f; as immoral, 173 f; innovation in, 146 f, 163 f; modern, 141, 160–63, 177 f, 326; motives in, 107 f, 145, 148, 163, 171, 173 n, 195 f; periods of, 145 f, 148, 160 ff, 167, 171, 195; reason and instinct in, 95, 104–11, 194–99; subordinated to life, 115 ff, 187 ff, 207; unconscious in, 145 f, 194 ff

as problem: 141–45, 168; descriptive study of, 142 ff; critique of, 28,

144 f, 170–87; reconstruction of, 165, 187–205

types of: 143; absolute, 162 f, 170, 175, 187, 199, 250, 270 n, 356, 367; flock, 114, 152 ff, 158–61, 175 f, 191; group and individual, 152, 191 f, 200–5; healthy and decadent, 148–52, 160 ff, 175 f; master and slave, 149, 155–61, 175 f, 198, 342 f, 370; mores, 146 ff, 153 n, 168 f, 249. *See also* Conscience; Ethics

Motion, 89, 271 ff, 275

Mozart, 226, 235

Multiplicity, 31, 46, 327, 368

Music, 47 n, 212 f, 224, 230, 234 f

Mystic experience, 303

Myth, 217, 234, 336 ff, 341, 365 f

Napoleon, 153, 348, 353, 359

Nationalism, 200 f, 353, 355, 358

Naturalism in art, 228

Naturalness, 188, 335, 352 f

Nearest things, good neighbors of, 199, 377

Necessity, metaphysical, 282 ff, 289; vital, 22, 136, 219, 229 n, 230, 232 f

Need, 71, 74 n, 79, 101, 108 f, 158, 199, 359. *See also* Coercion

Nero, 122

Nervous system, 93 n

Nietzsche, health of, 6 ff, 10 f; how to read, 17 ff; comment on own work, 16–20, 23–28, 34, 41, 43; continuity and consistency of his thought, ix f, 20–29, 36 n, 64 f, 215 n, 339 n; importance of, vii, 3–6; life and character, 6–11, 20, 35 f, 40, 54 ff, 66 f; loneliness, 9 f, 15, 39, 43 f; manner and purpose of writing, 10, 13–20, 143; as psychologist, 84 f, 90; relation of his thought and life, viii f, 6, 11, 26 ff, 32, 150 n; sense of vocation, 8 ff, 28, 31, 35 f, 103, 284 ff, 303

periods: 13, 25–29, 165, 266 f; early, 8, 35 n, 47, 182 n, 205, 206 f, 214 n, 327 n, 348 n, 364; middle, 48, 54 f; last, 37, 40 n, 212, 311 f. *See also* Free Spirit

works: 12 f; *The Birth of Tragedy*, 24 f, 36 n, 47 n, 49, 51 f, 208 n, 266, 267 n; *Ecce Homo*, 36 n, 286 n; *Revaluation of All Values*, 36; *Toward the Genealogy of Morals*, 18, 112 f, 143, 161 f; *Untimely Views*, 25 f, 39 ff,

44, 136; *Thus Spake Zarathustra*, 10,
17 f, 24, 302 f, 373 n

Nihilism, 52–56, 59, 115, 117 n, 162 f,
165, 169, 242, 267, 295 f, 299 ff, 303 f,
320, 340 f, 350, 352; active, 54, 356 f;
answer to, 362; in morals, 175, 178,
330, 354; in philosophy, 250; in science, 325; as sign of decadence,
329 ff; as sign of strength, 356

Nineteenth century, *see* Modern culture

Nobility, 119 f, 127, 128 n, 133 ff, 137 n,
158 n, 225 f

Noon, the Great, 361

Novelty, 81, 112 ff, 163 ff, 270, 283 f,
287 f. *See also* Creation and destruction; Values

Obedience, *see* Command and obedience

Objectivity in art, 207 ff, 228; in history and science, 319 ff, 325; of
knowledge, 251, 261 f, 264; in philosophy, 22, 32 ff

Offenbach, Jacques, 231

Old Testament, 235, 342, 370 n

Opposites, *see* Antagonism; Synthesis
of opposites

Optimism, 49, 100, 234, 299 f, 326, 328,
340

Order, 21, 77, 269, 281–84, 289; explanation of, 72 ff, 82; in history,
321–24

Organism, functions of, 75 f, 275; as
society, 72–75; unity of, 68 n, 71–75,
116, 279 f

Organization, 60 f, 73 f, 125 ff, 134, 279,
301. *See also* Integration; Power, dimensions of; Will to power

Orient and Occident, 334 f, 356

Originality, 218 f

Ortega y Gasset, José, 6

Ought, 120. *See also* Conscience; Duty;
Thou shalt

Over-civilization, 132, 157 n, 185, 341

Over-work, 220, 325 ff

Overbeck, Franz, 10

Overcoming, *see* Self-overcoming; Self-
mastery

Overflow, *see* Abundance; Excess; Will
to power

Pacifism, 328, 355 ff. *See also* Peace

Paganism, 115 n, 118, 342, 348 f. *See
also* Religion

Pain, 307–11. *See also* Cruelty; Hedonism; Suffering

Pantheism, 314

Parsifal, 375

Parsimony, 274 ff

Pascal, Blaise, 179, 210, 222; *Pensées*, 22

Passion, 99 f, 102 ff, 185, 188, 261 f,
367 f. *See also* Urge

Past, redemption of, 313, 364 f

Past, present, future, relations between, 30 f, 69 f, 165 f, 171 f, 176,
178, 180, 183, 319 ff, 325. *See also*
Memory; History

Pathos, *see* Passion

Paul, Saint, 3, 344 f

Peace, 35, 68, 100, 154, 160, 343, 377

Pederasty, 332

Perfection, 42, 104, 120, 126, 137 ff, 200,
206 f, 226, 230, 374; higher and lower,
139, 231; new, 301. *See also* Wholeness

Persons, 102, 105, 201

Perspectives, 26, 68 f, 88 f, 118, 173,
222, 255 f, 259–62, 266, 269, 276 ff,
293 ff, 321, 367 f

Pessimism, 25, 27 f, 41, 45, 47, 53, 299 f,
302, 371; romantic, 223 f; of sensibility, 117 n, 307 f; of strength, 309,
314, 335, 340

Phenomenology, 72, 86–89, 93 f, 95 n,
275

Philosopher, as bad conscience of his
time, 34, 43; development of, 31–34;
as educator, 19, 351 f; as lawgiver,
30 f, 360, 363, 366

Philosophers, anti-sensualism of, 206,
263 f; contemporary, 34 f, 326, 353;
moral, 142 f, 162, 202; pre-Socratic,
136, 337 f

Philosophies, as methods of education,
26

Philosophy, esoteric and exoteric, 16,
19; as mask, 14 f; method of, 21 ff,
59, 251 n; and science, 34 f; task of,
30–36; as transfiguration, 33

Physiological contradiction, 137, 160

Pirandello, Luigi, 6

Pity, 138 f, 147, 152, 154, 163 f, 177 ff,
186 f, 214 f, 312, 319, 326, 371

Plato, Platonism, 23, 31, 51, 135, 141,
162, 243, 250, 290 n, 295, 338 f, 342,
345, 360

Play, 215 f, 230

Pleasure, as value, 116 f; psychology of,
117 n. *See also* Hedonism; Joy

Pluralism, metaphysical, 248 n, 268 f.
See also Ethics
Polytheism, 335
Port Royal, 198
Positivism, 35, 49 n, 66, 253
Possibilities, 55, 339 f; of the individual,
40, 105 f; of man, 112 ff
Power, accumulation of, 63 f, 79 f, 105,
128, 217 f, 232 f; dimensions of, 122,
125–33, 186, 209, 215, 217, 219, 225,
229, 231, 234, 262, 289; feeling of,
60 n, 117 n, 119, 139, 200, 221 f, 233;
intrinsic vs external, 120–25, 127–30;
meaning of, 119–33, 368; as right, 192,
368; settling of, 72 f, 80, 283 f; stand-
ard of value, 118 f, 121–40, 221 f,
225, 262. *See also* Strong; Will to
power
Power structure, 74, 127, 279
Pragmatists, 6
Pride, 133, 156 f
Priests, 98, 113, 151, 161 f, 174, 186,
333 n, 336 n, 342 ff, 361
Probability, 251, 254, 256
Probity, *see* Integrity
Problems of Nietzsche's philosophy, 25,
32, 35, 38, 41, 47, 51–56, 137 n, 141–
45, 236, 241 ff, 307, 330 f
Progress, 45, 321 f. *See also* Evolution
Projection, psychology of, 97 f
Property, 123
Protestantism, 194
Psychoanalysts, 6
Psychology, Chap. IV; of art, 208–24;
clairvoyant, 90, 320, 331 f; of conflict,
96–100; method of, 84–90, 94; moral
prejudices in, 84 f; purposive, 95 f;
of tragedy, 308. *See also* Feeling; In-
stinct; Sublimation; Urge; Will to
power; etc.
Punishment, 129, 163, 193, 306
Puritans, 198, 349
Purity, *see* Integrity
Purpose, *see* Goal; Teleology
Pyrrho, 150, 340

Quanta, 273, 279 f
Quixotism, 40 n, 345

Race, 332 f
Racine, 235
Rangordnung, *see* Gradation; Rank
Rank, order of, 68, 73, 82. *See also*
Gradation

Raphael, 23, 210
Rationalization, 110
Rausch, *see* Frenzy
Readers, good and bad, 3, 15–19
Realism in art, 208, 211, 227 f
Reality, escape from, 50 f, 97; given,
274; as gradations of appearance,
258 ff; hatred of, 342 ff; irrational,
49, 258; primary intuitions of, 132,
266–71, 277; seen from within, 275,
277. *See also* Existence; Truth; Value
Reason, 51, 95 f, 194 f, 268 f; historical
critique of, 243–51; as independent
urge, 111; and passion, 91, 95; pure,
247; trust in, 49, 141, 250. *See also*
Mind
Recapitulation, 70, 324 n
Redemption, 150 f
Rée, Paul, 143
Reich, *see* Germany
Relations, 255 f, 273, 276 f
Relativism, 50 f, 142 n, 187, 243, 252,
255 f. *See also* Perspectives
Religion as foundation of culture, 335 f,
341, 364 f; as foundation of morals,
168 ff, 330, 354; Greek, 334 ff; substi-
tutes for, 37 n, 189, 197, 236 f, 285 f,
304, 365 f
Religious history, 52
Religious will, 184
Renan, Ernest, 320
Repentance, 151, 174
Repose, 229, 233, 377
Resistance, *see* Antagonism
Responsibility, 30 f, 39, 133, 156 f, 170 f,
189 f, 370 n
Ressentiment, 97 f, 120, 149–52, 159 f,
175, 223 f, 250, 343 ff, 356. *See also*
Revenge
Restraint, 98, 188, 198, 219 f, 232 f.
See also Coercion; Discipline
Revaluation, *see* Truth; Values
Revenge, 176, 306. *See also* Ressenti-
ment
Reverence for others, 134 n, 156 f; for
self, 133, 156, 204
Revolution, 36, 115, 168
Rhythm, of becoming and being, 138 ff,
219; of individualization and sociali-
zation, 205; of knowing and erring,
264 f; of life, 63 f, 323 n. *See also*
Life; Will to power
Right, 33 f; as power, 190–93, 293 n,
368

INDEX

Ripeness, 120, 138

Rivalry, 185 f, 336 f

Rôles, 102, 105 f, 298, 360

Romantic School, 322 n

Romanticism, 223 f, 227 ff, 300, 301 n. *See also* Nietzsche, periods

Rome, 122, 154, 336 n, 341, 345 f, 348; vs Judea, 323 n

Rosenstock-Huessy, Eugen, 6

Rousseau, 178, 348

Rubens, 223, 225 f

Russia, 353 n

Sacred, 43, 119, 140, 311

Sacrifice, 64 f, 81, 83, 156, 173, 355

Saint, 28, 36, 351

Salomé, Lou, 10

Sameness, *see* Identity

Satyr, 99

Scepticism, 24, 27 f, 34 n, 47–50, 165, 285 f, 299; German, 254

Schauspielerei, 102, 119, 137, 194, 216, 226 f, 327, 340

Scheler, Max, 6

Schlecht, *see* Worthless

Scholarship, 320 n

Schooling, *see* Discipline

Schopenhauer, 8, 13, 19, 25, 28, 39, 41 n, 45, 47 f, 53, 66, 91 f, 124, 172 f, 177, 182 n, 207 f, 214, 217, 223 f, 255 n, 267 n, 274

Schweitzer, Albert, 6

Science, 19 n, 48–53, 66, 255 ff, 267, 325, 340, 352; and the future, 59, 196 n, 202, 261, 263 f, 364; gay, 28, 230, 312; method of, 21 f, 35 n, 251, 274, 340 n, 346; psychological origins of, 104; social origins of, 248–51

Scientist, 34 f, 181, 210

Selection, 81, 178; natural, 73 f, 78, 104, 244 f, 247

Self, 85 n, 88 f, 106; escape from, 183 f, 204, 223; higher and lower, 40 f, 103 f, 202 ff; integration of, 102 ff; seeking and finding, 27 f, 202 f

Self-admiration, 203 f

Self-affirmation, 155 f

Self-confidence and self-doubt, 9, 33 f, 54 n, 110, 124, 133, 146 f, 152, 204, 327, 342, 347, 350, 352, 357

Self-consciousness, 51, 56, 181; cosmic, 307, 322; in evolution, 110 f, 243, 364 f; of history, 319; and instinct, 110 f, 194 f, 327; polemic against,

86, 92 f, 95, 106 ff, 116, 171, 292 n; involves simplification, 109, 246, 258; social theory of, 108 f; vs unconscious, 23 f, 31, 93 f, 110 f, 203. *See also* Phenomenology

Self-contempt and self-love, 31, 41, 114, 179, 183 f, 203 f, 302, 307 n

Self-denial, *see* Selflessness

Self-expression, 181, 183 f

Self-knowledge, 23 f, 99, 148, 202 f, 252. *See also* Introspection; self-consciousness

Self-mastery, 65, 72 f, 104 f, 124 n f, 129, 135, 156, 219, 347, 353, 359 f, 375

Self-overcoming, 34, 63 ff, 67, 81 f, 114, 154, 157 f, 163–67, 205, 262 f, 270, 299. *See also* Christianity; Self-mastery

Self-preservation, 62, 64, 277

Self-realization, 31, 39–43, 49 f, 102–6, 181 ff, 202 ff

Self-redemption, 236

Self-respect, 33. *See also* Reverence

Self-sufficiency, 133 f, 158, 205

Selfishness, *see* Egoism

Selflessness, 152, 163, 170, 172 ff, 181 f, 184, 208, 222, 296

Selves, series of, 203, 368

Sensation, 88 f, 109, 245 f, 272 f, 278; activity in, 246; aesthetic qualities of, 221; implicit valuations in, 242, 246

Senses, belief in, 206, 263 f

Sensitiveness, 31, 309, 312, 320

Sensualization, 130

Separateness, 72, 279 ff

Seventeenth century, *see* History

Sex, 99 f, 111, 209 f, 213

Shakespeare, 124, 214 n

Similarity, 280 ff

Simplicity and complexity, 90, 92, 95, 279 f

Simplification, 49, 69, 76, 88, 126, 244–47, 266 n, 278; levels of, 245 ff, 258 ff. *See also* Error; Fiction; Perspective

Sin, 150 f, 168, 179, 306 f, 335, 342 ff; substitute for, 307 n. *See also* Guilt

Sincerity, *see* Integrity

Slavery, 81, 159, 161, 176, 332, 355, 359, 372. *See also* Command; Morals, types of

Social hygiene, 178 f, 350, 371

Socialism, 151 f, 200 f, 354 f, 359

Society, 67, 72–75, 88 f, 362, 370; classless, 153; means, not end, 123, 129 f, 200; as organism, 200 f

Sociology, 328 n

Socrates, 5, 49, 52, 100 n, 127, 162, 194 f, 200, 210 n, 229 n, 264, 327 n, 338, 339 n

Solidarity, *see* Community

Solitude, 39 ff, 55, 202, 226. *See also* Nietzsche

Sophocles, 214 n, 339

Soul, 85, 88 f, 112 f, 275

Space, 245 n, 276, 280 n, 287

Sparta, 130 n, 336 n

Specialization, 33 ff, 293, 325, 360, 372, 375 f

Species, 78 ff, 373 n

Spencer, Herbert, 45, 60, 177

Spengler, Oswald, 6

Spinoza, 277

Spirituality, 119; as power, 122, 127, 134, 374 f

Spiritualization, *see* Sublimation

Stability, 78 ff, 130, 189. *See also* Order

Stagnation, 79 f, 132, 158 f, 161, 354

State, 64, 74, 127, 200, 336, 340 f, 347; idolatry of, 120, 325; and culture, 373

Steigerung, *see* Enhancement

Stendhal, 90

Stoicism, 150 n, 198, 340, 342

Storage, *see* Power, accumulation of

Strife, *see* Antagonism

Strong, the, 21, 23, 78, 103, 110, 118 f, 122, 135, 153, 158, 300 f, 303, 305, 308, 311, 333, 353, 356 f; defined, 124; effortless power of, 124 n f, 129, 153, 360, 368

Struggle for existence, 59, 62. *See also* Antagonism

Stupefaction, 79 f, 130

Stupidity, 99, 110 n, 198

Style, 134 ff, 217, 224, 228 ff, 337, 339, 347, 362, 364 f; the Great, 228 f, 232 f

Subjectivism, 257 f, 274 f

Sublimation, 98 ff, 128 ff, 180 f, 185, 209 f, 341

Sublime, the, 180 f, 231

Substance and process, 90, 95, 172, 243, 245, 249, 272 f, 276 n, 277

Success, worship of, 120, 321 f

Suffering, 150, 370 n, 375; discipline of, 178 f; meaning of, 124, 307–11. *See also* Cruelty; Tragedy

Suicide, 350, 356, 371, 376

Superman, 114, 123, 324, 357 f; genesis of, 369, 373 f; life of, 265, 374 ff;

nature of, 138 f, 266, 301 ff, 312 f, 373 n; as source of meaning, 299, 361 f, 365, 377. *See also* Genius; Individual

Supernatural, 116, 144, 162, 304, 342

Superstition, 146

Surfaces, living on, 216, 295

Symbolism, 72, 248, 253, 271 f

Symbols: abyss, 14, 302, 305, 312 f; Ariadne, 306 n; bridge, 113, 373 n; Caesar, 78, 366, 369; cavern, 14; child, 204, 298, 307; dawn, 55 n; Dionysos, 302 f, 306 n, 311; flying, 204, 291, 312; hermit, 14, 68; labyrinth, 14, 258, 375; land, country, 25, 28, 55 f; lion, 204, 298; lion and doves, 369 n; ocean, 306 n; ring, 314; sea, 25, 27 f, 30, 55, 197; singing, 312; snake, 313; star, 80, 114; sun, 306 n; voyage, 10, 55; wilderness, 27. *See also* Apollinian-Dionysian; Dance; Free spirit; God; Hero; Heaviness; Laughter

Sympathy, 73

Symptoms, 86, 106, 108, 144 f, 196, 273, 275

Synthesis of opposites, 31 ff, 36, 114, 131 f, 186, 225, 231, 290, 301 f

System, 21–29

Taming and training, 157 ff, 188 f, 197 ff. *See also* Discipline

Taste, 36 n, 292 n, 294 f, 297 f

Tautology, 49, 283

Technology, 322 n, 352

Teleology, 81 f, 95 f, 103 f, 269, 282, 286–89, 306 f, 321 ff

Tension, *see* Antagonism

Teutons, 346

Theater, 226

Theodicy, 314

Thermodynamics, second law of, 286 ff

Thinking, feeling, willing, 68 n, 89, 91, 108

Thou shalt, 138, 169, 190

Thought, phenomenal, 246; symptom of passions, 91, 261 f, 274 f

Time, 137 f, 280 n, 286 f, 290. *See also* Duration; Moment; Past, present, future; Rhythm

Titans, 333, 336

Tolerance, 153 f, 156 ff, 304, 327, 367

Tradition, 69, 232 f, 324, 327, 338 f, 347, 353, 363. *See also* Continuity; Instinct

Tragedy, 180, 213 ff., 224, 231, 308–11, 313
Tragic disposition, 42 f
Truth, absolute, 47 ff., 51, 106, 169, 241 f, 250–57, 260 f; created, 263, 274; criteria of, 251, 262; as courage, 32, 50, 262; not pragmatic, 244, 247, 264; relative, 252, 254–57, 262; revaluation of, 251 f, 257, 262 ff., 295, 367; subordinate to life, 241, 259 f, 262–65; there is no, 49, 254 ff; two senses of, 50; is ugly, 50 n; value of, 52, 241–44, 247, 249–52; will to, 47, 49 ff., 242, 249 ff., 263 ff., 310. See Also Knowledge; Perspectives; Relativism; Scepticism
Twentieth century, see Future
Type, see Morals; Species

Überwindung, see Self-overcoming
Ugliness, 50 n, 206, 221 f, 231, 309
Unconscious, rôle of, 84, 98 f, 103 f, 106 f, 110 f, 145 f, 203. See also Instinct; Self-consciousness
Uniformity, 79, 134 n, 362
Uniqueness, 39 ff, 119, 268
Unity, cosmic, 268 f, 279 ff; cultural, 336, 362–65; organic, 71–75, 278 f
Universal validity of morals, 163, 187, 191; of truth, 49, 250, 252
Unselfishness, see Selflessness
Urges, 94 f; activity of, 95 f; conflict of, 96–100; indirect expression of, 97–100; learned, 101; nourishment of, 96 f; relation to self, 102–6, 172 f, 181
Urphänomen, 81 n, 97 n, 211, 213 n
Use, 82
Utilitarianism, 156, 160, 189, 191, 195–98
Utopianism, 351, 363

Vaihinger, Hans, 6
Valuation, 68 f, 292; function of power, 222, 259 f, 295 n
Value, as appearance, 216, 295; distinctions of, 174, 187, 293, 314; of existence, 299 ff; intuition of, 42 f, 140, 361 f; nature of, 162 f, 166, 187 f, 243, 291–96; objective, 116, 125, 292 n: quantitative treatment of, 119 n; and reality, 53, 56, 59, 291–96; standard of, 42, Chap. V; as taste, 292 n, 294 f, 297 f
Values, absolute, 162 f, 241 f, 292 f; biological, 207, 220 ff; compulsive

sway of, 297; creation of, 30 f, 115, 128, 155, 165 f, 180, 292–99, 311 f; not deduced from life, 117 n, 293 f, 299 n; dialectical evolution of, 163–67, 179 f, 189, 297, 346, 348 f; express will to power, 65, 68, 94, 118, 293 ff; false, 292 n; moral, 141, 147, 342, 354; revaluation of, 25, 27, 31 ff, 56, 59, 115, 141, 148, 151 f, 175, 194 f, 199, 243, 257, 285, 298 f, 306, 342 f, 356 f, 360; scale of, 139, 141; spring from life, 22, 294, 299; variety of, 119 f, 133–40; as vital perspectives, 293 ff. See also Evil; Good; Ideal; Life; Morals
Van Dyck, 225 f
Variation, 79 f, 153, 157, 201
Verinnerlichung, see Introversion
Voltaire, 348
Vinci, da, Leonardo, 23, 353
Violence, 64, 121, 132, 209, 231, 298, 359. See also Coercion; Force; Power; Will to power
Virtue, 104 f, 124, 148 f, 176, 189, 194 ff; lavish, 139, 183 f
Virtues, Apollinian, 133–40, 225–32
Vitalism, 71 f

Wagner, Cosima, 8
Wagner, Richard, 8 f, 13, 17, 19 f, 25, 27 f, 47, 67, 124, 204, 206 f, 217, 219 f, 223 f, 226 f, 229 ff, 235, 267 n, 333 n, 338, 348 n; Parsifal, 224 f
War, see Antagonism
Weak, the, 46 f, 103, 110, 118, 129, 135, 158, 160 n, 178, 186 f, 228, 311, 327, 355, 371; defined, 124; master strong, 78, 122, 153 f; need leaders, 124 n, 153
Weakness, value of, 81, 124, 130, 186
Wealth, 122 f
Well bred, 130 f, 136, 182, 195, 301
Whitehead, A. N., 6
Wholeness, 41, 74, 77, 127, 133, 136 n, 202 f, 368. See also Perfection
Why, see Goal; Ends and means
Will, 52, 68, 118, 280; analysis of, 90–94; artist's, 219 f; as cause, 92 f, 274 ff; strong and weak, 103, 124, 134, 327; substitute for faith, 189 f, 197. See also Free will
Will to power, aggressive, 60 f, 75, 173; centers of, 88 f, 273, 276 f, 279 f; dictates values, 65, 68, 94, 118, 293 ff, 298; differentiation of, 60, 71, 75 f, 81 n, 85, 94, 118, 211, 274 ff; in evolu-

tion, 60, 81 ff; explains becoming, 277; explains teleology, 72 ff, 81 f; formative and destructive, 60 ff, 64, 73 f, 126, 208; generous, 62–66, 139; illustrations of, 66 ff, 336 f, 342, 360; involves perception, 68, 276, 278; lapse of, 76 f, 355; lethargy of, 71, 80; mitigated, 73; origin of the theory, 59, 164 n; rhythm of, 63 f, 76, 79 f, 183 f, 281; senses of, 60

applications: to art, 184, 208 f, 211, 213, 215, 219 f, 220 ff, 229, 231; to organism, 71–77; to cosmology, 259 f, 266–71, 273–84, 288 ff, 315; to history, 323; to knowledge, 244 ff, 259 f; to morals, 68, 149–67, 173 f, 180,

192 f; to psychology, 68, 85, 94 ff. *See also* Domination; Power; Will

Wisdom, 368 f

Wishful thinking, 35, 37

Wishing, 97

Women, 324, 332, 371 n

World become perfect, 314; external, 257 n f, 260, 274 f, 278; which concerns us, 246 f, 258 f, 263 f, 295 f

Worthless, 152, 155 f, 160, 183, 185, 195

Wrong, 193

Yes, *see* Affirmation and negation

Zeus, 113, 307

Zola, Émile, 206